Endoscope Reprocessing Manual

First Edition

Disclaimer

This publication is designed to provide accurate and authoritative information in regard to the subject matter covered. It is sold with the understanding that the publisher is not engaged in rendering legal, accounting or other professional service. If legal advice or other expert assistance is required, the services of a competent professional person should be sought.

From the Declaration of Principles jointly adopted by the American Bar Association and a Committee of Publishers and Associations.

The authors are solely responsible for the contents of this publication. All views expressed herein are solely those of the authors and do not necessarily reflect the views of the International Association of Healthcare Central Service Materiel Management (IAHCSMM).

Nothing contained in this publication shall constitute a standard, an endorsement or recommendation of IAHCSMM. IAHCSMM also disclaims any liability with respect to the use of any information, procedure or product, or reliance thereon by any member of the healthcare industry.

©2017
By the International Association of Healthcare
Central Service Materiel Management
55 West Wacker Drive, Suite 501
Chicago, IL 60601

The International Association of Healthcare Central Service Materiel Management is a non-profit corporation.

Printed in the United States of America

ISBN 978-1-5323-4208-0

Foreword

The Endoscope Reprocessing Manual was developed in response to a need for enhanced endoscope education. The purpose of the textbook is to provide information that enhances the knowledge of those responsible for reprocessing endoscopes and those who manage that process.

This manual follows a similar layout and design used in other IAHCSMM textbooks, which readers have found to be user friendly and invaluable. Some of those design elements include:

- Learning objectives that introduce the chapter and briefly outline the learning expectations in each chapter;

- Extensive use of the "green box" key terms that define new and important terms throughout the text;

- Use of sidebar "blue boxes" that contain additional information, clarifications and helpful tips;

- Pictures and diagrams to enhance learning and provide real-world examples of processes and practices;

- Information on current standards and regulations; and

- A glossary that not only contains all the terms introduced in the manual, but also many other terms important in today's dynamic endoscope reprocessing environment.

This textbook will assist readers in learning the science behind the discipline, as well as the why's and how's of endoscope reprocessing tasks. That knowledge will help those working in the discipline to succeed on the job and keep quality and patient safety at the forefront of every process.

Acknowledgments

Developing any textbook relies heavily on the latest standards, regulations and guidelines that drive the industry. For the Endoscope Reprocessing Manual, these include:

- The Association for the Advancement of Medical Instrumentation (AAMI), including standards ST91, ST79, ST41 and ST58.

- Surveying agencies, including the Centers for Medicare and Medicaid Services (CMS) and The Joint Commission (TJC).

- Federal agencies, including the Centers for Disease Control and Prevention, the U.S. Food and Drug Administration (FDA) and the Occupational Safety and Health Administration (OSHA).

- Professional organizations, including the Association of periOperative Registered Nurses (AORN) Inc., The Society for Gastroenterology Nurses and Associates (SGNA) Inc., and the Association for Professionals in Infection Control and Epidemiology (APIC) Inc.

In addition, no successfully developed textbook would come to fruition without the assistance of many dedicated, knowledgeable and talented contributors. Numerous association members, medical product and device representatives and other professionals devoted their knowledge, time and expertise to help ensure that this text would become a valuable resource for endoscope reprocessing professionals.

The process to develop this text began approximately 24 months ago as the need for specialized education in endoscope reprocessing was identified. The content was determined by needs surveys conducted with IAHCSMM members' input, evolving standards and guidelines and the results of research studies that evaluated current endoscope reprocessing practices and needs.

The following authors, researchers and photographers generously donated their time and expertise to the development of the Endoscope Reprocessing Manual (listed in alphabetical order):

Cheri Ackert-Burr

Gregory Agoston

Lindsay Brown

Curtis Champion

David Craig

Scott Davis

Gail Doyle

Mary Ann Drosnock

John Eiland

Amanda Hayes

Susan Klacik

Stephen Kovach

Cori Ofstead

Rod Parker

LeeAnn Purtel

Cathy Rocco

Richard Schule

Ashley Small

Peggy Spitzer

Kevin Stephenson

Rich Stroligo

Larry Talapa

Lynne Thomas

Grace Thornhill

Wava Truscott

No publication can be finalized until it is reviewed by subject matter experts to help ensure the content is accurate and current. The following individuals were instrumental in reviewing this text (listed in alphabetical order):

Cheri Ackert-Burr

Susan Adams

Gregory Agoston

Stacey Barber-Walker

Nola Bayes

Lindsay Brown

John Eiland

Marcia Hardick

Michele Juan

Susan Klacik

Patti Koncur

Natalie Lind

Cori Ofstead

LeeAnn Purtel

Cathy Rocco

Ashley Small

Lynne Thomas

Wava Truscott

Cindy Turney

Julie Williamson

The development of this textbook required significant time and input from the following healthcare companies and organizations who provided authors, reviewers, researchers, information and photographs, including (listed in alphabetical order):

3M Health Care

Advanced Sterilization Products (ASP), a division Ethicon Inc.

Capital Medical Resources

Censis Technologies

Certol

Healthmark Industries Company Inc.

Inspektor

Integrated Medical Systems International (IMS), a subsidiary of STERIS Corp.

Key Surgical

Medivators, A Cantel Medical Company

Mobile Instrument Service and Repair Inc.

Ofstead and Associates

OneSOURCE Document Site

Pull Thru

The Society of Gastroenterolgy Nurses and Associates (SGNA)

STERIS Corporation

Stryker Corporration

Truscott MedSci Associates, LLC.

IAHCSMM would like to thank all who contributed to the development of the Endoscope Reprocessing Manual, including CS departments, Endoscopy departments and healthcare facilities that shared photographs or allowed us to take photographs for inclusion in this manual. These facilities were instrumental for enhancing the visual content of this manual. It is because of each and every contributor that the Endoscope Reprocessing Manual will surely become a valuable and trusted educational resource for professional development and knowledge enhancement.

Contents

Table of Contents

Chapter 3
Microbiology Basics for Endoscope Reprocessors 27

Chapter 4
Work Area Design 51

Chapter 5
Cleaning Basics

Chapter 6
Point-of Use Cleaning, Transport and Leak Testing

Table of Contents

Chapter 7
Cleaning Processes for Flexible Endoscopes

Chapter 8
Endoscope Inspection and Preparation

Chapter 9

Chapter 10

Chapter 11

Chapter 12

Chapter 13

Endoscope System Maintenance

The International Association of Healthcare Central Service Materiel Management

The International Association of Healthcare Central Service Materiel Management (IAHCSMM) is the premier organization for professionals working in the Central Service (CS) discipline. IAHCSMM was established in 1958, as a non-profit corporation headquartered in Chicago, Ill. IAHCSMM represents more than 24,000 CS professionals in the U.S. and abroad. These individuals work throughout the healthcare industry—in hospitals, ambulatory surgery centers, clinics and dental offices, and as CS consultants and representatives for medical device manufacturers and third party reprocessors. IAHCSMM is committed to promoting patient safety by providing educational and professional development opportunities to the CS profession and any area that reprocesses medical devices.

A BRIEF HISTORY

One of IAHCSMM's primary roles is to provide education to Central Service professionals. Prior to the mid-1940s, sterilization services for hospital departments were performed by surgical nurses in the surgery department. The American College of Surgeons began a movement to standardize and centralize the preparation, sterilization, handling and storage of all surgical instruments and supplies into one unit. As a result, CS departments were created.

The CS profession continues to evolve at a rapid pace, with new medical devices being introduced regularly. The processing of robotic, endoscopic and complex orthopedic, spinal and other related instruments and equipment require special skills and knowledge of decontamination, disinfection and sterilization processes.

IAHCSMM MISSION STATEMENT

IAHCSMM's mission is to promote patient safety worldwide by raising the level of expertise and recognition for those in the Central Service profession. IAHCSMM accomplishes this:

- By providing educational, professional development, certification, communication and representation opportunities for Central Service professionals;

- Through collaboration efforts with allied partners, members and associates; and

- Through advocacy initiatives for public policy changes.

IAHCSMM EDUCATIONAL OPPORTUNITIES

The Association's mission statement emphasizes that the provision of educational opportunities for its membership is a high priority. Held in the spring of each year, IAHCSMM's Annual Conference and Expo combines the annual membership meeting with five days of educational offerings for technicians and managers and others affiliated with the field of Central Service.

IAHCSMM chapters also provide educational seminars to reach as many CS technicians as possible. Together, these educational offerings help technicians and managers keep up-to-date on the latest trends, standards, regulations and recommended practices and provide an opportunity for these individuals to network with other CS professionals in their region. Below, members of IAHCSMM's Minnesota Chapter attend a chapter-sponsored local educational seminar. (**Figure 1**)

At both the national and local level, vendors play a significant role in making educational offerings possible for CS professionals. Along with sponsoring exhibits where they bring the latest information on products and services available to CS, they also provide financial support for many of IAHCSMM's educational offerings, such as continuing education lessons, educational videos and online education.

Figure 1

The vast majority of IAHCSMM's educational offerings are developed for CS professionals by CS professionals. The result is practical and useful information that has a direct application to the field of CS.

IAHCSMM PUBLICATIONS

IAHCSMM publishes several comprehensive and informative textbooks for the CS profession. These publications are developed as needs are identified by the membership and as new processes and technologies enter the workplace.

Central Service Technical Manual, Eighth Edition, is designed to provide information on decontamination and sterilization theories and basic CS practices.

Central Service Leadership Manual provides valuable information for CS leaders at all levels of leadership.

Central Service Instrument Resource provides detailed information about the proper inspection, care and handling of commonly-used instruments, as well as specialty instruments.

The CS Dictionary is a useful pocket reference for all CS professionals.

The texts are used in the United States and several other countries. *The Central Service Technical Manual, Seventh Edition*, is available in Chinese, Japanese, and Spanish translations. *The Central Service Leadership Manual* is available in Chinese.

This text, *Endoscope Reprocessing Manual*, has been developed to provide additional education on the reprocessing, care and handling of endoscopes.

IAHCSMM INFORMATION EXCHANGE

Reprocessing professionals require the most current information to remain at the "top of their game." This information is vital for keeping them informed about new products and changes in recommended practices. IAHCSMM provides several methods for the sharing of information and ideas.

Communiqué is the Association's bi-monthly publication. With features such as "President's Message," "Technician's Exchange," "Self-Study Lesson Plans," "Hot Topics," information about upcoming meetings, and news from IAHCSMM chapters—not to mention articles on a wide variety of CS-related subjects, Communiqué is a valuable tool for every reprocessing professional.

Central Source is the Association's bi-monthly electronic publication that provides news and information that enhances CS professionals' knowledge and keeps them abreast of changes that impact the field. Popular features include: "Ask the Expert," "Certification Corner," "Educator Update," "Orthopedic Council Query," and "Breaking News".

IAHCSMM's website, www.iahcsmm.org, is an immediate source of a wide variety of helpful professional information. The website allows members and certificants to renew certifications, complete online lesson plans, purchase publications, access resources and references and stay abreast of late-breaking news, upcoming events, advocacy initiatives and much more.

One of the most popular features of the website is the Discussion Forum. This real-time feature allows members to post questions about many issues CS professionals encounter each day. Responses are provided by other forum users, many of whom face the same challenges.

IAHCSMM CERTIFICATION AND PROFESSIONAL DEVELOPMENT

Attaining certification is a positive first step in one's personal professional development efforts. Those pursuing a career in medical device reprocessing continually strive for recognition as professionals. IAHCSMM supports certification and recognizes it as an important component to patient safety. Professionals work in an occupation that requires extensive knowledge and skills and a profession involves membership limited to individuals with formal education in a specialized body of knowledge. A profession is typically controlled by licensing, registration, and/or certification. Individuals working in the Central Service profession certainly meet those requirements.

IAHCSMM maintains high educational and certification standards. As the professional and technical requirements of the medical device reprocessing profession have become more demanding, IAHCSMM has developed certification programs to address these evolving demands.

For many reprocessing professionals, the right combination of education and experience has lead to certification. Certification is the formal recognition of specialized knowledge, skills and experience. It is demonstrated by successful completion of a multiple choice exam, which tests knowledge needed to perform everyday tasks in the CS profession. Certification assures the public that minimum competency standards were met and recognizes those who have met those standards.

IAHCSMM offers several certifications including:

- **Certified Registered Central Service Technician (CRCST)**—emphasis is on reprocessing concepts and current standards and practices. Attaining CRCST status also requires a minimum of 400 clinical hours of hands-on experience and successful completion of the CRCST certification exam.

- **Certified Instrument Specialist (CIS)**—emphasis is on identifying, handling and processing surgical instrumentation. One

must first have the CRCST credential before attaining this certification.

- **Certification in Healthcare Leadership (CHL)**—emphasis is on supervisory responsibilities, including recruitment, selection, orientation and training, communication, leadership, motivation and other related concepts. One must first have the CRCST credential before attaining this certification.

- **Fellowship in Central Service (FCS)**—is available to CS professionals. By demonstrating professional accomplishments and writing a research paper, and successfully completing an oral interview, applicants may achieve the FCS, which is the highest designation for Central Service professionals.

Maintaining each of these certifications requires proof of continuing education that must be earned and then submitted at the time of annual certification renewal.

To learn more about IAHCSMM certifications and Fellowship visit: www.iahcsmm.org.

In addition to certification, IAHCSMM provides several additional opportunities for professional development. Opportunities for involvement include local IAHCSMM chapters and serving on national committees, projects, events or the IAHCSMM Executive Board. These opportunities provide an ability to learn, grow professionally and network with professional colleagues.

IAHCSMM ORGANIZATIONAL STRUCTURE

Active membership in IAHCSMM is open to anyone employed in healthcare CS or Materiel Management departments. Associate membership is open to anyone who, by virtue of their occupation, has an allied relationship with CS Materiel Management departments.

Although it is not required for membership, many IAHCSMM members form local chapters that offer independent meetings and provide educational offerings.

Figure 2

Information about local chapters or about forming a chapter can be found at www.iahcsmm.org.

The elected local chapter Presidents, or their designees, serve as chapter representatives and comprise the IAHCSMM Board of Directors. This Board convenes during the Annual Conference and elects representatives to the Executive Board from among its members.

The Executive Board is comprised of the Association's President, President-Elect, Secretary- Treasurer and Executive Director, as well as the elected representatives from the Board of Directors. Responsibilities of the Executive Board include transacting administrative and financial business of the Association, planning the Annual Conference, updating educational materials, maintaining working relationships with allied associations and interacting with committees, chapters and members.

IAHCSMM's Education Department is responsible for developing and monitoring all IAHCSMM educational programs to ensure that all materials are timely, consistent and accurate. The Executive Board, the Education Department, and Subject Matter Experts (SMEs) work together to:

- Provide various types of education, as identified by member needs;

- Develop the educational program for the Association's annual Conference; and

- Develop and update all the Association's educational resources.

These teams of experts, like the team pictured above, bring a real-world feel to educational offerings and help ensure that the information provided meets the needs of today's medical device reprocessors. (**Figure 2**)

Another important facet of education is the Corporate Advisory Committee (CAC). The Association's elected officers and Executive Director meet with the CAC to plan annual vendor exhibits and education and consider other issues relating to corporate sponsors.

IAHCSMM AND ALLIED HEALTHCARE ASSOCIATIONS

IAHCSMM represents the CS profession and fosters relationships with several allied associations, such as The Association for the Advancement of Medical Instrumentation (AAMI), Society of Gastroenterology Nurses and Associates (SGNA), the Association of periOperative Registered Nurses (AORN), Association of Surgical Technologists (AST), and the Association of Professionals in Infection Control and Epidemiology (APIC).

These allied healthcare associations focus on patient safety and infection prevention goals. Improving patient outcomes requires that all healthcare professionals within each specialty work together to achieve these goals.

IAHCSMM AND THE FUTURE

IAHCSMM leadership strives to improve the professional status of individuals working in the CS profession. They are continually looking for ways to enhance skills and knowledge. Current issues include:

- Advocating certification for CS technicians in all 50 states;

- Continually updating and improving educational resources;

- Advocating standards and best practices that protect the patient; and

- Providing opportunities for career growth and professional development.

When the need for education arises, IAHCSMM steps forward to provide the tools necessary to enable medical device reprocessors to provide safe and functional devices to meet the needs of healthcare providers and keep patients safe.

Medical device reprocessing is dynamic and fast-paced, and the work is challenging and highly technical. Inefficiencies in productivity, errors, and poor quality outputs are costly to healthcare facilities and can be life-threatening to patients. The performance of every person has a direct impact on patient and employee safety. The profession is truly an evolving occupational discipline. Reprocessing professionals should take great satisfaction in knowing that their efforts, service, special skills and commitment to doing what's right are a part of every surgical procedure, diagnostic procedure, patient recovery, birth and patient discharge. IAHCSMM's motto, "Instrumental to Patient Care®," accurately reflects our collective contributions and commitment.

Chapter 1

Introduction to Endoscopes

Learning Objectives

Upon completion of this chapter, readers will be able to:

1. Explain the importance of endoscopic procedures, what they entail and the various trained medical personnel involved in endoscopic procedures

2. Identify relevant historical milestones in the development of endoscopes/endoscopy

3. Explain the reprocessing challenges surrounding complex medical devices, such as flexible endoscopes

4. Examine the benefits of endoscopic procedures to a patient and a healthcare facility

5. Explain the importance of a technician's role and quality of work during endoscope processing

6. Identify key staff competencies necessary for successful and safe endoscope processing

INTRODUCTION

In today's healthcare environment, there is great emphasis placed on technicians' ability to fully understand and apply reprocessing techniques to a variety of medical devices that range from the simplest surgical instruments to the newest and most complex forms of medical technology. To allow for successful procedures, complex medical devices have certain reprocessing requirements that involve numerous steps and the reprocessing technician's detailed knowledge of the device's sophisticated and intricate design. One of the most complex and expensive medical devices found in today's healthcare environment is the flexible endoscope.

From 2014 to 2016, endoscope reprocessing garnered significant media attention because improper processing of endoscopes led to infection and, in some cases, death.

A January 2014 article published in *The Seattle Times* noted that more than 100 patients who had undergone colonoscopies at a Washington hospital between 2011 and 2013 were advised to be tested for HIV and hepatitis B and C after the hospital discovered equipment used in the procedures had not been properly cleaned.

In 2015, the *Los Angeles Times* reported that two endoscopy patients died and five more were infected by the *Carbapenem-resistant Enterobacteriacae* (CRE) superbug after being exposed to contaminated endoscopes; 179 more patients who underwent procedures between October 3, 2014, and January 2015, were also advised to be tested.

In addition to several other news stories devoted to contaminated endoscopes, a 2016 Senate investigation found America's system for ensuring medical device safety failed repeatedly to prevent dirty endoscopes from spreading deadly superbugs. The number of patients harmed far exceeded previous estimates from federal regulators.

Reprocessing endoscopes is a serious responsibility that comes with very real challenges and potentially serious consequences, if not performed correctly. Because reprocessing can result in cross contamination, infection and even death, the emphasis on proper training is critical. The steps in endoscope reprocessing must be understood and diligently and consistently followed by reprocessing technicians to protect patients. Proper reprocessing also protects staff from possible exposure and helps protect physicians and the facility from liability risk.

There are inherent challenges associated with reprocessing endoscopes, including:

- Flexible endoscopes' intricate and complex design.

- Complex reprocessing instructions by the manufacturer; lack of knowledge and sufficient training for those responsible for reprocessing endoscopes.

This, coupled with the lack of inventory and pressure to turn over equipment quickly for the next case, can increase the chance of errors or shortcuts.

The purpose of this text is to help technicians learn about the importance of reprocessing endoscopes and the good work practices needed to be successful. It is imperative that personnel who handle these complex and expensive medical devices have received proper training, passed competency requirements and receive ongoing education in their field. A competent and well-trained endoscope reprocessing professional is an invaluable member of the team. Endoscope reprocessing staff and endoscopy managers will also have standards for which to test competencies of staff working with endoscopes. Whether an individual has been working with endoscopes for 20 years or is a new technician, this manual will serve as a detailed guide to help ensure safe patient-outcomes during every endoscopic procedure.

WHAT IS ENDOSCOPY?

Endoscopy is the visual examination of interior structures of the body using an endoscope.

Endoscopes are specially-designed medical instruments used to view the interior of an organ or body cavity. The endoscope can be flexible, rigid or semi-rigid and vary by function, design and size, depending upon the area of the body being examined.

An endoscopist is a medical specialist trained in the use of an endoscope.

The Endoscopy or Gastrointestinal (GI) Lab is a dedicated department where many of the common endoscopic procedures, such as colonoscopies and gastroscopies, are performed. These self-contained units may clean, reprocess and high-level disinfect their own endoscopes or the endoscopes may go to the Central Service (CS) department for cleaning and reprocessing. Other procedures, such as bronchoscopy and cystoscopy, may be performed in the surgical unit or a specialized department, such as Urology. It is critical that ALL staff follow the same guidelines, regardless of where the endoscopes are used or reprocessed.

Other staff members who work in the GI Lab may include endoscopy technicians and gastrointestinal (GI) nurses. From set up to take down, endoscopy technicians support and assist endoscopists with exploratory procedures of the stomach, colon and esophagus. Some of these endoscopic procedures include colonoscopy preparation and biopsy specimen collection.

GI nurses assist endoscopists during endoscopy procedures. The GI nurse is often the patient's first contact and the one who answers the patient's questions. This is a specialized position covering pre-endoscopy and post-endoscopy care.

Endoscopists, GI nurses and endoscopy technicians work as a team to provide the best patient care possible. This team relies on the endoscope reprocessing technician to provide safe, properly processed and functional devices for each procedure. Failure to provide a safe and functional endoscope may result in patient injury, infection, delayed procedures, and missed or inaccurate diagnoses.

Endoscope reprocessing technicians must be familiar with a wide variety of endoscopes. Each is a complex device and each has different reprocessing instructions. **Figure 1.1** provides a diagram illustrating some common types of endoscopes in use today.

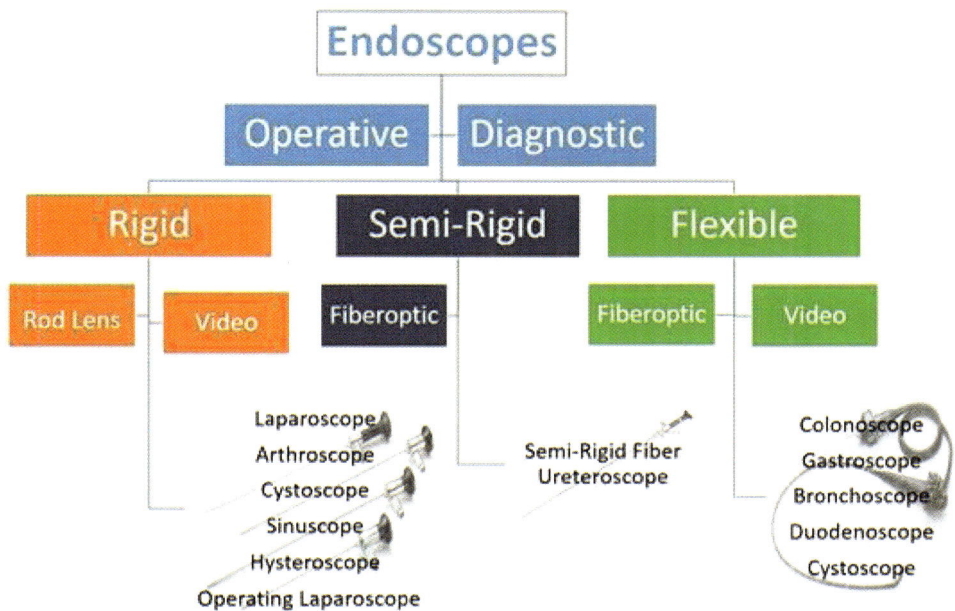

Figure 1.1

WHY ARE ENDOSCOPES USED?

Depending upon the patients' need, endoscopes may be used for:

- Routine screenings: For example, colonoscopies for cancer screening are typically recommended every 10 years, beginning at age 50 or earlier for high-risk individuals.

- Diagnostic treatment: To determine the source of pain or bleeding, obtain biopsy specimens, etc.

- Therapeutic treatment: Such as polyp removal (polypectomy), stone removal, etc.

ABOUT FLEXIBLE ENDOSCOPES

All endoscopes pose a challenge for technicians when it comes to reprocessing, but flexible endoscopes pose the greatest challenge because they are comprised of many moving and non-moving components. This text will focus largely on flexible endoscopes, with an emphasis on the importance of following reprocessing steps and properly caring for these complex medical devices.

A flexible endoscope is designed so the endoscopist can maneuver in and around the anatomy being examined (such as the curvy structure of the colon). The insertion tube that goes into the body is a flexible, tube-like structure that houses a video chip or fiber optic imaging bundle to allow for visualization by the eye or a video camera and monitor. Inside the insertion tube are light fibers, instrument channels and air/water and suction channels allow for the passage of instruments, such as biopsy forceps, and air and water to irrigate and keep the tip of the endoscope clean. The suction channel is used for aspiration — the action of drawing fluid by suction from a vessel or cavity. The tip or bending section of the endoscope is usually flexible and houses the terminal end of the air/water ports and biopsy port where instruments are introduced to the body cavity; this tip is operated by controls on the body of the endoscope. The bendable tip and flexible insertion tube allows for increased maneuverability and a wide angle of view, so all areas of the structure can be seen. Flexible endoscopes can use video or fiber optic visualization to capture real-time video footage and static images of internal body cavities. Some technology even enables 3-D imaging. **Figure 1.2** provides an example of a flexible endoscope. **Figure 1.3** provides a diagram of a flexible endoscope. Note the complexities within the endoscope's construction.

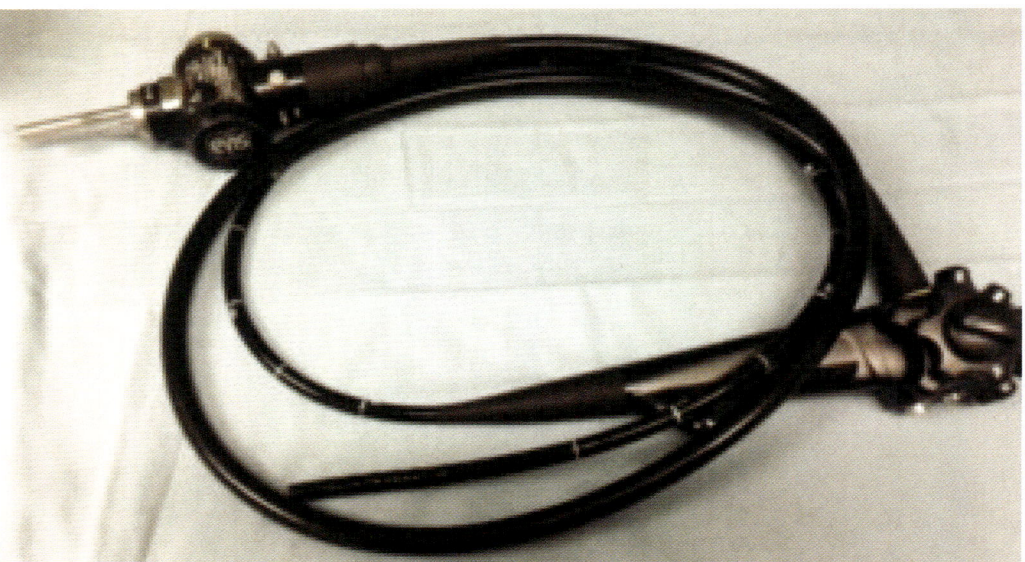

Figure 1.2

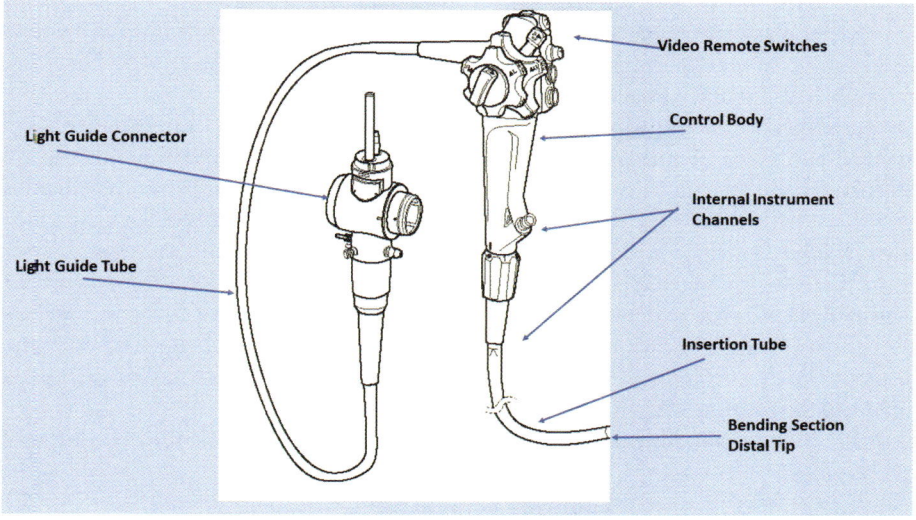

Figure 1.3

Historical Overview

Many people believe that endoscopes are a relatively new medical device. While there have been many advances in recent years, the concept of visualization of the body's interior has been around for a long time. **Figure 1.4** traces the evolution of endoscopes.

Benefits of Endoscopy

Due to technological advancements in endoscopy and in the medical device industry, many procedures that once required opening a body cavity have transitioned to **minimally invasive surgeries (MIS)** using endoscopes. MIS offers significant benefits to the patient, including a very small incision (or

A Brief History of Endoscopes

1800's	1900 - 1950	1960's – 1980's	1990's	2000's
• Phillip Bonzini makes an attempt to view the human body using a tube he calls the "Lichleiter (Light Guided Instrument). • Pierre Salomen Segales d'Etchepare develops an instruments to examine the urinary tract and bladder. He calls it an "endoscope". • Dr. Adolph Kussmail of Germany develops a "gastroscope" to look inside the stomach of a living human being.	• Georg Wolf, a Berlin manufacturer of rigid endoscopes produces the Sussman Flexible Endoscope. • The first endoscope image is transmitted over a flexible glass bundle. • Karl Storz and Harold Hopkins develop the rod-lensed endoscope. • Researchers unveil the first prototype of a gastrocamera which could take images of the digestive tract. • Basil Hirschowitz invents the first fiberoptic endoscope which becomes the standard visualization device.	• Fiberscopes completely replace gastrocameras. • The first robotic-assisted surgery is performed.	• Charge-coupled devices are introduced to modern flexible video endoscopes. • A 3D video system is developed in Germany.	• The first capsule endoscope is developed in Israel by Dr. Iddam. This "pill cam" includes LED lights and a camera. It is swallowed by the patient and tracks through the gastrointestinal tract. • The first High Definition endoscope system is developed. • Endoscopic Ultrasonography (EUS) or Echo-endoscopy is developed. It enables the endoscope to be combined with an ultrasound.

Figure 1.4

no incision at all) and, in many cases, the ability to perform the procedures on an outpatient basis, which allows the patient to go home the same day. These procedures generally have limited complications and are sometimes performed with conscious sedation, rather than general anesthesia, resulting in a much faster recovery time for the patient.

In the U.S. alone, at least 11 million endoscopies are performed every year—a number that continues to increase. Along with benefits to the patient, there are also many benefits to a healthcare facility that incorporates endoscopic procedures into its daily case load. MIS procedures are generally performed quickly; the average colonoscopy, for example, only takes about 30 minutes.

> **Minimally invasive surgery (MIS)** Minimally invasive surgery uses state-of-the-art technology to access body cavities and reduce the damage to human tissue during procedures.

ENDOSCOPE-RELATED CHALLENGES

Evidence shows that more healthcare-associated infections have been linked to contaminated endoscopes than any other medical device. ECRI Institute listed inadequate reprocessing of flexible endoscopes as the number one health technology hazard of 2015.

Pressure to turnover equipment quickly, coupled with lack of endoscope inventory and other resources, can make it tempting for endoscope reprocessing technicians to skip steps, rush the process or make other potentially life-threatening mistakes. Following best practices and standards is critical for endoscope reprocessing technicians to be successful and confident in their role.

Importance of the Technician's Role and Quality of Work

Endoscopes are very expensive devices, ranging from $7,000 for a fiber optic endoscope, up to $40,000 for a video endoscope and more than $60,000 for a flexible ultrasound endoscope. Proper care, correct handling and a thorough understanding of the equipment will not only improve patient safety, it

will also help protect this equipment investment and reduce unnecessary repairs and premature equipment replacement.

Due to increasing numbers of endoscopic procedures and the common demand for rapid device turnover, it is essential that endoscope reprocessing technicians diligently adhere to best practices and industry standards. Training and competencies are a key component to helping ensure endoscope reprocessing technicians have the necessary tools, knowledge and skills to properly clean, care for, store and handle endoscopes.

It is important for ALL reprocessing professionals to:

- Know the difference between flexible and rigid endoscopes, and understand the anatomy of each endoscope.

- Understand the risks involved with improper reprocessing of endoscopes, including cross-contamination, infection and death.

- Understand basic microbiology and which factors play a role in determining whether a patient will acquire an infection.

- Understand the importance of preventing **biofilm** on medical devices.

- Understand point-of-use preparation and handling of endoscopes, including scope handling and transport.

- Understand how to properly leak test endoscopes and know the steps to take if an endoscope fails a leak test.

- Understand and follow each step in the manual and mechanical cleaning processes, and know the detergents necessary for this process, along with any cleaning verification techniques.

- Understand proper high-level disinfection (HLD) safety measures and protocols to ensure safety of use.

- Understand the various inspection points to evaluate the basic condition of endoscopes.

- Understand types of sterilization processes and considerations when determining if an endoscope can/should be sterilized.

- Understand the necessary quality assurance testing documentation requirements necessary for endoscopes in the healthcare facility.

- Understand proper handling, storage and transportation of both flexible and rigid endoscopes.

- Understand the personal protective equipment (PPE) necessary for staff during endoscope reprocessing.

> **Biofilm** A collection of microorganisms that attach to surfaces and each other to form a colony. The colony produces a protective gel that is very difficult to penetrate with detergents or disinfectants.

If any person fails to understand any of the aforementioned competencies, patient safety may be at risk. When 100% patient safety is the goal, 99% is simply not good enough.

Technicians must also possess personal skills and traits, such as integrity, attention to detail and effective communication skills to help ensure a quality process for every endoscope and effective teamwork across all members of the team.

CONCLUSION

GI or CS technicians responsible for reprocessing endoscopes are faced with many challenges; however, given the right tools, these individuals can and will be successful in preventing infection, cross contamination and death due to improperly-processed endoscopes.

Endoscopy procedures will continue to increase in both frequency and urgency. Because endoscope reprocessing is a major patient safety concern, the need for proper training of endoscope reprocessing technicians will continue to grow. Technicians have

an opportunity to advance their professional skills by becoming experts in endoscope reprocessing. This involves understanding the anatomy of endoscopes; the various steps involved with proper precleaning; transporting; leak testing; cleaning, disinfecting; inspecting; sterilizing; and storing endoscopes. Understanding the risks and recognizing there are very clear steps and instructions that lead to successful endoscope reprocessing will help technicians become successful in their role.

Knowledge is the key to success for any endoscope reprocessing technician. Detailed knowledge about the anatomy of endoscopes and the critical steps in reprocessing that must be followed every time is essential for ensuring a safe device for each patient.

RESOURCES

Terhune C. Hospitals Grapple with Safety of Scopes after UCLA Outbreak. Los Angeles Times. Feb. 20, 2015.

Bartley N. Children's Patients May Be at Risk of Infection after Colonoscopies. The Seattle Times. Jan. 22, 2014.

Murphy P. US Senate Health, Education, Labor and Pension Committee. Jan. 13, 2016. Preventable Tragedies: Superbugs and How Ineffective Monitoring of Medical Device Safety Fails Patients. US Senate Minority Staff Report.

Rutala, WE, Weber DJ. 2008. Healthcare Infection Control Practices Advisory Committee. Guideline to Disinfection and Sterilization in Healthcare Facilities.

ERCI Institute. 2015. ECRI Institute Announces Top 10 Health Technology Hazards for 2015.

American Cancer Society. 2013. What is Endoscopy?

Association for the Advancement of Medical Instrumentation. 2015. ANSI/AAMI ST91: Flexible and Semi-rigid Endoscope Processing in Health Care Facilities.

TERMS
Minimally invasive surgery (MIS)

Biofilm

Chapter 2

Overview of Flexible Endoscopes

Learning Objectives

Upon completion of this chapter, readers will be able to:

1. Identify the purpose of flexible endoscope procedures

2. Review the basic anatomy of flexible endoscopes

3. Discuss specific flexible endoscopes and identify the procedures they support

4. Identify challenges endoscope reprocessing professionals face when cleaning flexible endoscopes

INTRODUCTION

The advent of flexible endoscopes provided a new way of examining and treating patients; it was no longer necessary to gain access to certain areas of the body through an incision. Certain areas of the body that had previously been impossible to see were made accessible through the use of a flexible endoscope that would bend to navigate body contours and project light to enhance visualization. Flexible endoscopes quickly became a valuable tool for detecting disease and treating conditions before they became major health problems. The instruments' popularity stemmed from the fact that they could offer improved visibility and, in some cases, provide minimally-invasive treatment, while reducing healing time for the patient.

Flexible endoscopes are one of the most complex medical devices used in **diagnostic** and **therapeutic/ operative** procedures. The physical complexity of general flexible endoscope design makes the device difficult to clean. The many types of flexible endoscopes further add to the complexity and cleaning challenges. An important step in successful reprocessing is to develop an understanding of how the endoscopes are designed. That knowledge will help identify and address reprocessing challenges. This chapter will provide basic information about common flexible endoscopes and the types of procedures they support.

> **Diagnostic** The process of attempting to determine or identify a possible disease or disorder.
>
> **Therapeutic/Operative** Used to perform procedures (e.g. the removal of a rectal polyp), tumor ablation, dilatation.

INTRODUCTION TO FLEXIBLE ENDOSCOPES

Flexible endoscopes are often used to:

- Screen for cancer;

- Take a closer look at abnormalities found in radiologic imaging;

- Search for the causes of specific symptoms;

- Obtain tissue samples;

- Perform operations to remove stones from the kidney, urethra and bladder and open strictures; and

- Remove some forms of cancer.

Common Endoscopic Procedures

Endoscopic procedures are quite common. It is likely that every reader of this text has either undergone an endoscopic procedure or knows someone who has. Examples of common endoscopes and their applications include:

- Arthroscopes, which examine joints;

- Bronchoscope, which examine air passages and lungs;

- Colonoscopes, which examine the colon;

- Cystoscopes, which examine the urinary bladder;

- Gastroscopes, which examine the small intestine, stomach and esophagus; and

- Hysteroscopes, which examine the uterus.

Flexible and Video Endoscopes: What is the Difference?

Endoscopes look alike and share similar construction. The primary difference is how each endoscope transmits images. Flexible endoscopes may require external equipment. Other equipment may include a video monitor that allows the physician (and others) to view the image on a monitor, and water and suction containers used for irrigating and aspirating during the procedure. **Figure 2.1** provides an example of a flexible video endoscope used for gastrointestinal (GI) procedures with the common equipment needed for a basic procedure.

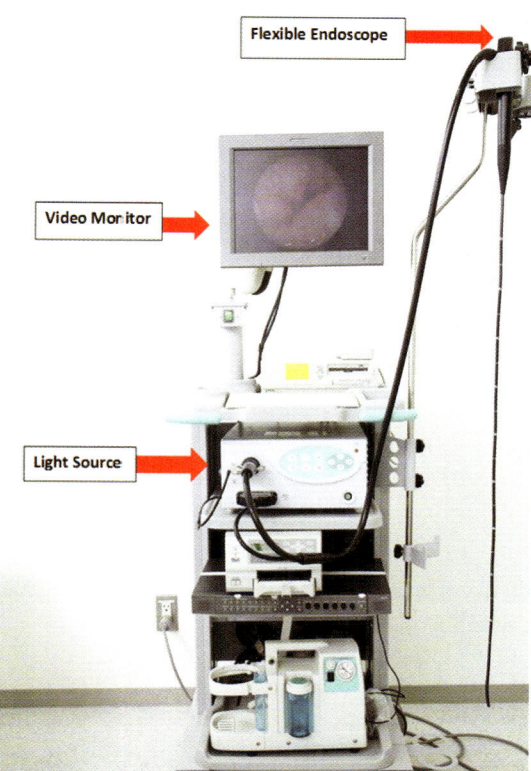

Figure 2.1

Basic Flexible GI Video Endoscope Components

Each flexible endoscope type has a unique design that enables it to be used effectively for its main purpose; however, there are some general components that are common to most flexible video endoscopes.

1. **Light Guide Tube (Light Connector)**
    The light connector is the end of the endoscope that connects to the light source.

2. **Universal Cord/Light Tube**
    This tube connects the light connector to the control body.

3. **Control Body**
    This section of the endoscope contains the hand controls: angulation control knobs, elevator/ lifter, air/ water, suction control valves, remote video switches, biopsy port and focus mechanism for the fiber optic endoscope.

4. **Internal Instrument Channel (Working Channel)**
    The instrument channel allows instruments to be inserted and enables the physician to perform certain procedures, such as polyp removal and biopsies. (See **Figures 2.2 and 2.3**) *Note: Some flexible endoscopes do not have an instrument channel.*

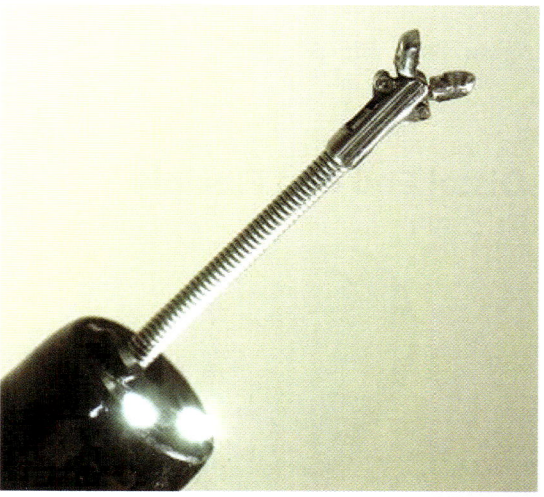

Figure 2.2

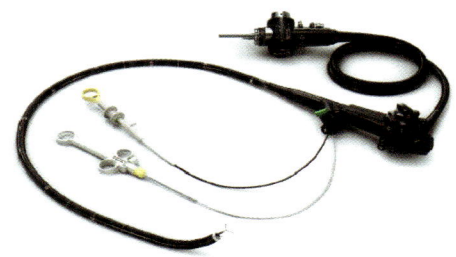

Figure 2.3

5. **Insertion Tube**

   This tube houses the internal components, such as the air, water and instrument channels and the fiberoptic system. This is the component that is inserted into the body. The insertion tube provides protection for each channel.

6. **Bending Section (Distal Tip)**

   As its name implies, the bending section of the insertion tube articulates to aid insertion into curved areas. Its ability to bend also provides enhanced viewing for the physician. While all flexible endoscope components are delicate, improper handling makes the bending section especially vulnerable to damage.

Figure 2.4 provides an example of the distal end of a flexible endoscope.

Distal End of a Flexible Scope

Figure 2.4

The distal tip of a flexible endoscope contains the critical components that enable the endoscope to:

- Shine light into the body;

- Transmit images from inside the body;

- Enable instruments to be inserted and removed;

- Enable air and water to be injected into the body; and

- Suction.

The distal tip can be manipulated to enable the physician to view the targeted area from several angles. (See **Figure 2.5**) Understanding the functions of the distal tip can help endoscope reprocessing professionals protect the endoscope from damage and help ensure that all components of the endoscope are reprocessed properly. **Figure 2.6** provides a cross-section diagram of a distal tip.

Figure 2.5

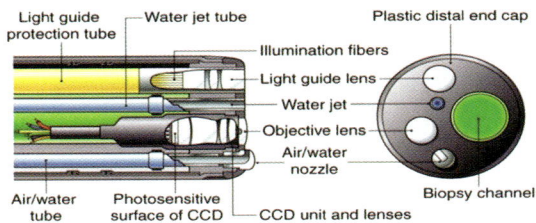

Figure 2.6 Distal Tip Diagram

The distal tip is protected by a metal sheath. (See **Figure 2.7**) If this area is kinked, crushed or damaged, it can render the endoscope unusable. Special care must always be taken to prevent damage to the distal tip. Failure to do so may delay procedures and will increase repair costs.

Figure 2.7

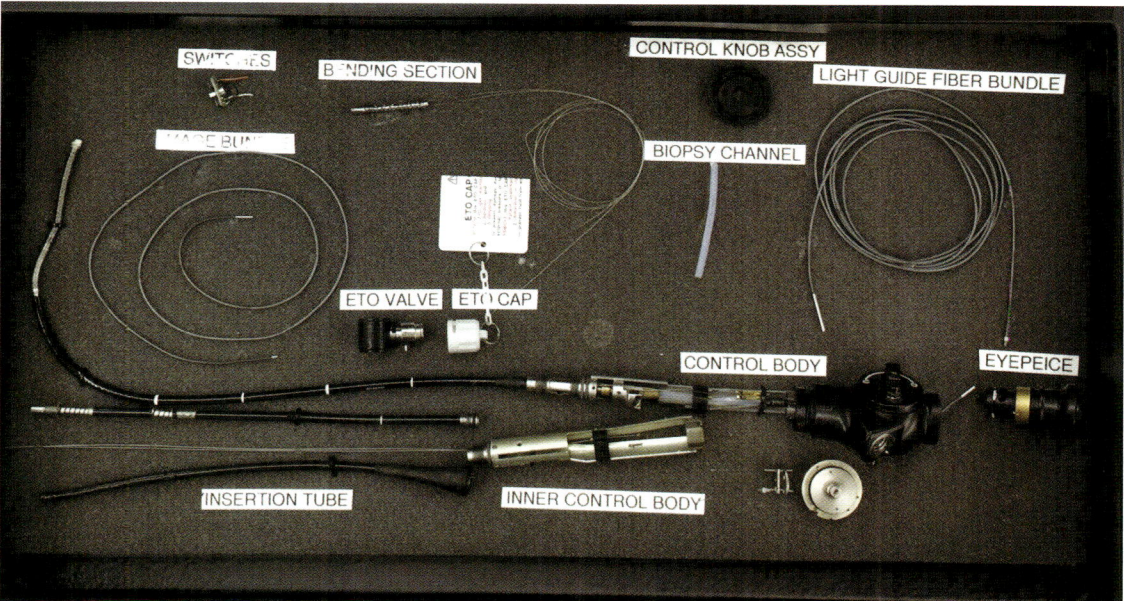

Figure 2.8 Small-diameter Endoscope

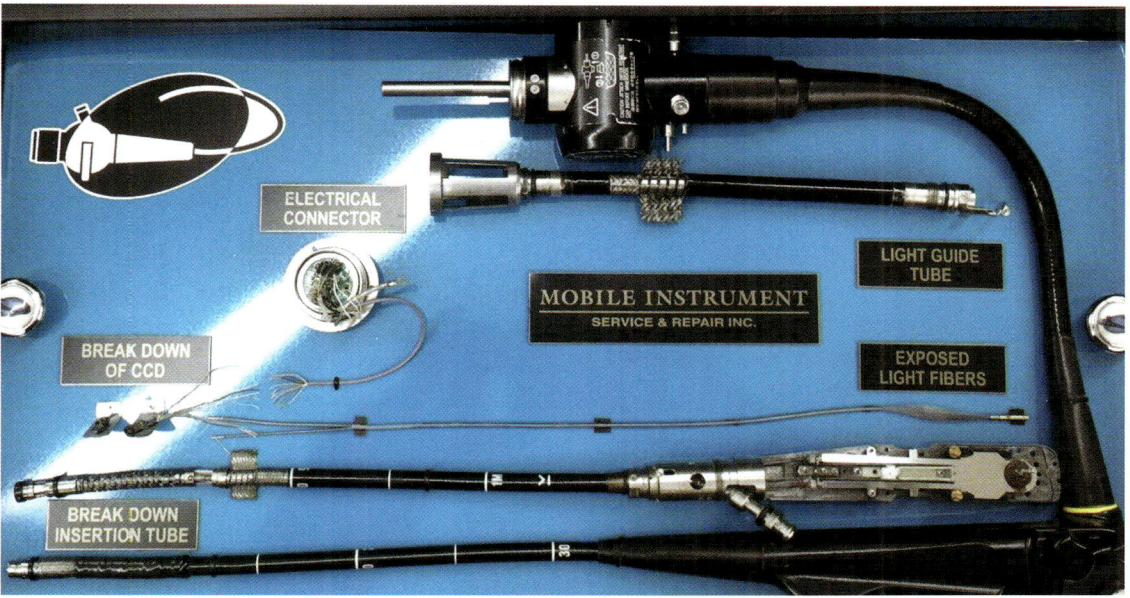

Figure 2.9 Large-diameter Endoscope

The distal tip is not the only area of the endoscope that requires careful handling and meticulous cleaning. Proper care and functioning of each section of an endoscope is critical for the success of each flexible endoscopy procedure. **Figures 2.8 and 2.9** provide a glimpse of deconstructed flexible endoscopes, which helps demonstrate the instruments' complexity.

COMMON ENDOSCOPES AND THEIR APPLICATIONS

While flexible endoscopes share some basic characteristics, each type is designed for a specific use. The following section identifies some common flexible endoscopes and their uses.

Gastroscope/Gastroscopy

A gastroscope is a flexible endoscope designed to view the interior of the stomach. Characteristics of gastroscopes include:

- Diameters ranging in size from 4.9mm (neonatal) to 13.2mm Working length ranging from 1030mm to 1100mm with 120-to140-degree field of view;

- Degrees of **deflection** 210/90 degrees up/down; 100/100 degrees left/right; and

- Working channel diameter ranging from 2.0mm to 3.7mm.

Figure 2.10 provides an example of a gastroscope.

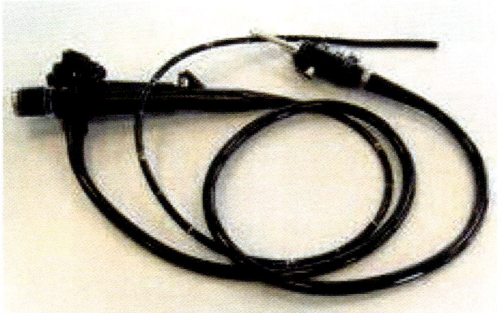

Figure 2.10

> **Deflection** The ability of the tip of a flexible endoscope to bend (using control knobs) to increase the area that can be accessed by a physician, visually or with an instrument.

Gastroscopes are used in gastroscopies, an examination of the upper digestive tract (including the esophagus, stomach and duodenum). Gastroscopies are commonly performed to diagnose abnormalities of the esophagus lining and stomach, remove polyps, control bleeding and obtain tissue samples for biopsy. Gastroscopy procedures are often referred to as upper GI or esophagogastroduodenoscopy (EGD) procedures. **Figures 2.11 and 2.12** provide illustrations of an upper GI gastroscopy.

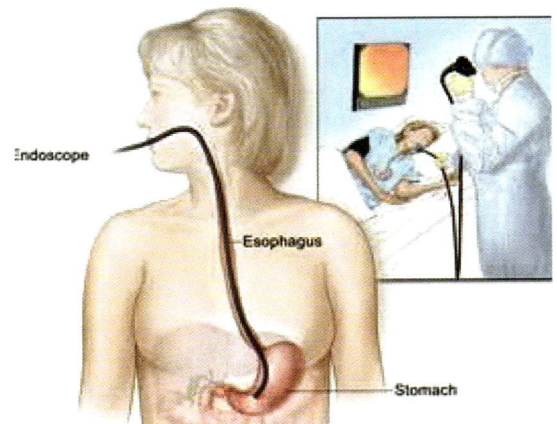

Endoscope

Esophagus

Stomach

Upper GI Endoscopy

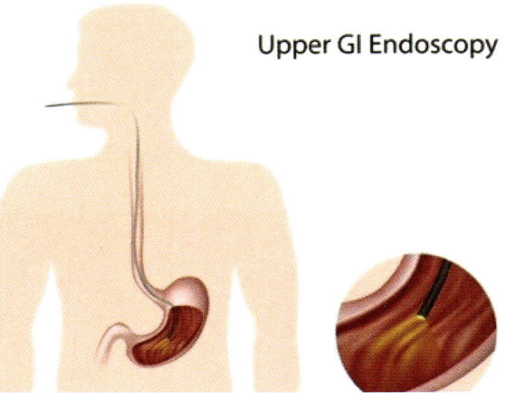

Figures 2.11 and 2.12

Duodenoscope/Duodenoscopy

A duodenoscope is a flexible endoscope used to diagnose and treat abnormalities in the duodenum. Characteristics of duodenoscopes include:

- Diameter ranging from 10.8mm to 11.3mm;

- Working length ranging from 1240mm to 1250mm with 100- to 140-degree field of view;

- Degrees of deflection are 120/90 degrees up/down; 110/90 degrees left/right;

- Diameter of working channel ranging from 3.2mm to 4.8mm; and

- An elevator mechanism and side-viewing camera that allows the physician to view the duodenum.

Although all flexible endoscopes pose complex cleaning challenges, duodenoscopes have been identified as particularly challenging to clean. The elevator channel at the distal tip is very difficult to access for cleaning. In 2016, ECRI Institute, which posts an annual top ten list for health technology hazards, listed duodenoscopes as the number one health technology hazard. Fatal *Carbapenem-resistant Enterobacteriaceae* (CRE) infections that attracted national media attention in 2014 and 2015, combined with ECRI Institute's own studies that explored endoscope cleaning and disinfection practices, prompted ECRI's safety engineers to place flexible endoscope reprocessing at the top of the 2016 health technology hazards list. **Figure 2.13** provides a close look at a duodenoscope elevator channel.

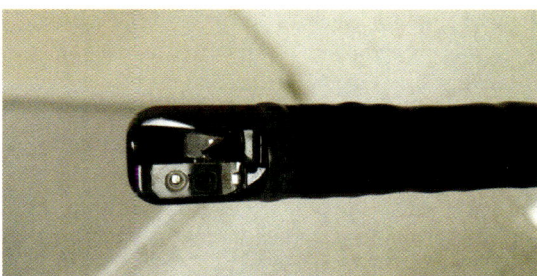

Figure 2.13

> **ECRI Institute** A nonprofit organization dedicated to using applied scientific research to discover which medical procedures, devices, drugs and processes are best to improve patient care. ECRI Institute aims to keep healthcare professionals abreast of challenges and concerns regarding medical devices.

Esophagogastroduodenoscopy

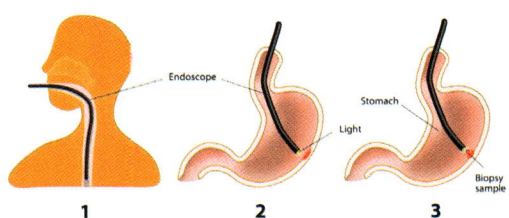

Figure 2.14

- Duodenoscopy is performed to diagnose and treat ulcers and diverticulitis. It may also be performed to examine, diagnose and treat several conditions, including: dysphagia (difficulty swallowing); upper abdominal pain or chest pain of a noncardiac origin; gastroesophageal reflux disease (GERD); GI bleeding and esophageal varices (enlarged veins in the esophagus); tumors (benign or malignant); hiatal hernia; upward movement of the stomach (either into or alongside the esophagus). Also performed for anemia, vomiting, epigastric or chest pain, suspected cancer, caustic ingestion and ulcers. A side-viewing (oblique view) endoscopy is primarily used for cannulating the biliary duct or pancreatic duct also called endoscopic retrograde cholangiopancretography (ERCP). The duodenoscope is designed with an elevator channel that assists the endoscopist with cannulating the duct(s). There are no accessories that are passed through this elevator channel, but its intricate design makes it very difficult to adequately clean and reprocess. An end-viewing EGD scope is generally used to examine the proximal (first portion) duodenum (beyond the stomach/pylorus)".

An EGD may be performed therapeutically to control bleeding; remove tumors or polyps (growths); dilate narrowed areas in the upper GI tract (e.g., esophagus); remove foreign objects; perform laser therapy; and place a percutaneous gastrostomy tube (a tube used for tube feeding into the stomach).

Figure 2.14 illustrates an EGD, a diagnostic procedure that allows the physician to diagnose and treat problems in the upper GI tract.

1. Insertion of endoscope;

2. Examination; and

3. Obtaining a biopsy.

Colonoscope/Colonoscopy

A colonoscope is used to examine the lower GI tract. Characteristics of colonoscopes include:

- Diameter of insertion tube ranging from 11.6mm to 13.7mm;

- Working length ranging from 730mm to 1700mm with 120- to 170-degree field of view;

- Degrees of deflection are 180/180 degrees up/down; 160/160 degrees left/right; and

- Diameter of working channel ranging from 3.2mm to 3.7mm.

During a colonoscopy, the physician examines the colon for tumors, polyps and other abnormalities that could lead to or indicate colorectal cancer. Colonoscopies can also be used to diagnose inflammatory bowel disease (IBD), diverticulosis and some forms of colitis. Colonoscopies are very common procedures. The American Cancer Society recommends colonoscopy (or some form of screening) for everyone over the age of 50. **Figure 2.15** provides an illustration of a colonoscopy.

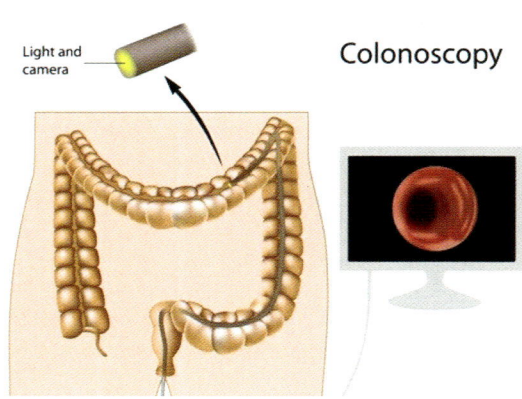

Figure 2.15

Enteroscope/Enteroscopy

An enteroscope is used to examine the small intestine to investigate irregularities such as blocked bowel passages and small bowel tumors. Characteristics of enteroscopes include:

- Diameters ranging in size from 9.2mm to 11.6mm;

- Working length ranging from 2000mm to 2200mm with 140-degree field of view;

- Degrees of deflection are 180/180 degrees up/down; 160/160 degrees left/right; and

- Working channel diameter ranging from 2.8mm to 3.8mm.

- Small bowel enteroscopy allows examination of the small bowel beyond the ligament of Treitz (the suspensory ligament of the duodenum). It is a limited exam because of the inability to examine the entire length of the small intestine. Enteroscopy may be performed because of suspected GI bleeding in the small bowel, small bowel biopsy for diagnosis of celiac disease and any suspected abnormality that is out of reach of the standard EGD endoscope. **Figure 2.16** provides an example of an enteroscope.

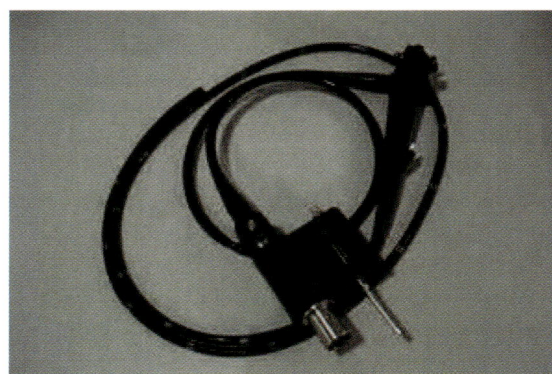

Figure 2.16

During an enteroscopy, a balloon is inserted into the small intestine. **Figure 2.17** provides an illustration of a double balloon enteroscopy.

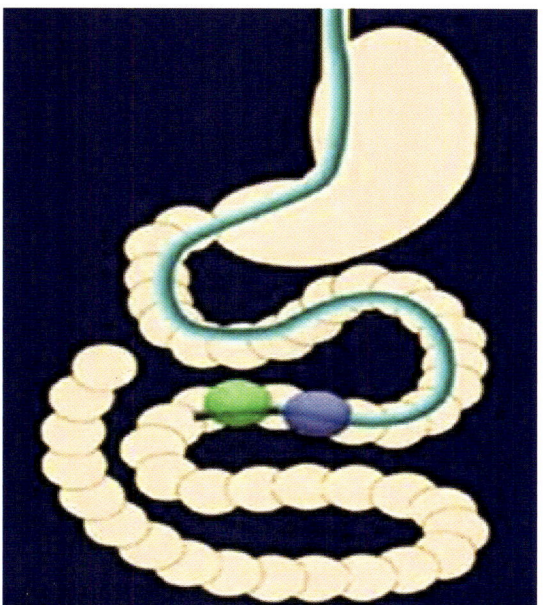

Figure 2.17

Bronchoscope/Bronchoscopy

Bronchoscopes are used to examine the throat, larynx, trachea and lower airways. There are two types of bronchoscopes: flexible and rigid. Flexible bronchoscope procedures are performed more often than rigid bronchoscope procedures. Rigid bronchoscopes are usually used when the patient is under anesthesia. **Figure 2.18** provides an example of a flexible bronchoscope.

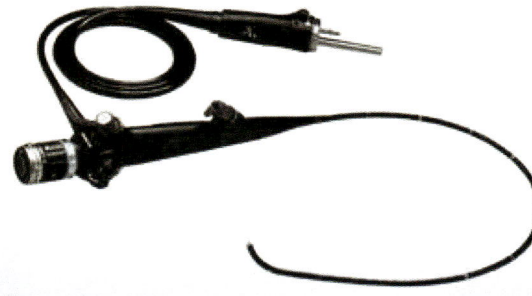

Figure 2.18

Bronchoscopy involves the direct visualization of the tracheobronchial tree and can be used for procedures to:

- Secure uncontaminated secretions for culture;

- Perform biopsies;

- Remove foreign bodies; and

- Excise small tumors.

The diameter of this flexible scope is small enough to reach into the bronchi of upper, middle and lower lobes for examination and/or biopsy.

Figure 2.19 provides an illustration of a flexible bronchoscopy procedure.

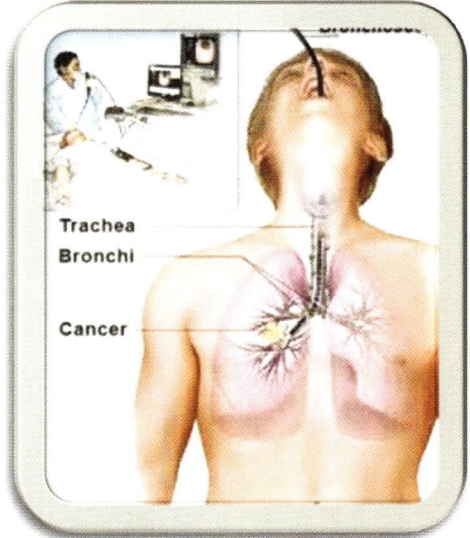

Figure 2.19

Rhinolaryngoscope/Rhinolaryngoscopy (Ear, Nose and Throat)

Rhinolaryngoscopes are used to examine upper airways, such as nasal passages, nasopharynx, oropharynx and larynx. Characteristics of rhinolaryngoscopes include:

- Diameters ranging in size from 2.4mm to 5.2mm;

- Working length ranging from 260mm to 600mm with 75- to 140-degree field of view;

- Degrees of deflection are 130/130, 180/90, 210/120 or 210/210 degrees up/down; and

- Working channel diameter ranging from 1.2mm to 2.6mm.

Rhinolaryngoscopies are often performed by allergists and Ear, Nose and Throat (ENT) physicians. **Figure 2.20** provides an illustration of rhinolaryngoscopy procedures using a flexible and rigid endoscope.

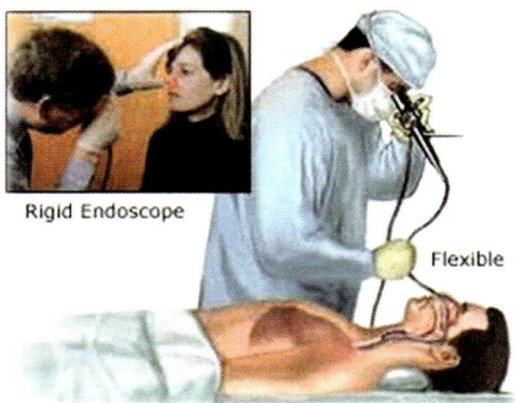

Figure 2.20 Direct Visualization via a Flexible Fiber Optic Rhinolaryngoscope

Choledochoscope/Choledochoscopy

Choledochoscopes are used to visualize the interior of the biliary tract. A choledochoscope is used to visualize gallstones and has a channel that allows for accessories for removal of stones. Characteristics of choledochoscopes include:

- Diameter ranging in size from 2.5mm to 5.6mm;

- Working length ranging from 300mm to 700mm with 75- to 140-degree field of view;

- Degrees of deflection are 160/130 degrees up/down or 180/130 degrees up/down; and

- Working channel diameter ranging from 1.2mm to 2.2mm.

Figure 2.21 provides an illustration of a choledochoscope.

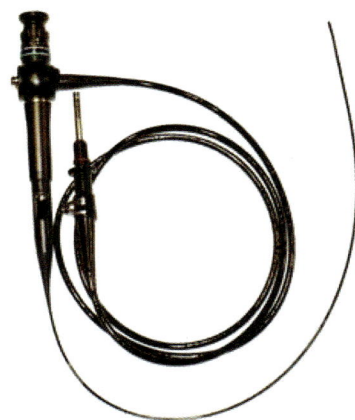

Figure 2.21

Choledochoscopy procedures are often performed to remove gallstones. **Figure 2.22** provides an illustration of a choledochoscopy procedure.

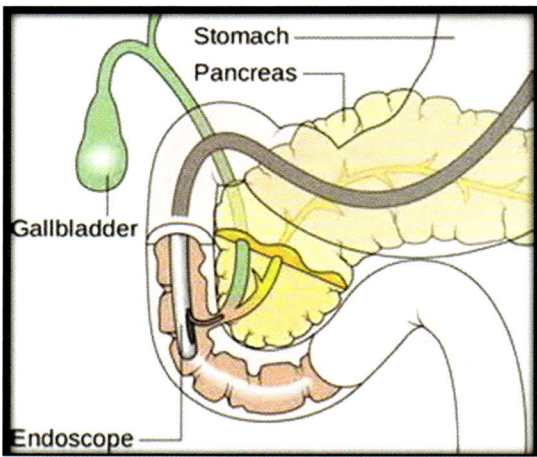

Figure 2.22

Ureteroscope/Ureteroscopy

Ureteroscopes are designed to provide visualization of the ureters that connect the kidney to the urinary bladder. Ureteroscopy is defined as retrograde instrumentation performed with an endoscope passed through the lower urinary tract directly into the ureter and calyceal system. Flexible ureteroscopy allows entry into all parts of the kidney to visualize any tissue abnormality, and aid in stone removal. Characteristics of ureteroscopes include:

- Diameter ranging in size from 2.5mm to 4.1mm;

- Working length ranging from 650mm to 700mm with 75-to 120-degree field of view; and

- Working channel diameter ranging from 1.2mm to 1.8mm.

Ureteroscopy is often used to treat kidney stones and tumors. **Figures 2.23 and 2.24** provide illustrations of ureteroscopies.

- Diameter ranging in size from 4.8mm to 5.4mm;

- Working length ranging from 550mm to 400mm with 90- to125-degree field of view;

- Degrees of deflection are 130/130, 180/170, 210/90, 210/120, 210/140, and 220/90 degrees' up/down; and

- Working channel diameter ranging from 1.2mm to 1.8mm.

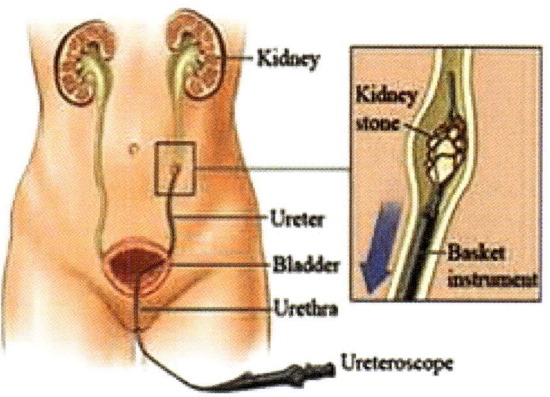

Figure 2.23 Fiberoptic Ureteroscope

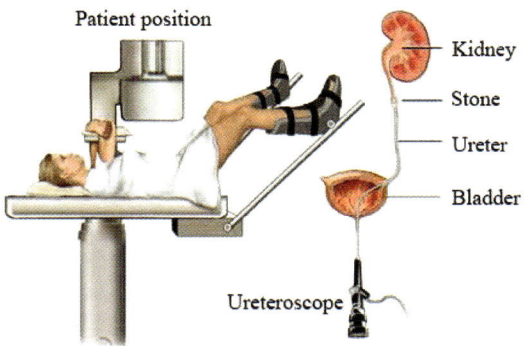

Figure 2.24

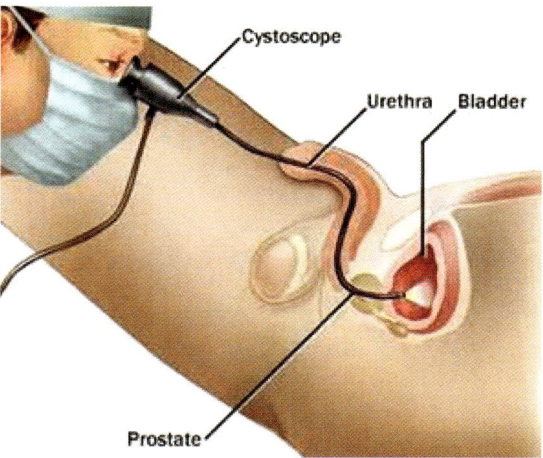

Figure 2.25

Cystoscopy procedures are performed to detect abnormalities in urinary tract organs. **Figure 2.25** provides an illustration of a cystoscopy being performed with direct visualization via a flexible fiberoptic cystoscope. *Note: Most procedures today are performed via video using either a flexible video cystoscope or a camera and video system with a flexible fiberoptic cystoscope.*

Hysteroscope/Hysteroscopy

Hysteroscopes are used provides visualization of the uterus. Characteristics of hysteroscopes include:

- Diameter ranging in size from 3.1mm to 4.9mm;

Cystoscope/Cystoscopy

Cystoscopes are used to examine the inside of the bladder. A flexible cystoscopy allows examination of the bladder to identify causes of pain, blood, rrepeated infections or an irritable bladder. Characteristics of cystoscopes include:

- Working length ranging from 240mm to 300mm with 90- to 120-degree field of view;

- Degrees of deflection are 100/100, 120/120, 130/130 degrees up/down; and

- Working channel diameter ranging from 1.2mm to 2.2mm.

Hysteroscopy procedures are performed to diagnose and treat abnormal bleeding inside the cervix or uterus. **Figure 2.26** provides an illustration of a flexible fiberoptic hysteroscopy. *Note that the attached cable to this fiber optic hysteroscope is the light guide. Some fiber optic endoscopes incorporate the light guide as shown here while other manufacturers allow for a standard light guide to be attached to the endoscope.*

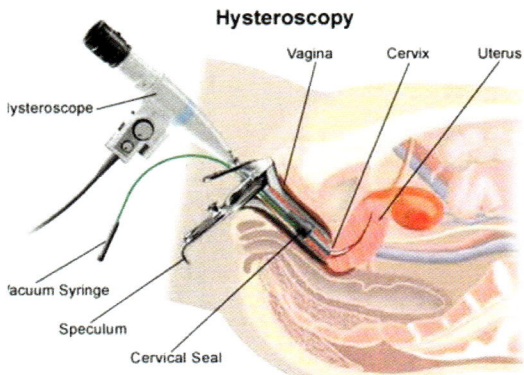

Figure 2.26

CHALLENGES

This sampling of endoscopes illustrates some of the various functions and styles of common flexible endoscopes. There are some similarities, such as lumens and working elements; however, there are also differences in configuration. Each type of endoscope presents its own unique challenge for endoscope reprocessing staff.

It is safe to say that the term "endoscope" is a broad one, much like "automobile" only broadly conveys "car." While there are some basic commonalities in automobiles, each make and model is unique.

When approaching endoscope reprocessing, it is important to keep in mind that each type of endoscope is unique and must be reprocessed according to its specific reprocessing requirements, as stated by the manufacturer in the instructions for use (IFU). The challenge for each endoscope reprocessing technician is to understand the features of each flexible endoscope and consistently process the device according to their unique requirements.

CONCLUSION

Flexible endoscopes are designed to perform different functions. These devices' differences are evident in their configurations. Knowing that reprocessing requirements are different for each type is the first step in successfully reprocessing flexible endoscopes. Understanding the different types of flexible endoscopes and their appropriate processes that must be followed during each reprocessing step improves the likelihood for positive patient outcomes.

RESOURCES

International Association of Healthcare Central Service Materiel Management. Central Service Technical Manual, Eighth Edition. 2016.

ECRI Institute. *Infections from flexible endoscopes, missed alarms, and opioid-related deaths lead the Top 10 Health Technology Hazards List for 2016.* https://www.ecri.org/press/Pages/Dirty_Endoscopes_Top_ECRI_Institutes_2016_Technology_Hazards_List.aspxhttps. Accessed Nov. 2016.

American Cancer Society. *Types of Endoscope and Procedures.* https://www.cancer.org/treatment/understanding-your-diagnosis/tests/endoscopy/what-is-endoscopy.html. Accessed Nov. 2016.

TERMS

Diagnostic

Theraputic/Operative

Deflection

ECRI Institute

Chapter **3**

Microbiology Basics For Endoscope Reprocessors

Learning Objectives

Upon completion of this chapter, readers will be able to:

1. Explain the importance of protecting patients from infection

2. Review basic concepts of microbiology

3. Discuss biofilm formation and its hazards

4. Identify infections associated with specific endoscopic procedures

5. Discuss survival of pathogens on environmental surfaces and cloth

INTRODUCTION

The purpose of reprocessing is to remove microorganisms and bioburden that are present on an instrument or device following patient use. Effective device reprocessing helps prevent cross contamination and subsequent patient infection. Reprocessing staff are an extremely important part of the endoscopy team. Every task performed during endoscope reprocessing either reduces or increases the risk of patient infection; from controlling the environment by donning personal protective equipment (PPE) (See **Figures 3.1** and **3.2**) to meticulously decontaminating endoscopes, each task is critical to patient safety. Controlling microorganisms within endoscopes and the reprocessing environment requires attention to detail. Every endoscope provides an opportune hiding place for microorganisms, which makes endoscope reprocessing a challenge. If microorganisms remain on or in an endoscope after processing, they can infect the patient during the next procedure.

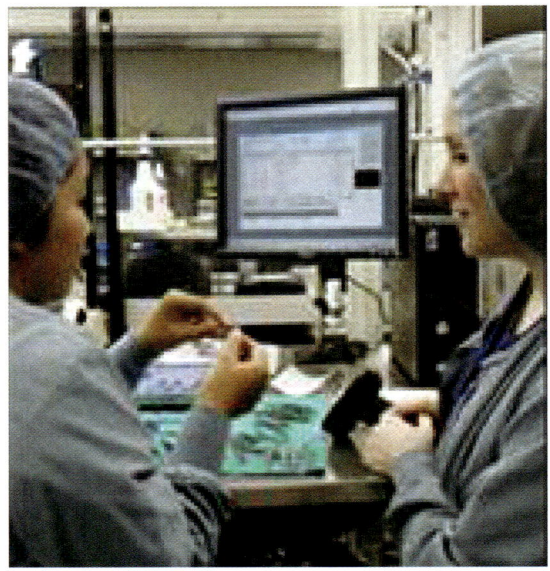

Figure 3.2 Every aspect of reprocessing impacts patient safety.

It is critically important that endoscope reprocessors use the most appropriate products and consistently apply best practices and the most effective techniques for each reprocessing task.

Don't be Discouraged: A Story

Endoscopes are complex devices that are difficult to reprocess. Even the smallest error can mean failure. It is the job of reprocessing professionals to meet the challenge and do what they can to prevent infection.

Let's take an example of another profession. Picture a city infected with a high level of crime. Some of the criminals are much more violent than others, but they are all hurting their victims. The police work hard to capture the criminals and prevent further victims, and the level of crime is dramatically decreased. Life is improved in the city; however, some crimes still occur. If the police become discouraged and fail to perform due diligence in their job, crime will increase again.

The point is we all have an important job to do. Whether an individual is fighting crime or infection, prevention requires sustained effort. It does make a difference!

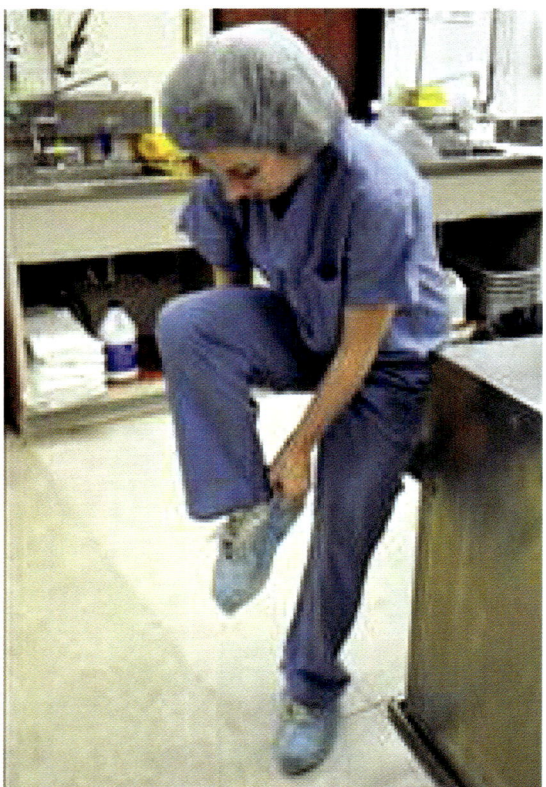

Figure 3.1 Every activity performed by reprocessors is designed to reduce the risk to the patient.

BACKGROUND

Endoscopes have been in use for the past 100 years; however, it was not until 1986 that these devices could magnify and project the images onto a monitor screen. It was this significant technological advancement that made endoscopes more practical and led to the rise in endoscopic procedures. Over time, endoscopes became increasingly complex, delicate and expensive. Flexible endoscopes were introduced, which allowed for their use across a range of specialties and applications. With the advent of these more sophisticated devices, cleaning and disinfection also became more intricate and difficult, which led to increased risk for patient infection.

Individual **microorganisms** cannot be seen without a microscope; however, they all possess the natural drive to survive. Most exist where their needs are met, where they are undisturbed and where they can proliferate. Microorganisms thrive in various environments, including in and on humans. Many **bacteria** that live inside the body are helpful. For example, humans have about one trillion "good" bacteria that live in the large intestines. Some bacteria produce substances that aid the digestion of food, while others play a vital role in the production of vitamins, such as B and K. Beneficial bacteria are known as **symbiotic bacteria**.

It is important to recognize, however, that even symbiotic (good) bacteria can lead to **infection** and other health complications if it migrates to areas of the body where it doesn't belong. Although humans are equipped with physical barriers to prevent inappropriate migration of symbiotic bacteria (See **Figure 3.3**), there are instances where bacterial migration can still occur. For example, minor injury can occur during an endoscopic procedure if an endoscope scrapes the surrounding tissue surfaces when it is being pushed or pulled into position. This friction injury can allow local bacteria to pass into the tissue, enter the "restricted area," and lead to subsequent infection. An infection that originates this way is called an opportunistic infection.

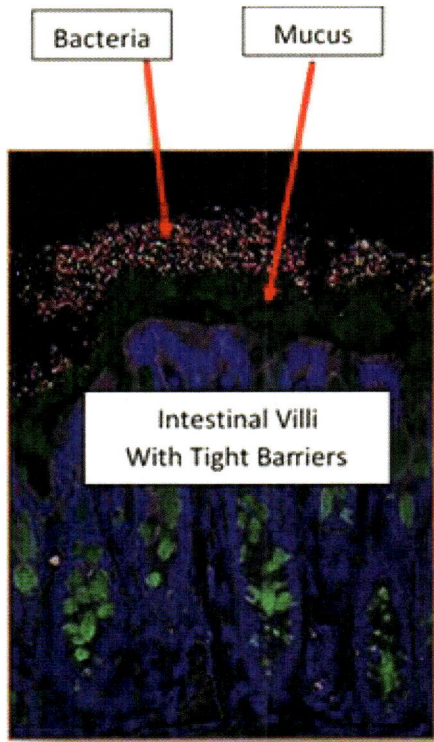

Figure 3.3

Microorganisms Organisms that can only be seen with the aid of a standard or electron microscope. *Note: Viruses are not considered to be alive and, as such, are often not included in the term microorganism; however, we include them here for simplicity.*

Bacteria Single-celled microorganisms that multiply by splitting. Bacteria can be helpful, such as those that aid food digestion in the intestines, or those used to break down waste in sewage treatment plants; however, bacteria can also be disease-causing pathogens or germs. *Note: A single bacteria is called a bacterium.*

Symbiotic Bacteria "Good bacteria" that help us in some way. A symbiotic relationship means that both sides benefit: bacteria can live and thrive and the human body is helped by the bacteria's presence.

Infection Invasion of body tissue by microorganisms that then multiply. The invading microorganism may be a recognized pathogen (germ) or a normally helpful microorganism (such as one that normally lives in the intestine) that invades a different part of the body, such as the bloodstream, kidneys or lungs. Things that cause infections are often called infectious agents.

There are many harmful bacteria, called **pathogens**, that do not help living beings, and cause infections. In addition to bacteria, **fungi**, **viruses** and **parasites** can also be pathogens. Pathogens can come from individuals who are ill, or from contaminated objects, including endoscopes. Endoscopes may remain contaminated due to inadequate reprocessing, use of contaminated automated reprocessing units, rinsing with contaminated water, excessively intricate endoscope design, inadequate reprocessing instructions from the endoscope manufacturer, endoscope damage, placing reprocessed endoscopes on contaminated surfaces, or endoscopes being handled with contaminated hands.

> **Pathogens** Capable of causing disease. Disease-causing bacteria, fungi, viruses, protozoa and helminths are called pathogens.
>
> **Fungi** A diverse group of microorganisms and plants that include microscopic fungi and yeasts, such as *Candida albicans* and *Aspergillus fumigatus*. Fungi also includes molds, mushrooms, mildews and smuts.
>
> **Virus** One of a group of infectious agents that can only reproduce using the mechanisms inside a living cell. Viruses can cause infections ranging from the common cold to hepatitis (A, B and C) to Ebola and small pox. Because they cannot reproduce outside a living cell, viruses are not considered to be alive. They are too small to be seen using a standard microscope, so an electron microscope must be used for their detection.
>
> **Parasites** Organisms that live off or in another organism (called the host). Parasites obtain nourishment and protection from the host, but give no benefit in return. Parasitic infections in human hosts often cause disease.

The more **aggressive** the pathogen, the fewer of them are needed to cause an infection. Pathogen aggressiveness can also be referred to as **virulence**. Less virulent pathogens require more bacteria to overcome the human defense systems and initiate an infection. Less virulent infections generally cause less severe infections; however, the physical condition of the person being infected plays a huge part in whether an infection occurs and how severe it will become.

Patients are much more vulnerable to infection. Many patients whose bodies may be fighting illness or injury have a suppressed ability to fight infection. The trauma of surgery and impact of anesthesia further increases their vulnerability. Reduced effectiveness of a patient's immune defenses makes it easy for even a few pathogens to cause an infection.

Figures **3.4 through 3.6** provide examples of patients who are more vulnerable to infection than healthy people.

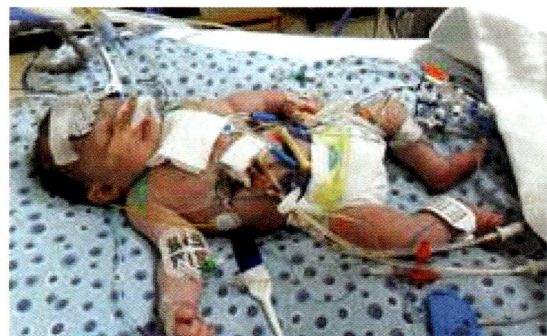

Figure 3.4

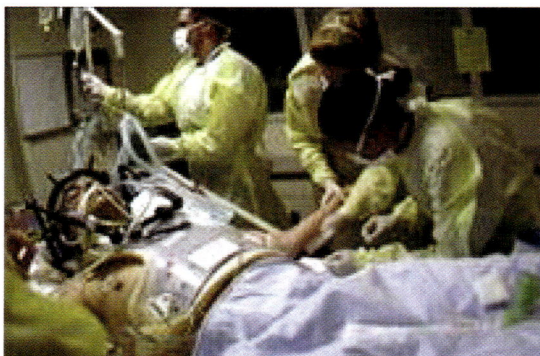

Figure 3.5

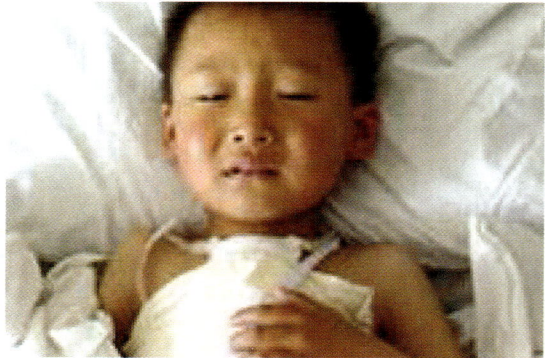

Figure 3.6

Elderly patients are generally at greatest risk for acquiring infection. Many have diabetes, respiration or heart problems, and less effective immune systems generally. (See **Figures 3.7 to 3.9**) Often, elderly patients arrive at hospitals from long-term care facilities where antibiotic-resistant pathogens are common. Endoscopes used for procedures on these elderly patients are more likely to be contaminated with **antibiotic-resistant** pathogens following use.

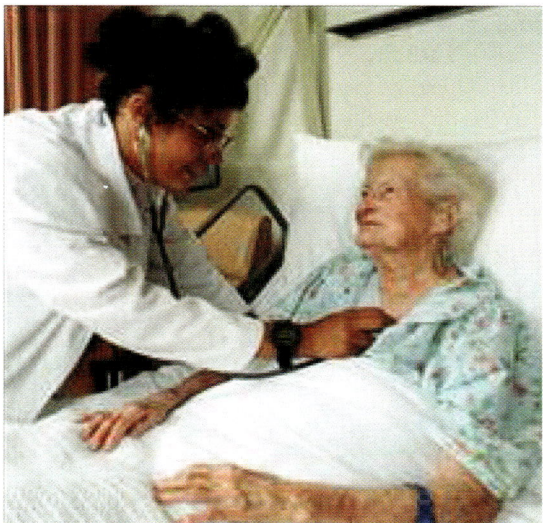

Figure 3.9

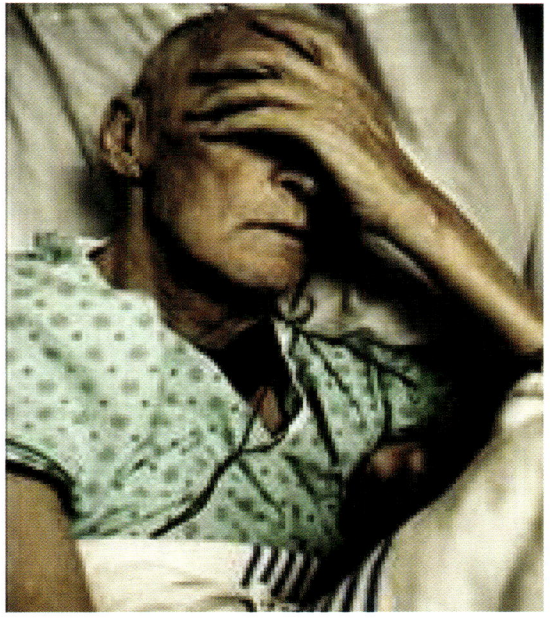

Figure 3.7

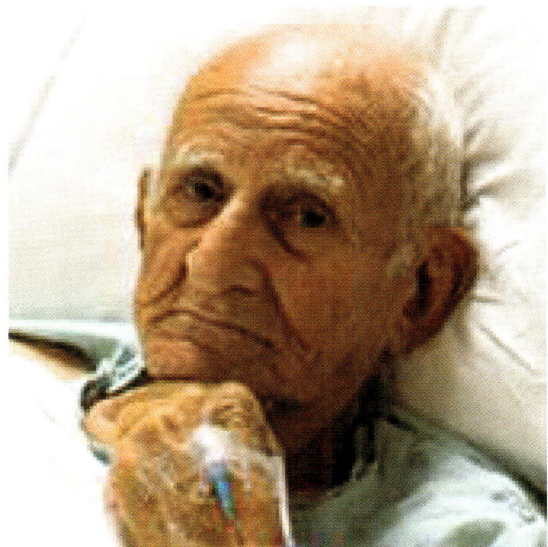

Figure 3.8

The more endoscope professionals learn about these microorganisms, the more they can understand how critical each step of endoscope reprocessing is to patient safety and infection prevention. It is important to remember that even a few pathogens can infect vulnerable patients; therefore, no reprocessing shortcuts are acceptable.

Aggressive The ability of a microorganism to invade, survive and multiply in tissues.

Virulence Ability of a microorganism to overcome a person's immune defenses and cause disease. The faster the infection progresses, or more severe the symptoms are, the more virulent the pathogen is rated.

Antibiotic-resistant Antibiotic resistance is the ability of pathogens to resist the effects of antibiotics that would normally be used to kill the microorganism. Antibiotics are ineffective against viruses, so anti-viral medications may be needed for their treatment. Viruses that resist the effects of these medications are often called drug-resistant viruses.

MICROBIOLOGY BASICS

Microbiology basics are important for endoscope professionals because they help provide an understanding of how to identify and destroy pathogens before they can lead to infection. (See **Figure 3.10**) If an infection does occur, knowing microbiology basics can help professionals investigate how the infection may have occurred.

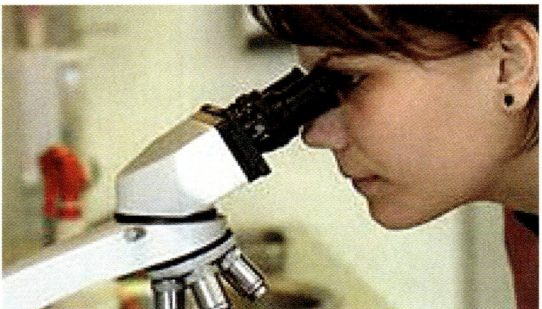

Figure 3.10

Bacteria

Bacteria are primarily divided into groups based on the color they stain, their shape, how they cluster or form groups and whether they make endospores (extremely protective escape pods) or possess individual slime capsule shields. *Note: There are also other characteristics used to group bacteria; however, this textbook will only address those that could affect endoscope reprocessing.*

Staining

Bacteria are without color, so staining is necessary to allow bacteria to be seen under the microscope. There are four primary stains for bacteria that are important to reprocessing departments, endoscopy departments and anywhere else in the healthcare facility where endoscopes are reprocessed: the **gram stain** (See **Figure 3.11**), **acid fast stain**, **endospore stain** and **capsule stain**.

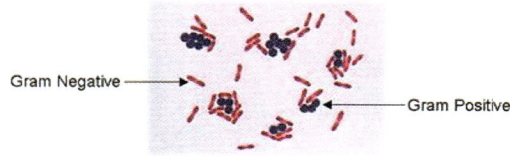

Figure 3.11

- Gram stain:. The structure of bacterium's outer surfaces determines which color the bacteria

will stain. This is important because the outer surface also helps determine which disinfectant would be most effective against it. Following gram staining, bacteria that are purple are called **gram positive** [or gram (+)] bacteria, and those that are red are **called gram negative** [or gram (-)] bacteria. (**Figure 3.12** provides a look at gram-stained bacteria.) Almost all bacteria fit into one of these groups. *Note: The gram stain was named after its inventor, Hans Christian Gram.*

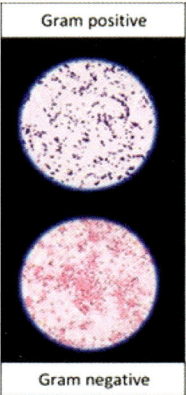

Figure 3.12

- Acid fast stain: Only two types of medically-important bacteria are acid fast, and both have caused endoscope-related infections. (See **Figure 3.13**) These bacteria are *Mycobacterium* and *Nocardia*. The structure of their outer surface makes them much more difficult to disinfect than gram negative or gram positive bacteria. A special disinfectant that kills these bacteria (called a tuberculocidal) is required. An acid fast stain is also called a Ziehl-Neelsen stain.

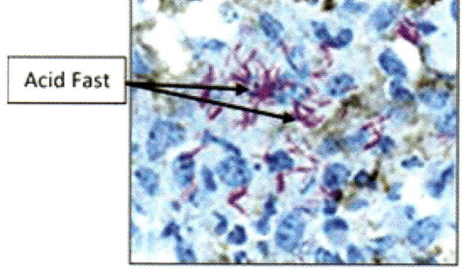

Figure 3.13

• Endospore stain: Only a few bacteria of medical importance produce endospores. These include *Clostridium* and *Bacillus*. An **endospore** forms inside the bacterial cell when it is threatened with starvation or exposed to extremely dry conditions or a lot of oxygen. (See **Figure 3.14**). Some bacteria, including *Clostridium difficile*, form endospores when exposed to oxygen which is poisonous to them. Bacteria that do not need oxygen to grow are called **anaerobes**. Endospores take about eight hours to form; then, the rest of the bacterial cell dies and the endospore is released. At that point, it is called a spore.

Under the microscope, the spore resembles a miniature golf ball. The bacteria's DNA is preserved inside. The spore goes into hibernation where it can survive extremely harsh conditions. Spores are

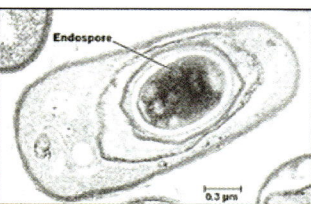

Figure 3.14

resistant to heat, chemicals, radiation and to drying out, all of which makes them extremely difficult to kill. They do not need food or water for survival.

A spore was found in the stomach of a bee that became trapped in amber 25 million years ago. By placing the spore in a favorable environment with the right food, scientists were able to **germinate** (grow) the spore into a fully functional, reproducing bacterial cell.

Endospores and spores look like white bubbles when gram stained and they are green when a special endospore stain is used. (See **Figure 3.15**) There are others stains that turn the spores other colors.

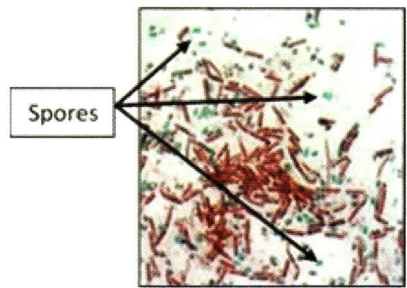

Figure 3.15

• Capsule stain: Some bacteria have slimy **capsules** around them that give bacteria added protection from the defensive attack of immune cells. Capsules also make it easier for bacteria to attack and invade human cells. Capsules are associated with bacterial virulence. In general, the larger the capsule, the more aggressive the bacteria. There are several capsule stains that can be used. (See **Figure 3.16**)

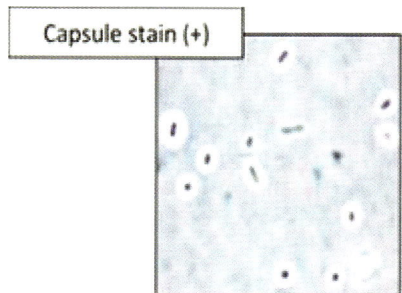

Figure 3.16

Gram stain Gram staining is usually the first test on a sample (specimen) taken from the patient when trying to identify bacteria that might be causing an infection. Most bacteria are either gram positive (hold on to a purple color) or gram negative (turn red or pink) when the staining is completed. The stain does not work for other non-bacterial microorganisms.

Acid fast stain A special stain used to identify mycobacteria and Nocardia. Also, called a Ziehl-Neelsen stain.

Endospore stain A stain used to identify the presence of spores. If spores are still covered with the membrane of the original bacteria, they are referred to as endospores.

Capsule stain A stain used to identify the presence of a capsule that surrounds individual bacterium.

Gram positive Bacteria that maintain a purple color after a gram stain is completed.

Gram negative Bacteria that cannot hold on to the purple color after a gram stain and are instead counter-stained red or pink.

Anaerobes Bacteria that do not require oxygen.

Endospore A tough dormant structure that some bacteria are able to form when cells find themselves in such extreme conditions that they are in peril of dying. The endospore allows the survival of bacteria's cell lines through harsh conditions that would kill a normal member of the species.

Germinate Refers to the spore process moving from the dormant, highly-protected spore state to an active bacteria in a favorable environment. Also, explained as moving from the spore form back to a vegetative (non-spore, vulnerable) form.

Bacterial capsules A gel-like coating that surrounds some bacteria. The capsule hides the identifying marks on bacteria, making them almost invisible to the immune system; this makes it difficult for immune cells to mount a successful attack.

Bacteria are segregated by shape. Under the electron microscope, shapes are significantly larger and appear more three dimensional (3-D). **Figure 3.17** provides examples of each shape.

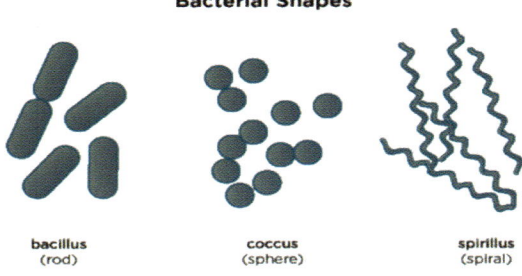

Bacterial Shapes

| bacillus (rod) | coccus (sphere) | spirillus (spiral) |

Figure 3.17

Figures 3.18, 3.19 and 3.20 provide clearer 3-D images.

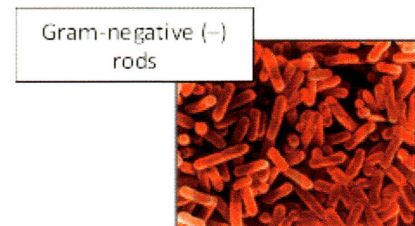

Gram-negative (−) rods

Figure 3.18

Gram-positive (+) cocci

Figure 3.19

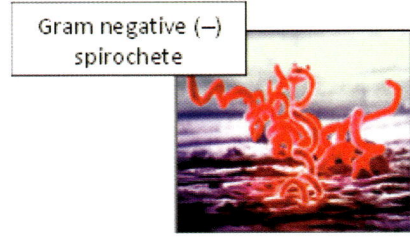

Gram negative (−) spirochete

Figure 3.20

When bacteria reproduce, many will form grouped patterns that can be seen through standard microscopes. They may be in long **chains** or in groups of two (**diploid**), four (**tetrad**), eight (**four on top of four = cuboid**), grape-like clusters, or as singles without a pattern.

In summary, one can describe gram positive bacteria as:

- *Streptococcus*: gram positive **cocci** in chains (illustration A).

- *Staphylococcus*: gram positive cocci in grape-like clusters (illustration B).

- *Tetrad:* gram positive cocci in groups of four (illustration C). Also called *Micrococcus.*

- *Clostridia*: gram positive rods as singles. Inside intestinal colon, *Clostridium difficile* has few, if any, spores (illustration D). After leaving the colon, they are exposed to oxygen in normal room air. This triggers endospore formation (illustration E). Endospores will later break free to be spores.

Figure 3.21 (below) provides illustrations of gram positive bacteria (A-E).

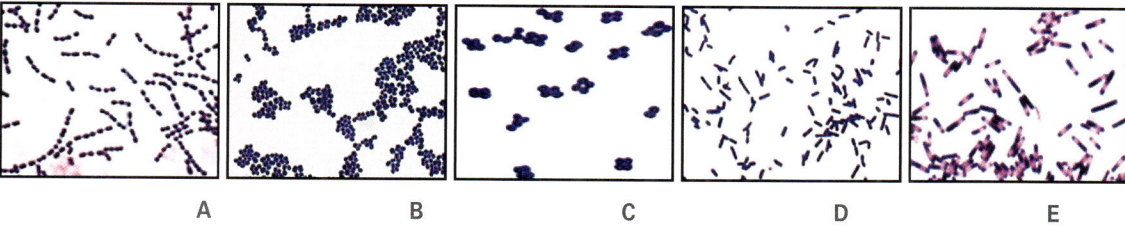

| A | B | C | D | E |

Gram negative bacteria as:

- *E. coli*: Large, gram negative **bacilli** that appear as singles (illustration A).

- *Klebsiella*: Small, gram negative bacilli with positive capsule stain (illustration B).

- *Neisseria*: Gram negative cocci in groups of two (illustration C).

- *Helicobacter pylori*: Tiny, gram negative **spirals** (illustration D).

Note: The altered staining of H. pylori is done to see the curves better making it appear purplish.

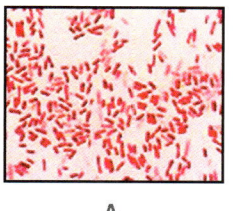 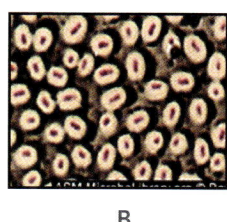 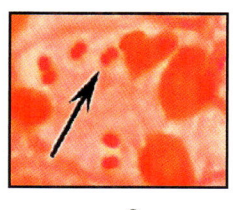 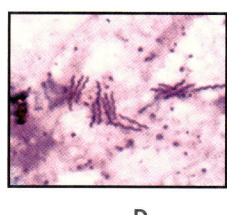

| A | B | C | D |

Figure 3.22 A-D provides photos of gram negative bacteria.

Chains Bacteria that are cocci appearing in single-file chains (like a necklace).

Diploid Bacteria that are cocci appearing in pairs.

Tetrad Bacteria that are cocci appearing in groups of four. Also called *Micrococcus*.

Cuboid Bacteria that are cocci appearing in groups of eight (like a box).

Cocci Spherical or ball-shaped bacteria.

Bacilli Rod-shaped bacteria.

Spirals Curved, spiral or corkscrew-shaped bacteria.

In addition to stains, shapes and groupings, bacteria are also described by how much oxygen they need to stay alive and how they respond to specific chemical tests. This helps to predict how members of the same bacterial family will respond to different disinfectants, environments and treatment therapies. It is often helpful to think of one's own "family tree." Grandparents have a large family with their own children and their children's children (grandchildren). Within this large family, everyone has his or her own unique traits, but they also share many characteristics with the entire family tree. Similarly, classification of bacteria into the large category of Family, the smaller grouping called Genus, and the even smaller set, called Species, means that members share traits, as well as have their unique properties.

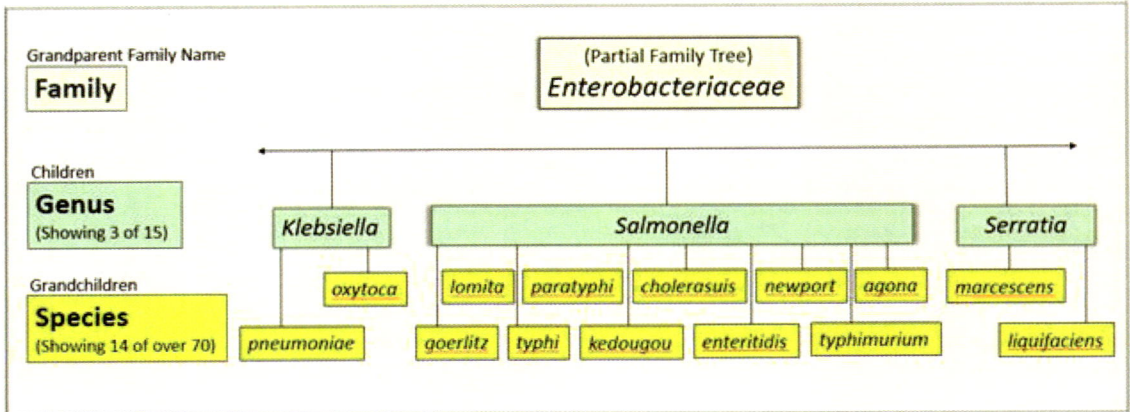

Figure 3.23

Example:

- Family: *Enterobacteriaceae*

- Genus: *Klebsiella*

- Species: *pneumoniae*

Note: The family and genus names are capitalized, but the species name is not. The first time the organism is mentioned in an article, it is normally spelled out with genus and species name. For example, when first mentioned in an article, Staphylococcus aureus would be spelled out. In the rest of the article, it often is only written as S. aureus.

Also, if referring to several species of the same genus, authors often use the abbreviation *spp.*, which is short for species. For example, one could see *Salmonella spp.* to refer to several or all species of the *Salmonella* genus, rather than writing out each species name.

Bacteria, fungi, protozoa and parasites are all italicized in print, but viruses are not.

Fungi

Fungi can cause human infections that are different than bacteria. Under the microscope, fungi look like tiny trees. The branches of Fungi provide great hiding places for bacteria and viruses. Some fungi start as small round balls, but then begin sprouting buds that form branches. *Candida* albicans is a good example. *Candida* can cause thrush as an oral

Candidiasis infection and is frequently a cause of diaper rash infections. *Candida* is also referred to as a yeast. (See **Figure 3.24**) *Candida spp.* go through three stages during infection: A) yeast stage; B) budding stage and C) thin densely-branched stage.

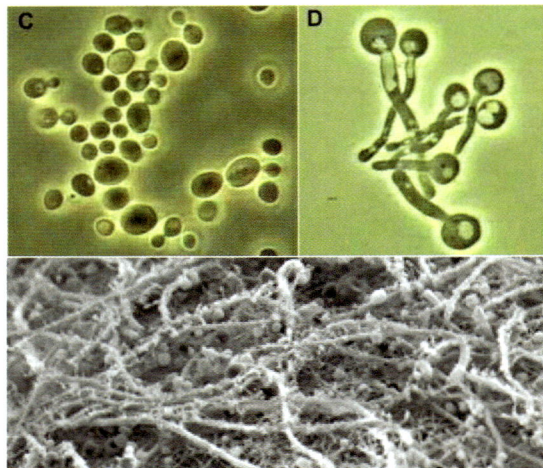

Figure 3.24

Viruses

Viruses are 100 to 1,000 times smaller than bacteria. They cannot be seen with standard microscopes, but can be seen with an electron microscope. Viruses have a core of genetic code (**DNA or RNA**) enclosed in a protective protein coat called a **capsid**. Viruses are unable to reproduce on their own. They must enter a living cell, insert their genetic code into that cell's code and force the cell to make viral copies of itself. Because viruses cannot multiply on their own, they are not considered to be alive; therefore, it is said that one can kill bacteria, but can only deactivate or destroy viruses. Viruses of human concern are divided into two major groups:

- **Enveloped viruses**: Viruses that are draped in a lipid envelope that is studded with proteins. These proteins perform functions, including locking onto cells to enable the virus to enter them and later, for the copies to exit. The lipid portion of the envelope is usually very easy to break or dissolve with soap, detergents or disinfectants. Once the envelope is broken, the virus is incapable of entering any cell, so no infection can occur. Hepatitis B is a good example of an enveloped virus. (See **Figure 3.25**)

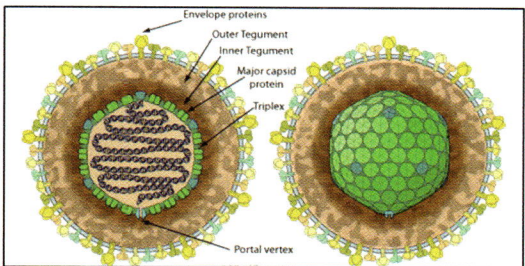

Figure 3.25

- **Non-enveloped viruses**: Viruses that do not have an envelope. Non-enveloped viruses are also referred to as naked viruses. They enter cells in a slightly different way and are much more difficult to disable. The capsid must be damaged and the genetic code must be destroyed to stop the virus from causing an infection. Adenovirus, a common respiratory infection that can be serious in infants and people with weakened immune systems, is a good example of a non-enveloped virus. (**See Figure 3.26**)

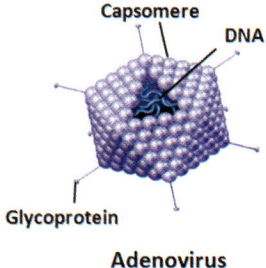

Figure 3.26

Note: Virus names are not italicized.

DNA Deoxyribonucleic acid that carries the genetic information of the organism.

RNA Ribonucleic acid is the messenger nucleic acid that normally carries the instructions from the DNA to the actual assembly line for proteins. RNA viruses are the only entities that carry only RNA (no DNA).

Capsid A viral capsid is the protective protein structure housing the virus DNA or RNA.

Enveloped virus Viruses that have a delicate membrane around the capsid.

Non-enveloped virus Viruses without an envelope around the capsid.

Biofilm

A wet or moist environment within a protected dark area is a great place for bacteria to grow and proliferate. This can take place in sewage pipes, on patient implants or in endoscopes, among other environments. If bacteria are left behind in any endoscope, one can be certain that some level of organic debris has also been left there; this provides nutrition and shelter for bacteria to rapidly multiply and form a biofilm. Depending on the type of bacteria, level of moisture, amount of organic debris, and type of protective surroundings, bacteria or fungi may attach to a favorable surface, or release and relocate elsewhere if the surroundings are not favorable for starting a colony.

Examples: Gouges and scratches create protected areas where organic debris and bacteria collect, and biofilms can rapidly form. The images in **Figure 3.27** are endoscope photos. 1 is a damaged area in an endoscope lumen. Photo 2, is a close-up view of the same area, showing a biofilm with mixed bacteria and organic debris. Photo 3 is mature biofilm in the lumen of an endoscope. Photo 4 is a thick, single-species biofilm found both on the inside and outside of the channel of another endoscope.

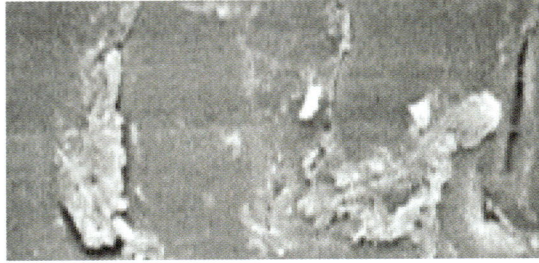

Figure 3.27

In the biofilm formation process, when bacteria attach and reside, their grip strength to the surface increases; this can take as few as 12 minutes to occur. The bacteria also send out messages to attract other bacteria to join the biofilm-forming community. In addition to the tight grip to the surface, they attach to each other in a way that is similar to how one might strap down before a storm. This does not just occur with one type of bacteria; many species join in and begin extremely rapid reproduction.

What constitutes rapid? In favorable conditions, some bacteria can double every 20 minutes (See **Figure 3.28**). For example, one *Escherichia coli* can multiply to 2 million in just eight hours.

How Fast Can Bacteria Multiply?	
Time from First survivor	Number of Bacteria
One survivor	1
20 minutes	2
40 minutes	4
1 hour	8
2 hours	64
3 hours	512
4 hours	4,096
5 hours	32,768
6 hours	262,144
7 hours	2,097,152!!
Depends on many variables, but an example	

Figure 3.28

Once attached, bacteria begin to ooze a gooey substance to cover themselves. This substance, called a matrix, traps any organic debris, including blood, tissue, fat and mucous left nearby, which gives the matrix added strength and a ready food supply. When the biofilm is mature, the matrix usually comprises about 50% to 85% of the structure, with bacteria taking up the remaining space. In the top portion of **Figure 3.29**, section 1, the bacteria can be seen gripping the surface and attaching to each other. In In the bottom portion of **Figure 3.29**, the gooey matrix of the biofilm is the green substance with yellow *Staphylococcus* suspended inside. This biofilm could not be seen with the naked eye, but larger, very mature biofilms sometimes can.

Viruses cannot make biofilms. Instead, they hide inside the biofilm built by bacteria and fungi. There they are protected and remain capable of causing infections.

Human biofilms

Biofilms also form inside the body. They can be initiated by bacteria or by fungi. They form on implants, in chronic wounds, in the nasal sinuses, on tonsils, and can even be seen as patches on the trachea, esophagus, colon and other tissues. One can imagine how easily the bacteria in these human biofilm colonies can attach to an endoscope that rubs over the biofilm surface, scraping portions off as the scope is inserted, manipulated into different positions and removed. **Figures 3.31** through **3.40** provide several human biofilm examples.

Figure 3.29

Finally, completed biofilm communities release individual bacteria, along with small chunks of detached bacteria-containing biofilm. Each start new biofilm communities and spread infection if it is inside the body. The released bacteria are often called pioneer or planktonic bacteria. The full cycle from attachment to mature biofilm is diagrammed in **Figure 3.30**.

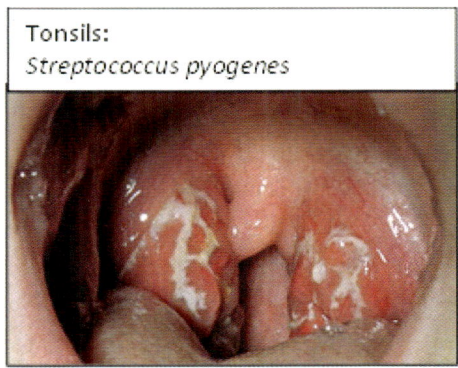

Tonsils:
Streptococcus pyogenes

Figure 3.31

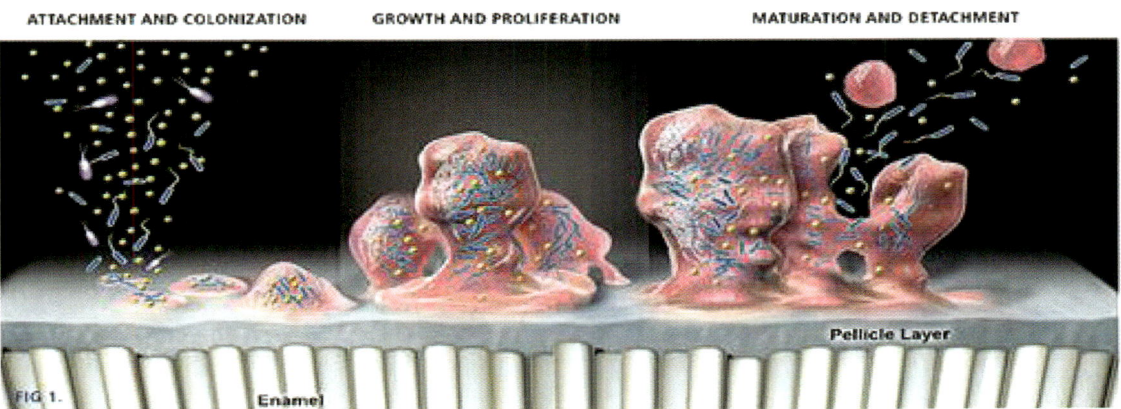

Figure 3.30

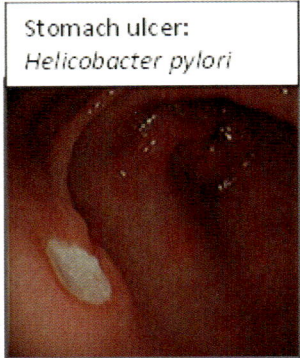

Figure 3.32

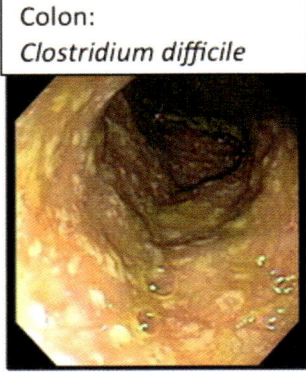

Figure 3.33

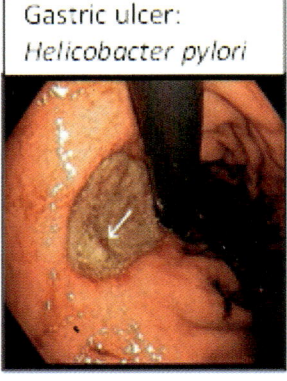

Figure 3.34

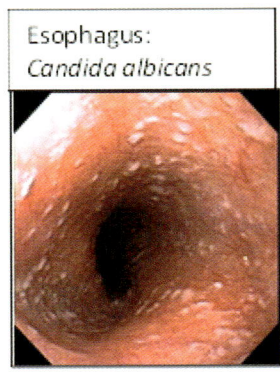

Figure 3.35

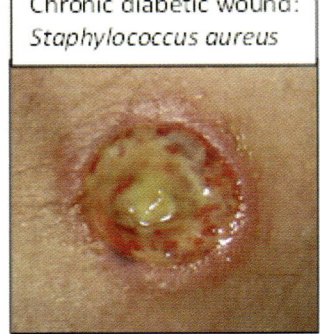

Figure 3.36

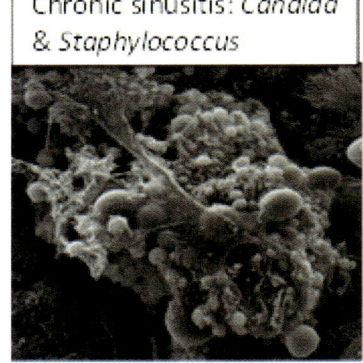

Figure 3.37

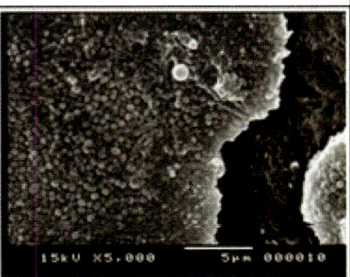

Uretal stent:
Klebsiella & Staphylococcus

Figure 3.38

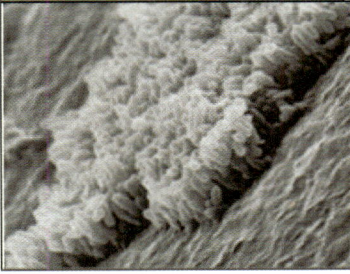

Urinary catheter:
24 hours - *Proteus mirabillis*

Figure 3.39

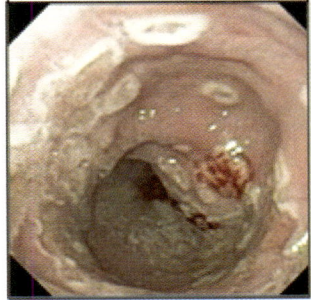

Esophagus:
Herpes virus

Figure 3.40

Important

Biofilm continues to increase in size and number of microorganisms. The longer it takes for an endoscope to be reprocessed, the more difficult it becomes to completely remove thickened, strongly-attached biofilm structures.

It is extremely important that endoscope reprocessing staff use a brush to remove biofilm; however, not any brush will do. Brushes used for endoscope cleaning must be the correct size and style for the specific endoscope.

Endoscope manufacturers must provide the U.S. Food and Drug Administration (FDA) with information that shows that their endoscopes can be cleaned. It is essential to use specific brushes that are the appropriate length, flexibility, shape and quality. The bristles themselves must also be the correct length, stiffness, density (number of bristles per area), and taper (narrowing shape) to correctly fit in the lumen. Brushes must also be able to fit through and clean intricate, hard-to-reach areas. It is important that the tip of the brush be cushioned with a plastic cap or something similar to prevent scratching or gouging the endoscope's inner surfaces. If a facility uses brushes other than those recommended by the manufacturer, the brushes chosen must be equal by comparison to help ensure the same "clean" results. Friction and the disruption accomplished by appropriate brushes are intended to physically remove the organic debris and strip away any biofilm structures, without damaging the endoscope surface.

Recent observational studies found that many reprocessing professionals who clean endoscopes push the brush straight down a channel on the endoscope and then pull the brush straight out. They believed they were performing the task correctly; however, this action alone is insufficient for removing biofilm or organic soil. Pushing a brush straight down and pulling it straight up will scrape "clean strips" straight down the channel, but soil and biofilm can still be present along the sides of the strips; therefore, technique is critical to success. Multiple passes through the channel — rotating the brush upon entry and removal, as well as repeating the process while ensuring the endoscope is extended (not coiled or bent) — is critical. Imagine the way one brushes his or her teeth. When teeth are not brushed regularly, the biofilm we call dental plaque forms. (See **Figure 3.41**) Now, imagine passing a brush straight down and then straight up once on a mature biofilm, such as dental plaque. If oral hygiene indicator tablets were used, one would see strips of cleaned areas on the teeth, and colored strips of biofilm. To be most effective, people are instructed to brush over the teeth multiple times, or use an electric toothbrush to reach all areas of teeth surface.

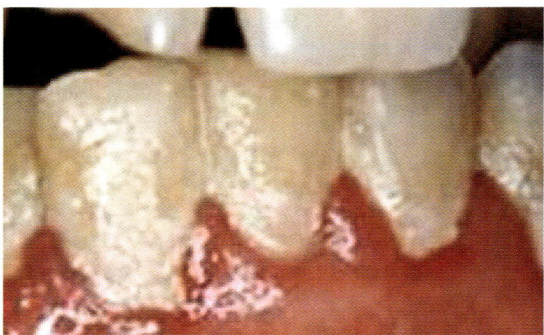

Figure 3.41

Cleaning is addressed in greater detail in chapter 7.

Biofilm resistance to disinfectants

If a biofilm is not removed during cleaning, one cannot be certain that disinfectants will kill or deactivate the microorganisms inside. In fact, it has been shown that bacteria inside a fully-developed biofilm can be 10 to 1,500 times more resistant to disinfectants than the same bacteria outside of the biofilm.

Important:

If ethylene oxide (EtO) is used as an added measure to make endoscopes safe, one cannot take shortcuts with the cleaning procedure. Even EtO gas under pressure has a difficult time penetrating a fully-formed biofilm, and EtO won't work if the endoscope is dirty or wet.

Biofilms in healthcare personnel

Pathogens can hide in skin rashes, psoriasis, plaques and the space between natural and artificial nails. Several patient infections have been traced to

contamination from these sources. It is important to treat and cover wounds and keep hands away from the face, head and any affected area, especially when there are scabs, pimples, boils, cold sores, rashes or other skin conditions where pathogens could live and potentially contaminate work items (see **Figures 3.42** to **3.44**).

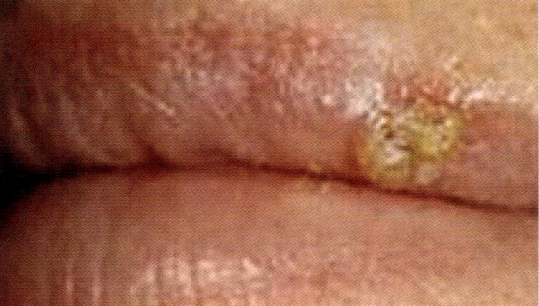

Figure 3.42

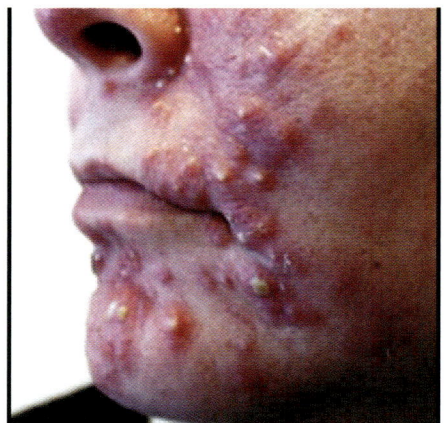

Figure 3.43

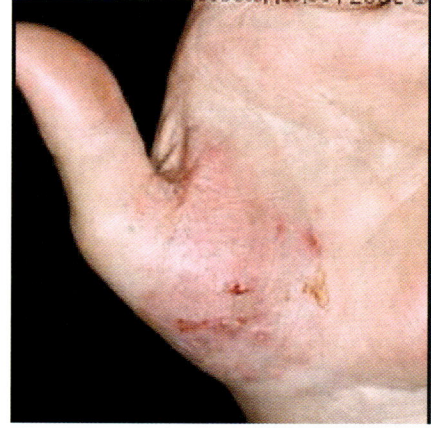

Figure 3.44

As noted earlier, fungus branches provide a protected hiding place for bacteria. Nail fungus is a great example. Hand hygiene practices do not destroy bacteria deep among the fungus branches. Several outbreak infections of *Staphylococcus, Streptococcus, Pseudomonas,* and *Serratia* have occurred when healthcare staff unknowingly transferred these bacteria from their fungus-infected fingernails onto items used on patients. Nail fungus affects 2% to 13% of adults and up to 90% of the elderly (finger or toenail fungus). If one has a fingernail fungal infection, it is necessary to have it treated and contained. It often takes a long time for the fungus to finally be eliminated, so treatment should be continued until the fungus is gone; otherwise the fungus remaining will expand again (See **Figures 3.45 and 3.46**)

become more difficult to destroy when they form cysts (their version of a spore). (See **Figure 3.47**) Standard procedures for cleaning and disinfection should eliminate them from the endoscopes, however. *Cryptosporidium parvum* is an example of a protozoa and has been a cause of cross contamination by endoscopes. The cyst version of *C. parvum* is called an oocyst; it contains sporozoites, the tiny worm-like stage of the protozoa that "hatches" out of the oocyst that burrows into the intestinal tissues and infects the patient. It then creates more oocysts containing more sporozoites which are deposited in the patient's feces. From there, the oocysts can try to gain access to another person potentially transported there by contaminated endoscopes. (see **Figure 3.48**)

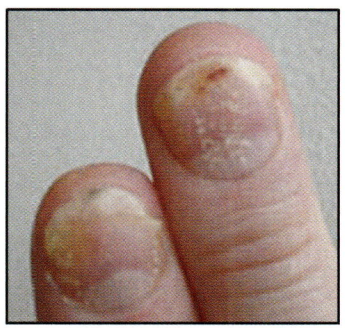

Figure 3.45

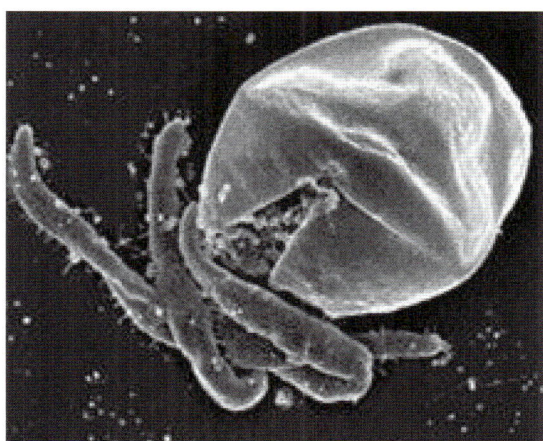

Figure 3.47

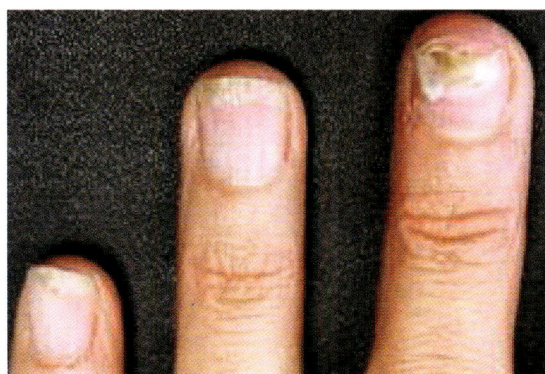

Figure 3.46

Protozoa

Protozoa are microscopic organisms that are not frequently associated with endoscope contamination; however it does occur. Protozoa are easy to kill, but

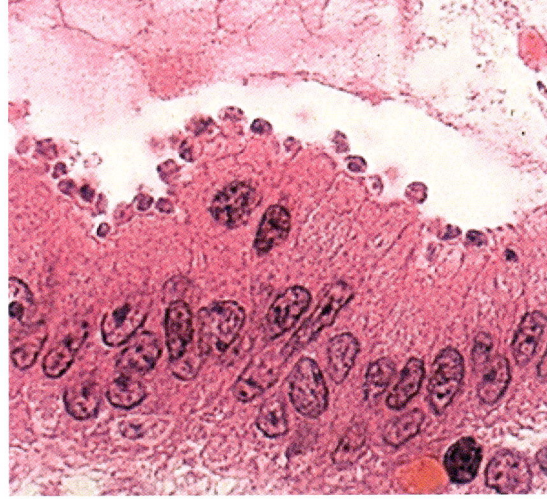

Figure 3.48

Protozoa that cause disease, like microscopic worms (helminths) can also be parasites and cause infections. Strongyloides is an example. (See **Figure 3.49**) Infections due to contaminated endoscopes have occurred.

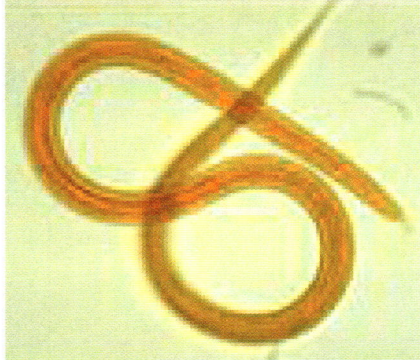

Figure 3.49

MICROBIOLOGY SPECIFIC TO ENDOSCOPE-ASSOCIATED INFECTIONS

When addressing infections that patients have acquired from specific endoscopic procedures, the discussion of microorganisms becomes much more focused. Historically, endoscope-associated infections have not been reliably reported. Efforts are increasing, especially with those associated with antibiotic-resistant infections, but there is still a long way to go. It is important to know which procedures and which endoscopes have caused infections and with which pathogens to be able to better understand and address the challenges associated with reprocessing. Different procedures present different infection risks. Infections associated with specific endoscopic procedures are presented in **Figure 3.50.**

Infections Associated with Specific Endoscopic Procedures

Procedure	Post-Procedure Infections
Bronchoscopy	• Bronchitis (infection of the large airways of the lungs) • Lung abscess (pocket of pathogens and pus in the lungs) • Pulmonary (lung) tuberculosis (TB): (severe lung damage can spread) • Pneumonia (infection of the air sacs in the lungs) • Sepsis (bloodstream infection and inflammation) • Sinusitis (infection in sinuses around the nasal cavity) • Wound infections
Colonoscopy/ Sigmoidoscopy	• Appendicitis (infection of the appendix) • Peritonitis (abdominal infection) • Endocarditis (heart valve infection from bacteria in bloodstream) • Gastroenteritis (infection of the stomach and intestines) • HBV infection (liver infection caused by hepatitis B virus; also in blood and body fluids) • HCV infection (liver infection caused by hepatitis C virus; also in blood) • Meningitis (infection of membranes covering brain & spinal cord) • Bacteremia (heart valve infection from bacteria in the bloodstream)
Cystoscopy/ Ureteroscopy	• Urinary bladder infection • Kidney infection • Heart valve infection (bacteria into bloodstream latch onto damaged or prosthetic heart valves)
Retrograde Cholangiopan-creatography Duodenoscopes (ERCP)	• Cholangitis (infection of biliary tube that carries bile for food digestion from the liver, through the gallbladder to the small intestine) • Gastroenteritis (infection of the stomach and intestines) • Hepatitis C infection (liver infection) • Liver abscesses (pus pockets in liver infection caused by hepatitis C) • Pancreatitis (infection of the pancreas) • Pneumonia (infection of the lung air sacs that caused the lungs to fill with fluids) • Sepsis (bloodstream infection and circulating inflammatory response) • Urinary tract infection (UTI) (infection in any part of the urinary system: kidneys, ureters, bladder, or urethra) • *Carbapenum-Resistant Enterobacteriaceae* (CRE) infections (40% to 50% death rate)
Upper Gastrointestinal Endoscopy	• Bacterial peritonitis (abdominal infection) • Cerebral abscess (pocket of pathogens and pus) • Cholangitis (infection of biliary tube that carries bile for food digestion from liver, through gallbladder to small intestine) • Endocarditis (infection of the heart's valves or inner lining; usually caused by bacteria). • Esophagitis (infection of the esophagus) • Gastritis (infection in the lining of the stomach) • Gastroenteritis (infection of the stomach and intestines) • Lung abscess (pocket of pathogens and pus in the lungs) • Meningitis (infection of membranes covering the brain and spinal cord) • Peritoneal abscess (pocket of pus and pathogens in the abdomen) • Pneumonia (infection of the lung air sacs that causes the lungs to fill with fluids) • Sepsis (bloodstream infection that causes systemic inflammation) • Urinary tract infection (UTI) (infection in any part of urinary system: kidneys, ureters, bladder or urethra)

Figure 3.50

Pathogens Causing Infections in Specific Endoscopic Procedures

Stain & Shape	Pathogens Causing Associated Infections	Bronchoscopy	Colonoscopy & Sigmoidoscopy	Cystoscopy & Ureteroscopy	ERCP Duodenoscopy	Upper GI Endoscopy
Gram Negative						
bacilli	Acinetobacter baumannii	X			X	
	Burkholderia contaminans				X	
	Bacteroides fragilis		X			
	Enterobacter cloacae		X	X		
	Escherichia coli	X	X	X	X	
	Klebsiella pneumoniae	X	X	X	X	X
	Legionella pneumophila	X				
	Methylobacterium mesophilicum	X			X	
	Morganella morganii	X				
	Proteus spp.	X	X			
	Pseudomonas aeruginosa	X		X	X	X
	Salmonella spp.		X		X	X
	Serratia spp.	X	X	X	X	X
	Stenotrophomonas spp.	X				
spirals	Campylobacter pylori				X	
	Helicobacter pylori				X	X
Gram Positive						
bacilli	Bacillus spp.	X				
	Clostridium difficile		X		X	
	Listeria monocytogenes		X			
cocci	Enterococcus spp.		X			
	Staphylococcus spp.			X		X
	Streptococcus viridans	X				X
Acid Fast						
bacilli (only)	Mycobacterium tuberculosis (TB)	X				
	Mycobacterium spp.	X				X
Virus						
	Hepatitis B (HBV)		X		X	X
	Hepatitis C (HCV)		X	X	X	X
	Human Immuno-deficiency virus (HIV)				X	
Fungi & Yeast						
	Aureobasidium	X				
	Blastomyces dermatitidis	X				
	Candida albicans	X				
	Rhodotorula mucilaginosa	X				
	Trichosporon spp.	X			X	X
Parasites						
	Cryptosporidium parvum				X	
	Strongyloides stercoralis				X	X

Figure 3.51

Investigations conducted to determine the causes of cross contamination and associated infections in endoscopy patients found the following to be primary factors: endoscope cleaning and disinfection lapses, insufficient cleaning/disinfection instructions from endoscope manufacturers, poor endoscope design, contaminated automated endoscope reprocessors (AERs) and accessories, contaminated rinse water, and environmental surfaces. These concerns will be discussed in detail in the chapters on endoscope cleaning and disinfection.

ENVIRONMENTAL CLEANING AND DISINFECTION

Surfaces in reprocessing areas must be cleaned and disinfected daily, as well as any time contamination is suspected. If an endoscope ready for patient use is placed on a contaminated surface, the microorganisms from that surface can attach to the endoscope.

Most people believe that bacteria die rapidly on dry surfaces; however, this is not the case. **Figure 3.52** displays survival times for many of the pathogens addressed in this chapter.

Survival on Dry, Non-living Surfaces

Type	Pathogen	Survival Time
Bacteria	*Acinetobacter baumannii*	3 days to 5 months
	Campylobacter jejuni	up to 6 days
	Clostridium difficile spores	5 months
	Enterococcus (including VRE & VSE)*	5 days to 4 months
	Escherichia coli (E.coli)	1.5 hours to 16 months
	Helicobacter pylori	1.5 hours
	Klebsiella spp.	2 hours to more than 30 months
	Listeria	1 day to months
	Mycobacterium tuberculosis	1 day to 4 months
	Proteus vulgaris	1 to 2 days
	Pseudomonas aeruginosa	6 hours to 16 months
	Salmonella	6 hours to 4.2 years
	Serratia	3 days to 2 months
	Staphylococcus aureus	7 days to 7 months
	Streptococcus pneumoniae	1 to 7 months
Fungi	Aspergillus conidia (fungal spores)	months or longer
	Candida albicans	1 to 120 days
Viruses	Adenovirus	7 days to 3 months
	HBV	2 hours to 60 days
	HIV	1 to 2 days
	Norovirus	Stable in the environment (no end found)

Kramer A, Schwebke I, Kampf G. How long do nosocomial pathogens persist on inanimate surfaces? A systematic review. BMC Infect Dis. 2006;16(6):130.

Figure 3.52

The Microbiology Basics section of this chapter addressed several stains that help identify bacteria into groups. Bacteria stain differently because of differences in the structure of their outer surfaces. That same outer surface structure determines how difficult it is to destroy them on working surfaces using different disinfectants.

Environmental cleanliness is an important part of preventing endoscope recontamination. **Figure 3.53** presents the major microbial pathogen categories, listed in the order of difficulty in regard to the pathogens' ability to be disinfected. The figure also highlights popular environmental surface disinfectants and ranks these disinfectants' performance against the microorganisms at recommended concentration levels. It is important to remember that whether disinfection is being performed at a U.S. hospital, ambulatory surgery center, clinic, physician's office or a third-party reprocessor, the surface disinfectants used must be approved for hospital use by the Environmental Protection Agency (EPA). Substantiated, unbiased information about each disinfectant can be obtained from the EPA website, along with compatibility on different surfaces (e.g., stainless steel; plastic, varnished or painted wood, vinyl, rubber, brass, chrome, copper, computer monitor screens, keyboards, mouse) at: https://www.epa.gov/pesticide-registration/selected-epa-registered-disinfectants If outside the U.S., please refer to the appropriate regulatory bodies.

The information in **Figure 3.53** serves as a general guideline. Surfaces must stay wet with the disinfectant for as long as the label instructions state for disinfection to occur. Only after the disinfectant has remained on the surface for the appropriate amount of time can the surface be wiped dry.

Surface disinfection must occur in decontamination, disinfection and assembly areas, as well as in and on endoscope storage cabinets. For complete step-by-step instructions, reprocessing professionals should refer to the manufacturer's instructions for use (IFU) and their facility's policies.

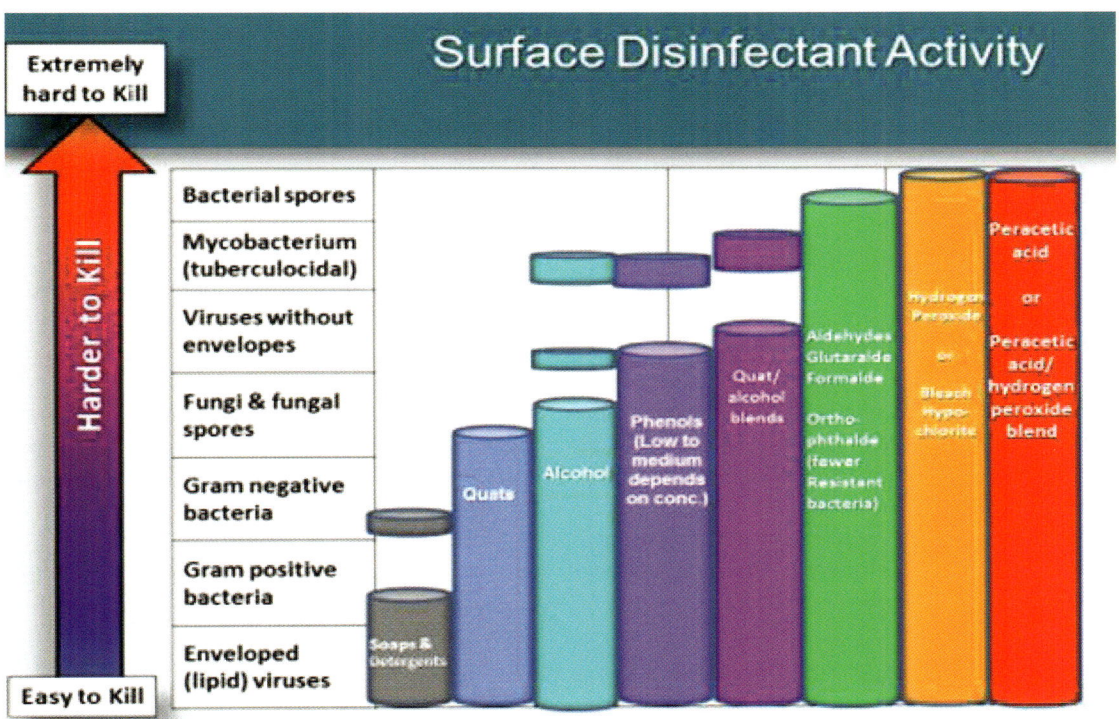

Figure 3.53

Survival of Enterococci & Staphylococci on hospital Fabrics & Plastics: Neely & Maley 2000

Fabric	Practical items	Survival up to approximate days	
		MRSA - days	VRE - days
Purified cotton	Clothing, linens	21	Greater than 90
Cotton	Terry cloth towels	14	Greater than 90
Cotton-polyester	Scrub suits, lab coats	3	Greater than 90
Polyester	Privacy curtains, clothing	40	Greater than 90
Polyethylene	Splash aprons	51	Greater than 90

MRSA: Methicillin-resistant Staphylococcus aureus (resistant to many antibiotics)

VRE: Vancomycin-resistant Enterococci (resistant to many antibiotics)

Figure 3.54

Survival of Pathogens on Clothing and Aprons

Reprocessing professionals may assume that bacteria die on lab coats or aprons overnight; however, that is a dangerous misconception. A study was performed at Shriners Hospital for Children in Cincinnati, Ohio, under a containment hood with the fan running. Even with this drying environment, pathogens survived an extended period. Spores, fungi and non-enveloped viruses would survive even longer. (See **Figure 3.54**)

It is important that reprocessing professionals wear clean clothing. If they touch contaminated fabrics, pathogens can be transferred to reprocessed, ready-for-use endoscopes.

CONCLUSION

Medical device reprocessing is a critically important part of quality healthcare delivery, patient safety and infection prevention. Endoscope reprocessing technicians play a vital role in infection prevention and other positive patient outcomes. Reprocessing endoscopes correctly requires a tremendous amount of work, focus, knowledge and attention to detail —and every step in the process should be performed with a commitment to vigilance and the desire to continually improve practices in the name of patient safety.

RESOURCES

Barbee SL, Weber DJ, Sobsey MD, Rutala WA. *Inactivation of Cryptosporidium parvum oocyst infectivity by disinfection and sterilization processes.* Gastrointest Endosc 1999;49:605–611.

Provincial Infectious Diseases Advisory Committee. *Best Practices for Cleaning, Disinfection and Sterilization in All Health Care Settings.* February 2010.

Provincial Infectious Diseases Advisory Committee. *Best Practices for Environmental Cleaning for Prevention and Control of Infections in All Health Care Settings.* December 2009.

Public Health Agency of Canada. *Infection prevention and control guideline for flexible gastrointestinal endoscopy and flexible bronchoscopy.* Modified 2011. http://www.phac-aspc.gc.ca/nois-sinp/guide/endo/index-eng.php.

Costerton JW, Stewart PS, Greenberg EP. *Bacterial biofilms: a common cause of persistent infections. Science* 1999;284:318–322.

DiazGranados CA, Jones MY, Kongphet-Tran T, White N, Shapiro M, Wang YF, Ray SM, Blumberg HM. *Outbreak of Pseudomonas aeruginosa infection associated with contamination of a flexible bronchoscope.* Infect Control Hosp Epidemiol. 2009;30(6):550-555.

Centers for Disease Control and Prevention. *Guidelines for Environmental Infection Control in Healthcare Facilities.* MMWR June 2003, Vol 52, No RR-10.

Centers for Disease Control and Prevention. The Healthcare Infection Control Practices Advisory Committee. *Guideline for Isolation Precautions: Preventing Transmission of Infectious Agents in Healthcare Settings*. 2007.

Kenters N, Huijskens GW, Meier C, Voss A. *Infectious diseases linked to cross-contamination of flexible endoscopes*. Endosc Int Open 2015;03:E259-265.

Kovaleva J, Peters FTM, van der Mei HC, Degener JE. *Transmission of Infection by Flexible Gastrointestinal Endoscopy and Bronchoscopy*. Clin. Microbiol. Rev. 2013;26(2):231-254.

Kramer A, Schwebke I, Kampf G. *How long do nosocomial pathogens persist on inanimate surfaces? A systematic review*. BMC Infect Dis. 2006;16(6):130. http://link.springer.com/article/10.1186%2F1471-2334-6-130.

Mah TF, O'Toole GA. *Mechanisms of biofilm resistance to antimicrobial agents*. Trends Microbiol 2001;9(1):34–39.

Mayhall CG. *Hospital Epidemiology and Infection Control, 3rd Ed*. Philadelphia. Lippincott Williams & Wilkins, 2004.

Neely AN, Maley MP. *Survival of enterococci and staphylococci on hospital fabrics and plastic*. J Clin Microbiol 2000;38(2):724-726.

Nickel JC, Ruseska I, Wright JB, Costerton JW. *Tobramycin resistance of Pseudomonas aeruginosa cells growing as a biofilm on urinary catheter material*. Antimicrob Agents Chemother 1985;27:619–624.

Ofstead CL, Wetzler HP, Doyle EM, Rocco CK, Visrodia KH, Baron TH, Tosh PK. *Persistent contamination on colonoscopies and gastroscopes detected by biologic cultures and rapid indicators despite reprocessing performed in accordance with guidelines*. AJIC 2015;43(8):794-801.

Pajkos A, Vickery K, Cossart Y. *Is biofilm accumulation on endoscope tubing a contributor to the failure of cleaning and decontamination?* J. Hosp Infect 2004;58(3):224–229.

Patterson DJ, Johnson EH, Schmulen AC. *Fulminant pseudomembranous colitis occurring after colonoscopy*. Gastrointest Endosc 1984;30(4):249–253.

Ramsey AH, Oemig TV, Davis JP, Massey JP, Török TJ. *An outbreak of bronchoscopy-related Mycobacterium tuberculosis infections due to lack of bronchoscope leak testing*. Chest 2002;121(3):976-981.

Rutala WA, Weber DJ. *The benefits of surface disinfection*. AJIC 2004;32(4):226-231.

Singh N, Belen O, Léger MM, Campos JM. *Cluster of Trichosporon mucoides in children associated with a faulty bronchoscope*. Pediatr Infect Dis J. 2003;22(7):609-612.

Spaner SJ, Warnock GL. *A brief history of endoscopy, laparoscopy, and laparoscopic surgery*. J Laparoendosc Adv Surg Tech A. 1997;7(6):369-373.

TERMS

Microorganisms

Bacteria

Symbiotic bacteria

Infection

Pathogens

Fungi

Viruses

Parasites

Aggressive

Virulence

Antibiotic resistance

Gram stain

Acid fast stain

Endospore stain

Capsule stain

Gram positive

Gram negative

Endospore

Anaerobes

Germinate

Capsules

Chains

Diploid

Tetrad

Cuboid

Cocci

Bacilli

Spirals

DNA

RNA

Capsid

Enveloped virus

Non-enveloped virus

Chapter 4

Work Area Design

Learning Objectives

Upon completion of this chapter, readers will be able to:

1. Discuss workflow requirements for endoscope reprocessing areas

2. Define environmental requirements for endoscope reprocessing areas

3. Identify requirements for the endoscope decontamination area

4. Discuss requirements for the endoscope high-level disinfection and sterilization area

5. Discuss requirements for the endoscope storage area

INTRODUCTION

Safe endoscope reprocessing begins with the work area. The design and quality of the work area has a significant impact on both patient and employee safety. Facilities that reprocess endoscopes range from smaller clinics to large hospitals.

Regardless of the type of facility, general guidelines for flexible endoscope reprocessing areas remain the same. This chapter will examine key areas of consideration when designing and equipping an endoscope reprocessing work area.

PHYSICAL SPACE DESIGN

The processing area should be physically separated from patient procedure rooms. To prevent cross contamination, the reprocessing area should be used only for reprocessing, and the design of this area should incorporate a one-way, dirty to clean flow from the receipt of soiled instruments all the way to storage. **Figures 4.1 through 4.5** provide examples of appropriate work area separation and workflow in various settings. Red arrows indicate the flow of soiled items and green arrows indicate the flow of clean items. *Note: Actual layout and flow may vary, but all reprocessing work areas should address separation and soiled to clean workflow.*

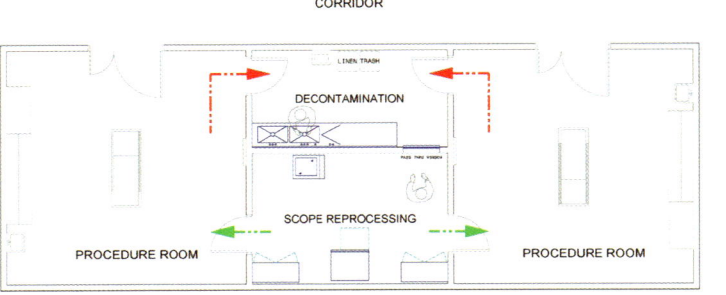

Figure 4.1 illustrates a design for a small scope reprocessing area in an office or clinic setting.

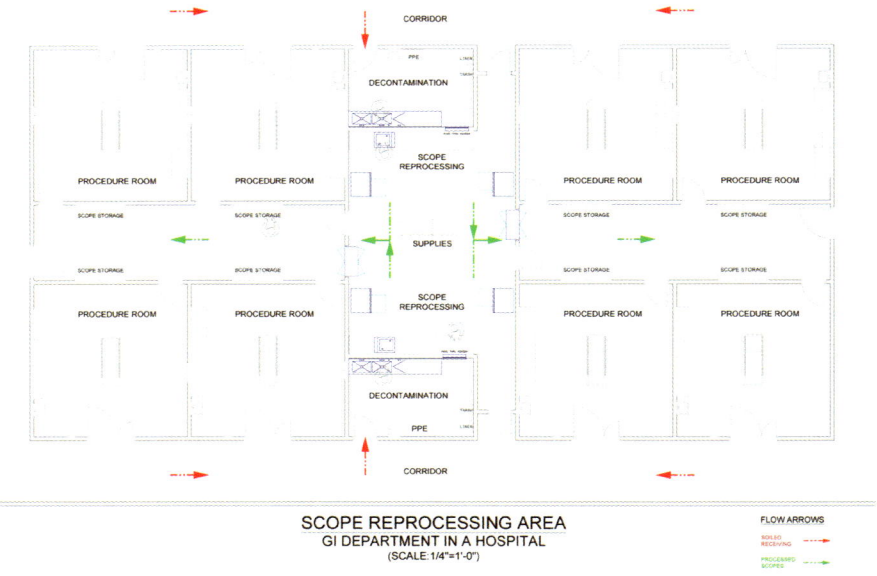

Figure 4.2 provides an example of an endoscope reprocessing area within a GI department in a hospital.

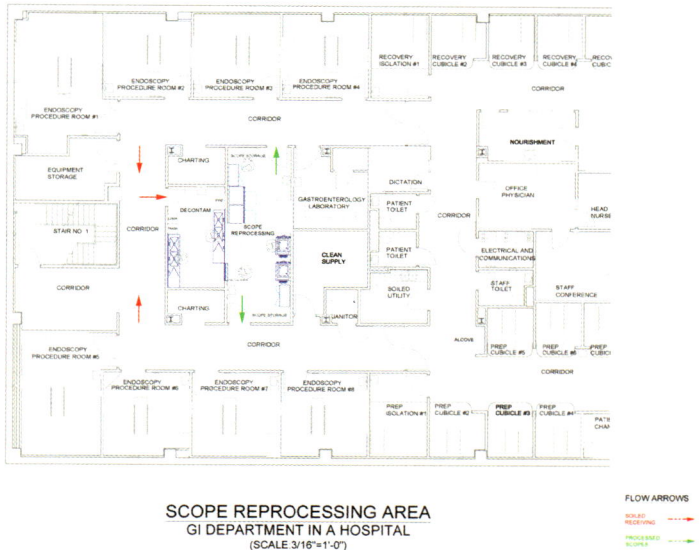

SCOPE REPROCESSING AREA
GI DEPARTMENT IN A HOSPITAL
(SCALE:3/16"=1'-0")

FLOW ARROWS

Figure 4.3 provides another example of an endoscope reprocessing area within a GI department in a hospital.

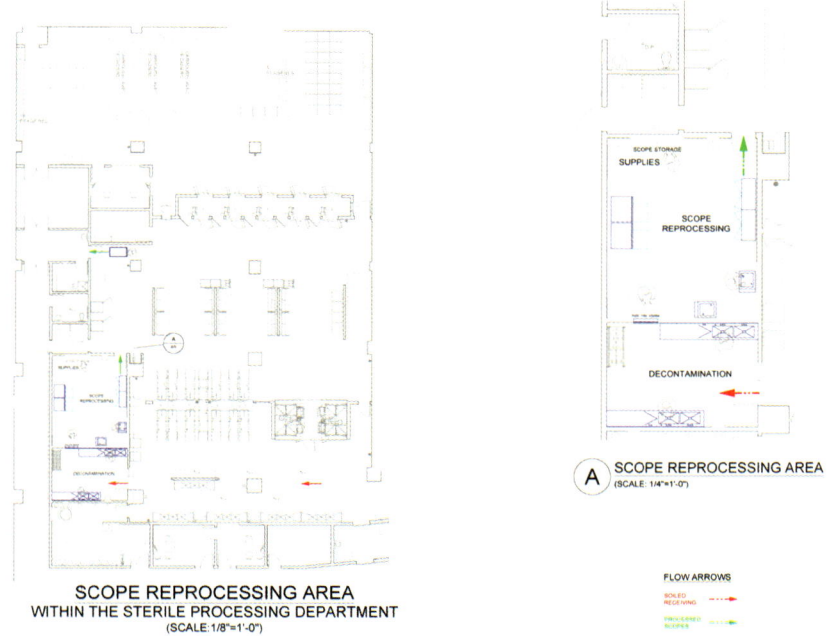

SCOPE REPROCESSING AREA
WITHIN THE STERILE PROCESSING DEPARTMENT
(SCALE:1/8"=1'-0")

SCOPE REPROCESSING AREA
(SCALE: 1/4"=1'-0")

FLOW ARROWS

Figure 4.4 provides an example of an endoscope reprocessing area within a Central Service/Sterile Processing department. Figure 4.4A provides an enlargement of the endoscope reprocessing area.

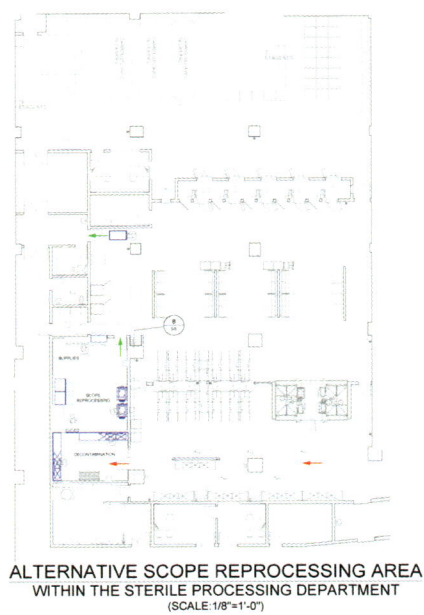

ALTERNATIVE SCOPE REPROCESSING AREA
WITHIN THE STERILE PROCESSING DEPARTMENT
(SCALE:1/8"=1'-0")

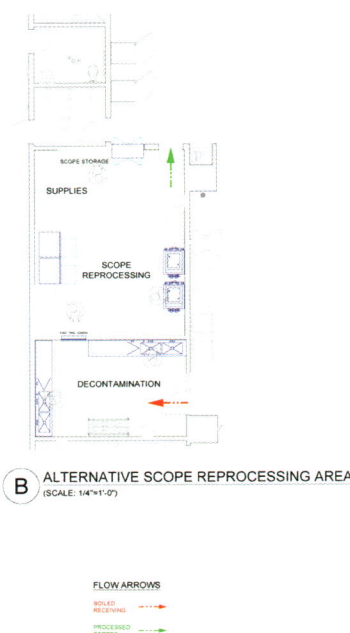

B ALTERNATIVE SCOPE REPROCESSING AREA
(SCALE: 1/4"=1'-0")

FLOW ARROWS
SOILED
RECEIVING
PROCESSED
SCOPES

Figure 4.5

Figure 4.5 provides another example of an endoscope reprocessing area within a Central Service department. **Figure 4.5B** provides an enlargement of the endoscope reprocessing area. The best method for preventing cross contamination is to have physical barriers separating the functional areas to maintain distinction between soiled and clean work areas. Physical separation prevents contaminated **aerosols**, **droplet nuclei** and dust particles from being carried by air currents from dirty to clean areas. Doors and pass-through windows separating the decontamination area from the adjoining disinfection/sterilization area should remain closed when not in use. Signage should be used to ensure that workflow and traffic reduces the risk of cross contamination and possible exposure to biohazard items. **Figure 4.6** shows a sign to control traffic and notify personnel of the requirement for personal protective equipment (PPE) in the decontamination room.

P.P.E. REQUIRED IN DECONTAMINATION ROOM

Figure 4.6

Aerosols A suspension of ultramicroscopic solid or liquid particles in air or gas; a spray.

Droplet nuclei Droplet nuclei develop when the fluid of pathogenic droplets evaporates. They are so small and light that they may remain suspended in the air for several hours. Airborne droplet nuclei can be widely dispersed by air currents.

In some facilities, physical separation may not be possible. To help ensure the one-way directional flow, a risk analysis should be performed to identify risks and then minimize those risks through policies and procedures and education and training of reprocessing personnel. Signage, color coding and other visual aids may help ensure that personnel follow uniform guidelines to prevent cross contamination.

Adequate space is another important consideration. Failure to provide adequate space for all reprocessing functions and equipment increases the risk of cross contamination and may impede good work practices. Inadequate space can also result in poor practices that damage endoscopes.

ENVIRONMENTAL CONDITIONS

The endoscope reprocessing environment should be controlled and monitored. Having the right environmental conditions promotes microbial control and employee comfort. ANSI/AAMI ST91, *Flexible and semi-rigid endoscope processing in health care facilities*, provides the following recommendations for temperature and humidity:

Humidity, Temperature and Airflow

Relative humidity requires monitoring. A high relative humidity, which is over 60%, can promote microbial growth. Relative humidity lower than 30% may permit absorbent materials to become excessively dry, which can adversely affect certain sterilization parameters (such as sterilant penetration) and the performance of some products, such as biological and chemical indicators. Relative humidity should not exceed 60% in all work areas; in the sterile storage area, the recommended minimum humidity level is 20%. *Note: Relative humidity lower than 30% can adversely affect the performance of some products. Check with product manufacturers to determine storage requirements.*

To help ensure that environmental conditions are maintained, humidity and temperature should be monitored daily. Environmental monitors are available that can record conditions; manual recording systems are also acceptable. Having a written record provides evidence that requirements were maintained and/or identifies the need for improvement. **Figures 4.7** and **4.8** provide an example of a computerized temperature/humidity monitoring system.

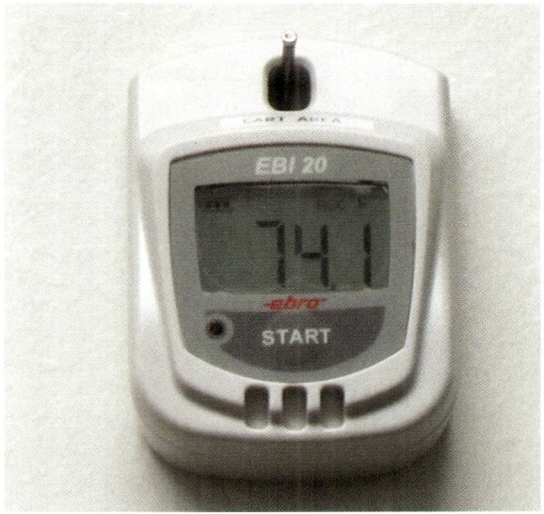

Figure 4.7

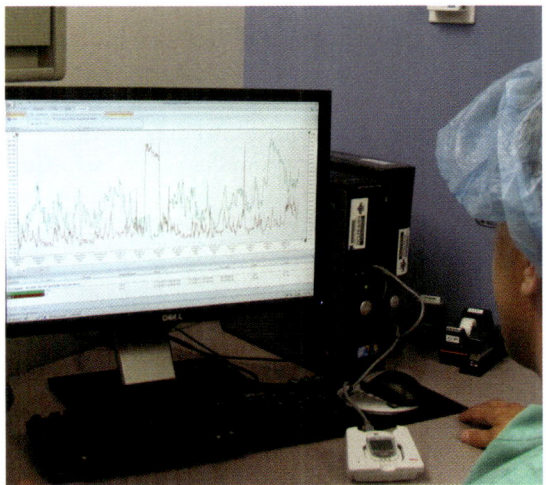

Figure 4.8

Along with temperature and humidity, air flow and air pressure should be monitored. Air should flow from positive pressure (clean) to negative pressure (dirty) areas. The soiled and decontamination (dirty) areas should be designed so air flows into the area (negative pressure), with a minimum of 10 air exchanges per hour, and so all air is exhausted to the outside atmosphere. **Figure 4.9** provides an example of an air pressure monitoring system.

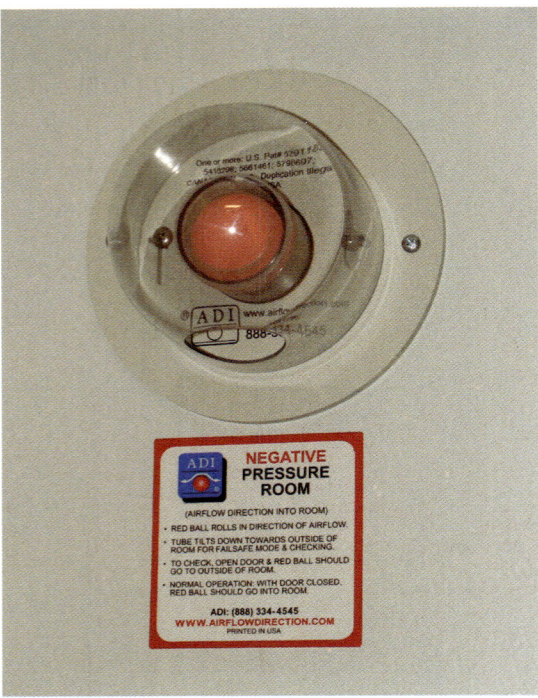

Figure 4.9

Whenever possible, dedicated local exhaust systems should be used in place of dilution ventilation to reduce exposure to hazardous gases, vapors, fumes or mists. Each functional area has its own requirements for airflow, number of air exchanges and exhaust (See **Figure 4.10**)

WORK AREA DESIGN

The endoscope reprocessing room should have adequate flat surfaces to allow endoscopes to be laid out for processing and inspection. All surfaces should be nonporous and cleanable. (See **Figure 4.11**) There should be adequate space for the manual cleaning and rinsing the endoscopes throughout the stages of reprocessing. The room should also have adequate lighting for inspection. Water and electricity should be provided in areas used for endoscope processing. The workflow in an endoscope processing area is important to keep soiled endoscopes and other instruments separated from clean endoscopes and instrumentation.

Figure 4.11

Environmental Controls

Area	Temperature	Humidity*	Air Flow
Decontamination	60°F and 65°F	20% to 60%	10 negative air flows
Preparation/Disinfection	60°F and 73°F	20% to 60%	10 positive air flows
Storage	60°F and 75°F	Above 20%	4 positive air flows

Note: Relative humidity lower than 30% can adversely affect the performance of some products. Check with product manufacturers to determine storage requirements.

Figure 4.10

Hand Hygiene Facilities

Hand sinks with soap and towel dispensers should be conveniently located and designed to allow good hand hygiene practices. Hand sinks should be designated for hand hygiene only. Employees hands should not be cleaned in the same sink with endoscopes and instruments. (See **Figure 4.12**) Hand hygiene facilities should be located in or near all areas where endoscopes and other devices are decontaminated and in the clean area where endoscopes are high-level disinfected or sterilized.

Transport to the Processing Area

Flexible endoscopes should be transported with their attachments in a closed container or system. (See **Figure 4.14**) Accessory instrumentation, such as bottles, forceps and wires used in the procedure, should be transported in their own containers to avoid puncturing or otherwise damaging the endoscope. The system should be marked with a biohazard label to identify potentially biohazardous material. The transport system should also be large enough to hold the flexible endoscope, without over-coiling the insertion or light guide tubes.

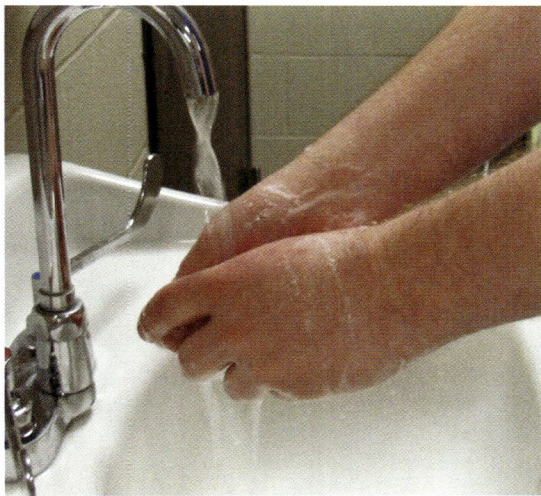

Figure 4.12

Figure 4.14

Handwashing Procedure

1	Remove all jewelry.
2	Turn on faucet using a paper towel.
3	Wet hands and apply liquid soap.
4	Work soap into a lather and scrub hands for at least 15 seconds.*
5	Keep hands at a lower angle than elbows to prevent dirty water from running back onto arms.
6	Interlace fingers to clean between them.
7	Dry hands with clean disposable towels.
8	Turn off the faucet using a clean disposable towel.

* Source: AORN

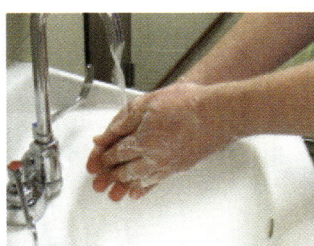

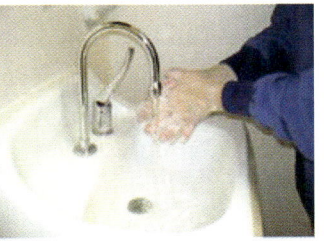

Figure 4.13

Decontamination Area

The decontamination area is where all soiled endoscopes and other items are received. Decontamination is the physical or chemical process that renders a contaminated medical device safe for further handling. It involves a thorough cleaning process. All items returned to this area are considered contaminated and potentially infectious.

Attire for the decontamination room or area

Personnel working in the decontamination area must be protected from potentially infectious materials and chemical agents used during cleaning and reprocessing. Policies and procedures must be developed and followed to ensure that work practices minimize employee injury and exposure to pathogens. Policies and procedures must also meet the facility's and Occupational Safety and Health Administration's (OSHA's) safety requirements to minimize exposure to bloodborne pathogens and other contaminates. **Figure 4.15** provides an example of appropriate PPE at a decontamination work station.

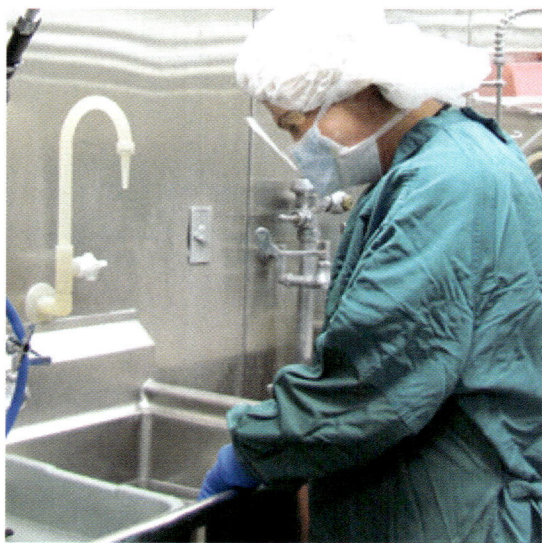

Figure 4.15

Storage areas should be located near the entrance of the decontamination area to provide access to PPE. Appropriate areas, with the necessary containers, should be provided for donning (putting on) and doffing (removing) protective attire.

Eye wash station

The decontamination area should also contain eye wash stations (See **Figure 4.16**) located within a 10-second walk of the work area to enable workers to reach them quickly in the event of a chemical splash. Eye wash stations should be operated and inspected per the manufacturer's instructions.

Work areas should also contain supplies that can be used in the event of a chemical spill or leak. Emergency spill kits should be designed for the specific chemicals being used. (See **Figure 4.17**)

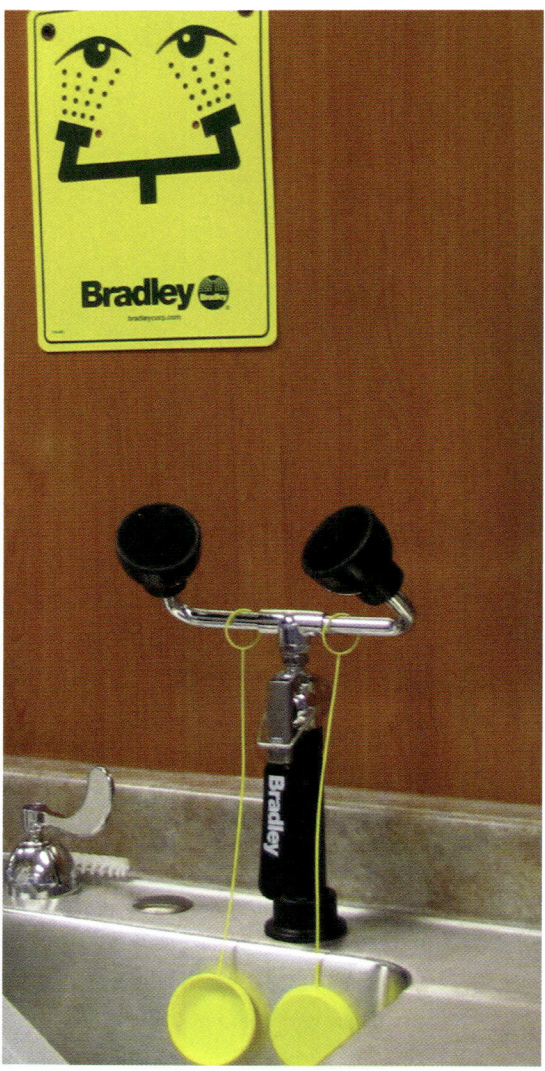

Figure 4.16 Example of an Emergency Eye Wash Station

Figure 4.17 Example of a Chemical Spill Kit

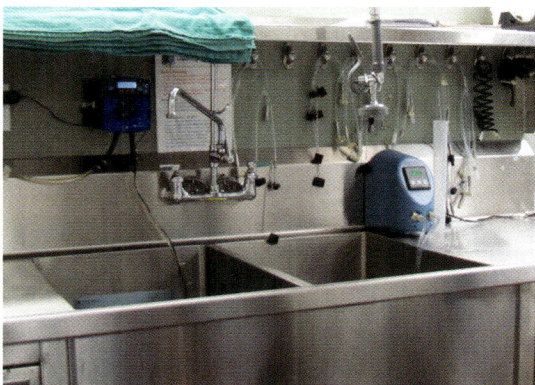

Figure 4.18

Decontamination equipment

There should be a minimum of two sinks in the decontamination area: one sink or sink basin for leak testing and manual cleaning and the other only for rinsing. Sinks should be deep enough to allow complete immersion of the endoscope to minimize aerosolization. The sink size should be adequate to position the endoscope without tight coiling, but not too deep to cause back strain to employees. Tight coiling of the endoscope could damage components, including image or light bundles, internal channels, tubes and/or angulation wires. The sinks should have faucets or manifold systems, adapters that attach to the faucet or other accessories, so the endoscope channels and accessories can be flushed. **Treated water** may be required as a final rinse for endoscopes (the requirement of using treated water would be documented in the endoscope **manufacturer's instructions for use (IFU)**. Using treated water prevents water contaminates from being deposited onto the endoscope.

> **Treated water** Water that has been processed to reduce impurities using filtration, distillation, deionization (DI) or reverse osmosis (RO) processes.
>
> **Manufacturer's instructions for use (IFU)** Written recommendations provided by the manufacturer of a medical device that provide instructions for safe and effective reprocessing methods for that device."

Figure 4.18 provides an example of an endoscope decontamination area sink set up.

Air and vacuum systems should be available to dry the endoscopes and accessories. (See **Figure 4.19**) If forced air is used, it is important to consult the endoscope manufacturer's IFU for an upper limit of pressure to avoid damaging the scope. The nozzle of the pressurized air source should be wiped, disinfected, and allowed to dry before use.

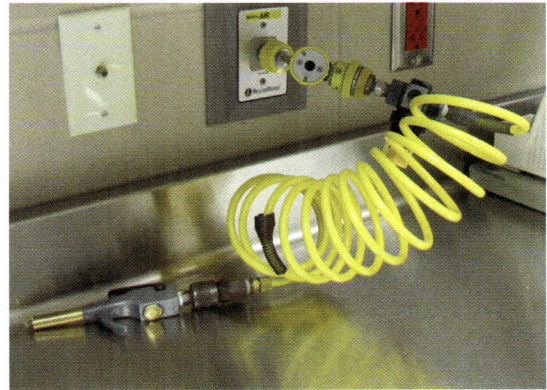

Figure 4.19

Cleaning implements should be easily identified and convenient. Different endoscopes may require a different type of brush. To assure the right brush is being used, refer to the endoscope manufacturer's IFU. Brushes should be labeled for efficiency, error prevention (to avoid using the wrong type of brush) and inventory control. Cleaning brushes should either be single use and disposed of after each use, or reusable and receive high-level disinfection or sterilization after each use, according to their written IFU. Cleaning cloths should be single use and lint free.

Leak testing is the first step in the decontamination process before the flexible endoscope is placed into fluids. Leak testing can detect damage to the endoscope. A hole or leak in the endoscope that is not detected can cause costly damage to the endoscope. The leak testing process requires a specific type of leak tester, as specified by the flexible endoscope manufacturer; the leak tester may be for manual (dry) leak testing or mechanical (wet) leak testing. Lighted magnification may also be used. *Note: Leak testing is discussed in detail in Chapter 6.*

Automatic flexible endoscope flushing equipment may be used to provide automatic flushing of the flexible endoscope channels with water and cleaning solutions. This equipment uses connection tubing; both equipment and tubing should be cleaned and disinfected per the manufacturer's written IFU. **Figure 4.20** provides an example of an automatic flushing device.

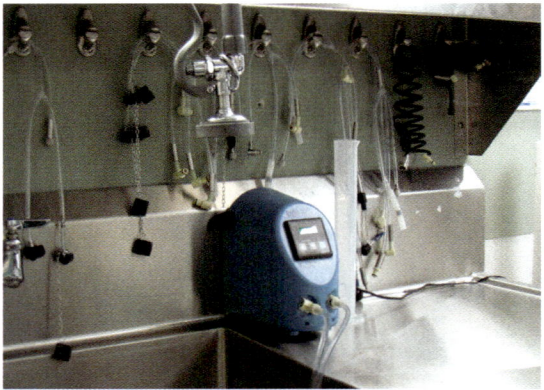

Figure 4.20

Quality assurance testing to assure endoscope cleanliness is performed in the decontamination area. If an endoscope is shown to have bioburden, it can be recleaned before being sent to the clean/preparation area for further processing. Equipment for cleaning verification includes protein tests, adenosine triphosphate (ATP) monitors and accessories, and a lighted magnification glass or system.

Technicians working in the decontamination area must be protected from the potentially infectious material that may be entering the work area. The physical layout of this area, as well as the cleaning equipment used in the area, must meet the appropriate standards of governmental agencies and the recommendations of professional organizations. Policies and procedures must be developed and followed to ensure that work practices minimize employee injury and exposure to pathogens. Again, to meet the facility's and OSHA's safety requirements, technicians must wear the appropriate PPE to minimize exposure to bloodborne pathogens and other contaminates. There should be dedicated facilities to allow for proper disposal of both biohazardous and regular waste.

Record-keeping materials and/or equipment may be required to document the endoscope processing information.

Preparation/Disinfection/Sterilization

Personnel working in the preparation, disinfection/sterilization area should wear facility-restricted attire, such as a scrub suit and hair coverings. Dress and operating practices protect the clean environment in this area from contamination.

The preparation/disinfection area should be separate from the decontamination area. If endoscopes are processed manually, a designated area must be provided for the immersion of the devices for high-level disinfection, followed by thorough rinsing, in accordance with the disinfectant manufacturer's written IFU (treated water may be required). Appropriate ventilation must be maintained. **Figures 4.21 and 4.22** provide examples of ventilation used for manual high-level disinfection.

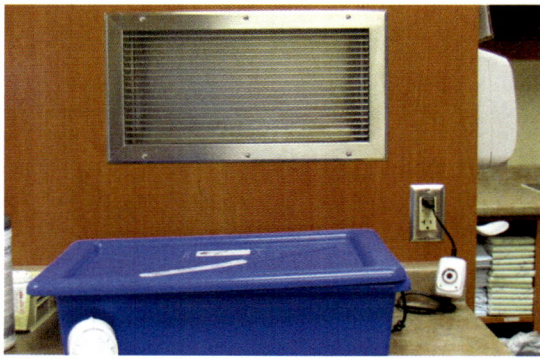

Figure 4.21

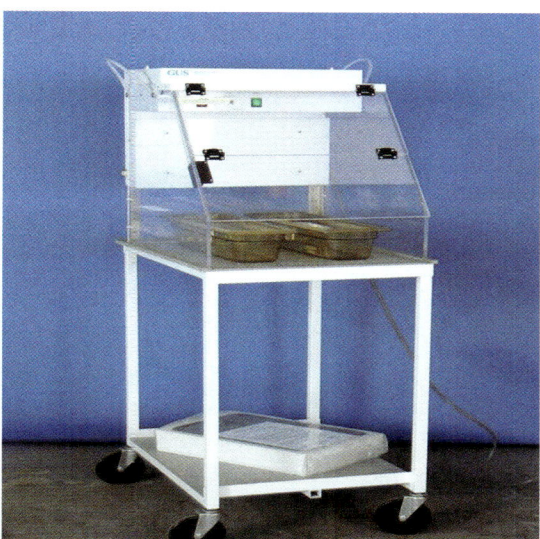

Figure 4.22

The automated endoscope reprocessor (AER) is located in the preparation/disinfection area. (See **Figure 4.23**) Strict one-directional reprocessing procedures should be in place to reduce risks of cross contamination. This area may include a designated drying area to dry the endoscope prior to patient use or storage, or in preparation for packaging and sterilization. A separate area should also be defined and controlled for the storage (temporary or longer term) of devices before patient use.

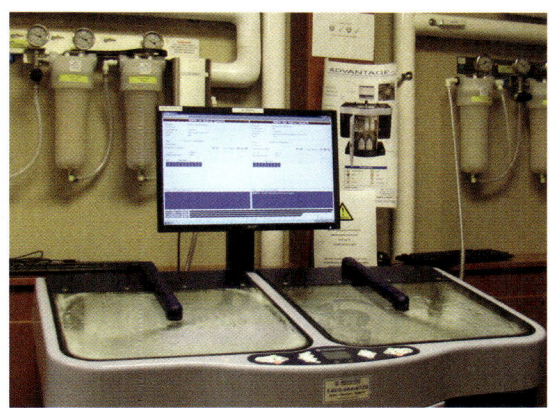

Figure 4.23

The safety data sheets (SDS) for the chemical sterilant or high-level disinfectant should be consulted for safety requirements. Some safety requirements may be the use of a ventilation hood or environmental monitor.

Work stations should be set up to facilitate the next steps in the processing cycle. At the workstation, each endoscope must be carefully inspected for cleanliness, proper function and possible defects; therefore, adequate lighting and magnification tools are essential. (See **Figure 4.24**)

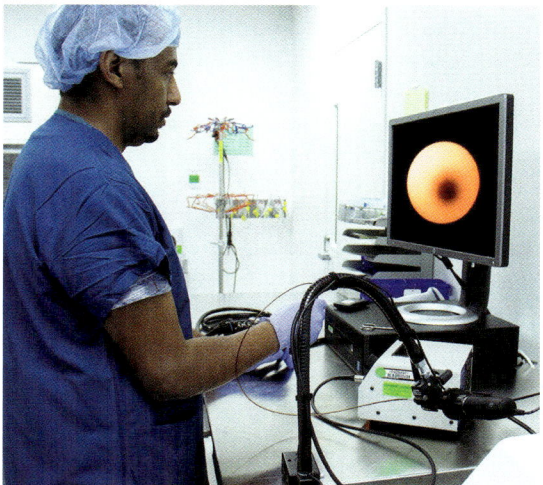

Figure 4.24

After the endoscope has been thoroughly inspected, supplies must be readily available to allow for the next step: high-level disinfection or sterilization.

For endoscopes undergoing sterilization, storage is needed for quality monitors, such as chemical and biological monitors and packaging and all packaging accessories, such as tape and labels; sterilization trays or containment devices may also be used. Some flexible endoscopes may require specific equipment, such as venting caps, for sterilization.

Storage

The endoscope and supply storage area is dedicated to the storage of sterile and clean supplies and endoscopes. A separate area for removing supplies from shipping cartons and containers should be provided. Floors, walls and ceiling surfaces should be constructed of non-porous material that will withstand frequent cleaning and wet conditions. Except for high-level disinfected endoscopes, the storage system may be open wire shelving, open solid shelving or enclosed cabinets. Endoscopes that have undergone sterilization will be stored in this type of environment. Sterilized endoscopes should be stored in the container or packaging in which they were sterilized. Steps should also be taken to ensure stock rotation occurs between all sterilized endoscopes.

A dedicated cabinet should be used to store flexible endoscopes that have undergone high-level disinfection. Flexible endoscopes should be hung vertically with the distal tip hanging freely in a well-ventilated, closed clean cabinet (in accordance with the endoscope manufacturer's written IFU for storage). **Figure 4.25** provides an example of a storage cabinet. The internal surfaces should consist of a material that can be cleaned. There should be sufficient space between and around endoscopes to prevent them from hitting into one another, which can cause damage to the endoscopes. The cabinet should also be of adequate height to allow endoscopes to hang without touching the bottom of the cabinet. *Note: Endoscope storage devices that allow for horizontal storage of flexible endoscopes are available. Check to ensure that the storage device is approved for horizontal storage.*

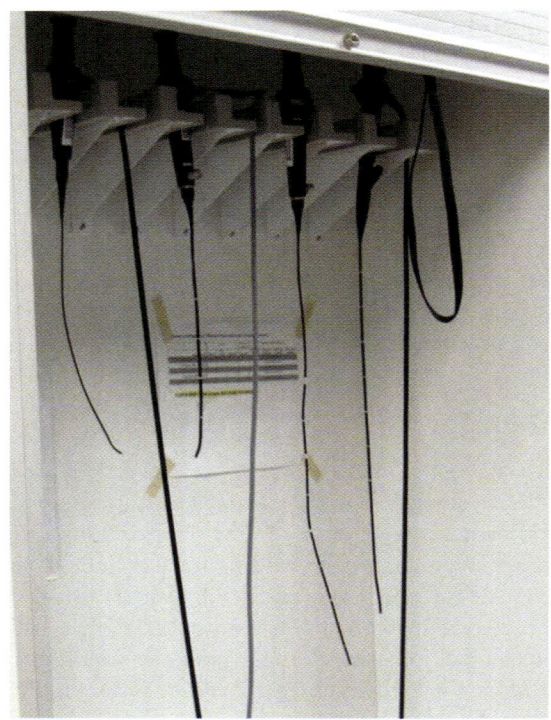

Figure 4.25

All removable parts (e.g., valves and caps) should be detached from the endoscope. To keep the parts together with the endoscope, a small bag or similar device may be used to attach the parts to the endoscope. (See **Figure 4.26**)

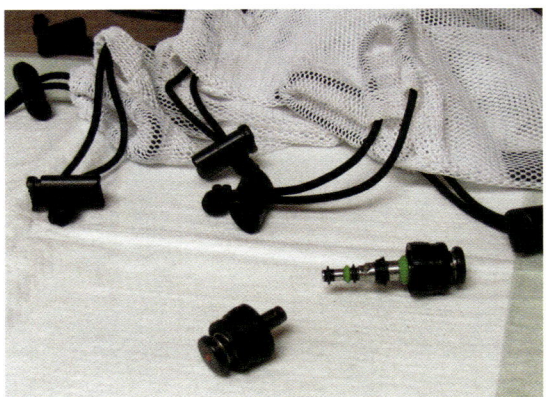

Figure 4.26

Special storage cupboards or cabinets designed for endoscopes are commercially available that assist the drying process by means of special ventilation methods (using filtered air or container systems). Regardless of whether a special cabinet is used, the temperature and humidity in the area where the endoscopes are stored should be monitored.

Maintaining the Work Area

Work areas must be meticulously maintained to help ensure that they remain clean and safe. The work environment must be cleaned regularly to reduce the risk of contamination. Work surfaces and floors should be cleaned at least daily and more often if they become visibly soiled. Other areas, such as cabinets, storage units, covers, etc., should be cleaned on a regular basis. Moveable objects, such as transport carts, should be cleaned regularly. It is important to document all cleaning processes to provide evidence that cleaning occurred.

CONCLUSION

The work area designated for endoscope reprocessing should be designed to prevent microbial cross contamination and allow reprocessing professionals to work safely, effectively and efficiently. The work area must provide adequate space and an effective workflow layout that facilitates good work practices. Careful planning and adherence to work area design recommendations increases the likelihood of successful reprocessing and positive patient outcomes.

RESOURCES

Association for the Advancement of Medical Instrumentation. ANSI/AAMI ST91:2015, *Flexible and semi-rigid endoscope processing in health care facilities.*

International Association of Healthcare Central Service Materiel Management. Central Service Technical Manual, Eighth Edition. 2016.

Association for the Advancement of Medical Instrumentation. ANSI/AAMI ST79:2010 & A1:2010 & A2:2011 & A3:2012 & A4:2013, *Comprehensive guide to steam sterilization and sterility assurance in health care facilities.*

Society of Gastroenterology Nurses and Associates. Standards of Infection Prevention in Reprocessing Flexible Gastrointestinal Endoscopes. 2015.

TERMS

Aerosols

Droplet nuclei

Treated water

Manufacturer's instructions for use (IFU)

Chapter 5

Cleaning Basics

Learning Objectives

Upon completion of this chapter, readers will be able to:

1. Define reprocessing

2. Explain the purpose of manufacturer's instructions for use (IFU)

3. Discuss the importance of cleaning

4. Review requirements for personal protective equipment when handling contaminated endoscopes

5. List strategies to prevent cross contamination

6. Discuss cleaning tools used for reprocessing endoscopes

7. Define the difference between cleaning and decontamination

8. Identify the key factors for selection and safe use of cleaning chemicals for endoscope reprocessing

INTRODUCTION

While many readers of this text will have training and experience in **reprocessing** many types of medical devices, others may have more limited experience. Both veteran and new medical device reprocessors will benefit from a review of factors that can impact the success of the overall medical device cleaning process. This chapter will examine basic cleaning information and identify the importance of using that information to develop good work practices.

Reprocessing is the process of rendering a clinically-used medical device safe and ready for reuse on another patient. Reprocessing is not a simple process. Medical devices are highly sophisticated and complex, and those design complexities often prove challenging when it comes to reprocessing; in fact, it is often said that the more complex a device is, the more complex reprocessing that device will be. Complex reprocessing steps may lead to errors that can jeopardize patient and staff safety. This chapter will examine basic cleaning information that applies to many types of medical devices, including flexible endoscopes.

> **Reprocessing** The process of rendering a clinically-used device safe and ready for reuse.

INFORMATION – THE FIRST STEP IN THE CLEANING PROCESS

Disease transmission from one patient to another can occur when medical devices, such as endoscopes, are not processed properly. Improper reprocessing can also damage medical devices and/or cause device failure. To help mitigate those risks, it is essential that reprocessing professionals have ready access to specific information before attempting to reprocess any medical device.

Device manufacturers provide specific instructions on how to reprocess each device. These manufacturer's instructions for use (IFU) are written recommendations provided by the manufacturer of a medical device that provide instructions for safe and effective reprocessing. Standards and guidelines from the Association for the Advancement of Medical Instrumentation (AAMI), Association of periOperative Registered Nurses (AORN),

Society for Gastroenterology Nurses and Associates Inc. (SGNA), and Centers for Disease Control and Prevention (CDC) state that manufacturers' IFU should be followed. Manufacturers not only understand exactly how their device is constructed, they have conducted tests to validate that the device can be successfully cleaned and disinfected or sterilized when processed in accordance with the instructions. This information serves as the basis for reprocessing. IFU can be maintained manually or electronically; however, regardless of how IFU are maintained, the information must be kept up to date. **Figures 5.1 and 5.2** provide examples of manual and electronic IFU.

Figure 5.1 Manual (Hard Copy) IFU System

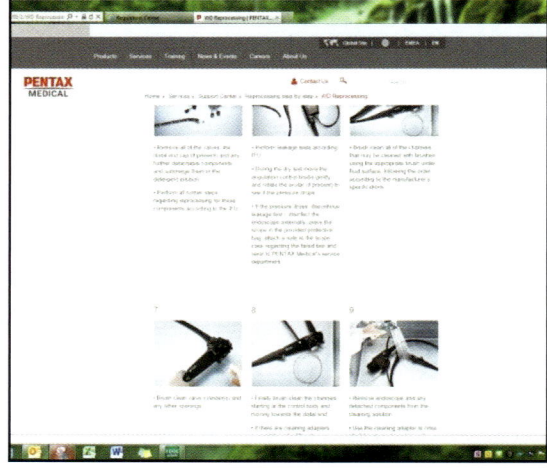

Figure 5.2 Electronic IFU

Prior to the development and availability of reprocessing standards and detailed manufacturers' IFU, healthcare facilities cleaned and sterilized devices based on their "best guess." Procedures varied from facility to facility and, in some cases, from technician to technician. Instructions from the device manufacturer were sometimes vague or nonexistent. In 2015, the US Food and Drug Administration (FDA) published "Reprocessing Medical Devices in Health Care Settings: Validation Methods and Labeling Guidance for Industry and Food and Drug Administration Staff," a more prescriptive document than the previous FDA document published in 1996. The purpose of the document was to identify specific requirements that medical device manufacturers should follow when developing reprocessing instructions to ensure that device users can successfully understand and follow them. The change required manufacturers to develop clear and thorough directions for the reprocessing of their products.

Manufacturers' IFU provide instructions for processes that have been proven effective for the specific device. Consistently following the manufacturers' IFU increases the likelihood that the medical device will be reprocessed successfully; in other words, following IFU is good for patient care and safety.

Following IFU is also good practice for the facility. In the event of an exposure or outbreak, the reprocessing professionals will be asked if the manufacturers' IFU were followed. Strict adherence to and ready availability of manufacturer's IFU will also be an area of focus during inspections and surveys.

Stringent and consistent adherence to IFU for endoscope reprocessing is a requirement for all reprocessing professionals. Technicians must perform each reprocessing step exactly as it is outlined in the IFU, without taking shortcuts. Managers and administrators must ensure technicians have adequate time for reprocessing, as well as the correct training and tools for the job. Managers must also audit processes to ensure that IFU are being followed. Physicians and clinical staff must also help ensure each IFU is carefully and consistently followed by scheduling cases at intervals that allow adequate time for endoscopes to be reprocessed between uses. Some facilities will also need to add additional endoscopes to their inventory if procedure volume makes it difficult for safe, effective reprocessing to occur. It is essential that all healthcare professionals involved understand that failure to follow the manufacturer's IFU puts patients and facilities at risk.

CLEANING BASICS

Endoscope manufacturers' IFU may vary with different types of endoscopes; however, the science behind cleaning, disinfection and sterilization remains the same for all medical devices.

The basics addressed in the following sections apply to Endoscope Reprocessing and must be a part of any Endoscope Reprocessing plan.

Employee Safety: Personal Protective Equipment (PPE)

Used endoscopes are contaminated medical devices. Personal protective equipment (PPE) is designed to protect employees from exposure to infectious materials and should be worn by anyone working with contaminated endoscopes. The use of PPE when reprocessing contaminated endoscopes is mandated (required) by the Occupational Safety and Health Administration (OSHA). Specific PPE required for handling biohazardous devices should be readily available in the decontamination area and must be worn by anyone working in that area.

The dress code for the overall Endoscope Reprocessing area should include the following:

Facility-supplied scrub wear or uniform. Attire should be donned (put on) upon entering the facility and removed before leaving at the end of the shift. If attire becomes soiled during the shift, it should be changed. All reusable attire should be laundered by the facility.

Hair Covering. Hair should be covered with a surgical hair covering. Facial hair (with the exception of eyebrows and eyelashes) should be completely covered with a mask or beard cover.

Jewelry and wrist watches should not be worn. Jewelry and wrist watches harbor microorganisms and are difficult to clean and make safe. In the endoscope decontamination area, jewelry and wrist watches can cause breaks in gloves and protective attire. Jewelry can also harbor microorganisms if it is contaminated.

In addition to the aforementioned standard dress code, more stringent requirements apply for anyone working in the endoscope decontamination area. Those who are assigned to the endoscope decontamination area must also wear:

Gloves. Gloves worn for decontaminating endoscopes should be long enough to prevent contact with contaminated water. Exam gloves should not be used for decontamination because their cuffs are not long enough to prevent contact with soiled water. The thickness and durability of gloves should be sufficient to prevent them from being easily torn when performing normal duties.

Gloves and Hand Hygiene

Gloves provide hands with a protective barrier, and prevent contamination when handling contaminated items; however, the use of gloves does NOT replace the need for hand hygiene.

A liquid-resistant covering with sleeves. A covering, such as a jumpsuit, backless gown, or apron made of a fluid-resistant material, should be worn to prevent the contamination of clothing, and to protect skin from exposure to contaminants. Arms should be completely covered.

Full face protection. A full-length face shield or a combination of mask and eye protection should be worn as a protective barrier during cleaning procedures to prevent mucous membrane exposure from splashes, etc. Face protection must protect from aerosols and splashes.

Shoe covers. Shoe covers should be worn to protect shoes from becoming wet and contaminated during cleaning procedures.

This protective apparel is a critical component of personnel safety. Its proper use will reduce the risk of an occupational exposure to bloodborne pathogens. **Figure 5.3** provides an example of a reprocessing technician in appropriate PPE. **Figures 5.4** to **5.6** provide information on the proper use of PPE.

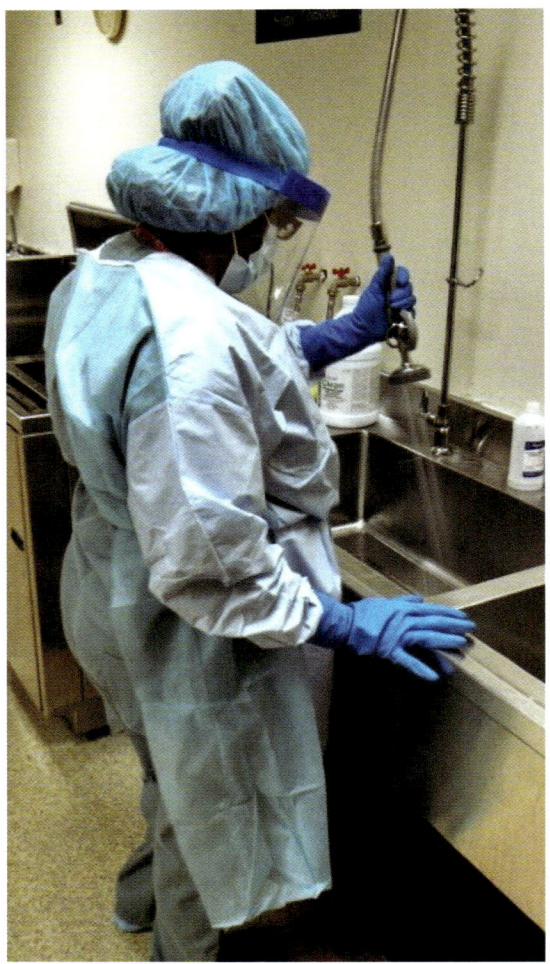

Figure 5.3

Types of PPE

Type of PPE	Protects	Why
Fluid-resistant gown, apron, jumpsuit	Protects skin and scrubs	Provides a barrier against splash or spray
Mask	Protects mouth, nose and chin	Protects respiratory tract from airborne infectious aerosols
Goggles	Protects the eyes	Protects eyes from infectious aerosols
Face shield-full length	Protects eyes, nose, mouth, face	Protects eye, nose, mouth, face from spray and infectious aerosols
Shoe covers	Protects shoes (boot length will protect calf to knee)	Protects the shoes (lower leg) from spray
Gloves	Protects hands	Protects hands from contaminated instruments, fluids and harsh chemicals

Figure 5.4

How to Put on (Don) PPE

*	Before Beginning	Don surgical scrubs, a head cover and appropriate shoes
1	Gown or Jumpsuit	Put on the impervious gown or jumpsuit-tie, snap or zip completely
2	Mask	Secure the ear pieces around the ears or tie the strings on the head area. Fit the mask over the nose area, ensure the nose and mouth areas are completely covered
3	Goggles or Face Shield	Put on goggles or face shield-adjust to fit properly, goggles should wrap around the side of the face
4	Shoe Covers	Put on shoe covers- make sure shoes are completely covered
5	Gloves	Put on gloves-make sure gloves are over the gown cuff

Figure 5.5

CDC Recommendations for Removing (Doffing) PPE

1	**Remove Shoe Covers**
2	**Remove Gloves**
3	**Remove Goggles or Face Shield**
4	**Remove Gown**
5	**Remove Mask**
6	**Remove Head Cover**
7	**Wash Hands**

Figure 5.6

Source: (Figures 5.5 and 5.6) Centers for Disease Control and Prevention Personal Protective Equipment in Healthcare Settings. www.cdc.gov 2010

Point-of-Use Cleaning

As soon as any procedure is completed, the cleaning process must begin. Soil that is allowed to dry is more difficult to remove than soil that is moist. **Figure 5.7** provides an example of a soiled instrument that has been allowed to dry. **Figure 5.7** shows a retractor with blood that is easy to see and accessible. Reprocessing professionals can imagine the difficulty removing dried blood from an endoscope channel with no clear visibility and limited access. Blood and soil that is allowed to remain on items can facilitate microbial growth and also increase the risk of biofilm formation (as discussed in Chapter 3).

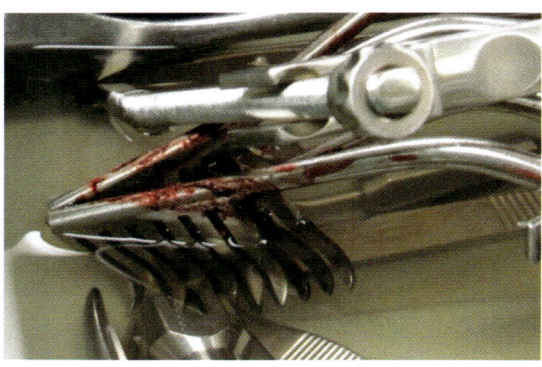

Figure 5.7

Transporting Soiled Items

Soiled items should be transported to the decontamination area as soon as possible after use so the cleaning process can begin. These items should be transported in a manner that minimizes potential exposure to employees and reduces the possibility of contamination in the environment. The transport container should be labeled "biohazard." Sharp items should be placed in a solid, puncture resistant, leak proof container to reduce the threat of injury.

Working against the Clock

Time is the enemy of soiled endoscopes. They should be precleaned, transported and reprocessed as soon as possible after use. As discussed in Chapter 3, failure to clean endoscopes in a timely manner enables biofilms to form and microorganisms to grow, and makes the cleaning process much more difficult. Increasing the risk of a failed cleaning process increases the risk to the patient!

Reducing Risks of Cross Contamination

There must always be a clear separation of clean and dirty items during all phases of endoscope handling. Cross contamination can lead to serious consequences for both patients and employees. Work flow should be identified and traffic should be controlled to help ensure that clean items are not contaminated by soiled items, as addressed in Chapter 4. There is another aspect that can impact cross contamination, however: the people who work in the reprocessing area.

Cross contamination can be avoided by ensuring that work flows one way in the decontamination area. For example, once an endoscope has been cleaned, it should not be placed on a surface where a soiled endoscope has been placed. When more than one person has access to the decontamination area, communication is a must. Everyone must understand the work flow and follow that same flow. If cross contamination occurs, it must be addressed immediately.

Learning to "See" Microbial Contamination

Since microorganisms cannot be seen without a microscope, the people reprocessing endoscopes must learn to see contamination with their "mind's eye."

Consider the following example: There are many types of plants and each type has different characteristics and requires specific conditions to grow. When the conditions are right, (e.g., proper sunlight, soil, moisture) the plants will grow.

Like plants, there are many types of microorganisms. Each has different characteristics and requires specific conditions to grow. Given the right conditions, microorganisms will also grow and thrive; however, because they can't be seen with the naked eye, reprocessing technicians must use their "mind's eye" to see them.

If microorganisms could be seen like plants, the decontamination area shown in **Figure 5.8** might look like the photo in **Figure 5.9**. A knowledgeable reprocessing technician "sees" the contamination and strives to control the spread of that contamination.

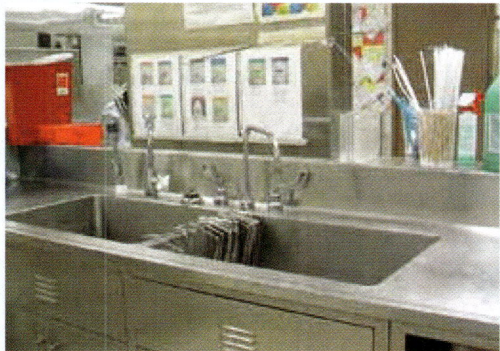

Figure 5.8

Figure 5.9

"If we could see microorganisms growing like plants, what would our cleaning area look like?"

Attire and gloves pose another significant danger for cross contamination. Handling clean items with contaminated gloves or touching handles, buttons, touch pads and other commonly touched items with contaminated gloves can lead to dangerous cross contamination issues. This is particularly true when clean and soiled areas are not physically separated and/or when reprocessing technicians move between clean and soiled duties. The extra time it takes to follow good work protocols is worth the level of safety it provides for patients and staff.

Reprocessing Tools

In addition to the need for a specially designed work area, proper reprocessing requires specific tools. Those tools vary depending on the device(s) being cleaned. It is important to note that the specific tools identified in the IFU must be used for cleaning processes. Common tools used for endoscope cleaning fall into two categories: reusable tools and disposable accessories. Reusable tools include leak testing devices that must be used prior to the cleaning process and mechanical flushing devices.

Disposable tools include items such as sponges, lint-free cloths and brushes. *Note: While some brushes may be reusable and are designed to be decontaminated and reused, they are not designated as long-term accessories; therefore, they must be discarded when they begin to show wear, and the brush manufacturer's IFU must be followed to ensure proper use.* The endoscope manufacturer's IFU will provide information on the specific size and style of brushes needed for cleaning. Using the wrong size brush can cause a cleaning failure and, in some cases, may even damage an endoscope. Brushes that are too large will not fit into the lumen. If a brush that is too narrow in diameter is used to clean a lumen, the brush will not have complete contact with the lumen walls and will, therefore, be unable to thoroughly clean the lumen. Brushes not specifically designed for cleaning an endoscope lumen may cause scratches and tears in the thin walls of the lumen. The brush materials must be softer than the channel to prevent damage. **Figure 5.10** illustrates the importance of brush size. Brush A is too large to fit into the lumen; brush B is too small to make proper contact with the sides of the lumen. The use of either brush A or B will result in inadequate cleaning. Brush C is the proper size for the channel to be cleaned. It is easy to make an error when selecting a cleaning brush. It is important to always check the manufacturer's IFU to obtain information on the correct brush style and size.

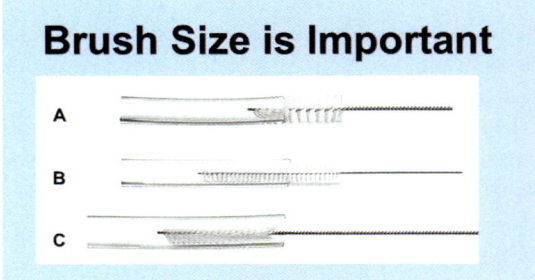

Figure 5.10

In addition to brush sizes, there will be more than one style and length of brush needed for each type of endoscope. **Figures 5.11** and **5.12** provide examples of some types of brushes designed for use with endoscopes. Brushes made for endoscope cleaning may have bristles, elastomer discs or other microfiber materials. **Figure 15.13** provides an example of a single-use endoscope cleaning device.

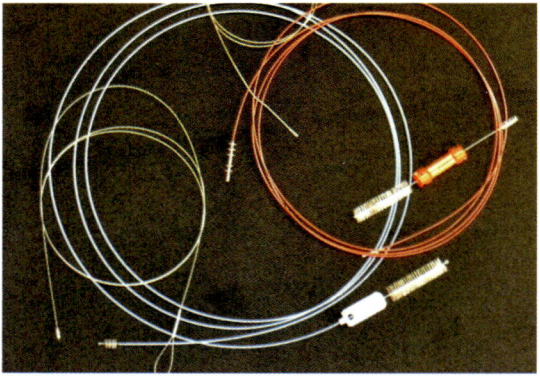

Figure 5.11

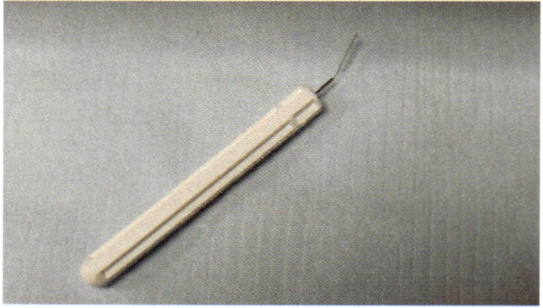

Figure 5.12

A Note about Brushes

It is important to dispose of brushes, as recommended, and keep reusable brushes clean. Remember, a soiled brush may redeposit microorganisms onto another endoscope.

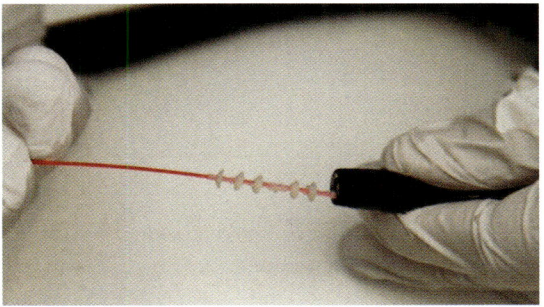

Figure 5.13 Disposable cleaning device designed for endoscope lumens.

Sponges used for endoscope cleaning should be designed for that use and addressed in the endoscope's IFU. **Figure 5.14** provides an example of a sponge designed for cleaning an endoscope insertion tube.

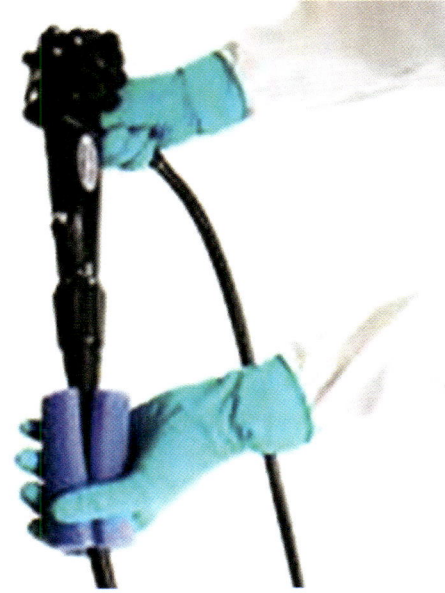

Figure 5.14

Cloths used for endoscope reprocessing should be lint free. (See **Figure 5.15**)

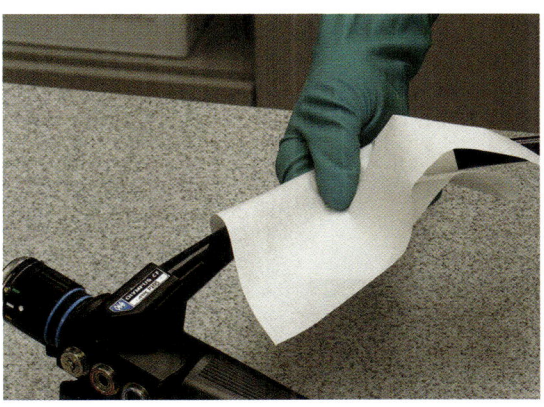

Figure 5.15

Cleaning

The terms cleaning and decontamination are often used interchangeably; however, they are not the same. The term "**cleaning**" refers to the removal of soil from the item being reprocessed. Cleaning is the most important step in the disinfection/sterilization process. Endoscopes must be thoroughly cleaned and rinsed for subsequent reprocessing steps to be effective.

The term "**decontamination**" involves removing or reducing contamination by infectious organisms or other harmful substances. Along with cleaning, decontamination is an important early step in reprocessing. These two steps must be completed in accordance with established principles and procedures, and in conjunction with the endoscope manufacturer's IFU.

One can clean without sterilizing, but one cannot sterilize without proper cleaning. Similarly, one can clean without disinfecting, but one cannot disinfect without cleaning. When soil remains on or inside an endoscope, that soil provides an environment for microorganisms to grow. That soil will also impede future sterilization or disinfection processes. Thorough cleaning is essential for every endoscope being reprocessed.

Because of the complex design of many flexible endoscopes, cleaning can be difficult. Lumens, difficult-to-access areas and areas that cannot be seen pose significant cleaning challenges. For that reason, meticulous attention to detail, good work practices and rigorous adherence to the endoscope's IFU are critical components of a successful cleaning process.

Cleaning The removal of soil from the item being reprocessed.

Decontamination Removing or reducing contamination by infectious organisms or other harmful substances.

Basics of Chemical Use

Various chemicals may be used during endoscope reprocessing. Whether those chemicals are cleaning agents or disinfectants, it is important to understand some basic information about chemicals used in reprocessing.

The most important fact about any chemical is that it will not perform as claimed if it is not used according to the manufacturer's IFU. Before using any chemical, it is essential to carefully read the label. Chemical manufacturers provide IFU for their products and those IFU must be diligently followed. The following are some basic guidelines for working with reprocessing chemicals:

- *Dilution*– Chemicals must be mixed properly. Accurate measurement to achieve the proper dilution is important. Solutions that are too strong or too weak will not be as effective as solutions that are mixed to the exact strength required. Measuring devices must be available for chemicals. Sinks and basins must be marked with water levels to help ensure that the amount of water in the sink or basin is accurate in relation to the chemical being used. Workflow should also be marked to reduce the risk of cross contamination. (See **Figure 5.16**)

Figure 5.16

- *Temperature*– Some chemicals must be used within a specific temperature range. Devices to measure temperature may be needed. (See **Figure 5.17**)

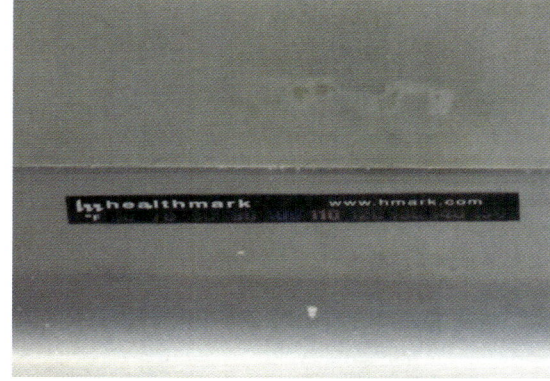

Figure 5.17 provides an example of a temperature marker in a decontamination sink. *Note: HLD solutions require more specific temperature markers*.

- *Contact*– Chemicals must make direct contact with all surfaces in order to be effective; that means ensuring that the endoscope is immersed properly in the chemical, and making certain that all lumens are flushed.

- *Time*– Many chemicals need a specific amount of time to perform as indicated on their label. Timers should be used, as necessary, to help ensure that required contact times have been met.

Selection and Safe Use of Cleaning Chemicals for Endoscopes

Complex design, manual processing and sticky soils combine to make endoscope cleaning a challenging process. The design features of most endoscopes limit direct access for physical scrubbing and brushing. The cleaning process for endoscopes depends on individual manual effort. The soils generated in endoscope procedures combine dried blood, fats and proteins with biofilm to create soils that resist simple cleaning processes. This combination of factors makes the selection and use of cleaning agents more critical.

The most important source of information for the endoscope reprocessing technician when selecting and using cleaning chemistry is the endoscope manufacturer's IFU. It is important to identify the correct instructions for cleaning a specific brand and model.

Manufacturers have typically tested a variety of cleaning agents under controlled conditions to confirm compatibility and validate their recommendations. If a product or product category is identified as compatible, this means the chemical will not cause damage to the endoscope and its components when diluted and used correctly.

Detergents are composed of several agents that aid in soil removal. Surfactants and sequestering agents loosen and break up soils and reduce soil reattachment. Chelating agents help bind minerals in "hard" water and improve rinsing action. The recommended or selected detergent for cleaning endoscopes may or may not contain enzymes.

The most common recommendations by endoscope manufacturers for cleaning chemicals are:

- Neutral-pH;

- Detergent/surfactant, with or without enzymes;

- Low foaming or no foam;

- Free rinsing; and

- Non-corrosive.

Neutral-pH detergents are generally mild and more likely to be compatible with an endoscope's many components. A detergent is considered neutral- or near-neutral-pH if the concentrated product is around 6.5 to 8.5 pH. (The pH scale for cleaning chemicals generally ranges from approximately 1.0 for acids to 14.0 for strong alkalines.) The pH of a product may be identified several ways. The product label may identify the product as neutral-pH. The pH of a detergent may be confirmed by reviewing the Safety Data Sheet (SDS). **Figure 5.18** provides a pH scale for reference.

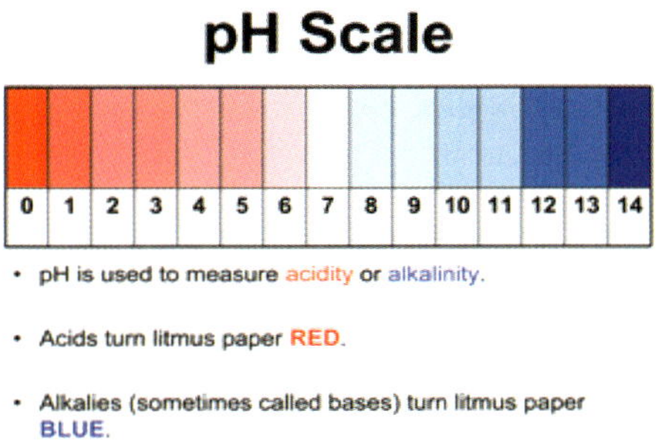

pH Scale

- pH is used to measure acidity or alkalinity.

- Acids turn litmus paper RED.

- Alkalies (sometimes called bases) turn litmus paper BLUE.

Figure 5.18

Low- or no-foam detergent is recommended due to the narrow channels and ports common to many types of endoscopes. The bubbles in a high-foaming detergent may also create a pocket on the surface that prevents direct surface contact. The detergent must be less viscous (less thick) and produce very little foam to easily penetrate narrow channels, and they must be free rinsing for complete removal. It is important to avoid over dosing detergents for endoscope cleaning to ensure complete removal during rinsing. If the detergent is not completely rinsed from the endoscope, residue may interact with high-level chemical disinfectants, creating a difficult-to-remove layer.

The application of pre-cleaning gel or foam sprays should be limited to the exterior of the endoscope. It is important to avoid inserting foam or gel pre-cleaning products into the smaller interior channels of the endoscope. Cleaning agents in the form of gels or foam may be more difficult to completely flush and rinse out of the channels.

Difficult soils are another issue that influences the selection of cleaning chemicals for endoscope reprocessing. Problem soils include fibrin proteins from dried blood, starches from mucous or feces, various types of fats, and biofilm.

A contaminated endoscope with moisture and human soils is a perfect environment to form biofilm.

Bacteria and other organisms live within a sticky gel matrix produced by the bacteria. The matrix serves as a home, a food source and a type of glue that keeps the biofilm attached to ports and inside channel walls. Biofilm can shelter viruses, bacteria and other pathogens, thereby, keeping them viable (able to infect). Biofilm may prevent the penetration of chemical and steam sterilants.

Complete removal of biofilm is essential to allow high-level disinfectants or sterilants to access all surfaces, especially within channels and ports. Biofilm removal requires physical effort (brushing, flushing) on every contaminated area and surface. Its removal also requires high-quality chemical cleaning agents and thorough, complete rinsing. Although many new cleaning formulas have entered the healthcare market, cleaning tests demonstrate that even the best cleaning chemistry must be combined with consistent step-by-step physical effort to remove biofilm.

Many endoscope manufacturers and most professional guidelines recommend the use of cleaning detergents with enzymes. Enzymes are organic protein substances that help break up complex soils, similar to human digestion. They work like a lock and key and target specific soils. Protease enzymes target proteins, amylase enzymes target starches and lipase enzymes target fats. For endoscope cleaning, a multi-enzymatic product with protease, amylase and lipase is especially useful for complex soils associated with most endoscope procedures.

Most enzymatic detergents are neutral-pH. Enzymes work best if allowed several minutes or more of contact time; therefore, they are especially useful in pre-soak or sonic applications with longer contact time.

Enzymatic detergents are organic and have several properties to consider for best action and safe use. Avoid prediluting enzyme products or using unit-dosed pre-diluted enzymatic products. Enzymes are protein and, upon dilution, the protease enzymes will attack and digest or break down other enzymes; this makes the diluted solution less effective after 12 to 24 hours. It is essential to use good inventory practices and rotate enzyme detergent stock to avoid expiration before use.

Organic enzymes are more active in lukewarm water, but will break down and may become ineffective if stored near boilers, sterilizers or washers — or if used in very hot water over 140° F. Refer to the specific detergent manufacturer's label for guidelines on temperature range.

The detergent manufacturer's IFU on the container label is the best source of information for dilution, temperature range, contact time, foaming or other properties, and safe use. Never remove product labels and never use detergent or other chemicals if the label is no longer present on the container.

For all types of cleaning chemicals used on endoscopes, it is recommended to discard the cleaning solution after use on each endoscope or set of endoscope accessories. Water is also considered a cleaning chemical and water quality is a major factor in the cleaning process. In addition to monitoring for adequate biological quality (presence of bacteria and endotoxin), the water used for cleaning should be tested periodically for hardness. Water used for cleaning at 200 total dissolved solids (TDS) or higher may inhibit cleaning and cause spotting. Chelation occurs when agents in detergents bind with calcium and other minerals in tap water.

Water is also a critical component of the rinsing process. It is important to follow the endoscope manufacturer's instructions for volume, water quality and rinsing requirements.

The endoscope reprocessing technician should look first to the endoscope manufacturer's instructions for cleaning a specific brand and model of endoscope, followed by the chemical manufacturer's label instructions for dilution, temperature and application. If a cleaning device such as an automated endoscope reprocessor (AER) with cleaning capabilities is to be used, those instructions must also be included when writing the processing protocols and training staff.

It is inevitable that conflicts will arise between the various instructions for use. Technicians and managers should contact manufacturers and resolve conflicts or possible errors by requesting revisions or updates in writing from the manufacturer. This letter should be on company letterhead, dated and signed by the company's management.

Another issue that may arise when selecting a cleaning agent is possible confusion over the choice of a disinfectant or detergent to be used. Each category of disinfectant and detergent has very different uses. The basic job of detergents is to help loosen soils and keep soils from redepositing on surfaces. Most detergents are not intended to be used as disinfectants and do not have claims to inactivate bacteria or viruses. Some concentrated disinfectants do have cleaning claims because they are diluted with water and contain surfactants. Any product with disinfectant or "bacteriostatic" claims must be registered with the U.S. Environmental Protection Agency (EPA), have independent testing that supports the claims, and include the EPA registration number on the label.

Disinfectants are not typically recommended as the primary cleaning agents for endoscopes. Ready-to-use disinfectants have a variety of chemicals intended to inactivate microorganisms that may interfere with soil removal. Alcohol, for example, is a common ingredient in disinfectants. If alcohol is used before the endoscope is clean, it will denature proteins and blood and make those soils stick tightly to the inside channel walls. At that point, removal of denatured protein soils may be nearly impossible.

Careful review of the product label will help determine if the product is a detergent or a disinfectant. Disinfectants must list the active agents and the EPA registration number on the label. If in doubt, it is important to refer to the endoscope manufacturer's instructions or contact the manufacturer via its technical help line.

In the past, some endoscope manufacturers have recommended household liquid dishwashing detergent as a special cleaning aid for artificial fat soils from colonoscopes used in gastrointestinal procedures. It is not generally recommended to use household products for cleaning and reprocessing a medical device. Household dishwashing liquid is very foamy and usually alkaline (with a pH of approximately 11 to 12). Both properties could harm the endoscope and make rinsing of detergent residue difficult.

The endoscope processing department must have ready access to the SDSs for each chemical product in use. Labels and SDSs should be reviewed to confirm that correct PPE is in use for each product. Latex gloves and human beings are both composed of protein. It is recommended to use non-latex utility gloves for manual sink procedures when using enzymatic detergents. Waterproof aprons, masks, goggles or face shields are appropriate PPE for all types of detergent products.

A recommended monitoring and quality review process for cleaning chemicals includes the following:

1. Periodic review of the chemical products in use. Verify that each product is the correct type for the application. Verify that the most recent SDS is on file for that brand and product.

2. Monitor materials management and stock control. Review expiration dates on cleaning chemistry; this is especially critical for disinfectants and enzymatic detergents.

3. Observe and evaluate use of PPE for specific chemicals. Use photography and /or log sheets to record compliance.

4. At each sink station, verify that dosing, temperature, soak time and cleaning device used comply with the device and detergent IFU.

5. For more complex devices, post the cleaning IFU. (See **Figures 5.19** and **5.20**)

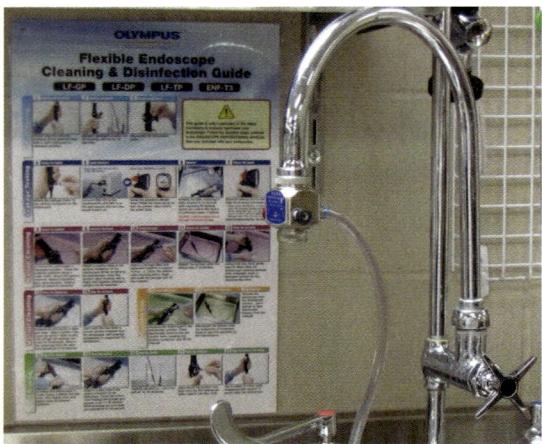

Figure 5.19

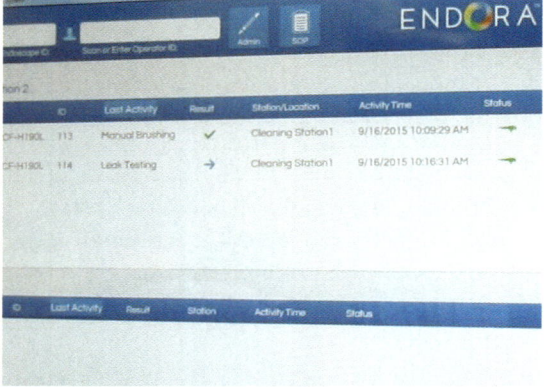

Figure 5.20

6. Measure staff knowledge of detergents and other chemicals by asking about the correct use of specific products, correct dosing and emergency spill exposure procedures for the higher-risk chemicals. Use periodic return demonstrations.

7. Monitor working conditions, equipment and accessories on a scheduled basis. If automated dosing devices are in use, periodically monitor that equipment is delivering the correct dose.

8. Review the department for secondary chemical containers, such as spray bottles. Ensure that any bottle of chemical product likely to be used by multiple staff members is adequately labeled for safe use.

9. Use cleaning tests, including protein and blood detection wands. Testing measures a combination of human effort and cleaning chemistry efficacy. **Figure 5.21** provides an example of a protein detection test. Protein detection tests will be discussed in Chapter 6.

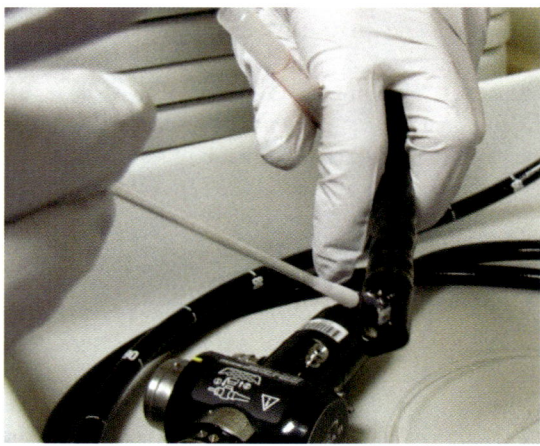

Figure 5.21

CONCLUSION

Infections resulting from improperly-processed medical devices are a threat in any facility. There are many tools designed to assist in the cleaning process, but effective cleaning is primarily impacted by people. At every phase of reprocessing, decisions are made that can impact the entire process. Good work practices make all the difference when cleaning endoscopes. An understanding of basic cleaning can reduce the risk of cleaning failure. During each step of reprocessing, knowing what to do, how to do it properly and what can happen if the process is not successful increases the likelihood that patients will receive a well-processed, safe and properly-functioning endoscope.

RESOURCES

Association for the Advancement of Medical Instrumentation. ANSI/AAMI ST79, A3 2012, A4 2013, section 6, *Comprehensive guide to steam sterilization and sterility assurance in health care facilities.*

International Association for Healthcare Central Service Materiel Management. IAHCSMM Central Service Technical Manual, Eighth Edition. 2016.

Association for the Advancement of Medical Instrumentation. ANSI/AAMI ST91: 2015 Flexible and semi-rigid endoscope processing in health care facilities.

Association for the Advancement of Medical Instrumentation. *ANSI/ AAMI ST65: 2008/(R) 2013 Processing of reusable Surgical textiles for use in health care facilities.*

Society for Gastroenterology Nurses and Associates. Standards of Infection Prevention in Reprocessing Flexible Gastrointestinal Endoscopes. 2015.

TERMS

Reprocessing

Cleaning

Decontamination

Chapter 6

Point-of-Use Cleaning, Transport and Leak Testing

Learning Objectives

Upon completion of this chapter, readers will be able to:

1. Explain the importance of point-of-use cleaning

2. List basic guidelines for the transport of soiled flexible endoscopes

3. Explain the purpose of leak testing

4. List the basic steps in wet and dry leak testing processes

5. Discuss the process for handling a damaged or leaking endoscope

INTRODUCTION

In previous chapters, we learned that failure to remove soil from a flexible endoscope in a timely manner can make the endoscope much more difficult to clean. The cleaning process for every flexible endoscope begins before the endoscope leaves the procedure room. This chapter will examine point-of-use cleaning, soiled endoscope transport and leak testing processes that should be performed before the manual cleaning process begins.

PRE-CLEANING AT POINT-OF-USE

Inadequate pre-cleaning can be a factor in patient infections. Pre-cleaning at the point-of-use, before transporting an endoscope to the decontamination area, helps remove organic materials, including blood and body fluids, on the endoscope's exterior and interior surfaces. The presence of these organic materials can prevent effective sterilization and high-level disinfection (HLD). Pre-cleaning also reduces the likelihood of biofilm formation, which can begin within minutes after completion of a procedure. Biofilm contains living and non-living microorganisms that can adhere to the surfaces of endoscopes. Biofilm is also difficult to remove, and sterilizing/disinfecting agents cannot easily penetrate and kill the microorganisms within biofilm.

Pre-cleaning begins in the procedure room (See **Figure 6.1**), immediately after removal of the insertion tube from the patient and before disconnecting the endoscope from the power source. Careful compliance with the manufacturer's instructions for use (IFU) is always important. *Note: The information that follows is representative of general recommendations.*

Every cleaning procedure requires tools and supplies. Items needed for point-of-use cleaning include:

- Personal protective equipment (PPE): This includes gloves, an impervious (fluid-resistant) gown with full sleeves and face shield or goggles and a fluid-resistant face mask. Fluid-resistant shoe covers should be worn where there is a chance for splashing.

- A container with an enzymatic or non-enzymatic detergent solution prepared according to the manufacturer's dilution and mixing instructions.

- Soft, lint-free cloths.

- Air and water channel cleaning adapters may be needed and should be used according to the manufacturer's IFU. **Figures 6.2** and **6.3** show examples of air and water channel cleaning adapters.

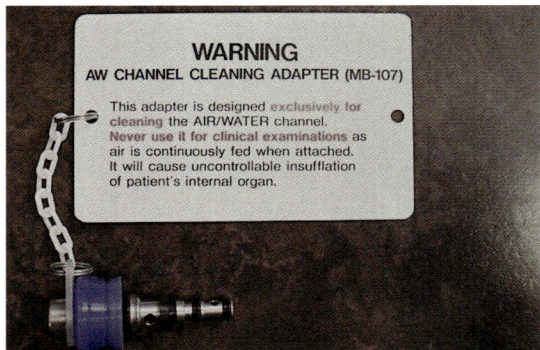

Figure 6.2

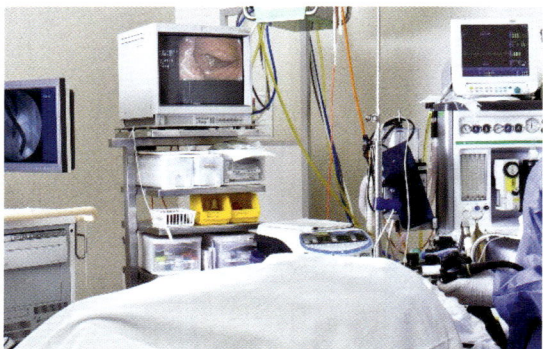

Figure 6.1 Pre-cleaning begins in the procedure room.

Figure 6.3

Steps in Point-of-Use Pre-cleaning

Step 1: Immediately after removing the endoscope from the patient, it should be moved away from him or her to prevent possible exposure to aerosolized (airborne) detergents and bioburden. To remove all gross soil, wipe the insertion tube with a wet cloth or sponge soaked in the freshly-prepared enzymatic or non-enzymatic detergent solution, in accordance with the manufacturer's dilution concentration and usage recommendations. (See **Figure 6.4**) To prevent cross contamination, this soft cloth or sponge should be disposed of or sent to linen services for reprocessing after use. *Note: Specialty cleaning cloths and foam devices designed for this purpose are available.*

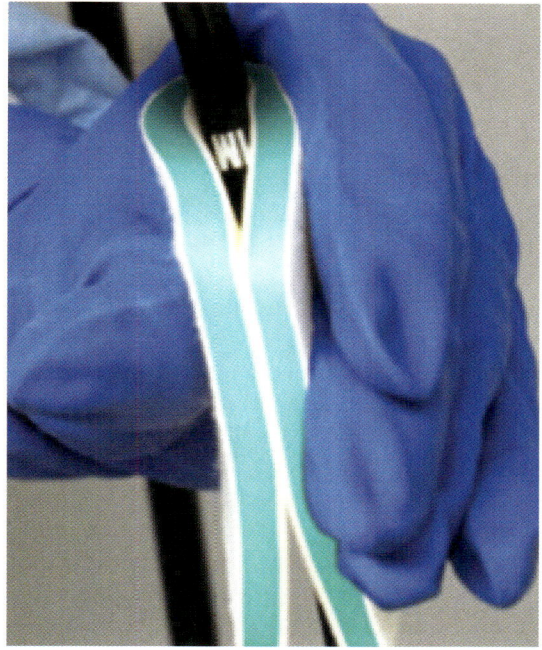

Figure 6.4

Step 2: Place the **distal** end of the flexible endoscope into the detergent solution. Suction the solution through the biopsy/suction channel. Alternate suctioning the detergent solution and air several times until the solution is visibly clean.

> **Distal** The end of an item that is farthest away from the point of origin; the end of the instrument farthest away from the operator; the distal end of the femur is closest to the knee.

Step 3: Attach the air and water channel connecters per the endoscope manufacturer's IFU and then flush or blow air from the water/air channel. *Note: The air and water channel is very small, and a miniscule amount of debris can clog it. Never use a needle or wire to clear the channel. The air and water channel adapter is the only tool that should be used to blow forced air out of the air/water channel.*

Step 4: Flush the auxiliary water channel.

Step 5: Detach the flexible endoscope from the light source and suction pump.

Step 6: If using a video endoscope, attach the protective video cap.

Step 7: Coil the endoscope and valves into a large circular configuration without kinks and carefully place it into a sealed container for transport to the reprocessing area. *Note: No other instrumentation or accessories should be placed in the container with the endoscope.* Valves should be kept with the endoscope to help ensure traceability of the endoscope components. The container should be leak proof and puncture resistant to protect the endoscope and the environment around it. **Figure 6.5** provides an example of reusable transport containers. The transport container must be labeled to indicate biohazardous contents. Proper labeling of the transport container informs others that the items are potentially infectious.

Figure 6.5

Disposable endoscope transport bags/kits are also available. **Figure 6.6** provides an example of disposable transport kits contained in a transport cart.

Figure 6.6

Step 8: All reusable accessories, such as biopsy forceps, snare wires or water bottles, should be gathered and placed into a separate container.

The endoscope should be immediately transported to the reprocessing area within 15 minutes of use. It should then be placed into the reprocessing cycle for continued processing no later than 60 minutes after pre-cleaning. Failure to do so increases the risk of the formation of biofilm, which can impede adequate cleaning and disinfection processes.

Transport of Contaminated Endoscopes

There are three main goals when transporting contaminated flexible endoscopes to the decontamination area:

- Deliver the endoscope in a timely manner;

- Prevent cross contamination as the endoscope is transported; and

- Prevent the endoscope from being damaged.

All personnel that handle endoscopes should be trained in endoscope handling techniques to help reduce the risk of damage to the devices.

Following pre-cleaning and transport, the remaining steps in the decontamination process are performed in the decontamination area in a dedicated location that has large side-by-side sinks for leak testing, cleaning and rinsing. The use of PPE is mandatory and failure to provide and/or use this protection may lead to staff exposure and/or injury, and citations by the Occupational Safety and Health Administration (OSHA). Personnel must receive training for PPE selection and use and information about all potential hazards related to endoscope reprocessing.

LEAK TESTING

Introduction

Once a flexible endoscope enters the decontamination room, leak testing is the first step in the reprocessing of the endoscope. Every endoscope that requires leak testing should be tested after each procedure, with no exceptions. The goal of a leak test is to detect damage to the exterior or interior of the endoscope that will cause fluid to leak into sections of the endoscope and contaminate the endoscope. Pockets of fluid that leak into an endoscope create a breeding ground for microorganisms. Due to the compromised integrity of the endoscope, those microorganisms may pose a danger to patients if they leave the endoscope and are introduced into the body of a future patient.

Fluid invasion may also cause significant damage to the endoscope's interior. Certain areas of the endoscope, such as the light bundles, electrical components and manipulation cables, should not be exposed to fluids. When fluids enter those areas, the endoscope's function and safety are impacted. Leak testing helps detect leaks that, when left unrepaired, can result in significant damage, repair costs and patent safety issues. **Figure 6.7** and **Figure 6.8** provide examples of the damage that fluid can cause to the interior of an endoscope.

HEAVY
CORROSION
IN
CONTROL
BODY

Figure 6.7

HEAVY
CORROSION IN
ELECTRICAL
CONNECTOR

Figure 6.8

Leak testing is the most effective method used to detect issues with endoscope integrity. **Fluid invasion** can cause significant damage to an endoscope. If the integrity of an endoscope is compromised and not detected, it can lead to cross contamination and patient infections.

Endoscopes should be leak tested in accordance with the manufacturer's IFU prior to immersion in any fluids. *Note: IFU do vary by equipment manufacturer and model.*

> **Fluid invasion** A situation where fluid invades internal sections of an endoscope. Fluid damage causes damage to working components of the endoscope and creates a situation where microorganisms are introduced to areas of the endoscope that cannot be cleaned.

Leak testing can be performed using wet or dry processes and manual or mechanical processes. Be sure to follow the IFU for each specific endoscope.

A leak test failure indicates that a channel is perforated, torn or twisted. If this occurs, the endoscope must be tagged for repair and the endoscope manufacturer's guidelines must be followed while it is cleaned, decontaminated and returned to the repair facility.

Note: It is illegal to knowingly transport an unlabeled contaminated item outside of the healthcare facility.

Leak testing must be performed before the endoscope is immersed in reprocessing solutions to minimize damage to the endoscope. The endoscope must be leak tested in accordance with the manufacturer's IFU. A basic leak testing protocol begins with consideration of necessary equipment, including:

- PPE: This includes gloves, an impervious (fluid-resistant) gown with full sleeves and face shield or goggles and a fluid-resistant face mask. Fluid-resistant shoe covers should be worn where there is a chance for splashing.

- Leak tester.

- Large basin/sink of clean water.

Types of Leak Detectors

There are numerous types of leak detectors available. Facilities should choose a leak detector that is appropriate for the endoscope model used.

The following is a general overview of basic types of leak detectors. *Note: Each facility will need to determine which leak tester is best suited for their reprocessing needs. Refer to the endoscope manufacturer's IFU to determine the most appropriate leak detector to be used.*

Leak Tester Type	Advantages	Disadvantages
Hand-held Tester (Dry)	Low cost, easy to use	No documentation features. Relies on operator observation
Electrically-powered pump, (Wet)	Can be used in reprocessing of a damaged endoscope	Does not document/record leak test. Relies on operator observation
Automated Leak Tester (Dry)	Documents leak test, minimizes chances of fluid invasion	May be cost prohibitive

The following is a general protocol for leak testing:

- Visually inspect the flexible endoscope for any tears and holes. Inspect joints for obvious signs of wear or damage. (See **Figure 6.9**) **Figure 6.10** provides an example of external damage to an endoscope.

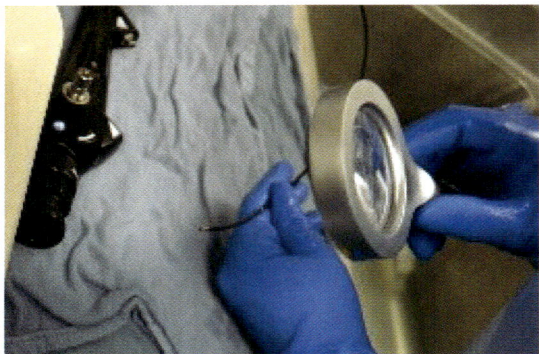

Figure 6.9

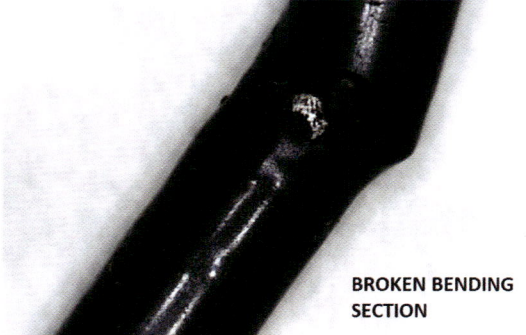

BROKEN BENDING SECTION

Figure 6.10

- Remove suction valves and air/water and biopsy valves, and discard the disposable parts. The endoscope must be completely disassembled so all surfaces can be accessed for thorough cleaning.

- Attach the leak tester to the venting connection that is usually located on the water-resistant cap. Always ensure that the cap is fully "on" and "locked." If using a manual leak test method, pressurize the endoscope before submerging it in clean water, without detergent. Detergent can produce bubbles that make the visual inspection for bubbles more difficult. (See **Figure 6.11**) Refer to the specific endoscope manufacturer's IFU to determine if other detachable parts must be removed before leak testing.

Figure 6.11 Leak tester connected to scope

- With the pressurized insertion tube completely submerge, (unless using the dry leak testing method, refer to IFU for proper dry leak process) flex the distal portion of the endoscope in all directions while observing for bubbles. Submerge the entire endoscope and observe the control head of the endoscope while depressing the freeze and release buttons. If the O-rings in the control knobs are damaged, air bubbles may escape when the control knobs are turned, so this should be done while the endoscope is fully submerged.

- Check the insertion tube and distal bending section, as well as the universal cord, for bubbles coming from the endoscope's interior. If a hole is present in the internal channel of the endoscope, air bubbles will exit via the distal tip. (See **Figure 6.12**) Therefore, it is vital that the internal channels are fully filled with water when submerging the endoscope while it is attached to the leak tester. The presence of air bubbles or the failure to maintain pressure during a manual or automated leak test is a positive indicator of an air leak. *Note: A continuous stream of bubbles indicates a leak.* (See **Figure 6.13**)

Figure 6.12

Figure 6.13

- Remove the endoscope from the water; drain.

- Turn off the leak tester, release the pressure from within the endoscope, and verify the deflation of the bending rubber.

- Disconnect the leak tester from the endoscope. *Note: Never disconnect the leak tester under water because water could enter the leak tester connector and invade the endoscope's interior.*

When a leak is detected, the leak testing device should remain attached to the flexible endoscope and under pressure until the endoscope is removed from the water. Maintaining continuous air pressure prevents water from entering the internal portions of the flexible endoscope, which may cause more extensive damage to the internal parts.

The protocol for computerized leak testing is:

- Remove suction, air, water and biopsy valves;

- Attach the leak tester to the computer following the IFU;

- Input data, including the endoscope's identification number and user's name;

- Move knobs and depress the freeze and release buttons, when indicated; and

- Following a "pass" result, reprocess the endoscope when the test is complete.

Follow the endoscope manufacturer's IFU if a leak or high humidity is detected or if the endoscope appears damaged.

INSTRUCTIONS FOR REPROCESSING A DAMAGED/LEAKING ENDOSCOPE

Required High-level Disinfection or Sterilization for Flexible Endoscopes

All endoscopes must be properly cleaned and high-level disinfected or sterilized before being sent to any repair facility. Always adhere to the manual cleaning and reprocessing guidelines that accompany each endoscope.

Endoscopes that fail a leak test must be handled with extra care to avoid additional damage due to fluid invasion. *Note: Additional information about protocols for shipping defective endoscopes is provided in, Chapter 13, Endoscope System Maintenance. If required, place the EtO venting cap on the endoscope prior to placing into the sterilizer.*

Manual Cleaning of a Leaking Endoscope

Endoscopes that fail a leak test, but have only a minor leak can be manually cleaned and high-level disinfected or sterilized without causing further damage to the endoscope by fluid invasion, if proper precautions are followed. A minor leak is characterized by a small stream of air bubbles emerging from the leak on the endoscope. Positive pressure must always be maintained on the endoscope during the manual cleaning cycle and HLD. This can be achieved by either leaving the endoscope attached to an automatic leak tester or manual leak tester. Ensure the automatic leak tester is turned on prior to submerging the endoscope in water. Do not turn off the automatic leak while the endoscope is submerged in water; a loss in air pressure will allow water to flow into the endoscope.

An endoscope with a major leak may have suffered severe damage, such as a torn bending rubber or insertion tube and, therefore, will not be able to hold any air pressure. A major leak appears as a large amount of air bubbles emerging from the endoscope. An endoscope with a major leak will not be able to be properly disinfected without fluid invading the endoscope, unless the damage is temporarily sealed.

Waterproof tape can be used to temporarily seal the endoscope and allow it to be disinfected. The steps for disinfecting a leaking endoscope include:

1. Remove the leaking endoscope from water;

2. Turn off the automatic leak tester or open the control valve on the manual leak tester and let the endoscope de-pressurize for approximately 30 seconds;

3. Thoroughly clean and dry the affected area, as directed by the manufacturer's IFU;

4. Wrap the affected area with waterproof tape. *Note: Colored tape may make it easier to distinguish.* (See **Figure 6.14**)

5. Pressurize the endoscope using the appropriate leak tester; and

6. Re-submerge the endoscope in water and continue with the manual cleaning and high-level disinfection steps.

Figure 6.14

High-level Disinfection or Sterilization of a Leaking Endoscope

Do not high-level disinfect the damaged endoscope in an automated endoscope reprocessor (AER), unless the manufacturer has certified that the endoscope will remain positively pressurized throughout the entire cleaning cycle, otherwise, the endoscope may not remain pressurized and therefore, fluid will invade the endoscope during the cleaning cycle. Use an appropriately-sized basin to accommodate the flexible endoscope with high-level disinfectant to disinfect the endoscope according to the manufacturer's recommendations. Ensure the endoscope is always attached to an automatic leak tester or physically pressurized with a manual leak tester throughout the entire disinfection cycle.

Ethylene oxide gas sterilization is acceptable if the leaking endoscope has been identified by the manufacturer to be compatible with the sterilization system. For leaking endoscopes where electrical tape has been applied, remove the electrical tape and clean with a germicidal cloth or lint-free cloth and 70% ethyl or isopropyl alcohol. The electrical tape must be removed to allow the sterilization gas to contact the affected area.

CONCLUSION

Flexible endoscopes are delicate, complex devices that require many reprocessing steps. If any of these steps are missed or performed incorrectly, endoscope damage can occur, microorganisms and biofilm may remain on the endoscope, and patient safety may become jeopardized.

Successfully completing point-of-use pre-cleaning, transport and leak testing will help ensure that the endoscope will be ready for cleaning and disinfection or sterilization.

RESOURCES

Association for the Advancement of Medical Instrumentation. ANSI/AAMI ST91: 2015. *Flexible and semi-rigid endoscope processing in health care facilities*.

International Association of Healthcare Central Service Materiel Management. *Central Service Technical Manual, Eighth Edition*. 2016.

Society of Gastroenterology Nurses and Associates. *Standards of Infection Prevention in Reprocessing Flexible Gastrointestinal Endoscopes*. 2015.

TERMS

Distal

Fluid invasion

Chapter 7

Cleaning Processes for Flexible Endoscopes

Learning Objectives

Upon completion of this chapter, readers will be able to:

1. Explain the importance of thorough cleaning of flexible endoscopes

2. List general steps in flexible endoscope cleaning

3. Discuss brushing requirements

4. Discuss reusable brush care and maintenance

5. Explain the impact that residues can have on patient outcomes

6. Discuss quality control for cleaning processes

INTRODUCTION

While every step of endoscope reprocessing is important, cleaning is especially critical. Soil that is allowed to remain in an endoscope cannot be removed by high-level disinfection (HLD) or sterilization. Failure to remove soil will result in failed disinfection and sterilization processes and will greatly increase the risk to patients. This chapter will provide general information about cleaning flexible endoscopes. Each specific endoscope model has specific cleaning instructions and the manufacturer's instructions for use (IFU) should be meticulously followed for each endoscope.

There are many steps to achieve proper cleaning of a flexible endoscope. Each required step is part of a cleaning process validated by the endoscope manufacturer. *Note: Facilities should not deviate from the specific steps outlined by the endoscope manufacturer.*

> **Validation** The U.S. Food and Drug Administration (FDA) defines validation as establishing by objective evidence that a process consistently produces a result or product that meets its predetermined specifications.

According to the Centers for Disease Control and Prevention (CDC) Healthcare Infection Control Practices Advisory Committee (HICPAC) guidelines, "Cleaning is the removal of visible soil (e.g., organic and inorganic material) from objects and surfaces, and normally is accomplished manually or mechanically using water with detergents or enzymatic products. Thorough cleaning is essential before HLD and sterilization because inorganic and organic materials that remain on the surfaces of instruments interfere with the effectiveness of these processes."

> **Centers for Disease Control and Prevention** The Centers for Disease Control and Prevention (CDC) is a federal agency that conducts and supports health promotion, prevention and preparedness activities in the United States, with the goal of improving overall public health. Established in 1946 and based in Atlanta, GA, the CDC is managed by the Department of Health and Human Services (HHS).

> **Healthcare Infection Control Practices Advisory Committee** The Healthcare Infection Control Practices Advisory Committee (HICPAC) is a federal advisory committee assembled to provide advice and guidance to the Centers for Disease Control and Prevention (CDC) and the Secretary of the Department of Health and Human Services (HHS). This advice pertains to the practice of infection control and strategies for surveillance, prevention and control of healthcare-associated infections, antimicrobial resistance and related events in U.S. healthcare settings. The primary activity of HICPAC is to provide advice on periodic updating of existing CDC guidelines, and development of new CDC guidelines.

Endoscopes are difficult to clean due to their complex design (long, narrow lumens) and delicate nature. The complete process of manual cleaning must be implemented each time the endoscope is reprocessed to prevent the spread of health-care-acquired infections. Inadequate cleaning of instruments has been reported as one factor responsible for transmission of infection by flexible endoscopes. Due to the variety of endoscopes available, it is important to refer to the endoscope manufacturer's IFU for the exact steps to follow for proper reprocessing. Endoscope IFU should be readily available for each reprocessing activity.

According to the Society of Gastroenterology Nurses and Associates Inc.'s (SGNA's) 2015 guidelines, *Infection control in reprocessing, cleaning of endoscopes*, manual cleaning of endoscopes is necessary prior to automated or manual disinfection. This is the most important step in removing the microbial burden from an endoscope. Retained debris may inactivate or interfere with the capability of the active ingredient of the chemical solution to effectively kill and/or inactivate microorganisms.

Meticulous cleaning must precede any sterilization or HLD process of these devices. Failure to perform good cleaning can result in sterilization or disinfection failure, and outbreaks of infection can occur. *The 2011 Multi-Society Guideline on Reprocessing Flexible Gastrointestinal Endoscopes* (2011) states that, "Before manual or automated high-level disinfection, meticulously clean the entire endoscope, including valves, channels, connectors and all detachable parts." Studies have shown that manual and mechanical cleaning of endoscopes achieves approximately a 4-log^{10} reduction of contaminating organisms; therefore, manual cleaning alone significantly reduces the number of microorganisms on contaminated endoscopic equipment.

What is a Log Reduction?

"Log" stands for logarithm, which is the exponent of 10. For example, Log-2 represents 102 or 10 x 10 or 100. Log reduction stands for a 10-fold (one decimal) or 90% reduction in numbers of live bacteria. For example:

- 1-Log reduction: Number of germs is 10 times smaller

- 2-Log reduction: Number of germs is 100 times smaller

- 3-Log reduction: Number of germs is 1000 times smaller

- 4-Log reduction: Number of germs is 10,000 times smaller

- 5-Log reduction: Number of germs is 100,000 times smaller

- 6-Log reduction: Number of germs is 1,000,000 times smaller

Manual cleaning begins immediately after leak testing is completed and should be conducted as soon as possible after use to prevent biofilm from forming and soil from drying on the device. Soil that remains on the endoscope may interfere with the disinfection or sterilization process's ability to effectively kill or inactivate microorganisms; it may also allow for biofilm development. If it is not possible to start the cleaning process immediately after the endoscope's use, the endoscope manufacturer's written IFU for delayed processing should be followed.

Delayed processing Reprocessing activities that begin more than one hour after an endoscope's use. A delay in reprocessing enables soil to dry on endoscope components and biofilm to form.

The following steps give a "general outline" of the process for manual cleaning of flexible endoscopes.

MANUAL CLEANING OF THE ENDOSCOPE

1. Completely submerge the endoscope in detergent or enzymatic solution.

2. Manually clean all internal and external surfaces; this includes brushing all internal channels that can be brushed.

3. Attach recommended cleaning adapters according to the endoscope manufacturer's instructions. (IFU).

4. Flush each internal channel with detergent or enzymatic solution.

5. Soak for the recommended time in detergent or enzymatic solution according to the detergent or enzymatic manufacturer's recommendation.

6. After soaking, rinse and submerge the endoscope in clean water and flush the channels.

7. Remove water from the channels by flushing internal channels with air.

The following steps are "general requirements" for proper manual cleaning of flexible endoscopes:

Note: Specific models of endoscopes may have different instructions for use. Carefully follow the manufacturer's IFU.

1. Don fresh personal protective equipment (PPE), including gloves and skin and eye protection. (See **Figure 7.1**)

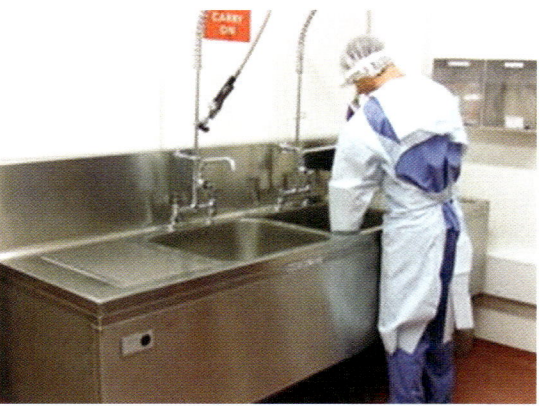

Figure 7. 1

2. Disconnect and disassemble endoscope components (e.g., air/water and suction valves) as completely as possible (See **Figures 7.2 and 7.3**)

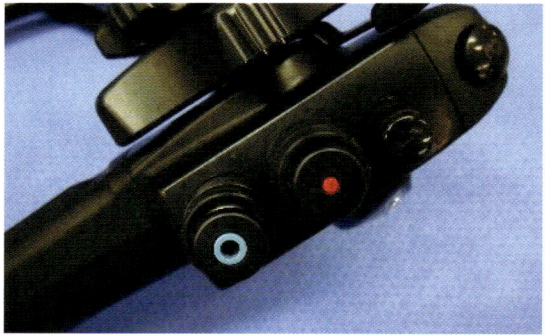

Figure 7.2

Figure 7.3

3. Fill a sink or basin with freshly-made solution of water and a medical-grade, low-foaming, neutral-pH detergent formulated for endoscopes (such detergent may or may not contain enzymes). Prepare fresh cleaning solution for each endoscope according to the solution manufacturer's written IFU for temperature (if applicable), concentration and water quality. The temperature of the cleaning solution should be monitored and documented.

Note: The Centers for Disease Control and Prevention (CDC) recommends use of a neutral- or near-neutral pH detergent solution for instrument cleaning because these solutions generally have good material compatibility and remove soil effectively. Alkaline-based cleaning agents are used for processing medical devices because they efficiently dissolve protein and fat residue; however, they can be corrosive to instruments.

4. Dilute and use according to the enzymatic or detergent manufacturer's instructions. *Note that:*

a) Freshly-prepared detergent solution should be used for each endoscope to prevent cross contamination.

b) Low-foaming enzymatic detergents are recommended so the device can be clearly visualized during the cleaning process, preventing personnel injury and allowing for complete cleaning of lumen surfaces. Excessive foaming can inhibit good fluid contact with the device surfaces.

c) Endoscopes exposed to synthetic lipids may require additional pre-cleaning with a detergent or enzymatic solution formulated to remove synthetic lipids.

5. Ensure the video cap is secure. Immerse the endoscope by placing it into the solution, keeping it below the fluid's surface level at all times. If using an enzymatic detergent, soak the endoscope and its internal channels for the period of time specified on the detergent's label.

The 2011 Multi Society Guidelines on Reprocessing Flexible Gastrointestinal provide provide more detail stating to completely immerse the endoscope and components in an appropriate detergent that is compatible with the endoscope, according to the manufacturer's instructions.

Clean the endoscope's exterior surfaces with a single-use, lint-free cloth or sponge. (See **Figure 7.4**) Remove all debris from the exterior of the endoscope by brushing and wiping the instrument while submerged in the detergent solution. As per ANSI/AAMI ST91 and SGNA Guidelines the endoscope should be submerged in the detergent solution when performing all subsequent cleaning steps to prevent splashing of contaminated fluid and aerosolization of bioburden. (ST91 and SGNA).

The 2011 Multi Society Guidelines on Reprocessing Flexible Gastrointestinal recommends completely submerging the endoscope and components in an appropriate detergent or enzymatic solution that is compatible with the endoscope and used in accordance with the manufacturer's instructions.

Clean the external surfaces and components of the endoscope by using a soft cloth, sponge or brushes.

Figure 7.4

6. Use a small, soft brush to clean all removable parts, including inside and under the suction valve, air/water valve, and biopsy port cover and openings. Use non-abrasive and lint-free cleaning tools to prevent damage to the endoscope. (See **Figures 7.5** and **7.6)**

Note: Disposable biopsy caps and air/water valves are on the market. Never reprocess a disposable component.

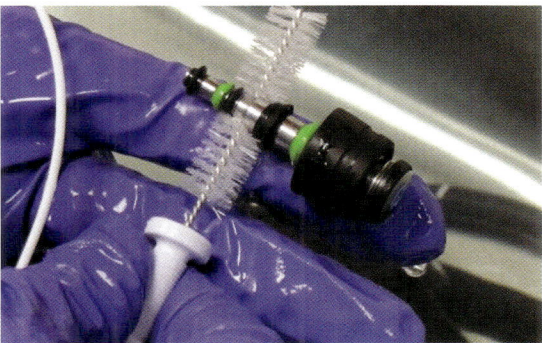

Figure 7.5

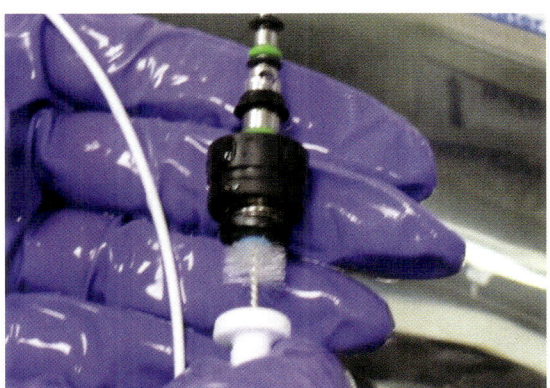

Figure 7.6

7. Clean all valve cylinders, openings and forceps elevator housings with a cleaning brush of the length, width and material designated in the endoscope manufacturer's written IFU.

Note: Endoscope valves must be manually actuated to ensure coverage of all internal parts.

8. Brush all accessible channels, including the body, insertion tube and the umbilicus of the endoscope. Use a brush size compatible with each channel. Be knowledgeable of the specific instructions for each model of endoscope being reprocessed. (See **Figure 7.7**)

Consult the manufacturer's IFU to determine appropriate brushes for the size of the endoscope channel, parts, connectors and orifices. Proper brush size is imperative for proper cleaning; bristles should contact all surfaces. If disposable cleaning tools are not used, each tool should be thoroughly cleaned and disinfected/sterilized between use.

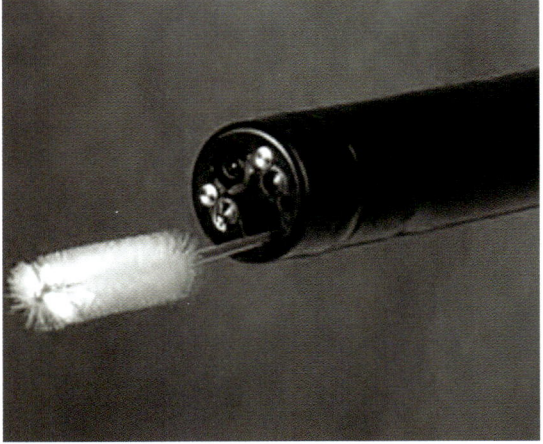

Figure 7.7 Brush exiting distal tip of scope

9. After each passage, rinse the brush or disc to remove any visible debris before retracting and reinserting it. Brush all channels according to the endoscope manufacturer's written IFU until there is no visual debris. (See **Figure 7.8**)

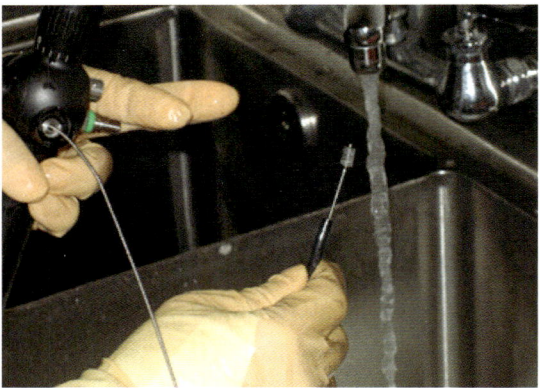

Figure 7.8 Rinse brush bristles or discs before pulling back through the channel.

BRUSH SELECTION AND MAINTENANCE

Proper brush selection is critical to thorough and effective cleaning. The key to efficiency in cleaning endoscopes is maximum bristle tip contact to the surface being cleaned and the proper type of bristle for the surface being cleaned. Always follow the manufacturer's recommendation for brush style and size. **Figure 7.9** provides information on the importance of proper brush selection. *Note: New technologies for brush design and lumen cleaning may be more effective and less damaging to the internal lumens of flexible endoscopes. Consult IFU for guidance.*

Feature	Consideration	Risk
Brush Diameter	Too large	• Bristles lay against walls of the lumen and don't produce enough friction for scrubbing • Brush becomes stuck inside channel, possibly damaging device and/or brush
	Too small	• Bristles don't touch the walls of the lumen, providing no scrubbing action/ friction necessary for cleaning
Brush Length	Too short	• Doesn't clean entire length of channel • Unable to push dirt through open end

Figure 7.9

10. Be sure to clean and high-level disinfect reusable brushes after the reprocessing of each endoscope. *Note: Reusable brushes should be inspected between uses and replaced when worn, frayed, bent or otherwise damaged. Worn bristles are ineffective in cleaning, and damaged brushes may damage endoscope channels.*

11. Attach the endoscope manufacturer's cleaning adapters for suction, biopsy, air and water channels, according to the solution manufacturer's written IFU.

12. Attach the manufacturer's cleaning adapters for special endoscope channels (e.g., elevator channel, auxiliary channel, and double-channel endoscopes).

Automated pumps are available for use during this step and eliminate the manual flush. **Figure 7.10** provides an example of an automated pump. Refer to the manufacturer's IFU for proper use of these devices, and also ensure that the device is used only with compatible endoscopes.

Note: It is important to follow the manufacturer's IFU for cleaning and disinfection of automatic flusher systems. Some manufacturers recommend disinfection of the flusher tubing at specific intervals.

Reusable vs. Disposable Cleaning Brushes

Each healthcare facility should have a specific policy about the reuse and disposal of cleaning brushes. Disposable brushes are intended for one-time use and are the safest and easiest way to minimize cross contamination. Reusable brushes can be reused after cleaning and HLD or sterilization, per their IFU. They are more cost effective and reduce waste but the drawback to using reusable brushes is that there is an increased risk of cross-contamination. Infection Prevention, management and reprocessing staff should work together to determine a brush policy for the endoscope reprocessing area.

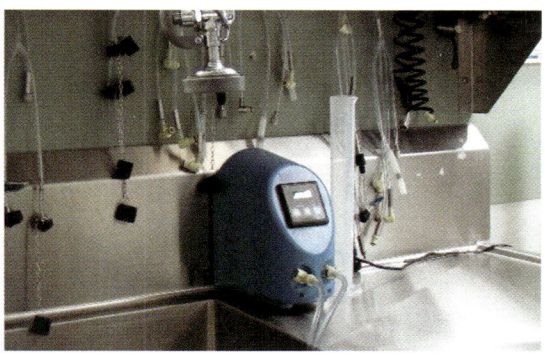

Figure 7.10

13. To achieve adequate flow through all lumens, various adapters or channel restrictors may be required. Refer to the manufacturer's IFU for specific instructions.

a) The Society of Gastroenterology Nurses and Associates (SGNA's) 2015 guidelines, *Infection control in reprocessing, cleaning of endoscopes*, states: "Because the elevator channel of a duodenoscope is a small lumen, this channel requires manual reprocessing (all steps) using a 2- to 5-milliliter syringe."

b) Other specialty endoscopes, such as endoscopic ultrasound scopes (EUS), endoscopic retrograde cholangiopancreatography (ERCP) scopes and double balloon endoscopes, may require additional steps to help ensure effective manual cleaning. Refer to specific manufacturer's IFU.

14. Flush all channels according to the endoscope manufacturer's written IFU and rinse exterior surfaces with potable water until all cleaning solution is visibly removed. Some cleaning solutions may require multiple rinses in fresh water. (See **Figure 7.11**)

Figure 7.11

15. Purge all channels with air.

16. Repeat cleaning, brushing, and rinsing steps until there is no visible debris or solution residual.

Note: All steps should be completed sequentially and immediately following the procedure. If this is not possible, refer to the manufacturer's IFU.

Note: Endoscopes that have been exposed to synthetic lipids or radiographic medium may require additional cleaning.

17. Soak, scrub, brush and rinse all reusable and removable parts (valves, buttons, port covers, tubing).

   Note: Parts designed for single use should never be reprocessed and reused.

18. Clean reusable endoscopy accessories (e.g., forceps, wires, baskets) according to their written IFU. If an automatic flushing system is used, personnel should follow the manufacturer's written IFU and ensure that it is compatible with the endoscope being processed. Fresh solution should be used with each endoscope. All connections should be secured. The connection tubing and equipment should be cleaned and disinfected according to the manufacturer's written IFU. Any quality assurance testing recommended by the manufacturer (e.g., daily volume verification) should be performed and documented.

19. Ultrasonic cleaning of reusable endoscopic accessories and endoscope components may be used to remove soil and organic material from hard-to-clean areas.

Enzymatic detergents should be discarded after each use because they are not microbiocidal and will not impede microbial growth.

MANUAL RINSING OF THE ENDOSCOPE

Manual rinsing of the endoscope's exterior surfaces and internal channels is performed after cleaning. Ensure that the endoscope, all components and accessories are thoroughly rinsed with potable water to help ensure all cleaning solutions and loosened debris are removed. Follow the endoscope manufacturer's and cleaning solution manufacturer's written IFU for the amount of water and psi and/or pressure needed to flush through each channel, as well as the recommended number of rinses. The following steps should be performed in accordance with ANSI/AAMI ST91:2015, *Flexible and semi-rigid endoscope processing in health care facilities* to help ensure proper rinsing:

1. Using the cleaning adaptors provided by the manufacturer, ensure adequate flow of potable water through each lumen.

2. Rinse all exterior endoscope surfaces with freely flowing potable water.

3. Purge channels with air using a syringe to evacuate residual rinse water. If compressed air is used, it should be oil-free and used at a pressure that does not exceed recommendations by the endoscope manufacturer. SGNA's 2015 guidelines, *Infection control in reprocessing, cleaning of endoscopes*, recommends using forced air to further purge water from all channels.

4. Rinse all valves and other removable components in accordance with the manufacturer's written IFU.

5. Dry the exterior of the endoscope with a lint-free cloth or sponge.

6. After cleaning, all detachable valves should be kept together with the same endoscope as a unique set. (See **Figure 7. 12**)

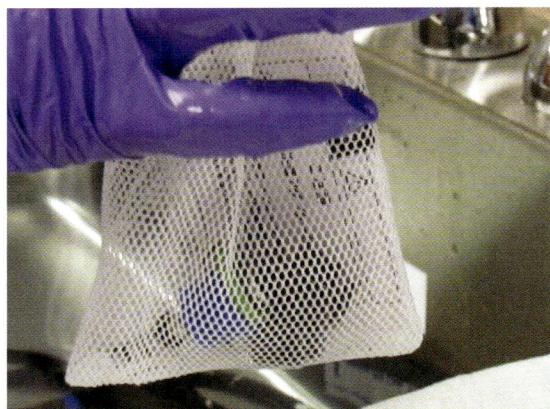

Figure 7.12

Automated Endoscope Reprocessors

Automated endoscope reprocessors (AERs) or endoscope washer-disinfectors are machines designed for cleaning and/or disinfecting endoscopes and their components. Many AERs have an integrated automated cleaning cycle. According to ANSI/AAMI ST91, "an automated process for cleaning and disinfection may be more efficient than manual processing. It may also result in less user exposure to toxic chemicals and help ensure repeatable results. The automated cleaning cycle is not intended to replace point-of-use pre-cleaning or thorough manual cleaning of the endoscope prior to placing it into the AER." AERs will be discussed in greater detail in Chapter 9. *Note: The FDA has cleared some AERs for cleaning. Check the manufacturer's IFU for specific information.*

ADDITIONAL INFORMATION ON REPROCESSING OF REUSABLE COMPONENTS

Processing of certain reusable endoscope components, such as air/water and suction valves, biopsy port covers, water bottles and tubing, require the same level of inspection, cleaning and HLD or sterilization as the endoscopes themselves. Before manual or mechanical HLD, remove and clean valves, connectors and all detachable parts. Disconnect and disassemble endoscope components and completely immerse the endoscope and components in a cleaning solution that is compatible with the accessories, according to the manufacturer's written IFU. Repeatedly actuate the valves during cleaning to facilitate access to all surfaces. Continue to brush and flush the valves until no visible soils remain. Alternately, consider the use of single-use, disposable valves.

Manually clean and high-level disinfect or sterilize the water bottle (used for cleaning the lens and for irrigation during the procedure) and connecting tube, in accordance with the manufacturer's written IFU, or at least daily.

THE RISKS OF RESIDUES

In the simplest of terms, "residue" is something unintentionally left on or in an endoscope that is not part of the endoscope itself. When discussing endoscope reprocessing, the first thing that comes to mind is the removal of organic soil, such as blood, mucous or feces. Those are common soils that are on and in the endoscope when it is returned to the decontamination area for reprocessing.

When the body is healing after an invasive or minimally-invasive procedure, the site is very vulnerable. In endoscopic procedures, the surfaces over which an endoscope is pushed and pulled across mucosal tissues rub off areas of protective mucus and leave the rubbed tissue surface with minor inflammation. In surgical procedures, the entry site often experiences severed blood vessels, abraded and cut tissues, exposure to air, and cell death. Such circumstances make the patient very sensitive to anything that could slow, interfere with or damage the healing process. Poor healing can result in excessive scarring, adhesions, blood clots (thrombosis), amplified inflammation, fever, swelling, weak tissue joining, dehiscence (splitting open of healing tissues) and reduced functionality. In sensitive areas like the eyes, brain, spinal cord, joints and reproductive organs, the damage can be devastating. All procedures involve some risk of infection and the goal of reprocessing is to reduce that risk.

Adhesions The holding together of two surfaces or parts; a band of connective tissue between parts that are normally separate; the molecular attraction between two contacting bodies.

Dehiscence The splitting open of a surgical wound along the surgical incision line.

Residues can seem minor and harmless, but they can be devastating. Resulting complications can occur almost immediately or not surface for years. Reprocessing staff expect to see some residues on a used flexible endoscope; however, careful attention to residues is very important to ensure proper cleaning and prepare an endoscope for HLD or sterilization. Residual matter can include:

- Bone, blood and other tissues (organic debris);

- Bodily secretions; and

- Water-soluble lubricants.

While removal of these common residues from an endoscope may seem simple, complete removal can be challenging. Blood that has been allowed to dry within an endoscope, for example, is difficult to remove. Water-soluble lubricants are designed to be removed with water and detergent; however, they do not completely dissolve upon contact with water and must be manually or mechanically cleaned.

Note: The common residues listed above are not a complete list of possible residues that may be found on an endoscope. Some endoscopes returned for processing may also contain **simethicone** *or* **olestra**.

> **Simethicone** An ingredient found in over-the-counter anti-gas medications. Simethicone drops are sometimes injected into water bottles or endoscope channels to reduce bubbles that can impede visibility. Residue from simethicone can remain in an endoscope even after reprocessing.
>
> **Olestra** A synthetic fat used in some foods labeled as reduced fat or fat free. Olestra may leave a waxy substance in the colon that may stick to the channels of an endoscope.

Specific cleaning processes may be required for endoscopes that have simethicone or olestra in their channels. Check the manufacturer's IFU for details. **Figure 7.13** provides an example of an endoscope channel with apparent residue after a procedure that included the use of simethicone.

In some cases, medications used during an endoscopic procedure may leave residues. It is important to communicate with the endoscopy team to identify possible residues that may be present on or inside endoscopes when they are returned to the decontamination area.

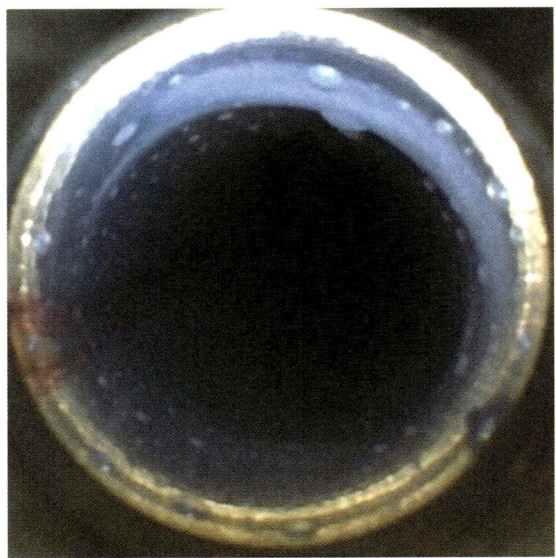

Figure 7.13 This gastroscope photo was taken with a borescope. It is the proximal end of the suction-biopsy channel near the port. Residual fluid droplets are visible along the top and sides of the channel. The fluid is translucent, thick, and white (assumed to be simethicone). There are also red streaks (unidentified substance) in the 8:00 position and a divet in the surface at the 4:00 position. This endoscope had positive cultures and high adenosine triphosphate (ATP) readings.

Residues That May Result from Reprocessing

In addition to the residues that may be received from the procedure area, endoscope reprocessing staff should also be aware of the danger of returning endoscopes with residues back to the procedural area. These residues can cause serious injury to the patient and interfere with the normal healing process.

Residues possibly generated by reprocessing include:

- Brush bristles;

- Debris from device corrosion;

- Endotoxin (from cell walls of dead gram-negative bacteria);

- Detergent residue;

- Disinfectant residue;

- Ethylene oxide sterilization residues:

  › ethylene oxide (EtO);

  › ethylene chlorohydrin (ECH);

  › ethylene glycol (EG);

- Glove powder;

- Hair strands;

- Hand lotion;

- Lint (from towels, wrap materials, instrument tray liners, clothes, head wraps, etc.);

- Working element lubricants (excess "spillage" beyond IFU required position and amount); and

- Minerals deposits (poor quality steam, tap water, cleaning solutions).

Most residues can be seen when guiding a lighted magnification device through the lumen of residue-contaminated endoscopes. Imagine that residue being inserted into a surgical wound, onto the scraped lining of an endoscope's path. Nearly every human being has experienced the pain of having dust or an eyelash fall onto the surface of an eye; beyond that, they have likely witnessed the red inflammation and fluids (tears) the eye produces in response to the presence of debris (See **Figure 7.14**).

Residues can have serious effects on the body. **Figures 7.15** and **7.16** provide examples of the effects of residues and underscore the importance of preventing residues from being introduced into any procedure. Endoscope reprocessing staff must make every effort to prevent residues from reaching patients.

In addition to potential consequences of tissue damage and poor healing, residues can also provide protection for biofilm formation. **Figure 7.17** shows

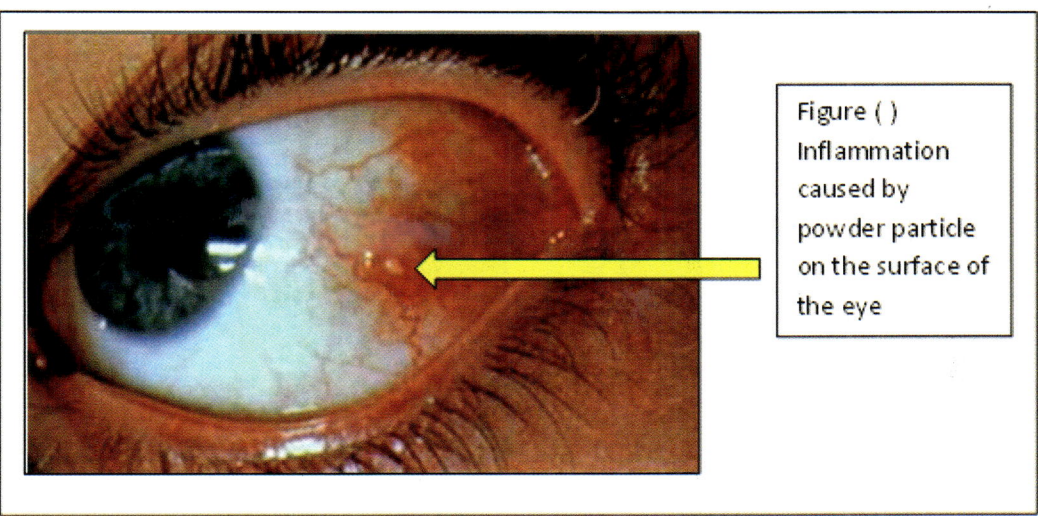

Figure ( )
Inflammation caused by powder particle on the surface of the eye

Figure 7.14

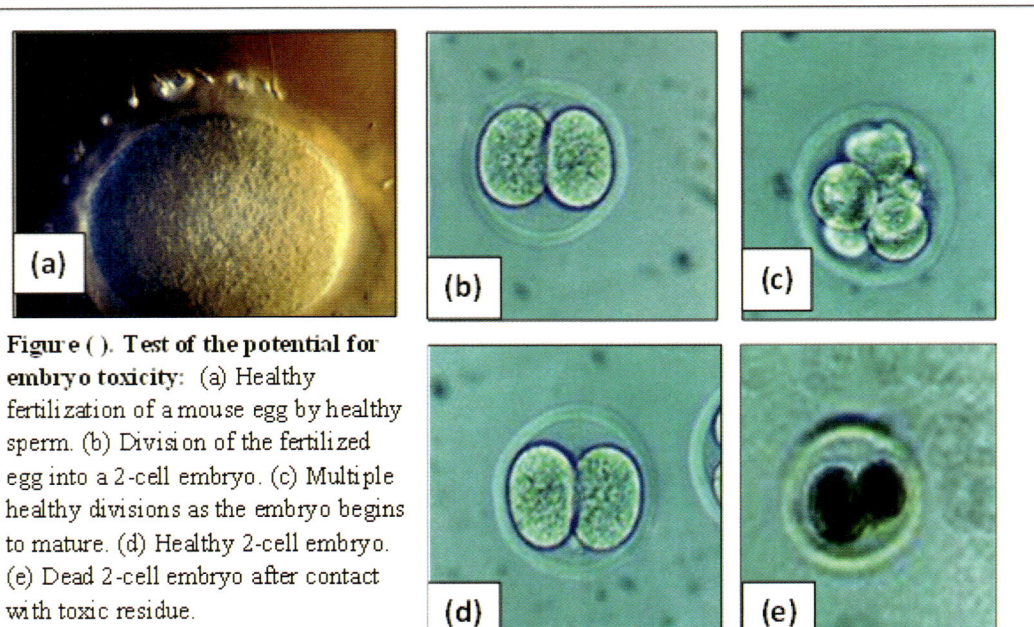

Figure ( ). Test of the potential for embryo toxicity: (a) Healthy fertilization of a mouse egg by healthy sperm. (b) Division of the fertilized egg into a 2-cell embryo. (c) Multiple healthy divisions as the embryo begins to mature. (d) Healthy 2-cell embryo. (e) Dead 2-cell embryo after contact with toxic residue.

Figure 7.15

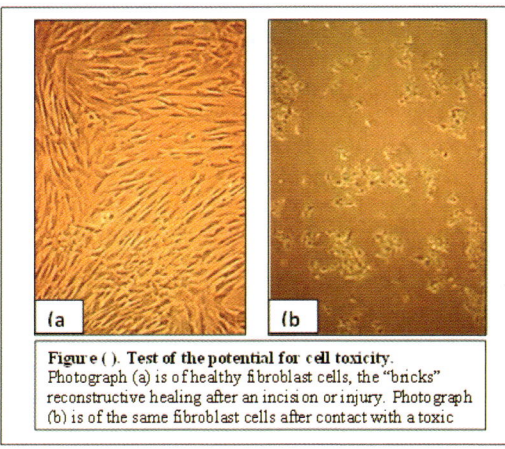

Figure ( ). Test of the potential for cell toxicity. Photograph (a) is of healthy fibroblast cells, the "bricks" reconstructive healing after an incision or injury. Photograph (b) is of the same fibroblast cells after contact with a toxic

Figure 7.16

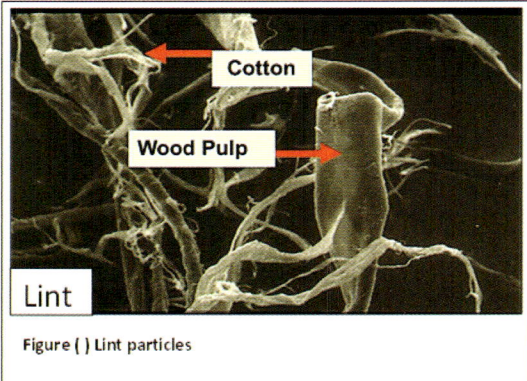

Figure ( ) Lint particles

Figure 7.17

a photograph of a magnification of lint particles. This photograph underscores the importance of using lint-free cleaning clothes and wipes.

Reprocessing staff can prevent many residues through careful cleaning, copious rinsing and the use of lint-free cloths (See **Figure 7.18**) for washing and drying.

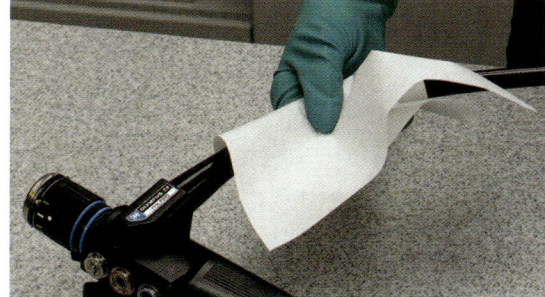

Figure 7.18

QUALITY CONTROL OF THE CLEANING PROCESS

It is recommended as part of ANSI/AAMI ST91:2015 to incorporate visual inspection and testing of equipment to identify issues that may affect the cleaning or disinfecting processes; this may include testing for leaks, inspecting for cracks, and checking the integrity of fiber optic bundles. Visual inspection alone may not be sufficient for assessing the efficacy of cleaning processes; therefore, the use of methods that measure organic residues unable to be seen using visual inspection should be considered in a facility's cleaning policy and procedures.

Meticulous manual cleaning is essential for the removal of organic contamination that can interfere with HDL. The manual cleaning step is prone to error and, therefore, should be monitored at least as frequently as is recommended for the cleaning equipment.

Verification and monitoring of the cleaning process includes:

- Cleaning verification tests are performed after cleaning. Their purpose is to verify the effectiveness of a cleaning process at removing or reducing to an acceptable level the organic soil and microbial contamination that occurs during the use of an endoscope.

- When developing a user verification procedure for the cleaning process, reprocessing personnel should ensure that:

  › The endoscope manufacturer has completed validation of the recommended cleaning process and provided written IFU detailing the process;

  › The facility has established, clarified and documented a standard cleaning process for the device;

  › Facilities should develop a defined program of cleaning verification that includes frequency of testing, number and types of endoscopes to be tested;

  › Cleaning verification results are documented;

  › The facility has established, clarified and documented a process to address cleaning verification failures; and

  › The facility has established an education, training and competency assessment program that verifies personnel are consistently achieving the expected level of cleaning.

Cleaning verification of flexible and semi-rigid endoscopes by users should include:

- Visual inspection combined with other verification that allows the assessment of both external surfaces and internal housing and channels;

- Testing of the cleaning efficacy of mechanical equipment; and

- Monitoring of key cleaning parameters (e.g., temperature).

Several methods can be used to monitor the cleaning process. The most common is visual inspection. Careful visual inspection should be conducted to detect the presence of any residual soil. Inspection using magnification and additional illumination might identify residue more readily than the unaided eye. (**Figure 7. 19**)

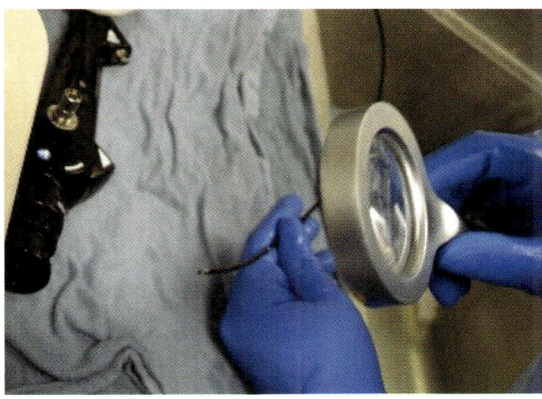

Figure 7.19 Visual Inspection of the External Surface of a Flexible Endoscope

Users should inspect every device for visible organic soil and contamination in a simple functionality test. **Figure 7.20** provides an example of an inspection work station.

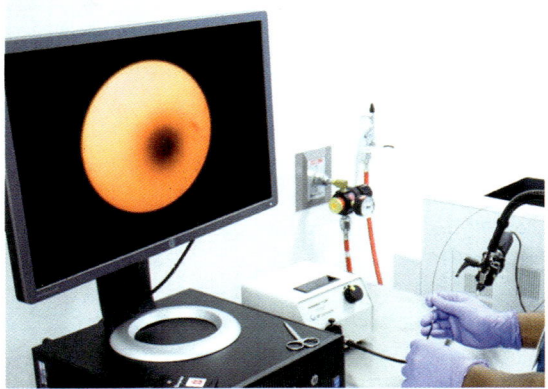

Figure 7.20 Visual Inspection Work Station for a Flexible Endoscope

Direct visual inspection is not possible for the inner channels of flexible endoscopes. Tools such as video borescopes of an appropriate dimension (length and diameter) may be used to visually inspect the internal channels of some medical devices. (See **Figure 7.21**)

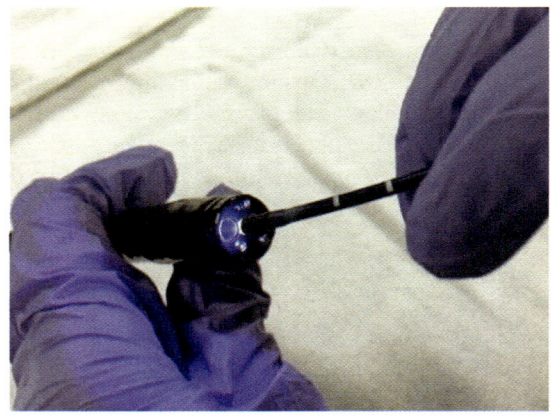

Figure 7.21 Inspection of a Flexible Endoscope Lumen using a Borescope

Figure 7.22 provides a borescope's view into a flexible endoscope lumen. This illustrates the value of borescope inspection to identify soil or damage within a lumen that cannot be seen by manual visual inspection.

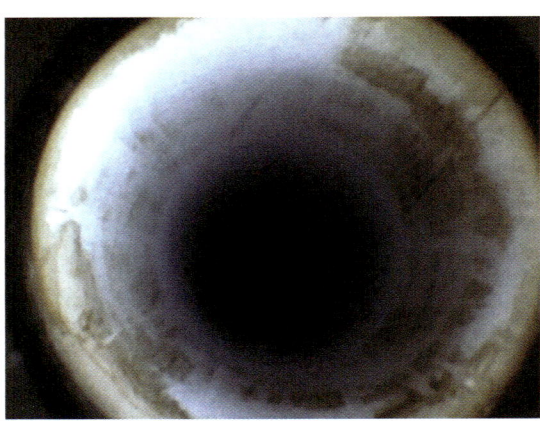

Figure 7.22

Residual organic soil and microbial contamination may be present on an accessible surface, even though the device looks clean. The use of methods that can quantitatively or chemically detect organic residues that cannot be seen in visual inspection should be considered and included in a facility's device cleaning policies and procedures.

CLEANING VERIFICATION TESTS FOR REPROCESSING PERSONNEL

ANSI/AAMI ST79, Annex D, provides information related to user verification of cleaning procedures and cleaning equipment. Tables D.1 and D.2 summarize the currently available testing methods that apply to in-use evaluation of the efficacy of medical device cleaning and the efficacy of washer-disinfectors used for flexible and semi-rigid endoscope processing.

Several technologies are available that can be used to measure the levels of organic soil and microbial contamination on a cleaned device. These include tests for residual protein, carbohydrate, hemoglobin (blood), adenosine triphosphate (ATP) and an enzyme that detects specific bacteria.

Testing the efficacy of the manual cleaning step should occur on a regular basis—weekly or, preferably, daily.

ATP testing is performed by swabbing sections of the endoscope and inserting the swabbing device into an ATP reader. (See **Figures 7.23, 7.24, 7.25** and **7.26**)

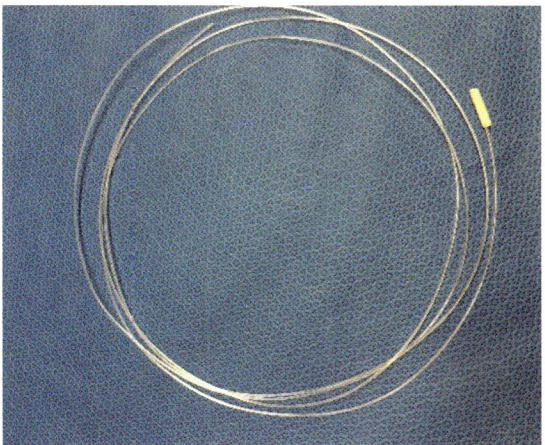

Figure 7.23 Example of a Lumen Swab for ATP Testing

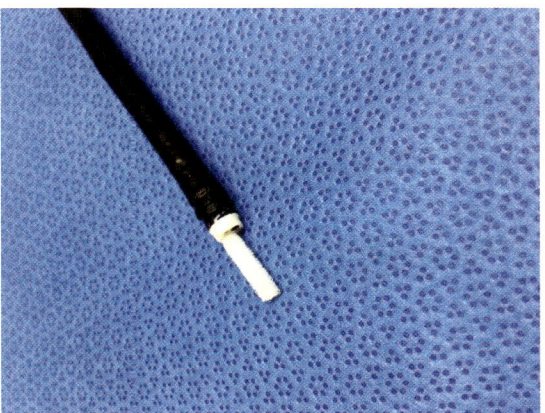

Figure 7.24 Lumen Swab Pushed through Lumen

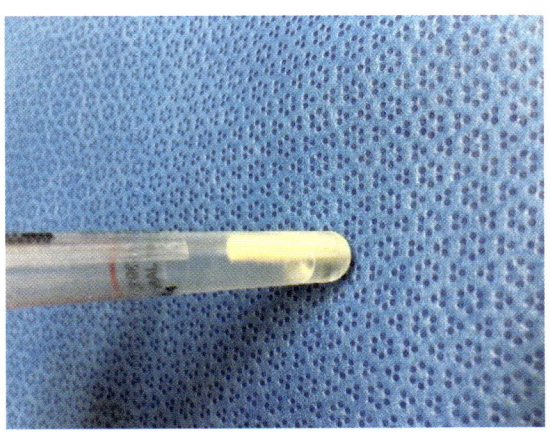

Figure 7.25 Swab Placed in ATP Vial

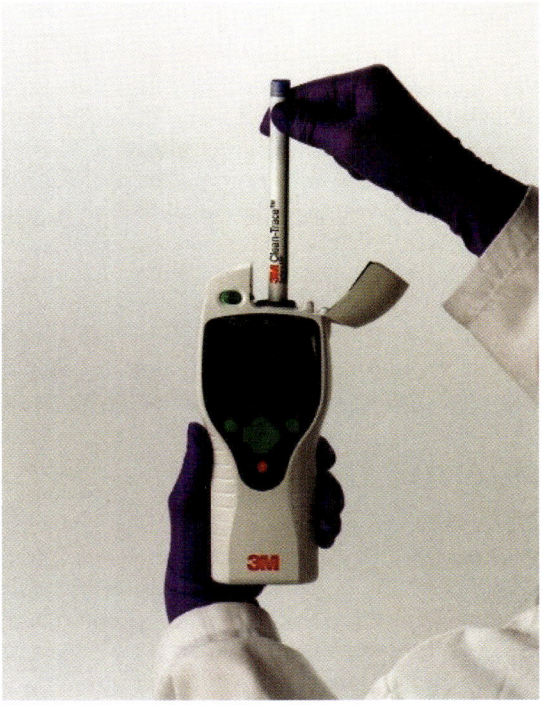

Figure 7.26 Swab Placed in ATP Reader

Realistic benchmarks for soil levels depend on what can be achieved by routine cleaning, as well as the limit of detection for the method used. Data indicate that for flexible endoscopes that have been cleaned after use on patients, the average levels of soil markers in the suction biopsy channel are as follows: protein, <6.4 µg/cm2, carbohydrate, <1.8 µg/cm2, hemoglobin, <2.2 µg/cm2, sodium ion, <1 µmole/cm2, endotoxin, <2.2 EU/cm2, bioburden, < 4 log10 CFU/cm2 and 200 Relative Light Units (RLU) for ATP.

Note: Different ATP manufacturers use different scales. Refer to the specific ATP manufacturer's written IFU for their recommended pass/fail threshold RLU values.

Benchmarks for residual soil and bioburden levels after cleaning might become more definitive as more data becomes available and/or as more efficient cleaning methods are developed. Users should review current literature, along with the test and endoscope manufacturer's data, to formulate policies and procedures for verification of cleaning efficacy.

Testing cleaning efficacy

The facility's policies should include ways to verify that the cleaning equipment used for processing of endoscopes is working. Testing the equipment upon installation; during routine use (daily) and on all cycles used, after repairs and when changing to a new type of cleaning solution allows the user to verify process efficacy. The manufacturer's written IFU should be consulted for recommendations of types and frequency of cleaning efficacy testing.

Efficacy testing of the manual cleaning step should occur on a regular basis — weekly, preferably daily.

Microbial Surveillance

In response to a series of outbreaks involving inadequately reprocessed duodenoscopes, the CDC issued the *Interim Duodenoscope Surveillance Protocol*. This protocol describes a procedure designed to determine the number and types of bacteria present on an endoscope (or any surface in question). Some healthcare facilities have opted to implement bacterial surveillance of their endoscopes in an effort to reduce the likelihood of pathogen transmission from one patient to another.

The endoscope is sampled by using a brush or flushing with water or another liquid medium. (See **Figures 7.27**, **7.28** and **7.29**) The bacteria in the sample are cultured (allowed to grow), counted and then identified and screened to determine if pathogenic organisms are present. This process may take several days to complete. If an endoscope is found to contain pathogens, it is recommended that it be quarantined, reprocessed and then retested for the presence of the pathogen. *Note: The endoscope should not be used again until it is demonstrated to be free of pathogens. There is currently no recommendation for frequency of testing using the surveillance protocol; suggestions range from testing after every use to only testing quarterly.*

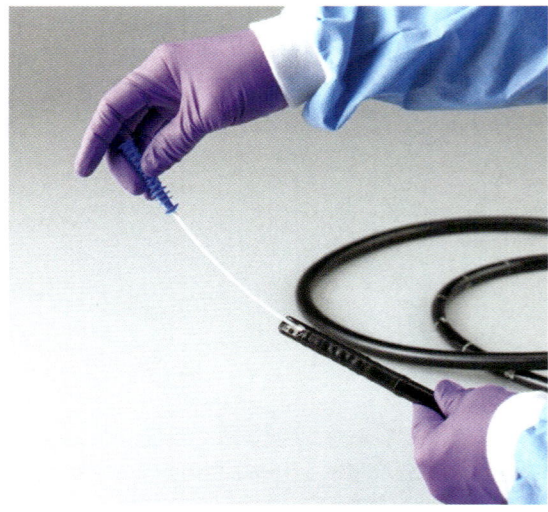

Figure 7.27

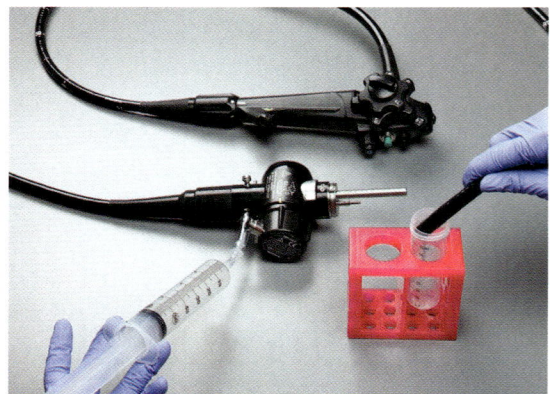

Figure 7.28

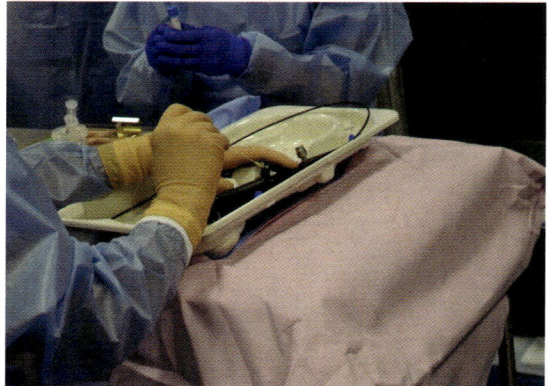

Figure 7.29

As with any testing procedure, it is important to understand the advantages and limitations. While bacterial surveillance may indicate the presence of pathogens, there are many limitations that should be taken into consideration when looking at test results. Bacterial surveillance results cannot be used to verify that an endoscope is sterile, and results can also not determine whether the endoscope is clean or has been properly high-level disinfected. Currently, the CDC is validating the sensitivity, specificity and limits of their protocol, so even negative results do not ensure that the endoscope is free of bacterial pathogens. The CDC surveillance protocol does not test for the presence of viruses (e.g., HIV), fungi or parasites—all of which can be transmitted by improperly reprocessed endoscopes. Because the CDC surveillance protocol is still under development, it is important to regularly check for updates to ensure the most current version is used in one's facility. Bacterial surveillance testing should be performed by trained personnel in facilities equipped to handle the special conditions under which sampling must be performed.

The choice of which quality control test to use to verify that endoscopes have been properly cleaned is a topic of ongoing discussion. It is often assumed that the choice between using a cleaning verification test (ATP, protein, hemoglobin, carbohydrate) and bacterial surveillance testing is an "either/or" decision. One test is not a replacement for the other because these tests answer different questions about the success of endoscope reprocessing. A cleaning verification test is typically performed after the manual cleaning step and before HLD or sterilization. The results indicate how much soil remains behind after an endoscope has been cleaned; the results are not an indication of whether the endoscope is safe for patient use. A bacterial surveillance test is typically performed after HLD and only provides information on the number and types of bacteria that have survived reprocessing. Bacterial surveillance results do not indicate whether an endoscope has been adequately cleaned and, therefore, should not be used as a cleaning verification test. Both cleaning verification and bacterial surveillance tests reveal important, but different, types of information and should be used and interpreted in accordance with current recommendations and guidelines.

CONCLUSION

The processes involved in cleaning flexible endoscopes include critical steps that can impact future biocidal processes. Understanding the steps in the process and the consequences of inadequate cleaning help produce a clean endoscope that is ready for subsequent biocidal processes. Current standards and guidelines recommend that the efficacy of cleaning be routinely monitored using both visual inspection and cleaning verification tests.

RESOURCES

Association for the Advancement of Medical Instrumentation. ANSI/AAMI ST91:2015, *Flexible and semi-rigid endoscope processing in health care facilities.*

International Association of Healthcare Central Service Materiel Management. *Central Service Technical Manual, Eighth Edition.* 2016.

Association for the Advancement of Medical Instrumentation. ANSI/AAMI ST79:2010 & A1:2010 & A2:2011 & A3:2012 & A4:2013, *Comprehensive guide to steam sterilization and sterility assurance in health care facilities.*

Society of Gastroenterology Nurses and Associates. *Standards of Infection Prevention in Reprocessing Flexible Gastrointestinal Endoscopes.* 2015.

CDC Interim Duodenoscope Surveillance Protocol. March 2015. http://www.cdc.gov/hai/organisms/cre/cre-duodenoscope-surveillance-protocol.html.

American Society for Gastrointestinal Endoscopy. (ASGE) *Multi Society Guideline on reprocessing flexible gastrointestinal endoscopes.* 2011.

American Society for Gastrointestinal Endoscopy. (ASGE) *Technologies for monitoring the quality of endoscope reprocessing.* 2014.

Association for Professionals in Infection Control and Epidemiology. American Journal of Infection Control. August 2015.

Ofstead CL, et al. *Persistent contamination on colonoscopes and gastroscopes detected by biologic cultures and rapid indicators despite reprocessing performed in accordance with guidelines* Am J Infect Control August 2015 Volume 43, Issue 8, p785-904, e39-e46

Alfa MJ, Olson N, Murray BL. Comparison of clinically relevant benchmarks and channel sampling methods used to assess manual cleaning compliance for flexible gastrointestinal endoscopes. Am J Infect Control 2014 Jan; 42(1): e1-5.

Alfa MJ, Fatima I, Olson N. Validation of ATP to audit manual cleaning of flexible endoscope channels. Am J Infect Control. March 2013; 41(3):245-248.

Alfa MJ, Fatima I, Olson N. The ATP test is a rapid and reliable audit tool to assess manual cleaning adequacy of flexible endoscope channels. Am J Infect Control. March 2013; 41(3):249-253.

Association of periOpetarive Registered Nurses. *Guideline for processing flexible endoscopes*, Revised February 2016 for publication in Guidelines for Perioperative Practice, 2016 Edition.

The Society of Gastroenterology Nurses and Associates Inc. 2015 guidelines, *Infection control in reprocessing, cleaning of endoscopes.*

TERMS

Validation

Centers for Disease Control & Prevention (CDC)

Healthcare Infection Control Practices Advisory Committee (HICPAC)

Delayed processing

Adhesions

Dehiscence

Simethicone

Olestra

Chapter 8

Endoscope Inspection and Preparation

Learning Objectives

Upon completion of this chapter, readers will be able to:

1. Describe the dangers of damaged endoscopes

2. Describe the dangers of soiled endoscopes

3. Discuss methods for visually inspecting endoscopes

4. Discuss preparation requirements for high-level disinfection of endoscopes

5. Discuss preparation requirements for sterilization of endoscopes

INTRODUCTION

As stated throughout this text, flexible endoscopes are complex, delicate medical devices that can easily become damaged at any point in their use cycle. Although employees should receive training in the proper care and handling of endoscopes, there are still instances when endoscopes are damaged through carelessness or lack of training. Endoscope reprocessing technicians should not only take steps to avoid endoscope damage, but they must also be on alert to identify any signs of wear or damage that may impact the safety and function of the endoscope.

DANGERS OF DAMAGED ENDOSCOPES

Like all other medical devices, endoscopes will eventually show signs of wear, even if they were well cared for throughout their life cycle. Every endoscope reprocessing technician must stay vigilant to avoid preventable damage and identify damage and/or wear as soon as possible.

Damaged endoscopes pose a significant threat to patients and to the facility's budget. Several examples of potential patient risks caused by damaged endoscopes include:

Sheath Damage/Fluid Invasion – When leak testing is skipped or not performed properly, leaks may go undetected and the fluid that enters the endoscope provides a breeding ground for microorganisms. The same leak that allowed the fluid to enter may allow the contaminated fluid to exit and be deposited into the patient's body.

Component Damage – Damage to any of the working components of an endoscope may cause the endoscope to malfunction. Damage may also make the endoscope's tip difficult to articulate, cause buttons to stick, etc.

Lens Damage – Damage to the lens may make the endoscope unusable, or cloud or distort vision. Impaired vision not only makes the endoscope difficult to use, but may also factor into a missed diagnosis.

Light Cord Damage – Endoscopes that use a fiber optic light cord may have reduced vision if the

damage is significant. **Figure 8.1** provides an example of a fiber optic light cord with significant damage. Each dark spot on the end of the cord represents a broken light fiber used to carry light. The more damage that is done to those fibers, the less light will be transmitted, thereby reducing the physician's visibility.

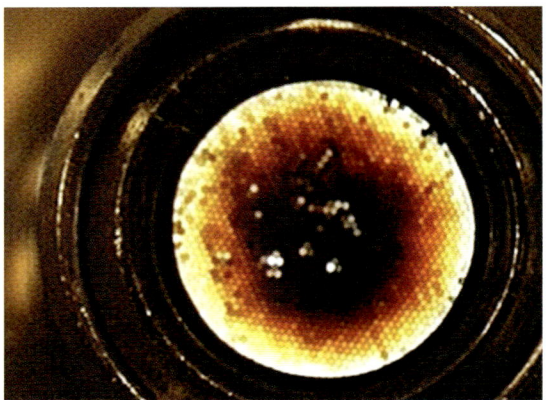

Figure 8.1

Channel/Lumen Damage – Scratches or other damage to the interior lumens/channels of a flexible endoscope can make the lumens/channels more difficult to clean and increase the risk of debris being left inside the endoscope. That debris will impede the high-level disinfection (HLD) or sterilization process and will result in a contaminated endoscope being used on future patients.

In addition to identifying issues to protect patients, early detection of endoscope damage can reduce repair and replacement costs. Endoscopes represent a significant financial investment for any healthcare facility; they are expensive to purchase, expensive to repair and expensive to replace. Endoscope reprocessing technicians have the opportunity (and obligation) to detect small issues before they become big ones.

DANGERS OF SOILED ENDOSCOPES

Inspection processes allow technicians to check for damage or wear as well as instrument cleanliness. After an endoscope has completed the cleaning process, it should be checked visually for soil that may have remained on the device after the cleaning process. Any soil that remains on a device will impede the disinfection or sterilization process that follows, and increase the risk of infection for patients. The best place to identify and remove soil is in the decontamination area.

The Dangers of Soil

Any soil that remains on a medical device after cleaning cannot be disinfected or sterilized. Additionally, soil acts as a shield to prevent the disinfectant or sterilant from making contact with the part of the device where the soil remains. Endoscopes (or any other medical device) with remaining soil must be considered contaminated and be reprocessed.

INSPECTION

Most opportunities for inspecting flexible endoscopes come during the reprocessing steps that take place after each use cycle of the endoscope.

Leak testing is an important part of the overall inspection process because it allows the observer to determine if the tubes and/or channels are intact. A successfully performed leak test prevents multiple types of endoscope damage and extends the useful lifespan of the endoscope. A hole can be detected by applying positive pressure to the endoscope, either manually or mechanically. It is imperative that all the steps are performed in their ordered sequence and that attention to inspection is uninterrupted. Physical and functional inspections are also conducted during leak testing. By slowly and individually rotating each directional knob to each extreme position while the endoscope is pressurized, the observer can determine if the O-rings or seals that support those knobs are properly seated. A monomeric drop (or bubbles seen coming from around the knobs) will alert technicians to an issue that, if left untreated, will lead to fluid intrusion. While rotating the knobs during the leak test, the observer is also able to determine if the knob is loose or overly tightened, or whether the endoscope is otherwise unable to attain the expected range of angulation. An endoscope with an elevator or forceps raiser should also be challenged during the leak test by moving its lever in both directions. A leak in this system is determined by a drop in pressure during a manual test (or bubbles from around the lever or

metal elevator may be evident during a mechanical test performed under water). If the endoscope is a video scope, the video function buttons can be massaged in a circular motion during the leak test. If an unseen hole is present in one or more of the switches, a pressure drop or bubbles will be seen.

Following the leak test and during the cleaning process, reprocessing staff are responsible for not only examining the endoscope for cleanliness, but also inspecting for damage. A cleaning brush in good condition and of the appropriate size for each channel should have no difficulty navigating the suction and biopsy channels to effectively clean. Restricted brush movement could be an indication of a kink in the channel.

Support for Visual Inspection of Flexible Endoscopes

Visual inspection of flexible endoscopes was always recognized as a "good idea," but in recent years, visual inspection of flexible endoscopes has received support from leading industry standards and guidelines providers. In 2015, the Association for the Advancement of Medical Instrumentation (AAMI) released ANSI/AAMI ST91: *Flexible and semi-rigid endoscope processing in health care facilities*. This standard recommends that visual inspections be conducted on every endoscope. In 2016, the Association of periOperative Registered Nurses (AORN) released its revised *Guideline for Flexible Endoscopes*, which recommended that endoscopes be inspected for cleanliness and function before use, during the procedure, after the procedure, after cleaning, and before disinfection or sterilization. Guidelines from the Society of Gastroenterology Nurses and Associates (SGNA) also recommend visual inspection of endoscopes.

Visual Inspection of Flexible Endoscopes

Visual inspection is an important part of the quality process and failure to detect endoscope damage or any soil that remains on the device following cleaning is a patient safety issue. It is important that inspection takes place in a well-lighted area. Flexible endoscopes are dark in color and it is difficult to see blood and other body substances;

therefore, ensuring there is adequate lighting is the first step in developing good visual inspection processes and practices.

Some endoscope damage is easy to detect. **Figures 8.2 thru 8.5** provide examples of damage that can easily be seen with a quick inspection. *Note: In each of these situations, the endoscope should be removed from service and sent for repair.*

CRACKED SWITCH HEAD IN CONTROL BODY

Figure 8.2

CRACKED COATING ON INSERTION TUBE

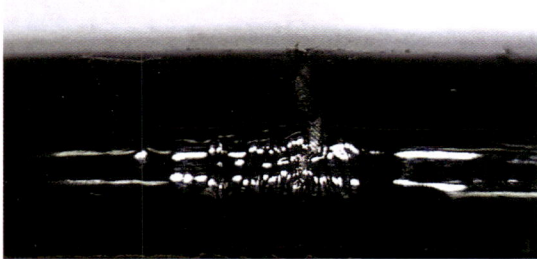

Figure 8.3

BROKEN INSERTION TUBE AT FITTING

Figure 8.4

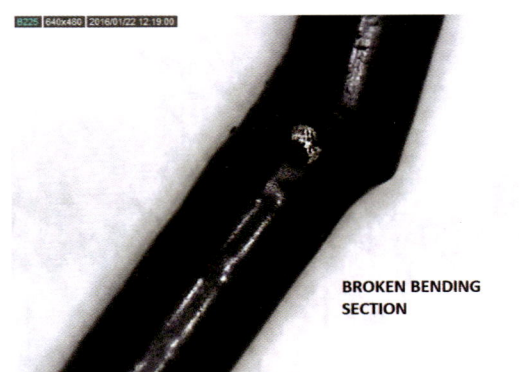

BROKEN BENDING SECTION

Figure 8.5

Not all endoscope damage is as clear as the damage shown in the preceding photos. Endoscope reprocessing technicians must be familiar the endoscopes they reprocess so they can identify damage or wear issues. **Figure 8.6** shows the distal tip of a new gastroscope and one that is damaged and in need of repair.

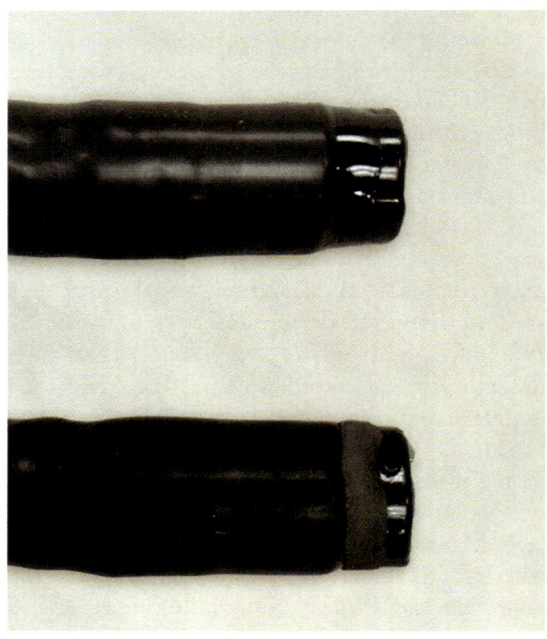

Figure 8.6

Changes in an endoscope's appearance should be questioned because any observed changes may mean that the endoscope has been damaged or improperly handled or reprocessed. In addition to careful examination of the endoscope's exterior sheath, distal tips must also be inspected carefully. This section of the endoscope can easily be damaged by improper handling or transport. **Figure 8.7** below provides an example of a cracked lens. The damage to the lens would make it impossible for the physician to see clearly.

Figure 8.7

Visual Inspection using a Borescope

As discussed in Chapter 2, endoscopes have many internal components. The most important areas for inspection are the lumens that run through the endoscope. Lumens pose a cleaning challenge because of their narrow structure that prevents visualization during cleaning; therefore, it is important to always check lumens for cleanliness after cleaning. Visual inspection of lumens can be accomplished using a borescope, a small flexible fiberoptic device that enables visualization of otherwise inaccessible areas within endoscope lumens. This inspection step can help identify debris present inside lumens and, in some cases, may reveal damage that could otherwise go undetected. **Figure 8.8** shows a borescope being inserted into an endoscope channel.

Borescope A device used for visual inspection in areas that are inaccessible by other means. Some borescopes are equipped with cameras that provide still images or video of inaccessible areas within endoscope lumens.

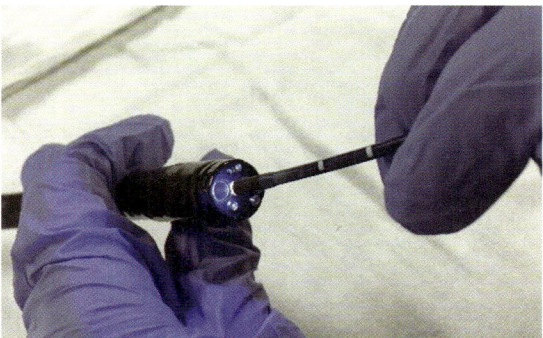

Figure 8.8 Using a Borescope to Examine the Suction/Biopsy Channel of a Colonoscope

Using an eyepiece (see **Figure 8.9**) or a camera system (see **Figure 8.10**), borescopes can be used to inspect lumens.

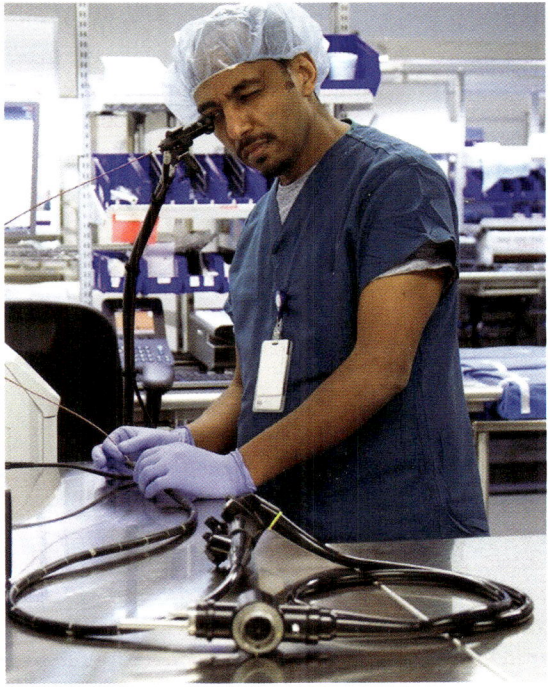

Figure 8.9

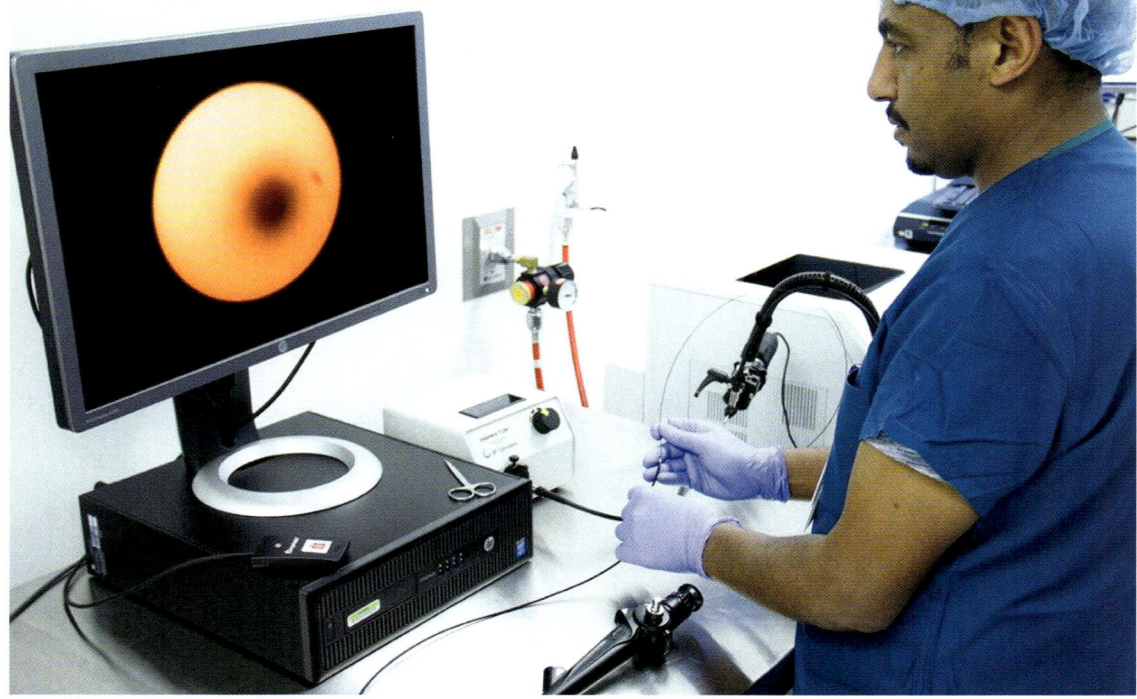

Figure 8.10 Using a borescope with a camera system can help provide evidence of endoscope damage and cleaning failures.

Borescopes can also help check for cleanliness or damage in difficult to inspect areas of an endoscope. **Figure 8.11** illustrates the use of a borescope to check the elevator area of a duodenoscope.

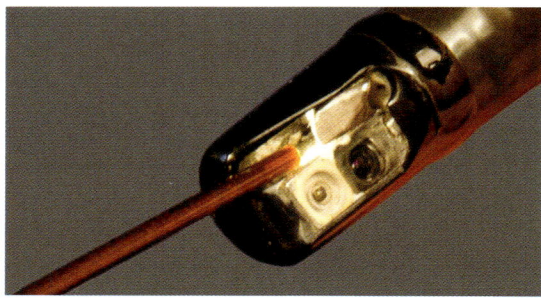

Figure 8.11 Inspecting the Elevator of a Duodenoscope

Using a borescope to inspect the lumens in an endoscope can find issues before they become a threat to the patient. **Figure 8.12** provides an example of a borescope image that indicates a clean, undamaged endoscope lumen.

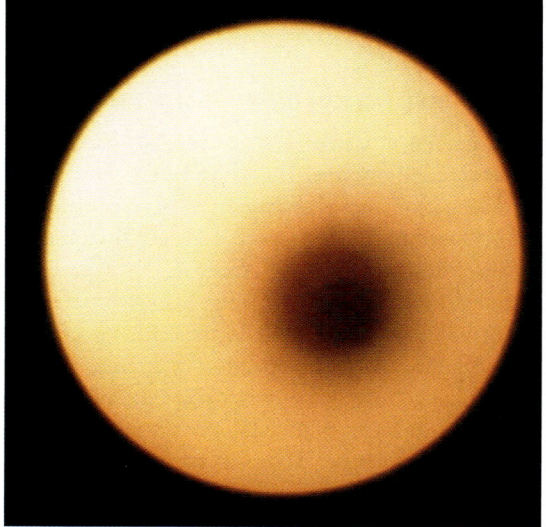

Figure 8.12

Figures 8.13 through **8.15** provide examples of endoscope lumens that have not been successfully cleaned.

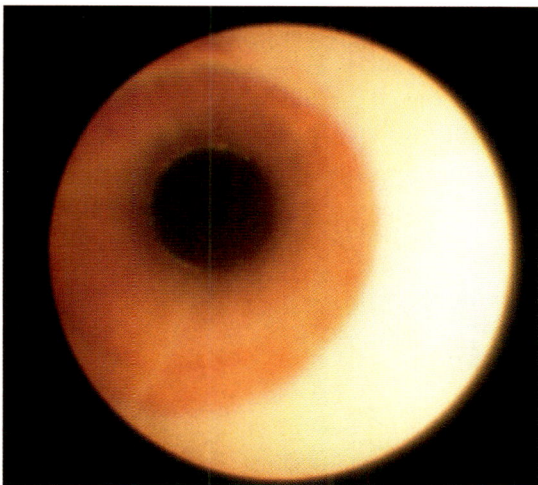

Figure 8.13

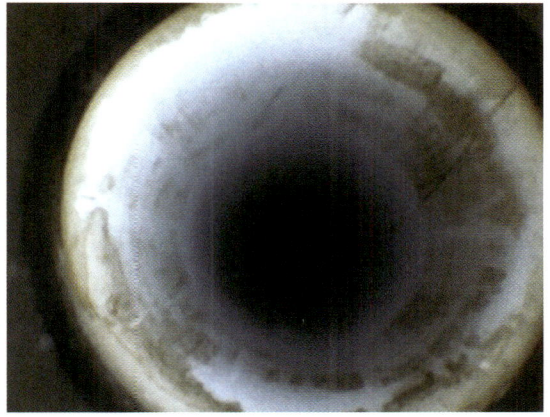

Figure 8.14

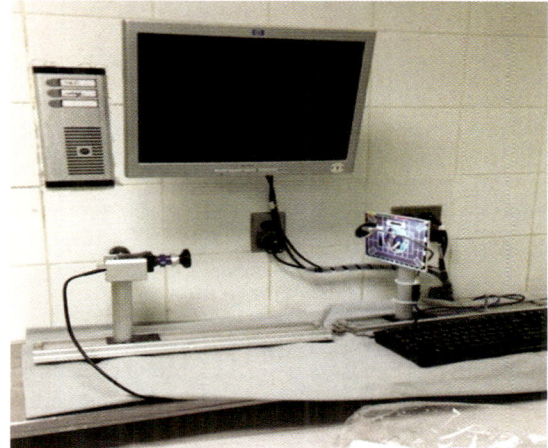

Figure 8.15

Inspection can be an invaluable patient safety tool. Inspecting endoscopes can prevent patient injury and physician frustration. **Figure 8.16** provides an example of an endoscope inspection station in a Central Service (CS) department.

Figure 8.16

PREPARATION FOR HIGH-LEVEL DISINFECTION OR STERILIZATION

Once an endoscope has been inspected and is deemed safe to reprocess, it will then need to be prepared for the process selected (HLD or sterilization). The specific endoscope's instructions for use (IFU) will indicate the type of biocidal process recommended. For liquid chemical processes, such as HLD and liquid chemical sterilization (LCS), the endoscope will need to be prepared in a manner that will allow the chemical to come in direct contact with all surfaces and lumens of the endoscope. Packaging is not used for these processes, but preparation is very important. Lumens should be open and detachable components should be removed to enable the liquid to enter the endoscope's lumens.

In automated endoscope reprocessors (AERs), the endoscope will need to be connected to the reprocessor to ensure fluid is pumped through the lumens. **Figure 8.17** provides an example of a technician placing an endoscope into an AER. *Note the numerous connecting tubes that must be attached to connect the endoscope to the AER. Each endoscope requires specific connectors to help ensure a successful process.*

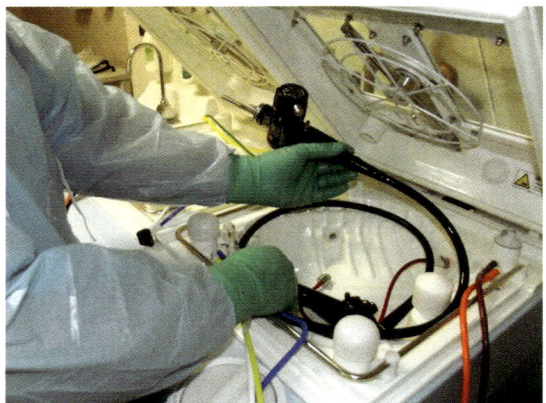

Figure 8.17

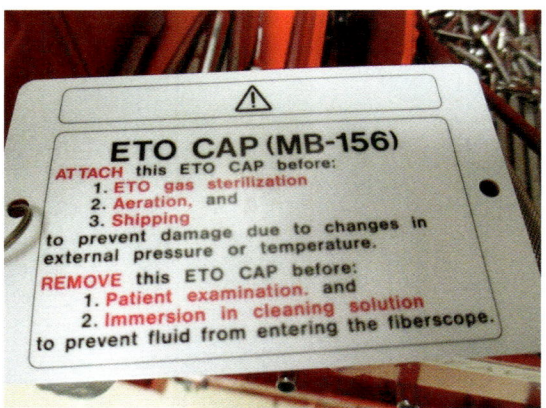

Figure 8.19

Whether using a manual or automated process, be sure to follow the manufacturer's IFU for proper processing. It is also essential to use the required quality checks, such as minimum recommended concentration (MRC) testing, etc.

Preparation for Sterilization

When the chosen process is high- or low-temperature sterilization, the endoscope must be packaged. The first step is to place the flexible endoscope in a container that will protect it from damage. **Figure 8.18** provides an example of a sterilization tray designed specifically for a flexible endoscope.

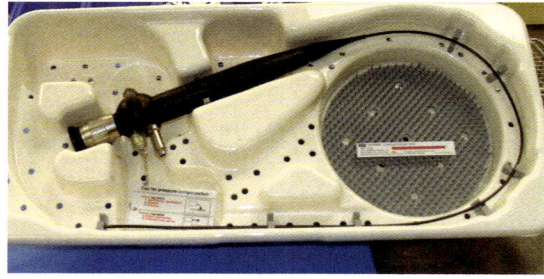

Figure 8.18

When the endoscope is placed in the tray, it is essential to check the manufacturer's IFU for any special sterilization instructions. Some endoscopes require additional preparation before they can be sterilized. For example, some endoscopes require venting caps before placing them in an ethylene oxide (EtO) sterilizer. (See **Figure 8.19**)

Failure to follow specific instructions for the sterilization of endoscopes can have disastrous results. **Figure 8.20** provides an example of an endoscope that was sterilized without its venting cap. The inability to vent the pressure in the sterilizer caused the endoscope's sheath to rupture (sometimes called a "blown scope").

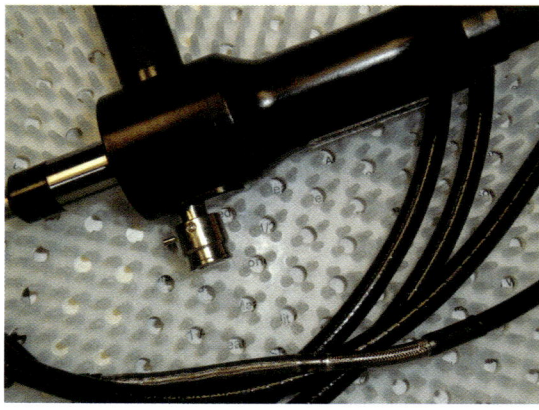

Figure 8.20

After the endoscope has been prepared for sterilization it must be packaged in approved packaging. The two most common types of packaging used for flexible endoscope sterilization are disposable flat wrap (See **Figure 8.21**) and rigid containers (See **Figure 8.22**). Technicians must be sure to follow the packaging method's application requirements and use chemical indicators as required. HLD and sterilization processes will be discussed in detail in chapters 9 and 10.

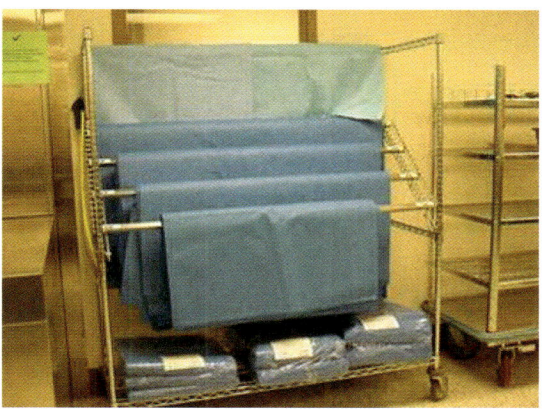

Figure 8.21

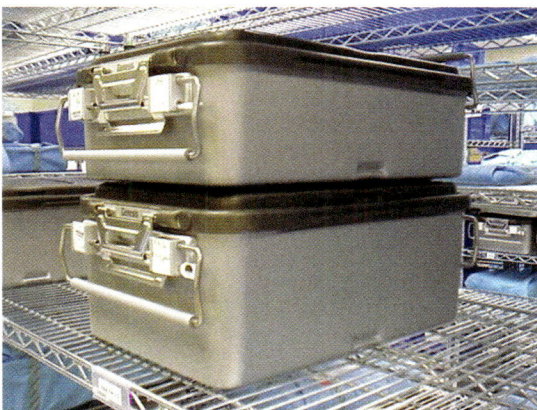

Figure 8.22

CONCLUSION

One thought should be foremost in the endoscope technician's mind during endoscope inspection and preparation: the next time the endoscope will be handled will be at the patient's bedside. Endoscopes must be safe and well-functioning to prevent patient injury. Diligently following IFU for each reprocessing step, carefully inspecting endoscopes for damage and any remaining soil, transporting, handling and storing endoscopes properly, and paying attention to detail will help ensure that endoscopes are safe, well-functioning and ready for use.

RESOURCES

Association for the Advancement of Medical Instrumentation. ANSI/AAMI ST91:2015, *Flexible and semi-rigid endoscope processing in health care facilities.*

International Association of Healthcare Central Service Materiel Management. *Central Service Technical Manual, Eighth Edition.* 2016.

Association for the Advancement of Medical Instrumentation. ANSI/AAMI ST79:2010 & A1:2010 & A2:2011 & A3:2012 & A4:2013, *Comprehensive guide to steam sterilization and sterility assurance in health care facilities.*

Society of Gastroenterology Nurses and Associates. *Standards of Infection Prevention in Reprocessing Flexible Gastrointestinal Endoscopes.* 2015.

TERMS

Borescope

Chapter 9

Disinfection Processes for Flexible Endoscopes

Learning Objectives

Upon completion of this chapter, readers will be able to:

1. Explain the theory of the Spaulding Classification System

2. List basic steps in manual high-level disinfection

3. Explain the importance of rinsing and drying processes

4. Discuss the use of automated endoscope reprocessors

5. Discuss high-level disinfection testing and documentation

6. List the steps in a recall

INTRODUCTION

There are many steps required to achieve proper processing of a flexible endoscope. To this point, this text has covered point-of-use cleaning, transport and cleaning of soiled endoscopes. The next phase of reprocessing is called disinfection. All flexible endoscopes must be subjected to an antimicrobial process before being used on the next patient. Most flexible endoscopes undergo **high-level disinfection (HLD)** and some endoscopes are **sterilized**. (The sterilization process will be addressed in Chapter 10). Each required step through the disinfection process must be validated by the endoscope manufacturer and/or automated endoscope reprocessor (AER) manufacturer. Meticulous attention to all steps involved in endoscope processing, as well as their removable components and accessories, is critical to ensuring they are safe for subsequent patient use. This chapter will cover the use of high-level disinfectants in the processing of flexible endoscopes.

Cleaning according to the specific manufacturer's written instructions for use (IFU) is required to ensure that patient soil and other materials are removed prior to the antimicrobial processes of HLD or sterilization. Soil that remains on the endoscope may interfere with the ability of the disinfectant or sterilant to effectively kill or inactivate microorganisms and may allow for biofilm development. (See **Figure 9.1**) Cleaning is followed by disinfection or sterilization to reduce or completely remove microbial contamination. At a minimum, it is recommended that endoscopes be subjected to HLD after each use. When possible and practical, flexible and semi-rigid endoscopes should be sterilized due to the greater margin of safety built into sterilization. HLD is a multi-step process and is expected to be able to inactivate most pathogenic bacteria, viruses and fungi; however, it may not reliably inactivate certain types of microorganisms, including bacterial spores. When these devices are used in sterile tissue procedures, sterilization is recommended.

High-level disinfection (HLD) The destruction of all vegetative microorganisms, mycobacterium, small non-lipid viruses, fungal spores and some bacterial spores.

Sterilization Process by which all forms of microbial life, including bacteria, viruses, spores and fungi, are completely destroyed.

No Soil

The action of high-level disinfectants is reduced by the presence of soil.

Endoscopes and accessories must be clean before any HLD process.

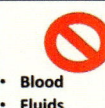

- Blood
- Fluids
- Feces
- Tissue
- Pus
- Lubricants
- Meds
- etc.

Figure 9. 1

THE SPAULDING CLASSIFICATION SYSTEM

The Spaulding Classification of medical devices and level of disinfection system is universally used to determine which type of disinfection or sterilization is appropriate for medical devices. Three classes—critical, semi-critical, and non-critical—stratify the risk of infection associated with each device. Critical devices break the mucosal barrier and should always be sterilized (e.g., reusable biopsy forceps). Semi-critical devices (e.g., endoscopes) come in contact with mucous membranes or non-intact skin and should be sterilized or undergo HLD. Non-critical devices are those that come into contact with intact skin (e.g., blood pressure cuffs and stethoscopes). These items can be cleaned with detergent and water, or disinfected with a germicide. HLD can be used in the reprocessing of semi-critical devices. Semi-critical devices can contact mucous membranes or non-intact skin and should preferably be sterilized or undergo HLD with a U.S. Food and Drug Administration (FDA)-approved high-level disinfectant prior to

Spaulding's Classification System

Level	Examples	Requires
Critical – Enters sterile tissue or vascular system.	• Implants • Surgical Instruments	Sterilization
Semi-Critical – Touches mucous membranes, except dental.	• Flexible Endoscopes • Laryngoscopes • Endotracheal Tubes	High-level Disinfection
Non-Critical – Touches intact skin.	• Thermometers • Hydrotherapy Tanks	Intermediate-level Disinfection
	• Stethoscopes	Low-level Disinfection

Figure 9.2

use on the next patient. **Figure 9.2** provides an overview of the Spaulding Classification System.

Endoscopes are considered semi-critical devices and should underdo HLD with an FDA-approved high-level disinfectant. Because endoscopes are used repeatedly, they must undergo reprocessing to ensure that all pathogenic microorganisms are removed before the endoscope is used on the next patient. Every patient must be considered a potential source of infection, and all endoscopes must be decontaminated with the same degree of rigor following every endoscopic procedure. An FDA-cleared high-level disinfectant or sterilant and 70% isopropyl alcohol are needed in the reprocessing room for HLD. HLD can be achieved either manually in a soaking tub or basin, or with the use of an AER.

Duodenoscope Caution

On August 4, 2015, the FDA listed supplemental measures to consider when reprocessing duodenoscopes. These measures include microbiological culturing, ethylene oxide (EtO) sterilization, use of a liquid chemical sterilant, and repeated HLD. The FDA recommended that healthcare facilities performing endoscopic retrograde cholangiopancreatogram (ERCP) procedures evaluate whether they have the necessary resources to perform these procedures; however, the agency did not mandate any changes at the time this document was published.

BASIC STEPS IN ENDOSCOPE HIGH-LEVEL DISINFECTION

Like all methods of disinfection, a successful HLD process has many steps. Each step has an impact on the process. Endoscope reprocessing professionals must follow IFU carefully to achieve desired results.

Figure 9.3 illustrates the relationship between a medical device and a successful disinfection process.

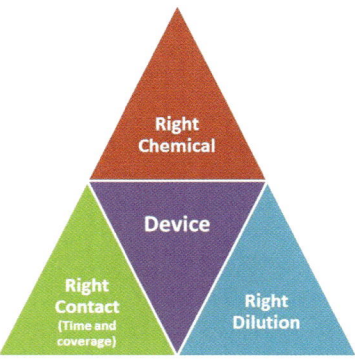

Chemical Disinfection: Doing It Right

Figure 9.3

According to ANSI/AAMI ST91: 2015 *Flexible and semi-rigid endoscope processing in health care facilities*, the following steps give a general outline of the process for manual disinfection of flexible endoscopes:

1. Precleaning at the point-of-use;

2. Transporting;

3. Leak testing;

4. Cleaning;

5. Rinsing;

6. Inspecting or testing for cleanliness, where applicable;

7. Disinfection/HLD and monitoring of the process, where applicable;

8. Rinsing;

9. Alcohol flush and drying; and

10. Storage.

Methods of High-Level Disinfection

As previously stated, HLD can be performed manually or mechanically. (**Figure 9.4**) Although the use of an AER is recommended, manual HLD is used when no AER is available.

High Level Disinfection Processes

Manual

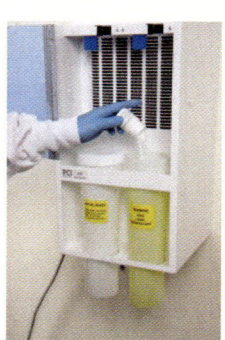

Mechanical

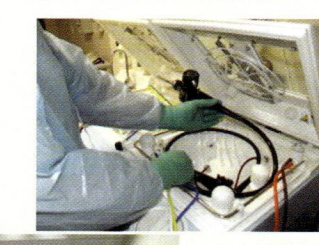
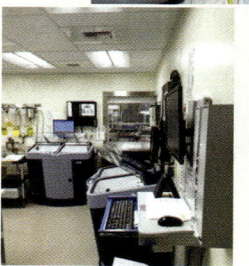
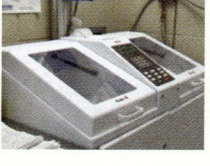

Figure 9.4

Manual High-Level Disinfection

Reprocessing professionals who perform manual HLD processes must closely follow each step in the process. In addition, an area must be provided where HLD can be performed. **Figure 9.5** provides an example of an HLD work station.

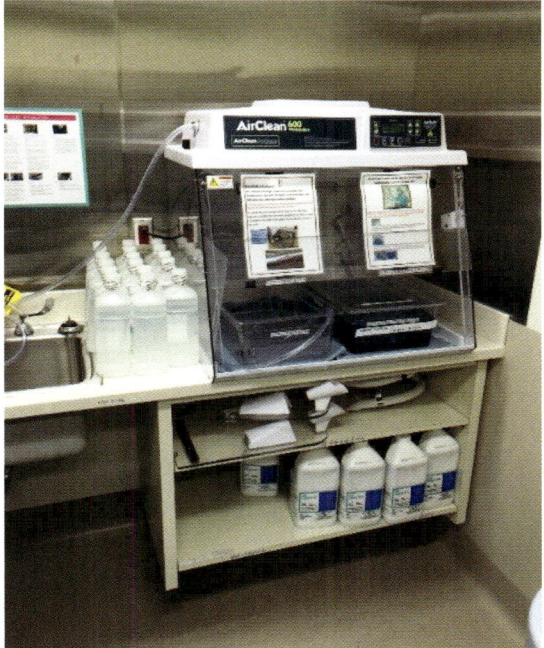

Figure 9.5

The following are general steps in the manual disinfection process:

1. Don fresh personal protective equipment (PPE), including gloves, skin and eye protection.

2. Use a closed container of sufficient capacity to completely immerse the endoscope in the HLD solution. The container should include a label that meets Occupational Safety and Health Administration (OSHA) requirements.

3. Prepare HLD solution according to the manufacturer's written IFU, noting the type, date of preparation, date of use, and expiration date.

4. Test the **minimum recommended concentration (MRC)** before each use with the disinfectant-specific (by type and concentration) test strip. Follow the label directions for the test strip and document results. **Figure 9.6** provides an example of a container of HLD test strips. A test strip from the container is placed in the solution. The color chart on the side of the container helps reprocessing professionals determine if the solution is ready for use.

Figure 9.6

> **Minimum recommended concentration (MRC)**
> Minimum concentration at which the manufacturer of a liquid chemical sterilant or high-level disinfectant tested the product and validated its performance.

Testing must be documented. **Figure 9.7** provides an example of a high-level disinfectant MRC testing log sheet.

5. Endoscopes must be purged with air and externally dried prior to immersion to minimize diluting the HLD. Excess water that remains on the endoscope after cleaning may dilute the HLD and render it ineffective.

6. Immerse the prepared endoscope and its removable components in the HLD solution, while maintaining a loose coil.

Example of a High Level disinfectant MRC Testing Log Sheet

Location/Dept.		High-Level Disinfectant				Equipment		
Warning: Do not use solution beyond its stated reuse life or below the designated MRC								
Date Solution Opened	Date Solution Expires	Date Test Strips Expire	Test Date	Test Time	Test Results + = Pass - = Fail	Tested By (Initials)	Comments	

Figure 9.7

- Completely immerse the endoscope and all removable parts in a basin of high-level disinfectant/sterilant. *Note: Ensure the endoscope is completely immersed.* **Figure 9.8** provides an example of a common error: failure to ensure that the entire endoscope is immersed.

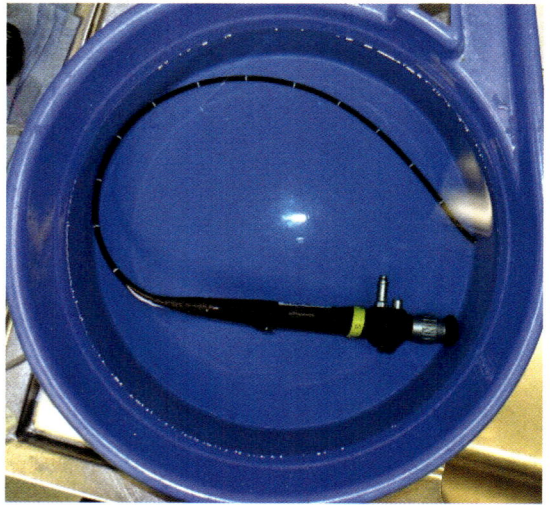

Figure 9.8 Shows an endoscope that is not completely immersed in the high-level disinfectant.

MEC or MRC?

The term "minimum effective concentration" or "MEC" may sometimes be used interchangeably with "minimum recommended concentration" or "MRC." Some older IFU may use MEC instead of MRC.

- The basin must be of a size to accommodate the endoscope without undue coiling and must have a tight-fitting lid to contain the chemical vapors.

- To prevent damage to the endoscope, the endoscope should not be soaked with other sharp instruments that could potentially damage the endoscope.

7. Flush disinfectant into all channels of the endoscope until it can be seen exiting the opposite end of each channel. Ensure that all channels are filled with the chemical and that no air pockets remain within the channels. *Note: Complete microbial destruction cannot occur unless all surfaces are in complete contact with the chemical.*

Since internal contact cannot be visually confirmed because of endoscope design, purging until a steady flow of solution is observed is necessary. Follow the endoscope manufacturer's written IFU for filling channels with the HLD solution.

8. Cover the soaking basin with a tight-fitting lid to minimize chemical vapor exposure.

Note: Exposure to chemical vapors may present a health hazard. The reprocessing area should have engineering controls to ensure good air quality.

Figure 9.9 provides an example of a portable system designed to manage fumes from HLD processes. **Figure 9.10** Provides an example of a wall ventilation system designed to manage fumes from HLD.

Figure 9.10

9. Soak the endoscope in the high-level disinfectant/sterilant for the time/temperature required to achieve HLD. Use a timer to verify soaking time. Do not exceed the manufacturer's recommended time for soaking (e.g., never soak an endoscope overnight).

10. Follow the HLD solution manufacturer's written IFU for contact time and temperature.

- Monitor process with a timer and thermometer. (See **Figure 9.11**)

- Document results.

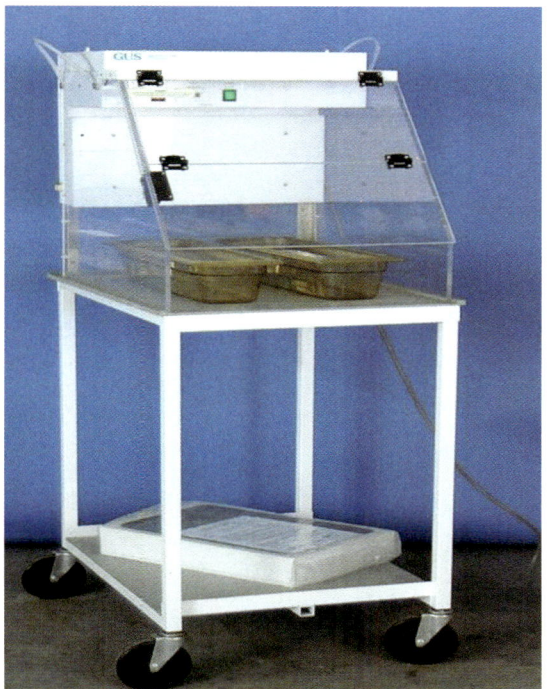

Figure 9.9

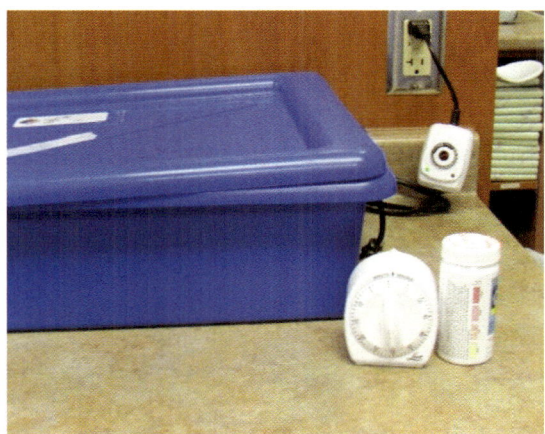

Figure 9.11 Soak Basin with Date of Solution on Top and a Thermometer inserted into the Solution.

- Purge all channels completely with air before removing the endoscope from the high-level disinfectant/sterilant. *Note: Purging the channels preserves the concentration and volume of the chemical, and prevents exposure from dripping and spilling.*

- Document the operator, date, time, make and model of the endoscope placed in the solution.

- Document the operator, date and time the endoscope is removed from solution. **Figure 9.12** provides an example of a documentation log sheet for manual HLD.

Manual Rinsing After High-Level Disinfection

The manual disinfection process must be followed by a manual rinsing process, as follows:

1. Don fresh PPE, including gloves, and skin and eye protection.

2. Thoroughly rinse all surfaces and channels of the endoscope and its removed components according to the endoscope and HLD solution manufacturers' written IFU to remove all traces of the disinfectant. *Note: Rinsing prevents exposure and potential injury of skin and mucous membranes from chemical residue.*

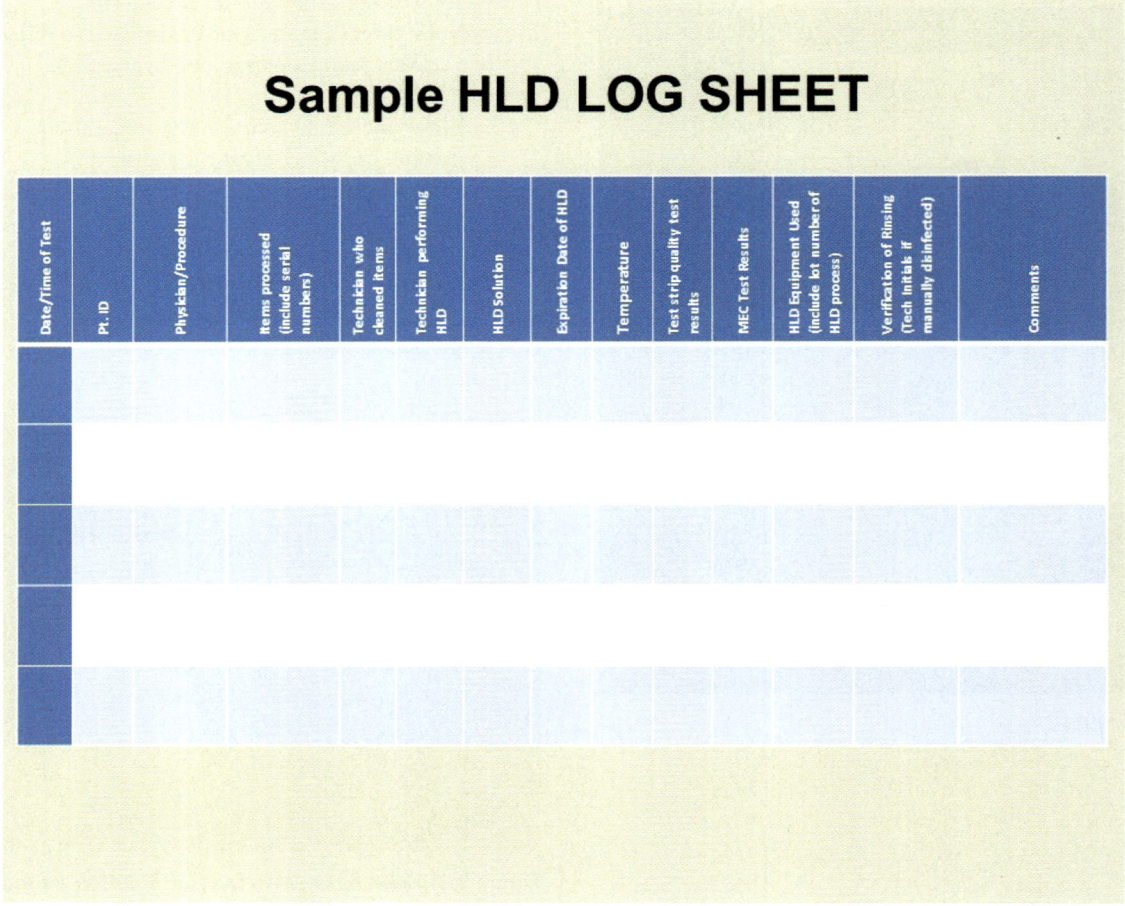

Figure 9.12

Use fresh water for each rinse (do not reuse the rinse water if multiple rinses are specified in the IFU). Follow the device manufacturer's written IFU for the specified rinse water quality. Rinsing is required for manual HLD, but it may be completed in the AER if using an automated endoscope reprocessor. According to endoscope reprocessing recommendations from AORN, published in their 2017 Guidelines for Perioperative Practice, Flexible Endoscope section; *"Following disinfection, the endoscope and endoscope channels should be mechanically rinsed and flushed with critical or sterile water. The final rinse should be performed with sterile water. Thorough rinsing and flushing with critical water helps prevent patient injury associated with disinfectant or sterilant retained in the endoscope. Utility water may contain microorganisms and endotoxins that can be deposited on the endoscope during the final rinse."*

Manual Drying After High-Level Disinfection

The manual rinsing process that follows HLD must be followed by a manual drying process. Drying is a critical element in reprocessing. Effective drying of endoscopes can reduce the risk of microbial contamination following HLD (e.g., recontamination of the endoscope by waterborne microorganisms during rinsing). Remaining moisture can allow microorganisms to survive and multiply; therefore, all channels and the surface of the endoscope must be thoroughly dried before storage. Certain waterborne microorganisms, such as *Pseudomonas aeruginosa*, can pose an infection risk to a portion of the endoscopy patient population. Even when reprocessing steps are performed meticulously, a few microorganisms may survive HLD. If any moisture remains in the endoscope channels or on its surface, those few microorganisms can multiply to over a million colony-forming units in just a few hours.

Figure 9.13, first shared in Chapter 3, provides a reminder of the speed that microorganisms can reproduce and illustrates the importance of thorough drying.

| How Fast Can Bacteria Multiply? ||
Time from First survivor	Number of Bacteria
One survivor	1
20 minutes	2
40 minutes	4
1 hour	8
2 hours	64
3 hours	512
4 hours	4,096
5 hours	32,768
6 hours	262,144
7 hours	2,097,152!!
Depends on many variables, but an example	

Figure 9.13

The presence of such microorganisms in conjunction with retained moisture can also lead to the development of biofilm and further increase patient risk. This is a particular concern when tap water is used to rinse the endoscope following HLD. Drying the endoscope after every reprocessing cycle, both between patient procedures and before storage, is crucial to preventing bacterial transmission and infection. Drying is as important to the prevention of disease transmission and nosocomial infection as cleaning and HLD.

Drying can be achieved by flowing air through all endoscope channels for a specified period of time. Drying should be followed by using 70–80% ethyl or isopropyl alcohol, which helps dry the channels. Alcohol will displace water and evaporates more easily than water. The alcohol mixes with the remaining water on the channel surfaces and encourages evaporation of the residual water as air flows through the channel.

When using alcohol, it is important to follow the endoscope manufacturer's written IFU regarding the volume of alcohol and method to be used for each endoscope lumen. Any remaining alcohol should be removed with forced air until no visual signs of moisture remain (or as otherwise recommended by the endoscope manufacturer). Reprocessing professionals should refer to the endoscope manufacturer's written IFU for guidance on correlating the force of air pressure in pounds per square inch (psi) or other measure to the channel size. The use of syringes to dry channels is not recommended. All removable endoscope parts should be thoroughly dried. To reduce the risk of trapping liquid inside the instrument, valves should not be attached to the endoscope during storage. Valves, including rinsing valves, should stay with a named endoscope as a set to prevent cross-infection and enable full traceability.

Manual drying should be performed by completing the following steps:

1. Flush all channels with 70% isopropyl alcohol until the alcohol can be seen exiting the opposite end of each channel. Alcohol flushes are necessary even when sterile water is used for rinsing.

2. Purge all channels with air.

- Use compressed air that has been filtered to remove microorganisms.

- Avoid the use of excessively high air pressure that can damage the internal channels of flexible endoscopes.

- According to AORN's 2016 Endoscope Reprocessing Recommendations, the endoscope channels should be dried by purging with instrument air or mechanically dried with a mechanical processor drying system.

3. Remove all channel adapters.

4. Dry the exterior of the endoscope with a soft, clean, lint-free towel.

5. Thoroughly rinse and dry all removable parts. Do not attach removable parts (e.g., valves, etc.) to the endoscope during storage.

Note: Storage of endoscopes with the removable parts detached reduces the risk of liquid becoming trapped *inside the instrument, and also facilitates continued drying of the channels and channel openings.*

USE OF HIGH-LEVEL DISINFECTANTS

HLD solutions are cleared by the FDA and include those formulated with glutaraldehyde, ortho-phthalaldehyde (OPA), peracetic acid, chlorine and hydrogen peroxide. Information on HLD solutions that are cleared by the FDA is listed on the FDA website at www.fda.gov. This list is updated periodically and provides information on the product's clearance for HLD, the contact time and temperature required for HLD, and whether the HLD solution is limited to use in an AER.

Most HLD solutions are reusable, which means the solution can be used repeatedly, until it has reached either its manufacturer-specified MRC determined by testing, or its maximum reuse life prescribed by the manufacturer and determined by testing, (whichever comes first). HLD solutions have been cleared by FDA for maximum reuse ranging from five to 30 days. Testing of the reusable HLD solution for the MRC should be performed and documented prior to each use, in accordance with the manufacturer's written IFU. It is unacceptable to "top off" the basin of HLD solution or AER reservoir containing the reusable HLD solution, unless the HLD solution manufacturer provides written guidance for doing so. Some volume loss of HLD solution occurs during each processing cycle. Topping off does not extend the use-life days of the solution, even if the MRC or MEC is still met.

Single-use HLD solution formulations are available for use with specific AERs. Some HLD solutions are formulated as a concentrate, which is metered and mixed in the AER just prior to the HLD cycle in the AER. Examples of these types of HLD solutions include concentrated OPA and peracetic acid. The MRC or MEC of the use solution for single-use HLDs that are prepared from a concentrate is determined either through use of a solution test strip or chemical monitoring device, or automatically, depending on the AER.

To be effective, the HLD solution should contact all surfaces of the endoscope, including the control body and the internal lumens of all endoscope channels; therefore, for manual processing, the endoscope and its components should be completely immersed in the HLD solution, ensuring that all channels are filled with solution and air bubbles are eliminated. Non-immersible gastrointestinal (GI) endoscopes should not be disinfected in liquids. The exposure time should be precisely measured.

Note. Air bubbles on the surface of the endoscope could interfere with the disinfectant's ability to function properly on that site. A lint-free cloth should be used to remove the air bubbles from the surface/exterior of the endoscope.

In all cases, the manufacturer's written IFU for each HLD solution should be followed, including information concerning the quality of water to be used in the formulation. For some HLD solutions, it might be acceptable to use tap water; for other solutions, softened water or other treated water may be needed. If a water treatment process is used, it

should be monitored to ensure that the appropriate water quality is achieved.

When an endoscope is to be processed in an AER using an HLD solution (including multi-use or single-use solutions), the device connectors should be correct for the specific brand and model of endoscope. (See **Figure 9.14**) Reprocessing personnel should ensure that all endoscope channels are connected according to the manufacturer's written IFU, and that any support tray or accessories used are for the endoscope brand and model being processed. (See **Figure 9.15**) If the sterilant is being used manually or if a reusable liquid chemical sterilant (LCS)/HLD solution is used, all quality control checks should be performed according to the manufacturer's written IFU. It is important to ensure in any manual process that all internal lumens and external surfaces of the device are in contact with the solution for the entire recommended exposure time.

Examples of AER Connectors

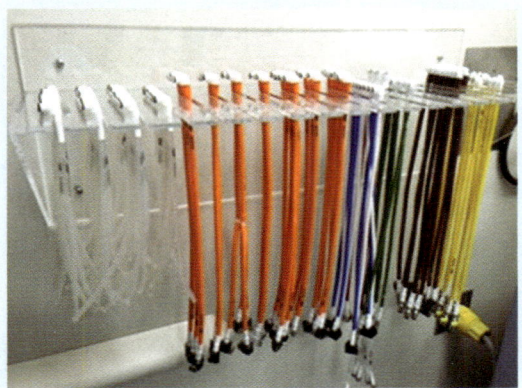
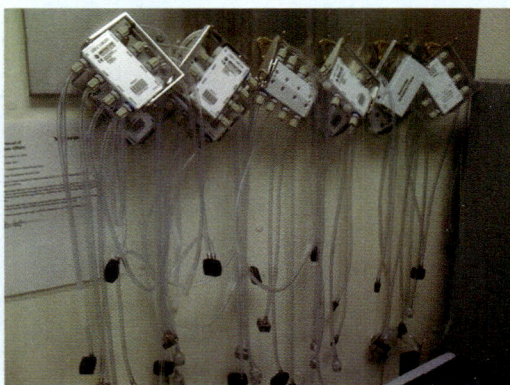

Figure 9.14 AER Connectors Designed for Specific Endoscope Models Hang in an Endoscope Reprocessing Area.

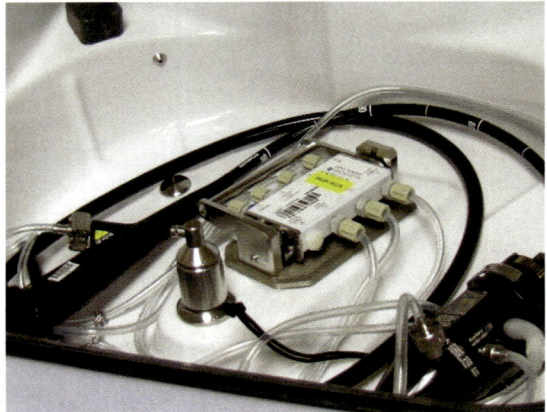

Figure 9.15 Connectors are used to ensure internal channels are flushed.

All items processed with HLD solutions should be thoroughly rinsed according to the manufacturer's written IFU. The IFU will include the quantity and quality of rinse water, as well as the number of rinses and the time required for each rinse to reduce chemical residues to safe levels. The microbial quality of the water used to rinse endoscopes processed with LCS/HLD solutions is an important aspect in the sterilization or HLD process. Users should follow the recommendations of the device manufacturer and the LCS/HLD solution manufacturer for the microbial quality of the water to be used for rinsing. If the device is not rinsed adequately, the safety of the device may be compromised.

A Word About Water

Water is a critical factor in effective endoscope cleaning, disinfection and rinsing. Additional information about water can be found in the *TIR34: Water for the reprocessing of medical devices.*

Reprocessing professionals should determine in advance whether the endoscope is to be used immediately after processing. If it is to be used immediately, it should be unloaded from the AER, transferred directly into an aseptic transport device and sent to the intended point of use. An HLD-processed endoscope will be wet and unwrapped at the end of processing. An endoscope reprocessed with HLD that will not be used immediately can become recontaminated during storage and should be carefully and properly placed in an appropriate storage cabinet. Endoscopes intended to be used in a normally sterile area should be reprocessed with HLD immediately before use and then transferred in an aseptic transport container or device with sterile technique to the patient for immediate use. Endoscopes should not be left in the AER to complete reprocessing the next day; endoscopes should undergo the complete HLD process and be properly dried and stored for its next use.

USE OF AUTOMATED ENDOSCOPE REPROCESSORS

AERs are machines used for the purpose of cleaning and/or disinfecting endoscopes and components. This disinfection process uses an HLD solution to achieve HLD. The AER includes automated immersion or spraying of the endoscope and filling of the endoscope channels with the HLD solution, followed by timing of the exposure period and rinsing of the endoscope's internal and external surfaces with water to remove HLD solution residues. **Figures 9.16** and **9.17** provide examples of AERs.

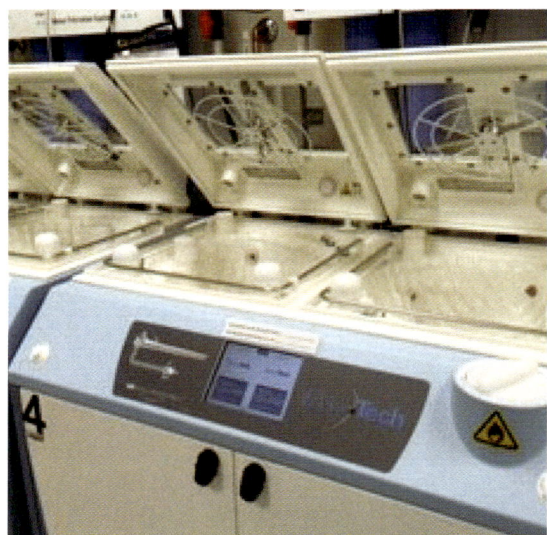

Figure 9.16

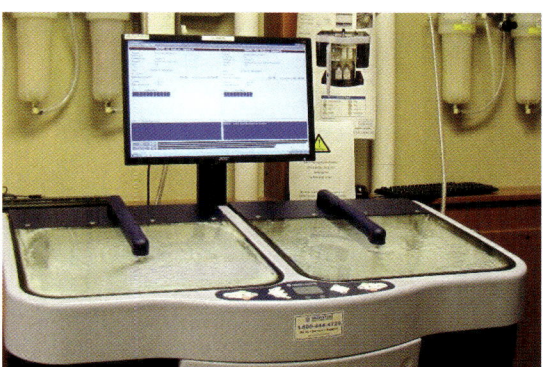

Figure 9.17

AERs must be effective, safe, reliable and able to handle endoscope design and throughput. Reprocessing personnel should diligently follow the AER manufacturer's instructions on the proper use and maintenance of the equipment. The AER must also be compatible with the endoscopes and accessories being reprocessed. Any special considerations for reprocessing not handled by the AER (such as the elevator on duodenoscopes) must be done following the manufacturer's instructions. Other factors that play a role in effective AER reprocessing include water quality and temperature, the chemical being used and its tested MEC, maintenance of filters, and contact disinfection time with the endoscopes. The use of cleaning monitors for automated washers may help to ensure adequate functioning. The chemical and microbial quality of water should be specified, controlled and monitored.

An automated process for cleaning and disinfection may be more efficient than manual processing. AERs standardize the disinfection process and decrease personnel exposure to HLD solutions. When used in strict accordance with the manufacturer's IFU, they may also result in less user exposure to toxic chemicals and help ensure repeatable results. Some AERs use high pressure and flow rates to perfuse the endoscope channels, bathe the exterior of the endoscope and circulate the HLD solution continuously during the exposure period. Most AERs also include automated cleaning and rinse cycles. The automated cleaning cycle is not intended to replace point-of-use pre-cleaning or thorough manual cleaning of the endoscope prior to placing it into the AER. In addition to improved cleaning and decontamination, mechanical processors may also

provide improved rinsing of disinfectants and reduce the potential for patient injury associated with residual disinfectants remaining in the endoscope.

Note: The AER manufacturer's written IFU should be compared to the endoscope manufacturer's written IFU. If there are discrepancies between the two, a decision should be made based on information that can be acquired from both companies.

Although mechanical processors provide many advantages compared with manual processing, AORN notes there are some disadvantages as well. AORN states: "Mechanical processors require preventive maintenance to ensure safe and effective operation. The use of contaminated or defective mechanical processors for cleaning, disinfecting or rinsing can result in inadequate processing that has been associated with outbreaks of endoscopy-related infections and pseudo-infections and patient injury. In addition, the presence of biofilm has been detected in mechanical processors."

AERs can automatically rinse the processed endoscope with water to remove toxic HLD residues. It is essential to only use HLD solutions whose recommended number of rinses can be programmed into the AER. Some AERs then flush the channels with forced air or with 70–80% ethyl or isopropyl alcohol, followed by forced air to aid in drying the endoscope channels. This practice also prevents growth of waterborne pathogenic microorganisms during storage that may have recontaminated the device during rinsing. **Figure 9.18** shows alcohol to be used in the drying process being added to an AER.

Figure 9.18 Alcohol Being Added to an AER That Uses Alcohol as Part of the Drying Process.

Some AERs have reservoirs with heating elements that will bring the temperature of the HLD solution to the indicated contact temperature for LCS/HLD. Some HLD solutions are indicated for use at elevated temperatures; thus, they can only be used with an AER with the capability of maintaining HLD solutions at the specified temperature.

If an AER cycle is interrupted, LCS/HLD of the device cannot be ensured; therefore, the cycle should be repeated. (See **Figure 9.19**)

The microbial quality of the rinse water will vary and may recontaminate the processed device, as explained in AAMI TIR34. To avoid recontaminating the device with the rinse water, the incoming AER water should be at least filtered using bacterial retentive filters, as recommended in the AER manufacturer's written IFU. (See **Figure 9.20**) The water handling systems, which do not come into contact with the LCS/HLD solution, should be disinfected on a regular basis, as directed by the manufacturer. Some AERs have self-disinfection cycles using either an LCS/HLD solution or thermal methods. The water filters should be changed according to the manufacturer's written IFU. In addition, the endoscopes should be flushed with alcohol and purged with pressurized air prior to storage.

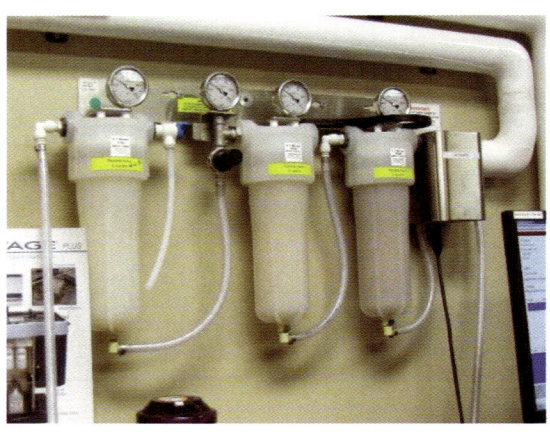

Figure 9.20 Example of an AER water filter system

AERs are designed to provide flow of solutions to internal channels. Quality testing devices are available for many of the AERs to ensure the solutions are flowing. To help ensure function of this equipment, testing should be performed at least weekly, after major repairs or whenever there is a concern about equipment function.

Depending on the make and model of the AER, additional features may include:

- A printer for documentation;

- Adjustable cycle times;

- Ultrasonic cleaning capabilities;

- Channel detection for obstruction;

- Leak testing;

- Automatic rinsing;

- Automatic alcohol flush;

- Automatic air purge; and

- Ability to process more than one endoscope at a time, either in the same chamber or in separate chambers.

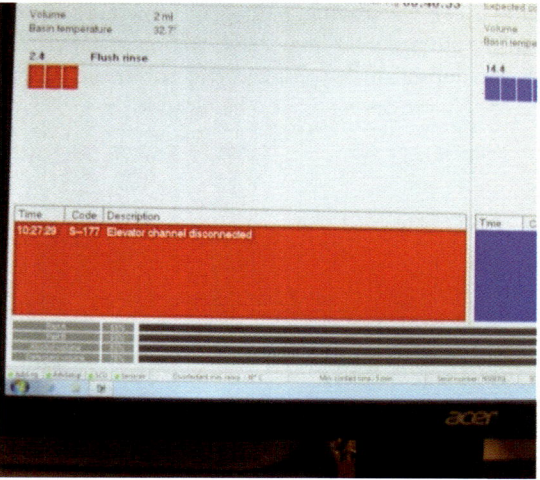

Figure 9.19 Notification of cycle interruption on an AER

Following disinfection, the endoscope and accessories should be removed from the solution or AER to prevent recontamination.

PPE that was used for decontamination should not be worn when handling an endoscope or any of the endoscope's accessories after they have gone through the disinfection process. PPE should be removed and hands should be properly washed. Clean, latex-free gloves should then be worn when handling the endoscope and accessories.

If the AER cycle is interrupted, HLD or sterilization cannot be ensured; therefore, the cycle should be repeated. A preventive maintenance plan should be in place for all AERs, equipment and accessories used to reprocess endoscopes. Quality controls recommended by manufacturers of AERs should be adhered to and documented.

The FDA has approved labeling some AERs as washer-disinfectors, which do not require prior manual cleaning and channel brushing. While the introduction of automated, brushless washing of endoscope channels represents a potentially significant advancement, manual cleaning and brushing are still required when a washer-disinfector is used in order to ensure the overall efficacy of HLD. The redundancy achieved by adding an automated washing step following manual cleaning can undoubtedly provide an extra level of safety. Users should continue to manually clean endoscopes as a precaution until the capabilities of the new machines are confirmed in independent studies and in clinical practice.

PROCESSING OF ENDOSCOPE ACCESSORIES

Processing of certain reusable endoscope components, such as air/water and suction valves, biopsy port covers, water bottles and tubing, require the same level of inspection, cleaning and HLD or sterilization as the endoscopes themselves.

Reusable endoscopic accessories (e.g., biopsy forceps and other cutting instruments) (See **Figure 9.21**) that break the mucosal barrier should be mechanically cleaned as described previously and then sterilized between each patient use. This means that HLD is not recommended. Before HLD is performed, remove and clean valves, connectors and all detachable parts.

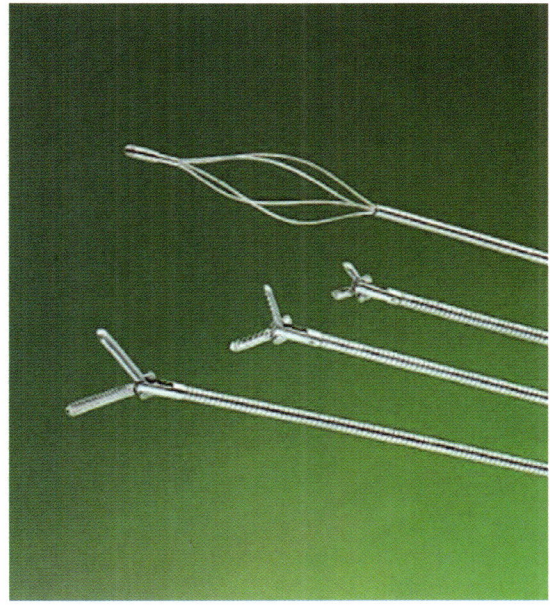

Figure 9.21

Valves may then be immersed in an HLD solution, following the manufacturer's written IFU for disinfectant contact time and rinse requirements. The valves should be repeatedly actuated during disinfection and rinsing to facilitate access to all surfaces. Alternately, valves may be placed in an AER (if it has been cleared for the processing of valves) and processed according to the AER manufacturer's written IFU.

At least daily and in accordance with the manufacturers' written IFU, the water bottle (used for cleaning the lens and for irrigation during the procedure) and connecting tube should be manually cleaned and undergo HLD or sterilization. (See **Figure 9.22**) Only accessories validated for processing in the specific AER should be processed in that AER. Water bottles may not drain completely, resulting in diluted HLD solution. Irrigation tubing requires flow of disinfectant and rinse water through the length of the tubing. Reprocessing professionals should consult the manufacturer of the peripheral accessory, or consider the use of disposable water bottle connectors or irrigation tubing, which are used with bottles of sterile water.

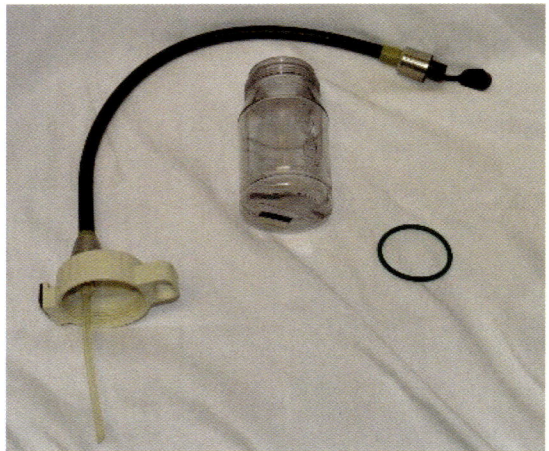

Figure 9.22

Between cases, reusable brushes should be cleaned and undergo HLD. *Note: Reusable brushes should be inspected between uses and replaced when worn, frayed, bent or otherwise damaged. Worn bristles are ineffective in cleaning and damaged brushes may damage endoscope channels.*

TRANSPORT OF HIGH-LEVEL DISINFECTED ENDOSCOPES

When transporting an endoscope that has undergone HLD, the endoscope should be protected from recontamination. Before removing the endoscope from the storage cabinet, new exam gloves should be donned (put on). The endoscope should then be transported using an impervious barrier method that will prevent recontamination. Examples would be a clean plastic bag, endoscope transfer system (an endoscope in a tote bin with a cover), or similar method. The endoscope should be loosely coiled to prevent damage.

QUALITY CONTROL

Incorporating visual inspections and testing of the equipment is necessary to identify conditions that may affect the cleaning or disinfecting processes; this includes testing for leaks, inspecting for cracks and checking the integrity of fiber optic bundles. Visual inspection alone may not be sufficient for assessing the efficacy of the cleaning processes; the use of methods that can measure organic residues that are not detectable during visual

inspection should be considered in facility cleaning policy and procedures. Process monitors should also be used, as recommended by the AER and HLD manufacturers. Reprocessing professionals should verify that all manufacturer-recommended maintenance schedules and services are performed for all endoscopes and processing equipment (e.g., AERs and sterilizers) used in the facility.

Product Identification and Traceability

Each item or package intended for use should be labeled with a lot control identifier. The lot control identifier should designate the following:

- Identification number or code of the sterilizer, AER or soaking container;

- Date LCS or HLD was performed;

- Sterilization or HLD cycle number; and

- Patient identifier.

Items processed for immediate use by means of an HLD soaking system require a means of identifying the items processed. Lot identification enables personnel to retrieve items in the event of a recall and to trace problems to their source. Quality control recordkeeping is critical and relies heavily on historical data, especially where quality control measures yield conflicting evidence. Recordkeeping is needed for both epidemiological tracking and ongoing assessment of the reliability of LCS and HLD processes.

Documentation for Flexible Endoscope High-Level Disinfection

For each HLD cycle, the following information should be recorded and maintained:

- Assigned lot number, AER or soaking container identification and cycle number;

- Specific contents of the lot or load, including quantity, processing area and description of the items;

- Patient's name or unique patient identifier;

- Procedure, physician and, if applicable, serial number or other item identification;

- Shelf-life date, if applicable, as well as lot number; date the original container of HLD was opened; use-life of the open container; date the product was activated or diluted; date the activated, diluted or ready-to-use solution was poured into a secondary container; and the reuse-life of the solution;

- Exposure time and temperature, if not provided on the physical monitors;

- Date and time of cycle;

- HLD type and concentration; pH test results, if required;

- Name or initials of the operator;

- Results of MRC or MEC solution monitoring strip, if applicable;

- Results of the quality control of test strips, if applicable;

- Any reports of low MRC or MEC testing results (as indicated by solution test strips or chemical monitoring devices); and

- Any reports of positive microbial contamination testing.

The recording chart, printer or tape, if applicable, should also be dated and maintained, and the operator should review and sign each cycle. A record of repairs and preventive maintenance should also be kept for each AER and soaking container. **Figure 9.23** provides an example of an AER cycle printout.

Other documentation essential for infection control includes information and audits about reprocessing activities, equipment performance and maintenance records, and records verifying that HLD solutions were tested and replaced appropriately. Audits should monitor all reprocessing steps and provide feedback to personnel regarding their adherence to cleaning and disinfection procedures.

Medical Center Endoscopy

1

Basin : A

Daily A Cycle#: 8 Total A Cycle#: 55 Total Cycle# : 105 Manufacturer : ABC

Model No. : EC–450HL5

Serial No. : 1C375A003 Scope ID : WHITE Patient ID : ABC123 Physician ID : Dr. F. Marsh Operator ID : M.T.

Process Start : 12/06/11 12:08:41 Process End : 12/06/11 12:38:42 Total Time : 30:01

Status : Completed
    CIDEX OPA–C Concentrate MEC : Pass
    Expiry : Feb 2018 Lot No. : 140710/450

Available : 32 Cycles Detergent Exp.: Jan 2018

Endoscope Leak Rate : 1.84 mBar/min

Stage Time

Leak Test 1 00:53

Wash 10:54

Disinfect 15:17
    HLD Time 05:10
    HLD Min Temp. 51.4 C HLD Requirements Achieved

Alc. Flush 01:28

Leak Test 2 01:27

Removed By:

Figure 9.23

Use of Physical Monitors for Reprocessing

Physical monitoring of manual HLD processes using a thermometer and timer should be completed for each cycle. The results of physical monitoring should be documented. Thermometers, timers and other monitoring equipment should have their calibration verified periodically, according to facility policy, to help ensure their accuracy and precision. The HLD solution should be visually inspected before each use and discarded if precipitates (e.g., crystallization, particulate matter) are observed, even if the solution is within its use-life (consult the solution manufacturer's written IFU for specific guidance). Visual inspection should also ensure that the solution container is covered to prevent evaporation of the solution and exposure to light, both of which can affect the efficacy of the chemical agent. Visual observations should be documented. If the interpretation of the physical monitors or visual inspection of the solution suggests inadequate processing, the items should not be dispensed or used. Follow-up measures should be initiated in accordance with facility policy.

Solution test strips are designed to determine whether the concentration of the active ingredient in the HLD solution is above or below the MRC or MEC for the HLD. (see **Figure 9.24**) These solution test strips assist the user in determining when the solution should no longer be used. All solution test strips or chemical monitoring devices should be used according to their manufacturer's written IFU. Processing personnel should use the solution test strip or chemical monitoring device cleared by the FDA for use with a specific HLD product. The manufacturer's written IFU should provide information on the reliability, safety and performance characteristics of the product, including the interpretation of the solution test strip or chemical monitoring device reaction, the MRC or MEC that the solution test strip or chemical monitoring device is designed to detect, and the shelf life and storage requirements. Any necessary efficacy testing of the solution test strip or chemical monitoring device should be performed according to the manufacturer's written IFU. The solution test strip or chemical monitoring device,

manufacturer's written IFU for testing, storage of the strips and reagents, interpretation of results, and expiration should be followed.

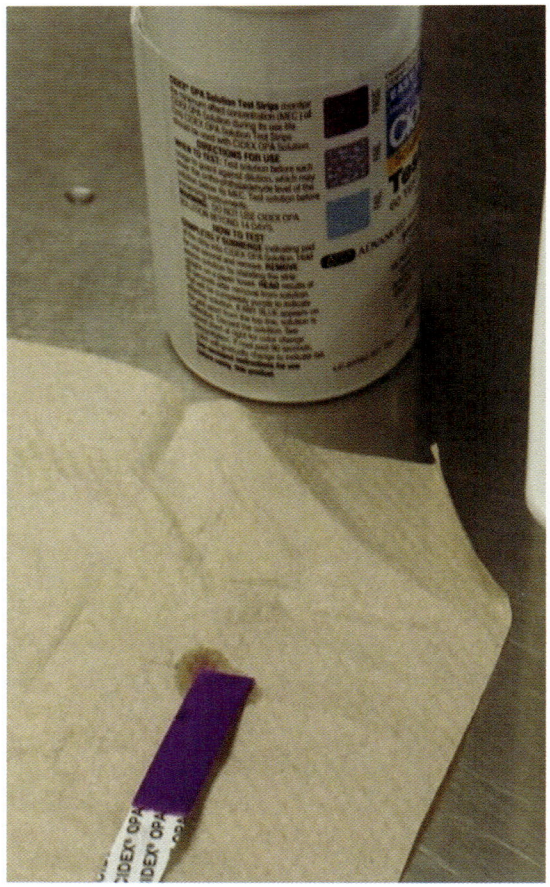

Figure 9.24 Solution Test Strip

The solution test strip should be read before the HLD solution is used. Processing personnel should receive education, training and complete competency verification regarding the performance characteristics of the solution test strip or chemical monitoring device to be used. Users should follow the manufacturer's written IFU when interpreting test strips. If the interpretation suggests that the concentration of active ingredients is inadequate, the solution should be discarded, even if it is within its use life. Suppliers of solution test strips that change color often provide visual color interpretation reference charts. If available, these charts should be obtained and used for education of and reference by processing personnel.

Recall Process

If the solution test strip device indicates that the concentration of the active ingredient is inadequate and if items have been processed in this ineffective solution and used, the following actions should be taken to identify these items:

1. The supervisor or other designated person and the designated infection prevention personnel should be notified immediately, and this notification should be followed by a written report. The report and notification should include:

   - The time and date of the questionable processing cycles;

   - A description of the soaking or processing container and the load, including lot control numbers, product and patient names, and other identifying information;

   - The results of physical monitoring and the solution test strip or chemical monitoring device obtained from the user; and

   - Any other information that could be useful in determining whether the results of the solution test strip or chemical monitoring device are valid or questionable.

2. Items processed since the last cycle for which the solution test strip or chemical monitoring device indicated an inadequate concentration should be considered unprocessed. They should be retrieved, if possible, and reprocessed. The HLD solution in question should be discarded.

3. After the cause of the processing failure has been determined and addressed, the HLD solution should be tested with a solution test strip or chemical monitoring device. If the solution test strip or chemical monitoring device indicates that the concentration of the active ingredient is inadequate, the solution should be discarded and replaced with freshly prepared solution.

4. Determine whether a product recall is necessary.

If using an AER, solution monitoring test strips should still be used to monitor the effectiveness of automated processing equipment that uses an HLD solution. These devices should be defined by the manufacturer of the chemicals and/or processing equipment and should be used and interpreted according to the manufacturer's written IFU. Solution test strips should be used to test automated equipment at the same frequency as for manual processes, which is before each use. The use and interpretation of these strips to monitor the concentration of active ingredients in HLD solutions are described previously. The devices to use should be determined based on the written IFU from the manufacturer of the chemicals and/ or automated processing equipment, because not all process monitoring devices are commercially available for all automated processes.

Use of Physical Monitors and Process Monitoring Devices

Physical monitors reflect the parameters of the automated processing equipment and include displays, digital printouts and gauges. The user should obtain information from the manufacturer of the monitoring device regarding the accuracy and precision of the monitor, which parameters are measured, and any maintenance required to ensure the continued adequate performance of the equipment.

At the end of the cycle and before items are removed from the processing equipment, the operator should examine and interpret the printout to verify that cycle parameters were met, and initial the printout to allow later identification of the operator. Automated processing equipment that does not have physical-monitor recording devices should not be used. Electronic software programs are also available that provide a real-time, paperless and permanent recording of physical parameters. Automated processing equipment without electronic data transfer, recording or printing capabilities should not be used.

If the interpretation of the physical monitors or process monitoring devices, such as solution test strips or visual inspection of the chemical solution, as defined by the manufacturer, suggests inadequate processing, the items should not be dispensed or used. The interpreter should inform the designated supervisor or delegated individual; this individual should then initiate follow-up measures.

If the physical monitoring records or process monitoring devices (solution test strips) indicate any malfunction or suspicious operation, the load should be considered inadequately processed and not be used. The processing equipment manufacturer's written IFU should be reviewed for troubleshooting information. After examination, if the malfunction cannot be corrected immediately, the cycle should be terminated in accordance with the manufacturer's written IFU, and the processing equipment should be removed from service. All items in the terminated cycle should be reprocessed. The healthcare facility engineer or maintenance contract service should then be notified and the malfunction should be corrected. Faulty processing equipment cannot be made operational without identifying and correcting the underlying problem; merely extending the cycle time, for example, is not sufficient.

Many HLD automated processing equipment computer programs are designed to detect inadequate cycle conditions. Computer-controlled equipment will often abort the cycle when the required parameters for the process have not been met. Some automated equipment will also provide various types of alerts regarding equipment performance. Equipment users should be educated and trained to distinguish between alerts that represent failure conditions and those that do not.

If any process monitoring device defined for use with HLD indicates the concentration of the active ingredients or specific process parameter during a cycle was inadequate, the following actions should be taken to identify the reasons for this failure:

1. Follow the manufacturer's written IFU to troubleshoot the problem.

2. If troubleshooting was unsuccessful, a description of the processing equipment should be included in a written report and notification.

3. Any processing equipment in question should be removed from service.

4. Infection prevention, sterile processing and facility maintenance personnel should attempt to determine the cause of the processing failure.

5. After the cause of the processing failure has been determined and corrected, the complete processing system should be tested according to the manufacturer's written IFU. This should include any associated diagnostic cycles and/or testing with process monitoring devices (such as biological indicators, spore test strips, chemical indicators, solution test strips or chemical monitoring devices). If the physical monitoring results and the process monitoring devices for the cycle are satisfactory, the processing equipment can be returned to service.

If there are any doubts related to improper cleaning, disinfection or contamination, the equipment should be taken out of service (e.g., endoscope, washer-disinfector, accessories, flushing pump, etc.) until corrective actions have been taken and satisfactory results have been achieved. Corrective actions such as repairs or improved training should be initiated to correct deficiencies in reprocessing. Any item that may not have been appropriately disinfected or sterilized must be reprocessed.

PERSONAL PROTECTIVE EQUIPMENT

PPE should be used when reprocessing endoscopes, as exposure to HLD solutions and body fluids may occur. Gowns, gloves, protective eyewear and/or face protection are recommended when handling any HLD solution.

1. Gowns should be impervious to fluid, have long sleeves that fit snugly around the wrist, and wrap to cover as much of the body as possible. Reprocessing professionals should dispose of or launder gowns if they become wet or are exposed to contaminated material.

2. Gloves should be impervious to the chemical, inspected for tears or holes before use, and appropriate for the task (i.e., chemical handling versus general use). Reprocessing professionals should not use an imperfect glove or reuse disposable gloves. The permeability of gloves varies considerably, depending on manufacturer; therefore, the recommendations of the glove manufacturer and the HLD solution manufacturer should be consulted. Gloves should be long enough to extend up the arm to protect the forearm or clothing from splashes or seepage. To avoid cross contamination, gloves should be changed and hands should be properly washed whenever moving from a dirty to clean task or environment.

3. Eye and/or face protection is necessary. Eye glasses or contact lenses are not sufficient eye protection. A face shield or safety glasses in combination with a face mask allowing for ventilation is recommended. High filtration masks should not be worn because they may trap vapors. Emergency eyewash stations must be accessible within a 10-second travel time.

PERSONNEL CONSIDERATIONS

Education and training of processing personnel should include procedures for cleaning, disinfecting or sterilizing, packaging, and storing each specific endoscope make and model, including equipment connections. Facilities must also verify that current versions of the manufacturer's written IFU for the endoscope models and AERs used at the facility are readily available to processing personnel.

Temporary personnel and persons new to endoscope reprocessing should not be allowed to clean or disinfect instruments in either a manual or automated reprocessing system until competency has been established. Individuals working in the setting must be trained in the safe handling of HLD solutions or sterilants, and spill containment procedures. Reprocessing professionals should refer to the manufacturer's IFU for information on the specific solution to be used. Personnel must also know which AERs, HLD solutions, etc. are compatible with a particular endoscope and then use the equipment and products according to the manufacturer's instructions.

CONCLUSION

High-level disinfection is a complex process that must be performed correctly in every step of the process. A solid understanding of each HLD method and attention to detail is required to help ensure a successful process and outcome. Routine testing and strict adherence to procedures and manufacturers' IFU reduce the risks for patients.

RESOURCES

Association for the Advancement of Medical Instrumentation ANSI/AAMI ST91: 2015. *Flexible and semi-rigid endoscope processing in health care facilities.*

Society of Gastroenterology Nurses and Associates. Standards of Infection Prevention in Reprocessing Flexible Gastrointestinal Endoscopes. 2015.

Rutala, WA and Weber, DJ. New developments in reprocessing semicritical items. *American Journal of Infection Control.* 2013. 41, 560-566.

Society of Gastroenterology Nurses and Associates. *Standard of Infection Prevention in the Gastroenterology Setting.* 2015.

United States Food and Drug Administration. *FDA-cleared sterilants and high level disinfectants with general claims for processing reusable medical and dental devices.* 2009.

Association of periOperative Registered Nurses. Endoscope Recommendations. Published in: *Guidelines for Perioperative Practice* by Burlingame, B, et al. Vol. 1. January 2016.

Miner, N. Cleaning, disinfection and sterilization of heat-sensitive endoscopes. In Endoscopy, S. Amornyotin, Ed. 2013.

Society of Gastroenterology Nurses and Associates. *Guideline for Use of High Level Disinfectants & Sterilants for Reprocessing Flexible Gastrointestinal Endoscopes.* 2013.

AAMI TIR 34: 2014 *Water for the reprocessing of medical devices.*

Centers for Disease Control and Prevention and U.S. Food and Drug Administration. CDC/FDA Health Update about the Immediate Need for Healthcare Facilities to Review Procedures for Cleaning, Disinfecting, and Sterilizing Reusable Medical Devices. 2015.

TERMS

High-Level disinfection

Sterilization

Minimum recommended concentration (MRC)

Chapter 10

Sterilization Processes

Learning Objectives

Upon completion of this chapter, readers will be able to:

1. Define sterilization and identify factors that can negatively impact the sterilization process

2. Discuss basic steps in preparing medical devices for sterilization

3. Discuss low-temperature sterilization methods, safety and sterility assurance monitoring processes

4. Discuss high-temperature (steam) sterilization and sterility assurance monitoring

5. Explain sterilization recordkeeping and documentation requirements

INTRODUCTION

A successful sterilization process depends on a successful preparation process, functioning equipment and the knowledge of the reprocessing technician. The goal is to create a pack (endoscope or accessory) that is free of any living microorganisms. There are several modalities that can be used to **sterilize** medical devices. This chapter will review commonly-used sterilization methods and identify requirements for successful sterilization processes.

> **Sterile** Completely devoid of all living microorganisms.

WHY STERILIZATION?

Although most flexible endoscopes undergo high-level disinfection (HLD), sterilization still plays an important part in the reprocessing of endoscopes and their accessories. To better understand how the selection to disinfect or sterilize is made, a review of the Spaulding Classification System (introduced in Chapter 9) is helpful.

The Spaulding Classification system for medical devices is universally used to determine what type of disinfection or sterilization is appropriate for medical devices. Three classes—critical, semi-critical and non-critical—stratify the risk of infection associated with each device. Endoscopes and their accessories are classified in the critical and semi-critical levels.

Critical devices contact the bloodstream or sterile body tissues and should always be sterilized (e.g., reusable biopsy forceps). Semi-critical devices (e.g., flexible endoscopes) come in contact with mucous membranes or non-intact skin and should be sterilized or receive HLD. High-level disinfection can be used in the reprocessing of semi-critical devices.

As minimally invasive procedures increase, flexible endoscopes begin to divide into two groups: the original classification as semi-critical and a critical designation for flexible endoscopes that enter directly or secondarily (e.g., via a mucous membrane) into sterile tissue and the vascular system. These endoscopes, including bronchoscopes, cystoscopes and duodenoscopes increase the risk of infection

if they are contaminated with microorganisms from a previous procedure when used. Most rigid endoscopes (arthroscopes, laparoscopes, etc.) are classified as critical items and must be sterilized. For those reasons, it is important that anyone reprocessing endoscopes be familiar with the basics of sterilization.

Processes that are appropriate for endoscope sterilization are determined by the endoscope manufacturer and instructions for sterilization are contained in the endoscope's instructions for use (IFU). Endoscope accessories also have IFU and it is important to note that their sterilization instructions may be different from the endoscope that was used with them.

STERILIZATION BASICS

To safely reprocess an endoscope or accessory there are several steps that must be performed correctly. Successful reprocessing of these items must follow sterilization standards and the instructions for use for all the components of the process. That includes the sterilizer, endoscope, packaging, cleaning agents and quality monitors. Cleaning is the first step in this multi-step process; if the endoscope or accessory is not clean when it enters the sterilizer, it will not be sterile even though the sterilizer cycle may indicate that the correct conditions were met.

The Myth of Sterilization

Many people believe that if an item is placed into a sterilizer and a cycle is run, the item will be sterile upon cycle completion. Nothing could be further from the truth! A successful sterilization process requires meticulous preparation (cleaning, inspection, assembly, positioning, packaging and loading) and a functioning sterilizer. Everyone involved in the process must perform their role according to manufacturers' IFU, industry standards and guidelines and the known science of sterilization.

Reprocessing staff performing any sterilization process have two goals: they want to achieve sterility and they want to do so in a manner that will not damage or shorten the life of the device they are sterilizing. The best way to attain those goals is to pay careful attention to detail during all steps of reprocessing. In the decontamination area, that means following the device's IFU and following the IFU of the chemical and equipment manufacturers used during the decontamination procedures. In preparation for sterilization, the device's IFU must be followed, along with the IFU for packaging systems, sterility assurance systems and equipment (sterilizers). Each IFU is developed by the manufacturer of the product or device. The endoscope and accessory manufacturer bases the IFU on a series of specific tests, called validations, that determine the best process to achieve sterility.

Sterilization Failure

Sterilization failures can happen with any type of sterilization process. No matter which modality of sterilization is used, there are many factors that can negatively impact outcomes. The following are some of the factors that can be barriers to successful sterilization:

- **The design of the medical device.** Devices that are dense, complex or have long narrow lumens, such as flexible endoscopes, present a challenge to the sterilization process.

- **The amount and type of soil present.** Soil acts as a shield to protect microorganisms.

- **Sterilizer loading.** Incorrect loading of a device into a sterilizer may cause a sterilization failure.

- **The type and number of microorganisms present.** Large numbers of microorganisms and highly-resistant microorganisms can make successful sterilization difficult.

Some endoscopes and accessory devices have complex designs that make cleaning difficult. Endoscope technicians are familiar with the cleaning challenges posed by endoscopes themselves however, other barriers to consider include types of **endoscope accessories**. The accessories can be very complex and often become grossly soiled during use. (See **Figure 10.1**)

Endoscope accessories Separate devices used with a flexible endoscope. Examples include water bottles, biopsy forceps and basket forceps.

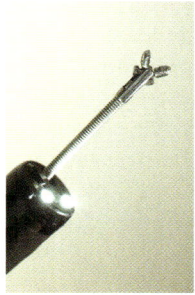 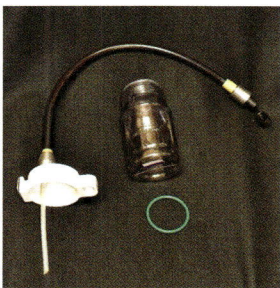

Figure 10.1 Examples of Endoscope Accessories

Figure 10.2 provides an example of the cleaning challenge posed by endoscopy forceps.

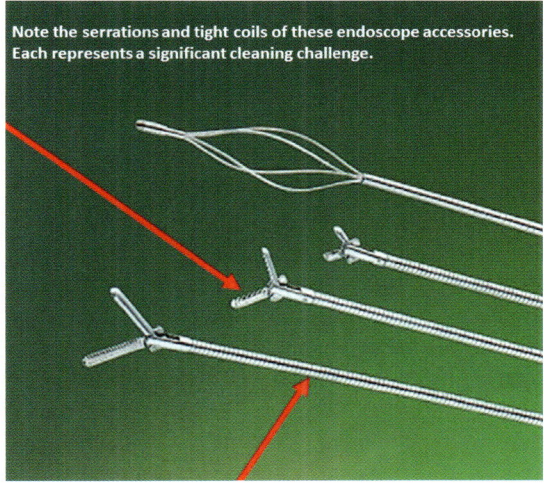

Note the serrations and tight coils of these endoscope accessories. Each represents a significant cleaning challenge.

Figure 10.2

The complexity of these devices underscores the fact that cleaning is the most important step in the sterilization process.

Effective training is another factor in the sterilization process. Before reprocessing an endoscope, an endoscope accessory or operating a sterilizer, it is important to be trained with documented competencies on sterilizer operation.

Preparing Endoscopes and Accessories for Sterilization

No matter which method of sterilization is used, endoscopes and accessories must be properly prepared before sterilization. To be effective, the sterilant must make direct contact with all surfaces of the item(s) being sterilized. For this to occur, all devices must be thoroughly cleaned, rinsed and dried before sterilization. In addition to cleaning used devices, devices that are new or returned from repair should also be cleaned before sterilization. Those devices may appear clean, but may have manufacturing oils and other debris or contamination on their surfaces.

Once a device has been cleaned and dried, it should be inspected and tested as indicated in the IFU. The goal is to ensure that all devices sterilized are clean and functional before sterilization. It is important to remember that the next time the device is handled will be at the start of the procedure and it must be safe and in good working order.

BASIC STERILIZATION PRINCIPLES FOR LOW-TEMPERATURE STERILIZATION AND HIGH-TEMPERATURE PROCESSES

Currently, most flexible endoscopes can only be sterilized with a low-temperature sterilization method. Either a low-temperature method or high-temperature method (steam) may be used to sterilize rigid endoscopes and some accessories. To make the correct selection, it is important to follow the manufacturer's IFU for the specific endoscope and its accessories. *Note: No endoscope should ever be placed in a sterilization process if it has not been validated for that specific endoscope.*

Low-temperature sterilization is typically used to sterilize devices made of heat- and moisture-sensitive materials, such as those with fiber optics or cameras. Many of these devices cannot withstand the heat and moisture associated with steam sterilization. Low-temperature sterilization methods differ in their mode of action and the method chosen is based on the process validated by the device manufacturer.

Each endoscope must be inspected or tested as per instructions. **Figure 10.3** shows a reprocessing technician checking a rigid endoscope to help ensure that there are no issues with visual clarity through the optics. **Figure 10.4** show inspection of the lumens of a flexible endoscope.

Figure 10.3 Checking a Rigid Endoscope for Clarity

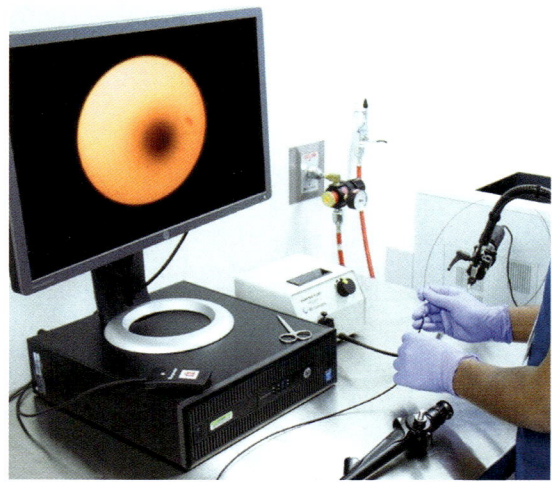

Figure 10.4 Checking a Lumen in a Flexible Endoscope

In general, if a device has more than one part, it should be dissembled. There are, however, some instruments that can be sterilized after being assembled, so it is important to check and follow the endoscope or instrument manufacturer's IFU.

Devices must be dry. This can be accomplished by using clean lint-free towels or filtered, instrument-grade compressed air (previously called medical grade air). *Note: Canned air is not an option as it contains chemicals.*

What is Instrument Air?

Instrument air is a medical gas that falls under the general requirements for medical gases, as defined by the NFPA 99: Health Care Facilities Code; is not respired; is compliant with the ANSI/ISA S- 7.0.01, Quality Standard for Instrument Air; is filtered to 0.01 micron; free of liquids and hydrocarbon vapors; and dry to a dew point of -40o F (-40o C).

No item should be sterilized without written instructions from the manufacturer. That information must be kept on file and readily available to all staff who reprocess the devices.

The sterilizer manufacturer recommends the type of instrument tray or tray/containment device that can be used. Instrument trays have multiple perforations or a mesh bottom. Containment devices house the device within a box-like structure approved for the sterilization method identified. **Figure 10.5** shows an example of one type of instrument tray, while **Figure 10.6** shows one type of rigid containment device.

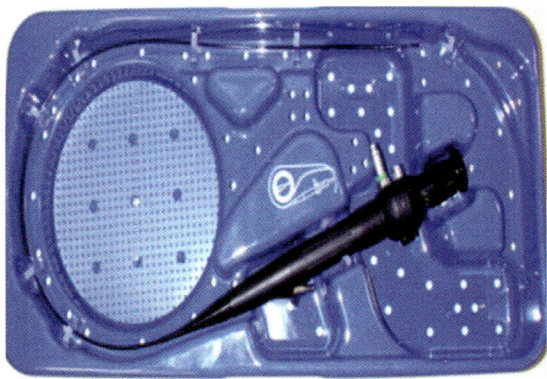

Figure 10.5 Endoscope instrument tray. This type of tray alone does not provide a barrier for contents and must be packaged using a flat wrap.

Additional packaging methods may be used to contain accessory devices. Each form of packaging or containment must be validated for the sterilization method used. Packaging methods may include sterilization containers, flat wrap and peel pouches. (See **Figure 10. 7**) Each method must be used according to the manufacturer's IFU.

Figure 10.6 Containment device (rigid sterilization container). This type of device seals to provide a barrier for contents. The container is the packaging, so it does not require wrapping.

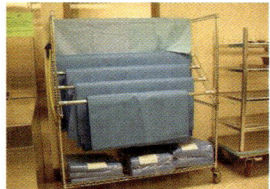

Figure 10.7 Additional types of packaging

When using flat wrappers, (see **Figure 10.7**), it is important to select the correct size wrapper to completely cover the item. There are two types of wrapping methods, either the envelope or the square method. *Note: For additional information on packaging techniques, refer to the packaging manufacturers' IFU.*

When using a flat wrap method, chemical indicator (CI) tape is used to seal the package and create an external indicator. Chemical indicator sterilization tape is designed to change color after the sterilization process to demonstrate that the package was exposed to a specific sterilant. Its main purpose is to help identify processed from unprocessed items. **Figure 10.8** provides an example of a commonly used low-temperature chemical indicator tape. *Note that on this specific indicator tape, the color change when the item has been processed. This only indicates that the item has been exposed to the sterilizing process.* It is not a guarantee that the contents are sterile. Packages that have not had a color change on the external indicator after sterilization must be reprocessed and repackaged.

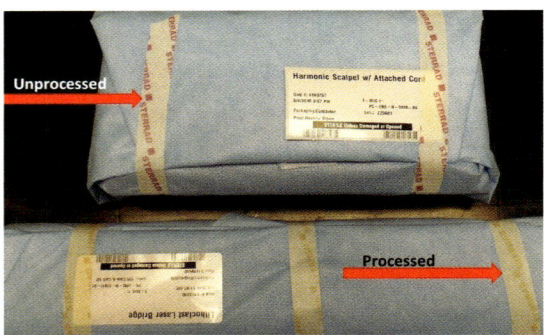

Figure 10.8

The CI tape should be checked after sterilization to ensure that proper processing has occurred. Sterilization tape is an external chemical indictor (CI). All packages that undergo sterilization have external indicators, most external indicators are in the form of CI tape. There are other types of external CIs, such as sterilization container locks and pouch indicators. (See **Figure 10.9**)

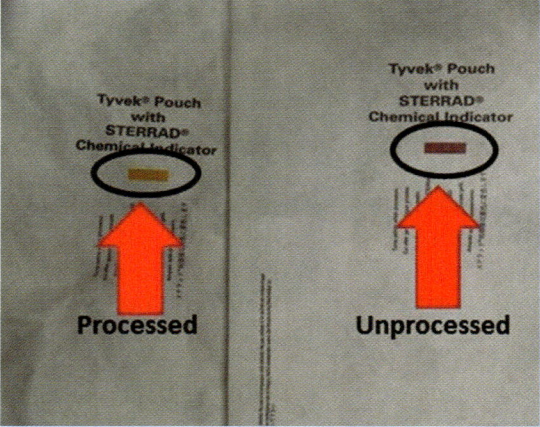

- **These peel pouches are designed to be used with a low-temperature sterilization process.**

- **Their external indicator changes color when exposed to the sterilant.**

Figure 10.9 External Indicators on Peel Pouches.

External package indicators vary with different methods of sterilization. Users should become familiar with the specific products used at their facility.

LOW-TEMPERATURE STERILIZATION

Low-temperature sterilization is used for medical devices that are heat and moisture sensitive. Low-temperature sterilization methods available to healthcare facilities that provide **terminal sterilization** are:

- Ethylene oxide EtO;

- Hydrogen peroxide gas plasma; and

- Vaporized hydrogen peroxide.

Liquid chemical sterilization is also a low-temperature option. However, since items are not packaged, items processed cannot be stored for later use.

> **Terminal sterilization** The process by which medical devices are sterilized in their final containers, allowing them to be stored until needed.

Chemicals used to sterilize instruments have toxic properties, though levels of toxicity and potential for exposure vary widely based on the sterilization method and sterilant used, therefore, personnel using these methods of sterilization must be trained on how to use them safely and effectively. Each sterilization method has advantages and limitations.

Medical devices such as endoscopes and surgical instruments are composed of a variety of materials that may be affected by the chemicals in the sterilants. When medical device manufacturers perform validation testing on their medical devices, some testing is devoted to assuring that the devices are compatible with the sterilization method. In addition, the sterilant must be compatible with the packaging being used. The following sections introduce common sterilization modalities, describe how each works and provide information on how to use each safely.

Terminal Sterilization of Endoscopes with Ethylene Oxide

Ethylene oxide (EtO)* gas is an effective sterilant with good materials compatibility. It is used for heat- and moisture-sensitive medical devices that cannot be steam sterilized. EtO is appropriate for use with flexible and semi-rigid endoscopes as indicated by the endoscope manufacturer's reprocessing validations and instructions for use. EtO, like all other chemical sterilants and disinfectants, must be used safely.

*EO or EtO?

The official acronym for Ethylene Oxide is EO. However, many documents and resources use the previous acronym, EtO. Both are correct and both refer to ethylene oxide.

To assure EtO residuals are removed from the device after EtO sterilization, devices are **aerated**. Aeration is part of the sterilization process during which EtO and/or its reaction products evaporate from the medical device until predetermined safe exposure levels are reached. This can be performed within the sterilizer (required in U.S. healthcare facilities) and/or in a separate chamber or room.

> **Aeration** A process by which sterilized packages are subjected to moving air to facilitate removal of toxic residuals after exposure to a sterilizing agent, such as ethylene oxide.

The EtO systems of today use single-dose cartridges of 100% EtO and have a proven track record of safe and effective use. EtO can be an environmentally sustainable technology with the advancements of pollution emissions control systems that convert EtO to carbon dioxide (CO_2) and water vapor before release in the atmosphere to duly protect our environment. In addition, any EtO that may be released into the environment will biodegrade naturally and is not expected to accumulate in the environment.

Ethylene Oxide Sterilization Cycle

The typical EtO sterilization cycle consists of progressed stages where the chamber is conditioned and load contents are exposed to the sterilant. The sterilant is then exhausted and after the sterilization cycle is complete, an aeration cycle removes any residual EtO from the medical devices per the IFU.

Facility Engineering Controls

the Occupational Safety and Health Administration (OSHA) states, EtO may cause bodily harm if the vapor is inhaled, if it comes into contact with eyes or skin or is ingested. Proper design of EtO sterilization areas will provide increased protection in the workplace as well as promote efficient work flow. All EtO sterilizers should be located in an area that is physically separate from all other work areas. It should be actively ventilated to ensure that under normal conditions, occupational safety requirements are routinely met.

Ethylene Oxide Area Monitors

EtO area monitors measure one point of the immediate environment and are not a replacement for personal (breathing zone) monitoring. While OSHA doesn't require the use of an area monitor, it does require employers to have a method to alert employees to emergency situations. A wall-mounted EtO monitoring system is an effective, practical method of satisfying this requirement. **Figure 10.10** provides an example of an area monitoring system. A detector is placed on the wall near the sterilizer and information is routed to a nearby computer away from the actual sterilization area.

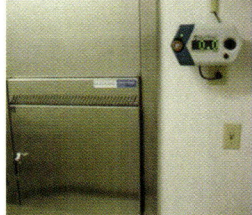 

Figure 10.10 Example of an Area Monitoring System

Preparing Endoscopes for Ethylene Oxide Sterilization

Always follow the endoscope manufacturer's IFU, including endoscope decontamination, cleaning, drying, packaging, sterilization parameters, and aeration.

- Meticulous cleaning is essential to achieve sterilization efficacy. The facility's Quality Assurance (QA) program should include a method to verify that cleaning equipment and processes are working effectively. Cleaning is prone to error and should be monitored.

- Always assure the endoscopes have passed the required leak testing before sterilization. Do not place damaged endoscopes into an EtO sterilization process.

- Always dry the endoscopes per the endoscope manufacturer's recommendations before sterilization and assure there are no pools or droplets of liquid remaining inside the channels of the endoscopes.

- Only sterilize medical devices that are manufactured with materials compatible with EtO sterilization processes.

- Do not sterilize devices with energy sources that could create a spark in the sterilization chamber during the sterilization cycle (e.g., batteries).

Ventilation Adaptors (Ventilation Caps) and Water-Resistant Caps (Soaking Caps)

Some brands and models of endoscopes require connecting a ventilation adapter (ventilation cap) before packaging and EtO sterilization (See **Figures 10.11** and **10.12**).

In some brands and models of endoscopes, failure to vent the endoscope can result in severe damage to the endoscope during the air removal or vacuum phase of the sterilization process. The ventilation adapter opens the endoscope to allow a balance of internal and external pressures during the vacuum phases of the sterilization process. The ventilation adapter can be removed after aeration just prior to use of the device. Never immerse in liquid or soak the endoscope with the ventilation adapter attached, as fluid invasion may severely damage the endoscope.

Always inspect the ventilation adapter before use to ensure the component is free from deterioration, breakage, and clogging. If any abnormality is found, replace it with a new ventilation adapter. Refer to the endoscope manufacturer's IFU for the proper location on the endoscope to connect the ventilation adapter.

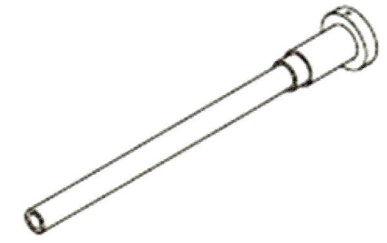

Figure 10.11 Example FUJIFILM® Ventilation Cap

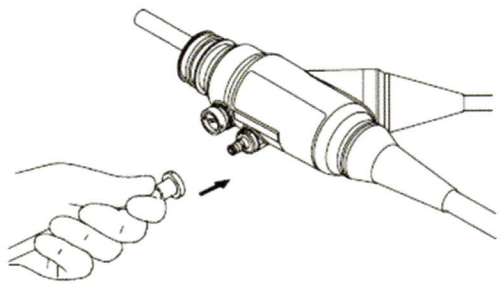

Figure 10.12 Example FUJIFILM® Ventilation Cap Connection

Some brands and models of endoscopes are vented by the removal of the water-resistant cap (soaking cap) before packaging and EtO sterilization (**Figures 10.13** and **10.14**). In some brands and models of endoscopes if the water-resistant cap is attached during sterilization, the air inside the endoscope will expand during the air removal or vacuum stage of the sterilization process which may cause severe damage to the endoscope.

The water-resistant cap is attached to the electrical connector on the endoscope to protect the connector from water penetration during reprocessing. Refer to the endoscope manufacturer's IFU to determine if the water-resistant cap must be removed before sterilization.

Figure 10.13 Example OLYMPUS® Water-Resistant Cap

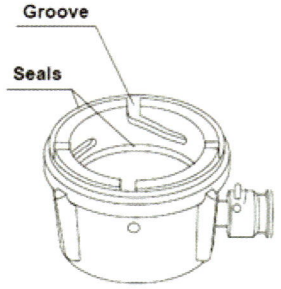

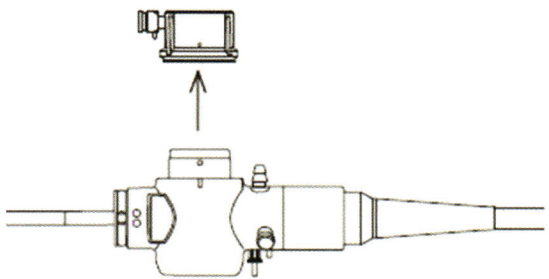

Figure 10.14 Example Removal OLYMPUS® Water-Resistant Cap for Sterilization

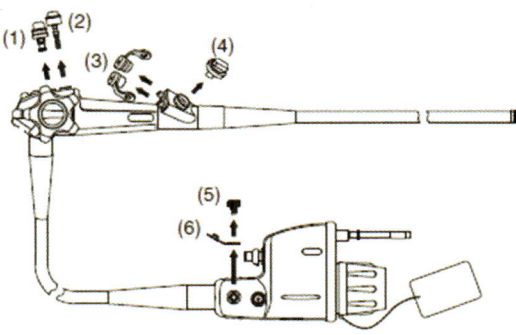

Figure 10.16 Example PENTAX® Removal of Subparts or Components before Packaging and Sterilization

Some brands and models of endoscopes require both REMOVING water-resistant caps (soaking caps) AND the connection of a ventilation adaptor (vent cap) before packaging and EtO sterilization. (See **Figure 10.15**) Always refer to the endoscope manufacturer's IFU to determine if the water-resistant cap must be removed before sterilization and to identify the proper location on the endoscope to connect the ventilation adapter.

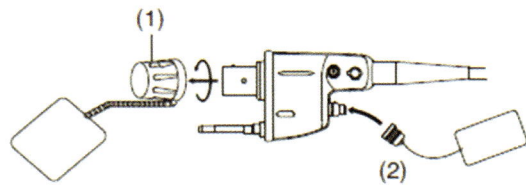

Figure 10.15 Example PENTAX® (1) Removal of Soaking Cap and (2) Connection of Ventilation Cap

Removal of Subparts or Components before Packaging and Sterilization.

Some brands and models of endoscopes require the removal of subparts or components before packaging and sterilization. (See **Figure 10.16**) Always refer to the endoscope manufacturer's IFU to determine what components or subparts (if any) should be removed from the endoscope before packaging and sterilization. Refer to the endoscope manufacturer's IFU to determine how the components or subparts are to be packaged and sterilized.

Preconditioning (Humidification)

The moisture levels in the materials, devices and packaging can significantly affect the EtO sterilization process. It is advisable to maintain relative humidity in the range of 35% to 60% throughout the preparation, processing, and storage areas. Visible moisture should be dried or wiped from the device before packaging. Porous and moisture-absorbent items should not be dried by heated forced air. Certain items might require special preconditioning procedures; the endoscope manufacturer should be consulted for instructions. Although the recommended humidity range for all work areas is 30% to 60%, ideal relative humidity in processing areas for EtO sterilization is 50% and should not be less than 35% for best results in achieving sterilization.

Packaging Endoscopes for Ethylene Oxide Sterilization

Each facility should identify appropriate packaging procedures with the endoscope manufacturer to ensure the endoscopes are suitably packaged in regards to endoscope positioning and bending radius inside the packaging system the facility chooses to use. (See **Figure 10.17**) Including the factors noted above, there are many options available to optimize packaging and the load configuration for endoscopes (e.g., number of endoscopes placed in the chamber).

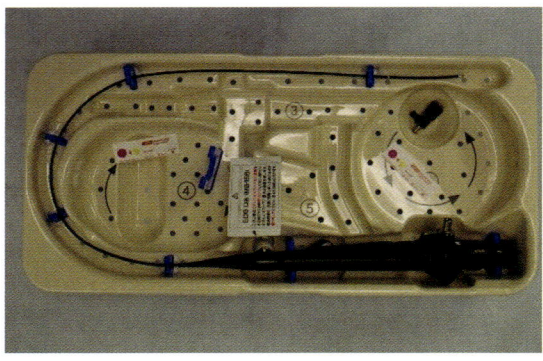

Figure 10.17 Molded Trays - Endoscope Manufacturer to Verify Acceptable Bending Radius

Using Proper Packaging Materials for Ethylene Oxide Sterilization

Non-compatible packaging may compromise the sterility of the processed devices. There is a large variety of packaging that is compatible for use in EtO sterilization. Use packaging that has been cleared by the FDA for processing in EtO sterilization and follow the packaging manufacturer's IFU.

The following packaging types have been recommended for use with EtO sterilization:

- Polyethylene plastic bags (designed for use as a sterile package and are not more than 5 mils thick)

- Peel pouches:

  › Spun-bonded olefin polyethylene-polyester laminate;

  › Paper/polyethylene-polyester laminate; and

  › Paper/polypropylene-polyester laminate.

- Wraps:

  › Woven textile;

  › Nonwoven textile;

  › Nonwoven polypropylene;

  › Paper, coated and uncoated;

- Rigid sterilization container systems;

- Plastic trays with paper or spun-bonded olefin lids; and

- Muslin.

Ethylene Oxide Package labels

Package labels (e.g., process indicators, labels for product identification and lot number, expiration statement labels) should remain securely affixed to packages throughout the course of their handling, from sterilization to use. If a marking pen is used to label paper–plastic pouches, the labeling information should be written only on the plastic side of the pouch. If a marking pen is used to label wrapped packs, the ink should be nontoxic, and the labeling information should be written on the indicator tape or affixed labels.

Loading the Ethylene Oxide Sterilizer

Always use loading baskets or racks when loading an EtO sterilizer. Do not overload the chamber. Arrange items in loading baskets to ensure water vapor and EtO can circulate freely between them. Place peel pouches on their edges. Arrange sterilization pouches so that the transparent side of a pouch faces the opaque side of the adjacent pouch. Ensure no devices are touching the sterilizer chamber walls. **Figure 10.18** provides an example of using baskets to help ensure that packages do not touch chamber walls.

To the extent practical, sterilize full loads consisting of items having a common aeration time. A full load can be comprised of sterilization pouches, wrapped trays, and rigid containers or a combination of various packs. Full load definition means the maximum number of items that does not impede proper air removal, humidification of the load, or sterilant penetration and evacuation in the sterilization unit (ref. 40 CFR 63.10448).

In the U.S., the Environmental Protection Agency (EPA) National Emission Standards for Hospital Ethylene Oxide Sterilizers requires hospitals that do not have an air pollution control device to adopt the management practice of running full loads except under medically necessary circumstances. The date and time of all EtO sterilization cycles should be documented and any loads not containing a full load for medically necessary reasons should be noted.

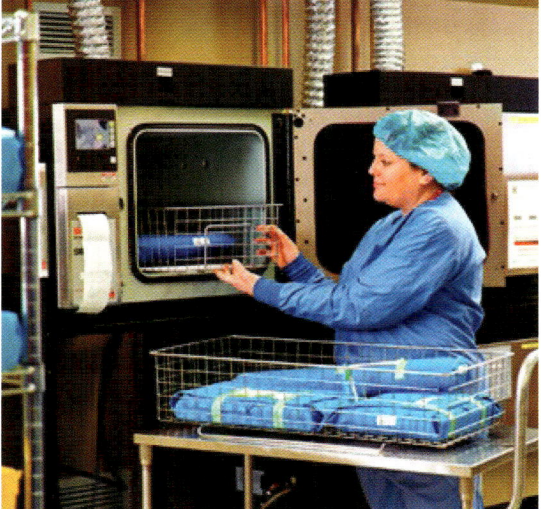

Figure 10.18 Example of Good Loading Practices

Operation of the Ethylene Oxide Sterilizer

It is the user facility management's responsibility to ensure that all personnel who operate or maintain the EtO sterilization equipment are trained in its operation and safe use. In addition, it is the user facility management's responsibility to ensure safety inspections are complete on the sterilizer before routine use. Contact your service personnel for required safety inspections.

The responsibility for EtO sterilization should be assigned to qualified individuals who have demonstrated competence in all aspects of device reprocessing: decontamination, preparation, packaging, sterilization, sterile storage, and distribution of sterile medical devices.

Before operating any sterilization equipment, read and always follow the procedures described in the manufacturer's Operator's Manual. Warnings and precautions should be observed to avoid unsafe actions that could result in personal injury or damage to the sterilizer or medical devices.

The critical process parameters for ethylene oxide sterilization include four parameters:

1. Cycle temperature;

2. Relative humidity (RH) at the end of conditioning;

3. EtO gas exposure time; and

4. EtO concentration.

Other process variables listed in the endoscope manufacturer's IFU typically are not the critical process variables routinely verified for the safe and effective use of ethylene oxide sterilization.

These other variables (e.g., conditioning pressure) are routinely controlled and monitored by the sterilizer to assure the four critical process parameters are consistently achieved. The performance of these non-critical parameters can vary slightly between sterilizer models, facilities, environmental factors and between load configurations. Always follow the endoscope manufacturer's critical process parameters for EtO sterilization.

Unloading the Sterilizer

Do not remove the load from the sterilizer until the total elapsed aeration time meets or exceeds the aeration time specified by the endoscope and packaging manufacturers' IFU. The U.S. EPA requires U.S. healthcare facilities to complete full aeration within the sterilizer chamber (single-chamber process) prior to transferring the load. This practice eliminates the potential for EtO exposure that might occur if the load were transferred to a separate aeration chamber prior to full aeration.

If it is necessary to access the chamber during the aeration stage, for example, to remove a biological indicator process challenge device (BI PCD), routine biological indicator (BI) test pack, an item that requires minimal aeration, take all precautions to minimize exposure to EtO. In the US the chamber should be locked so technicians are unable to retrieve unless the cycle is aborted as soon as possible to limit outgassing of into the sterilizer room. When it is necessary to handle individually packaged items that are not fully aerated, butyl, neoprene or nitrile gloves should be worn. The breathing zone of personnel should be monitored to verify the safety of the practices followed. Additional information can be found at www.osha.gov (section on Health and Safety of Ethylene Oxide).

Sterilization Documentation

For each cycle the following information must be recorded and maintained:

- Lot number, including sterilizer ID and cycle number;

- Time of day load was run;

- Specific contents of the load (noting implants);

- Exposure time and temperature;

- Name or initials of operator;

- Aeration time and temperature;

- Results of BI;

- Results of internal CI in BI PCD; and

- Any reports of CIs that did not turn color, as required.

The sterilizer cycle report or printout of the sterilizer physical parameters typically contain some of this information and is an acceptable record for the required documentation. Some sterilizer printers use paper where the print will fade over time. Photocopy, scan or electronically export these cycle reports for long-term storage.

Performance Monitoring and Routine Load Release

Always use chemical indicators (CI) and biological indicators (BI) for routine monitoring of the performance of the EtO sterilization cycles, as described in the sterilizer manufacturers Operator's Manual and as part of the recommended Quality Control program. Always use CIs and BIs per the manufacturer's IFU.

Monitoring recommendations for routine load release per ANSI/AAMI ST41:2008 (R)2012 (1) include:

- User verification of the physical parameters reported on the cycle report (i.e. print-out or electronic file); Do not use sterilizers that do not have a verifiable cycle report;

- Use of external and internal CI within each package, tray or containment device. ANSI/AAMI ST41:2008 (R)2012 (1) recommends the use of a Class 1 process indicator for external CIs. For internal CIs, Class 4 multi-variable or Class 5 integrating indicator CIs are recommended; and

- Use a BI PCD for every load, either the routine test pack described in ANSI/AAMI ST41:2008 (R)2012, or a commercially available equivalent. The BI PCD "should be placed in the area of the chamber and load that is considered to be least favorable to sterilization (usually the center of the load unless otherwise indicated by the sterilizer manufacturer)" (See **Figure 10.19**).

Figure 10.19 Placement of BI PCD in Center of the Load

In addition to verifying satisfactory results for all monitoring tools, load release should include verification that the prescribed aeration time is complete. Furthermore, any "packages containing implants should be quarantined until the results of the BI testing (early readout or spore growth) are available."

Device Use

The endoscope manufacturer validates the device is safe for patient use with EtO sterilization process parameters and aeration conditions supplied in the IFU. After the total aeration time is fulfilled, quality control monitoring tools are found acceptable and documented per facility policy, and sterilizer documentation and records are complete, the device is ready for patient use or sterile storage.

Health and Safety of Ethylene Oxide

The human body has several natural defenses to protect from contaminants in the air. Large particulates are trapped by nose, throat, and lungs. Absorbed gases and vapors are detoxified, metabolized, and eliminated. When chemical levels are above the Occupational Exposure Limits (OEL), there is a possibility that a body's natural defenses may be overcome.

Users of EtO, including those in healthcare, must follow the requirements of OSHA's occupational exposure standard for EtO (29 CFR 1910.1047). Commonly referenced sections of the standard include those on exposure limits, employee exposure monitoring, emergency planning, and employee training. Per 29 CFR 1910.1047 Subpart A, ethylene oxide may cause bodily harm if the vapor is inhaled, if it comes into contact with eyes or skin or is ingested.

Conduct personal breathing zone monitoring by having employees wear a clip-on, passive EtO monitor in their breathing zone for a specified period of time (See **Figure 10.20**) The monitor is then sent to a lab for analysis. This personal breathing zone monitoring is not accomplished by EtO area monitors which, OSHA clarifies, are used to detect leaks or spills.

A written plan for emergency situations is also a required element of the OSHA standard. Please reference the OSHA standard for more details required of the written plan for emergency situations.

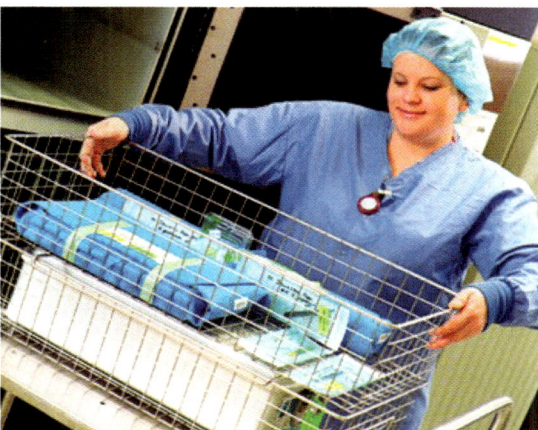

Figure 10.20 Example of Proper Placement for an EtO Monitoring Badge

Ethylene Oxide Resources

This section has provided an overview of ethylene oxide sterilization. Detailed information on EtO sterilization standards can be found in *ANSI/AAMI ST41: 2008 (R) 2012, Ethylene oxide sterilization in health care facilities: Safety and effectiveness.*

Additional information on EtO safety can be found at: https://www.osha.gov/SLTC/etools/hospital/central/central.html#exposuretoethyleneoxidegas.

Hydrogen Peroxide Sterilization Systems

There are different types of hydrogen peroxide low-temperature sterilization systems. While they have some similarities, there are also differences. Hydrogen peroxide is a highly effective oxidizing agent that affects sterilization by oxidation of key microbial cell components.

Hydrogen Peroxide Gas Plasma

Hydrogen peroxide gas plasma (using a hydrogen peroxide solution ranging from 59–95% for the sterilization cycle) is proven effective at killing microorganisms. Plasma is a state of matter different than solids, liquids or gases. Gas plasmas are highly ionized gasses, composed of ions, electrons and neutral particles that produce a visible glow. Hydrogen peroxide is a contact sterilant. As is true for all sterilization methods, it is important to check the medical device and scope IFU before using this sterilization method. Instrument designs, such as lumen diameter and length, must be considered to ensure adequate gas plasma penetration and efficacy for the various cycle parameters. Sterilization times vary from 24 minutes to 75 minutes. **Figure 10.21** provides an example of a hydrogen peroxide gas plasma system.

Figure 10.21

Sterilization Cycle Phases

The phases of hydrogen peroxide gas plasma include:

Vacuum. The load is heated while the vacuum system removes any remaining water as it evaporates. Air is removed from the chamber and packages until the pressure is reduced to below atmospheric pressure.

Injection. Once the correct pressure has been reached, a pre-measured amount of concentrated hydrogen peroxide is pumped from a cassette into the vaporizer bowl and vaporized into the chamber.

Diffusion. The diffusion stage drives hydrogen peroxide vapor into the small crevices and lumens of devices. The chamber returns to atmospheric pressure in order to accomplish this.

Plasma. A vacuum decreases the pressure and radio frequency (RF) energy is radiated within the chamber from an electrode screen. The RF energy ionizes the hydrogen peroxide, creating hydrogen peroxide gas plasma and the generation of free radicals and other chemical species. When the power is turned off, the radicals combine to form oxygen and water, reducing the potential for residuals. The injection/plasma phases are repeated a second time.

Vent. At the end of the second plasma sequence, the RF is turned off. Air is then vented into the chamber through bacterial-trapping HEPA filters, returning it to atmospheric pressure. The process byproducts are only water vapor and oxygen. No aeration is required.

OSHA regulations require that operators demonstrate competence in all parameters of hydrogen peroxide gas plasma sterilization.

Concentrated hydrogen peroxide liquid can irritate skin and, like other oxidants, is damaging to eyes if direct contact occurs. In the vapor phase, concentrated hydrogen peroxide is irritating to the eyes, nose, throat and lungs; however, several safeguards are built into hydrogen peroxide sterilizers to prevent personnel from contacting hydrogen peroxide in either the liquid or vapor phase.

The hydrogen peroxide is packaged in sealed cassettes with chemical leak indicators on each side of the package, which change from yellow or white to red when exposed to liquid or vapor hydrogen peroxide. The leak indicator is visible through a clear plastic over-wrap to protect personnel handling the cassette. (See **Figure 10.22**) Once the cassette has been placed in the sterilizer, it is automatically advanced by the machine, eliminating any danger of exposure to liquid hydrogen peroxide through handling of the cassette. After the cassette is empty, the cassette is automatically ejected into a collection box for safe disposal. To avoid exposure to hydrogen peroxide when removing items from a cancelled cycle, personnel wear latex, PVC (vinyl) or nitrile gloves. As with any chemical used for sterilization, healthcare workers should consult the Safety Data Sheet (SDS), follow all manufacturers' recommendations and department procedures.

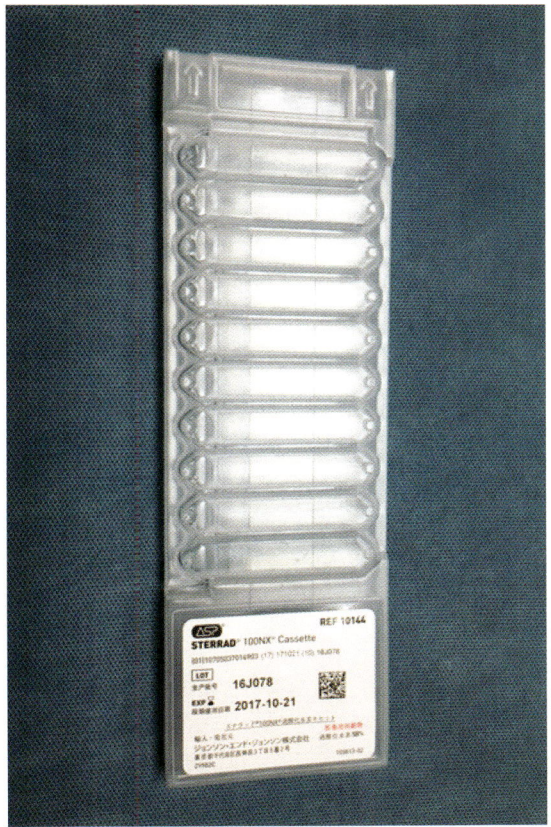

Figure 10.22

Using Proper Packaging Materials for Hydrogen Peroxide Gas Plasma Sterilization

Packaging materials can affect the penetration of hydrogen peroxide. Packaging materials used in the sterilizers should be designed to optimize diffusion of the hydrogen peroxide and not interfere with the radio frequency energy or absorb hydrogen peroxide. Trays and container systems from the sterilizer manufacturer and Tyvek pouches are compatible. Check with tray and sterilizer manufacturers before purchase and use of containers.

Cellulose-containing packaging materials, such as paper/plastic pouches, cellulose-based (paper) disposable wrappers, and muslin (cotton) wraps, should not be used with hydrogen peroxide gas plasma sterilizers because they absorb the peroxide and inhibit effective penetration of the sterilant.

The chamber should not be overloaded. As with other low-temperature sterilization technologies, hydrogen peroxide gas plasma sterilizers must be properly loaded for effective sterilization. If the available amount of hydrogen peroxide is reduced because it reacts or is absorbed before reaching all surfaces, a sterilization failure could occur.

Excess moisture remaining on devices can cause the cycle to abort. Consult manufacturer's IFU for suggested drying methods.

Sterilization Documentation for Hydrogen Peroxide Gas Plasma Sterilization

For each cycle, record and maintain the following information:

- Lot number, including sterilizer ID and cycle number;

- Time of day load was run;

- Specific contents of the load;

- Cycle;

- Name or initials of operator;

- Results of BI, if applicable; and

- Results of internal CI in BI PCD, if applicable.

The sterilizer cycle report or a printout of the sterilizer physical parameters typically contain some of this information and is an acceptable record for the required documentation. Some sterilizer printers use a type of printing that will fade over time. Photocopy, scan or electronically export these cycle reports for long-term storage.

Health and Safety for Hydrogen Peroxide Gas Plasma Sterilization

To minimize hydrogen peroxide risks, employees should be instructed about:

- Hazards of hydrogen peroxide;

- Storage, handling, and disposal of hydrogen peroxide cassettes;

- Handling cancelled cycles;

- Applicable OSHA standards;

- The use of personal protective equipment;

- Applicable Safety Data Sheets (SDS); and

- Recommendations for routine maintenance.

Exposure Monitoring

No personal or area monitors are required for hydrogen peroxide gas plasma sterilization systems. Monitoring of the area around the systems during operation has demonstrated that the concentration of hydrogen peroxide in the atmosphere is less than the OSHA-established limit of 1 ppm, 8-hour time weighted average

Vaporized Hydrogen Peroxide (VHP)

Low-temperature vaporized hydrogen peroxide (VHP) sterilization, utilizes an oxidative process and provides a rapid cycle time that improves the throughput of medical devices and surgical instruments. VPH is a contact sterilant. **Figure 10.23** provides an example of a VHP sterilizer.

There are two types of VHP sterilizers available for use. One system has a single, pre-programmed, 55-minute sterilization cycle for use with both lumened and non-lumened instruments and devices. The second system offers two pre-programmed cycles—a 28-minute cycle for non-lumened instruments including instruments with stainless steel diffusion restricted spaces, such as the hinged portion of forceps and scissors, and a 55-minute cycle used to sterilize instruments with lumens and non-stainless steel mated surfaces. The manufacturer's IFU provides details on instrumentation that can be processed in both systems and cycle types.

Figure 10.23

The sterilization cycle of VHP systems operates at low pressure and temperature. The hydrogen peroxide vapor is generated by injecting aqueous hydrogen peroxide into a vaporization chamber, where the solution is heated and converted to a vapor, and then introduced into the sterilizer chamber under negative pressure. **Figure 10.24** provides an example of a single-dose cup of Hydrogen Peroxide solution.

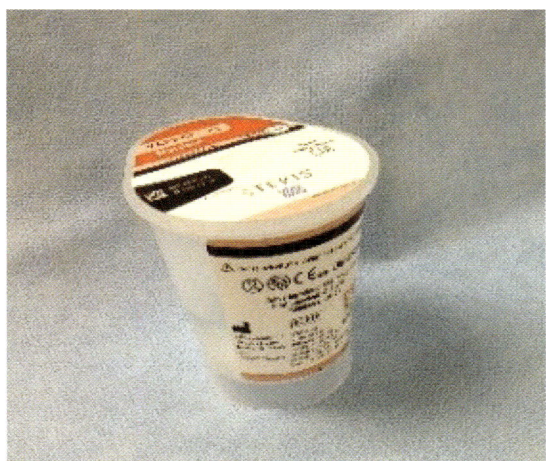

Figure 10.24

The phases of VHP systems include:

Conditioning. To remove air and excess moisture from the chamber and packaging, and to equilibrate product temperature, the chamber is evacuated and then recharged with dry, sterile air.

Leak test. Vacuum is held to assure a leak-tight chamber.

Sterilization. To enhance penetration, hydrogen peroxide vapor is injected into the chamber by a series of four pulses, each followed by a hold period.

Aeration. After completion of the last VHP injection hold period, the load is automatically aerated in the sterilizer. The chamber VHP is exhausted through a catalytic converter that decomposes the VHP to water and oxygen. No special venting is required.

Packaging Items for Vaporized Hydrogen Peroxide Sterilization

Packaging materials approved for use with VHP sterilization include polywrap, a nonwoven sterilization packaging made of 100% polypropylene. Tyvek also has been validated for use with VHP systems. Trays and organizers are available from the manufacturer that allow gas penetration and are compatible with the VHP process.

Sterilizer Performance Monitors

VHP sterilizers should be monitored with physical performance records, CIs and BIs. As previously stated, none of these indicators provide conclusive evidence of device sterility by themselves; however, when used in combination, they provide a high degree of sterility assurance.

Sterilizer performance monitors include:

- *Physical monitors*. Vaporized hydrogen peroxide sterilizers operate on fixed automatic cycles controlled by a microprocessor and are designed and validated to independently monitor key process cycle parameters;

- *Chemical indicators*. CI strips for VHP sterilization change color when exposed to the VHP process. They should be used in each pouch, pack or tray as a process indicator to show that items have completed a cycle; and

- *Biological indicators*. BIs are used for periodic biological monitoring of the VHP process. The microorganism of choice for VHP is the *Geobacillus stearothermophilus* spore. Biological monitoring is required each day the sterilizer is used, but recommended every cycle. Follow the sterilizer manufacturer's IFU for proper BI placement.

Sterilization Documentation for Vaporized Hydrogen Peroxide Sterilization

For each cycle, record and maintain the following information:

- Lot number, including sterilizer identification and cycle number;

- Time of day load was run;

- Specific contents of the load;

- Cycle;

- Name or initials of operator;

- Results BI, if applicable; and

- Results of CI, if applicable.

The sterilizer cycle report or printout of the sterilizer physical process parameters typically contain some of this information. Both are acceptable records for the required documentation. The print from some sterilizer printers will fade over time. Photocopy, scan or electronically export these cycle reports for long-term storage.

Health and Safety for Vaporized Hydrogen Peroxide

OSHA regulations require that operators demonstrate competence in all parameters of VHP sterilization. Personnel should use good work practices when working with all chemicals. This is true for VHP, which uses concentrated hydrogen peroxide. Concentrated hydrogen peroxide is corrosive to skin, eyes, nose, throat, lungs and the gastrointestinal tract. Under normal conditions of use, the VHP sterilizer operator is not exposed to the contents of the sterilant container. The sterilizer automatically dispenses and injects LHP into the chamber, and at the end of each sterilization pulse, hydrogen peroxide vapor is automatically removed from the chamber and converted to water and oxygen. An aeration phase facilitates the removal of hydrogen peroxide residuals from instruments and packaging. To avoid exposure to hydrogen peroxide when removing items from a cancelled cycle, central service technicians should always wear latex, PVC (vinyl)or nitrile gloves.

To minimize risks, employees should be instructed about:

- Hazards of hydrogen peroxide;

- Applicable safety data sheets (SDSs);

- Handling cancelled loads;

- Applicable OSHA standards;

- The use of personal protective equipment; and

- Storage, handling and disposal of hydrogen peroxide cartridges.

Exposure Monitoring

No personal or area monitors are required. Testing to check for hydrogen peroxide vapors in the environment around the sterilizer has shown acceptable VHP levels during typical sterilization cycle conditions. The levels were >20 times lower than the OSHA hydrogen peroxide gas Time-weighted average (TWA) limit of 1 ppm. Users should consult the SDS to better understand safe handling practices.

When unloading a low-temperature sterilizer, the packs are warmer than ambient air temperatures. Care is needed to ensure that they are moved out of the sterilizer to an appropriate cool down area. Placing the items or sets on an open wire rack in a room with proper temperature and humidity before transportation and storage is important.

LIQUID CHEMICAL STERILIZATION (LCS)

Liquid chemical sterilization (LCS) is used for heat-sensitive items that are moisture resistant. LCS is sometimes used for reprocessing flexible endoscopes. Mechanical liquid sterilization processors require that the endoscope be connected to the device to facilitate the proper flow of sterilant through the endoscope channels. The cycles use individual dose sterilant packs and highly filtered water, which is flushed through and around the endoscope during the cycle.

LCS is a liquid process, so no packaging is used. (See **Figure 10.25**) The items being processed must be placed in a tray that is designed for the medical device and the process.

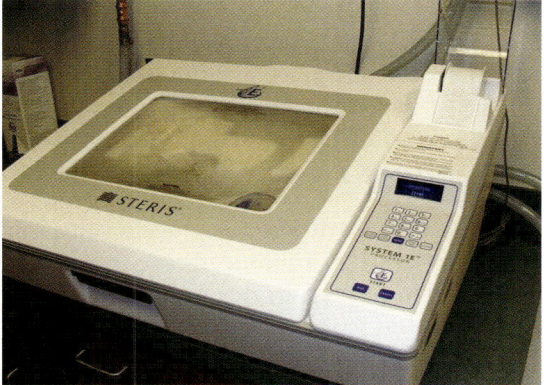

Figure 10.25 Example of a Liquid Chemical Sterilization Device

Documentation for Liquid Chemical Sterilization

For each cycle, record and maintain the following information:

- Cycle number;

- Load number;

- Date;

- Time;

- Item processed;

- Patient identification;

- CI results;

- Review of cycle printout; and

- Technician releasing items for use.

HIGH-TEMPERATURE STERILIZATION

Steam sterilizers all use a combination of air removal, steam and time to accomplish sterilization. They can range in size from tabletop size to floor load units. (See **Figure 10.26**) Steam sterilizers differ in design and operating characteristics, so the specific sterilizer manufacturer's written instructions should always be carefully followed. The following is a review of steam sterilizer types and requirements.

Figure 10.26 Floor Loading Steam Sterilizer.

Note: At this time, flexible endoscopes cannot be sterilized in steam sterilization processes, however, some accessories and many rigid endoscopes are approved for steam sterilization.

Gravity Air Displacement Sterilizers

In a gravity displacement sterilizer, steam enters the chamber and displaces the air. Steam is lighter than air, so as the steam enters the sterilizer chamber, it rises to the top and forces the cooler air to the bottom of the chamber and out the drain. Steam then fills the chamber.

There are limitations to gravity sterilization. Lumens, such as needles and tubing, pose a challenge to sterilant penetration, especially in certain types of gravity-displacement cycles, because they restrict diffusion.

Dynamic Air Removal Sterilizers

Dynamic air removal sterilizers are very similar in construction to gravity air displacement sterilizers, except that a vacuum pump or water ejector is used to remove air during the preconditioning phase prior to reaching the exposure temperature.

Dynamic air removal sterilizers have different types of preconditioning methods for air removal. There are prevacuum steam sterilizers and steam-flush pressure-pulse (SFPP). The preconditioning cycle is used to remove air from both the sterilizing chamber and the load before the chamber is pressurized with steam to a sterilizing exposure temperature. Effective air removal is critical to steam penetration.

Prevacuum Steam Sterilizers

In prevacuum steam sterilizers, the dynamic air removal cycle depends on one or more pressure and vacuum excursions at the beginning of the cycle to remove air during the preconditioning phase with pressure and vacuum pulses. Typical operating temperatures are 250°F to 253°F (121°C to 123°C) and 270°F to 275°F (132°C to 135°C).

To ensure the removal of air in prevacuum sterilizers, the integrity should be checked daily by processing a **Bowie-Dick (or Daily Air Removal) test**.

> **Bowie-Dick (or daily air removal) test** Test run daily to verify the vacuum cycle of a steam sterilizer. The test should be run in an empty load at the same time each day.

Steam-Flush Pressure-Pulse Sterilizers

SFPP sterilizers use a repeated sequence of a steam flush and a pressure pulse to remove air from the sterilizing chamber and processed materials. Air removal occurs above atmospheric pressure; no vacuum is required. Vacuum pulsing is not used because a series of steam pressure pulses forces air out the drain in a manner similar to that of air removal systems. Like a pre-vacuum sterilizer, this process rapidly removes air from the sterilizer's chamber and wrapped items.

Loading a Steam Sterilizer

When loading a sterilizer, packages must be positioned for complete sterilant contact and removal; the items should be loaded to facilitate air circulation and removal. The basic procedures for loading a sterilizer are to leave enough space for the sterilant to circulate. As the cart or shelf is being loaded, there should be visible space between packs to allow sterilant exposure. Instruments trays should have perforated bottoms that are placed flat on the shelf. (See **Figure 10.27**) Paper/plastic peel pouches should be placed on edge using a basket or rack. (See **Figure 10.28**) Placing them plastic side down may cause moisture to remain inside, and placing them plastic side up may cause water to stand on top of the plastic. Place them so that the sterilization pouches are placed paper-to-plastic for air and sterilant circulation.

Figure 10.27

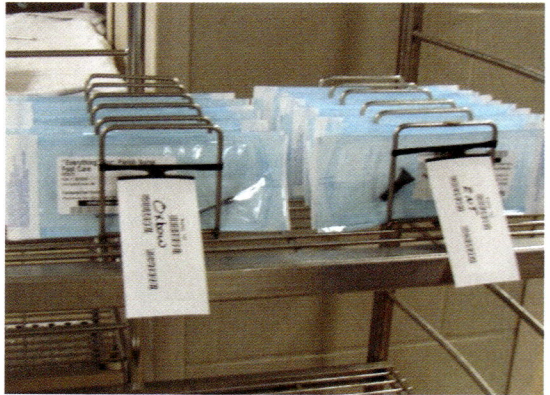

Figure 10.28

The sterilization cycle selection is based on the items undergoing sterilization. Both the sterilizer and endoscope or instrument IFU governs the cycle selection. The sterilizer IFU provides direction on how to operate the sterilizer.

All items that are placed in the sterilizer are recorded and the records are maintained. Recordkeeping for items undergoing sterilization includes the following:

- Date and time of the sterilizer load control number (sometimes called the lot number), which includes sterilizer information;

- Specific items sterilized, including quantity, department and item description (e.g., cystoscope, 2 Mayo Scissors);

- Exposure time and temperature;

- Sterilizer operator identification;

- BI results, if applicable; and

- CI results if a PCD is used.

Steam Sterilization Resource

This section has provided an overview of steam sterilization methods. Detailed information on steam sterilization standards can be found in ANSI/AAMI ST79: 2010 & A1:2010 & A2:2011, A3:2012, A4:2013, *Comprehensive guide to steam sterilization and sterility assurance in health care facilities.*

CONCLUSION:

Achieving sterilization can only be accomplished if all steps have been followed. There are no shortcuts to successful sterilization. It is imperative to follow the manufacturer's IFU provided by the endoscope and other medical device manufacturers, sterilizer, package and quality control devices, in conjunction with best practices. Following all the necessary steps is required when sterilizing any endoscope or endoscope accessory.

RESOURCES

ANSI/AAMI ST79:2010 & A1:2010 & A2:2011, A3:2012, A4:2013 *Comprehensive guide to steam sterilization and sterility assurance in health care facilities.*

International Association of Healthcare Central Service Materiel Management. *Central service technical manual. 7th ed.* Chicago: IAHCSMM, 2007.

International Association of Healthcare Central Service Materiel Management. *Central Service Technical Manual. 8th ed.* Chicago: IAHCSMM, 2016.

Occupational Safety and Health Administration (OSHA) United States Occupational Exposure Standard for Ethylene Oxide OSHA (29 CFR 1910.1047).

International Association of Healthcare Central Service Materiel Management. IAHCSMM, Lesson Plan CRCST 138 Low-Temperature Sterilization

Association for the Advancement of Medical Instrumentation ANSI/AAMI ST91: 2015 *Flexible and semi-rigid endoscope reprocessing in health care facilities.*

U.S. Environmental Protection Agency. Fact Sheet: Hospitals and Healthcare Facilities Must Use a Single-Chamber when Sterilizing Medical Equipment with ETO. March 2010. http://www.epa.gov/pesticides/reregistration/ethylene_oxide/ethylene_oxide_fs.html.

Federal Register / Vol. 72, No. 248 / Friday, December 28, 2007/ Rules and Regulations. Environmental Protection Agency. 40 CFR Part 63: *National Emission Standards for Hospital Ethylene Oxide Sterilizers.*

TERMS

Sterile

Endoscope accessories

Terminal sterilization

Aeration

Bowie Dick (air removal) test

Chapter 11

Endoscope Handling, Storage and Transport

Learning Objectives

Upon completion of this chapter, readers will be able to:

1. Describe proper handling procedures for flexible endoscopes

2. Explain considerations for proper endoscope transport

3. Describe the requirements for proper endoscope storage conditions

4. Identify factors that influence the expiration date (or" hang time") of a high-level disinfected device

5. Discuss proper storage requirements for sterilized endoscopes and their accessories

INTRODUCTION

As stated numerous times throughout this text, flexible endoscopes are delicate devices. Great care and attention to detail is needed to help ensure endoscopes remain in good working condition and are free from harmful microorganisms—from the time they are reprocessed, until they are used in a procedure.

Significant effort and energy goes into the reprocessing of flexible endoscopes, and specific steps must be diligently and consistently followed when storing the devices and transporting them to the user area. This chapter will outline proper handling, storage and transport requirements for flexible endoscopes.

ENDOSCOPE HANDLING

Endoscopes are complex medical devices capable of saving lives; however, patient lives can also be placed at risk if endoscopes are not properly cared for in-between uses. Each time a flexible endoscope is handled, care must be taken to ensure the device is not damaged. Rough handling may cause damage that can go undetected until the endoscope is placed into use. Flexible endoscopes should be handled gently during all phases of reprocessing. Damage may occur when flexible endoscopes are coiled too tightly, transported incorrectly, dropped or crushed by other equipment, or otherwise handled in a rough or careless manner. **Figure 11.1** provides an example of an endoscope properly coiled for transport.

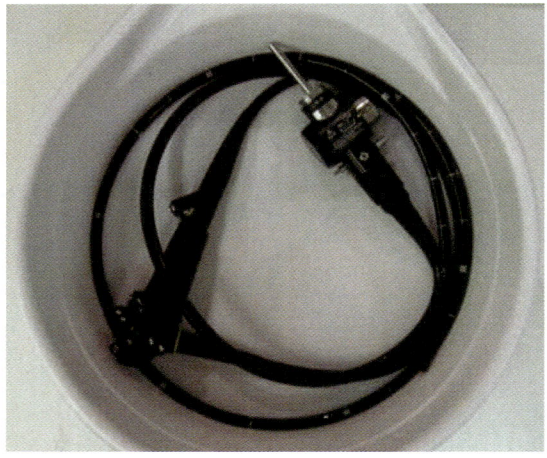

Figure 11.1

When transporting a flexible endoscope by hand, it is important to always carry it by the control head and support the insertion tube and connectors. (See **Figure 11.2**) A flexible endoscope should never be carried by the insertion tube.

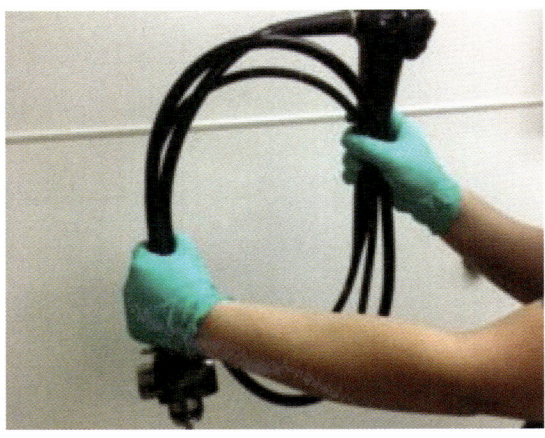

Figure 11.2

Preventing Contamination

When handling endoscopes, technicians must be aware of how microorganisms can impact the devices' safety. Prior to reprocessing, endoscopes must be handled in a manner that minimizes the risk of an endoscope cross contaminating the environment around it. This is accomplished by using a directional workflow, proper signage and containment devices, and by properly wearing personal protective equipment (PPE).

Figure 11.3 provides an example of poor endoscope handling and transport practices. This soiled endoscope is not clearly marked as "contaminated" and is not supported and protected from damage that may occur during transport.

Figure 11.3

Figure 11.4 Provides an example of a soiled endoscope transport container that is sealed and clearly labeled as "contaminated." The lock and signage alert individuals to the hazardous nature of the container's contents. Those working with endoscopes labeled as "contaminated" must wear appropriate PPE.

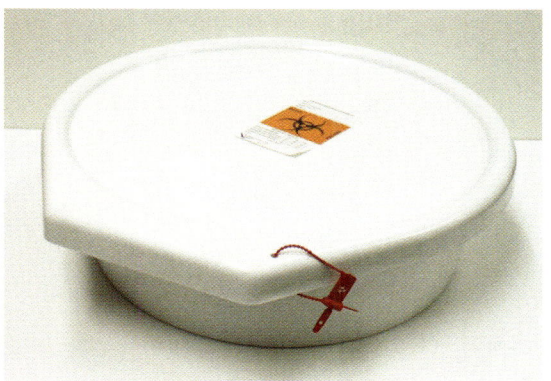

Figure 11.4

Transport carts should be designed to protect the endoscope from damage and protect the environment from contamination. **Figure 11.5** provides an example of endoscope transport carts.

Once an endoscope has been reprocessed, care must also be taken to prevent the environment from re-contaminating the endoscope. Endoscopes should be handled with clean, gloved hands and the device should be placed in a designated storage device. (See **Figures 11.6** and **11.7**)

Figure 11.5 Example of an Endoscope Transport Cart

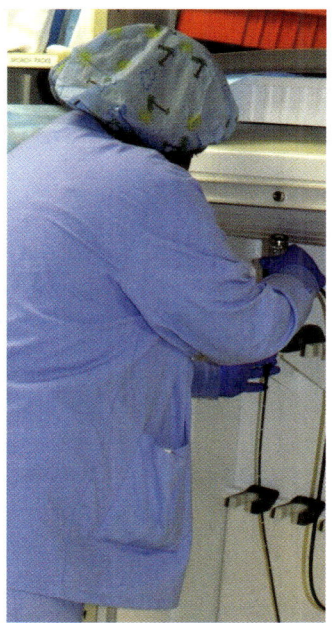
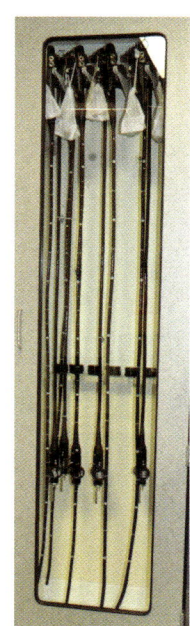

Figure 11.6   Figure 11.7

Moisture Danger

Once an endoscope has been properly cleaned and subjected to a high-level disinfection (HDL) process, it must be dried thoroughly. Moisture that remains in an endoscope provides an opportunity for bacteria to grow.

In the past, processed endoscopes were stored in cabinets. While those cabinets protected the endoscopes from damage and kept them "dust-free" until use, they did little to reduce internal moisture. (See **Figure 11.8**) In recent years, drying cabinets have been developed to keep endoscopes dry, both externally and internally. (See **Figures 11.9, 11.10** and **11.11**)

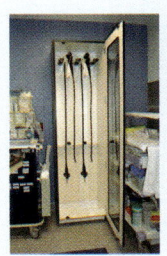
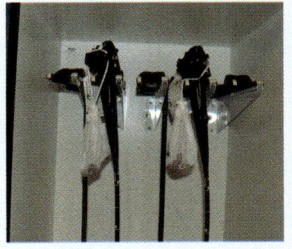

Figure 11.8 Endoscope Storage Cabinet

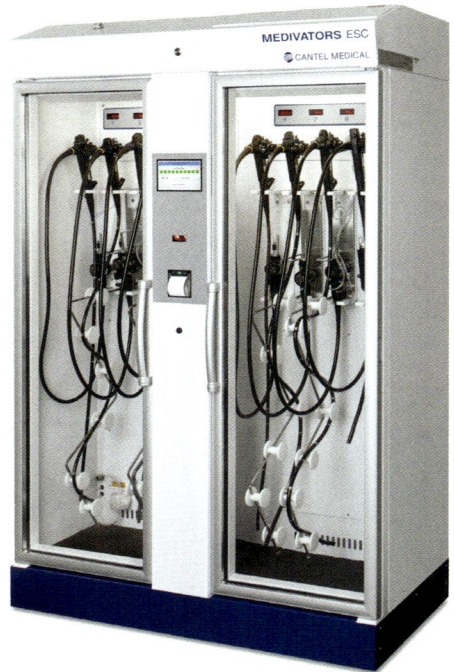

Figure 11.9 Endoscope Drying Cabinet

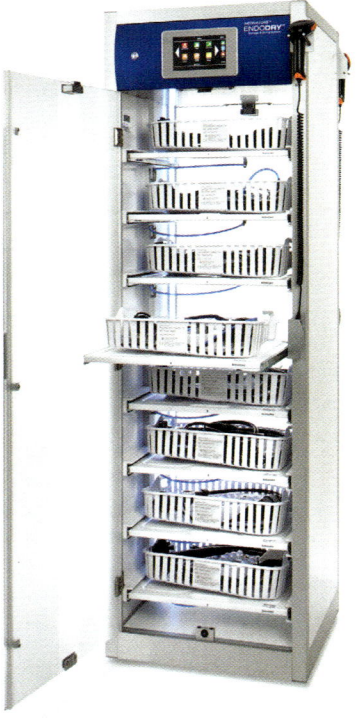

Figure 11.10 Hoizontal Drying Cabinet

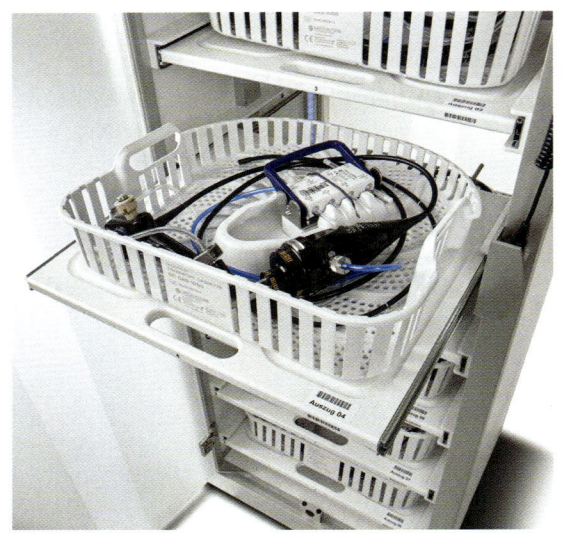

Figure 11.11 Hoizontal Drying Cabinet Drawers

STORAGE

As with all reprocessed items, specific storage conditions are required for flexible endoscopes. When placing a flexible endoscope into an endoscope storage cabinet, technicians must ensure that all caps, buttons and valves are removed. If left in place, these components may trap moisture and facilitate microbial growth. Moisture is the enemy of any clean flexible endoscope.

It is also important to ensure that any removable components remain with the endoscope throughout cleaning, high-level disinfection (HLD) or sterilization, and storage. Keeping components with each individual endoscope allows them to be easily identified in the event a specific endoscope is determined a possible source of contamination related to a healthcare-associated infection (HAI). When all components remain together, tracking and recall information is also more easily identified. **Figure 11.12** provides as example of endoscopes stored with their specific removable components.

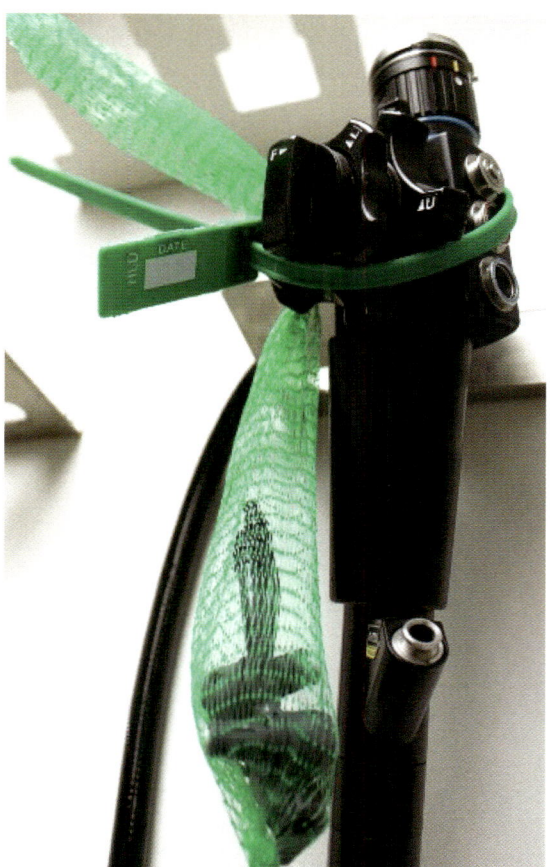

Figure 11.12

Endoscopes should be hung vertically, unless a storage unit validated for horizontal storage is used.

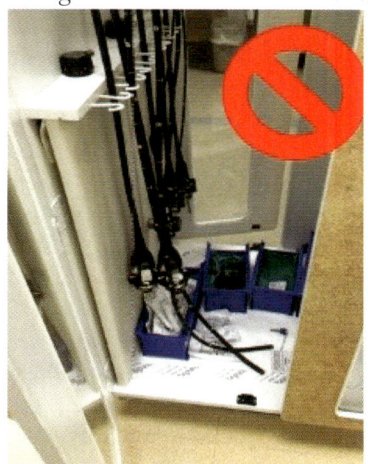

To reduce the risk of damage or cross contamination, endoscopes should be stored so they do not touch one another or the bottom or sides of the storage cabinet. (See **Figure 11.13**)

Figure 11.13 Poor Endoscope Storage. Flexible endoscopes should never touch the bottom of an endoscope storage cabinet.

Cabinets should be vented to control airflow within the cabinet. Many cabinets use high-efficiency particulate (HEPA) air to help reduce the risk for contamination.

Endoscopes placed into storage should be clearly marked to indicate they have been reprocessed in accordance with the manufacturer's instructions for use (IFU). The endoscope should also be marked with the reprocessing technician's name or initials, the date the endoscope was reprocessed, and the date that HLD was performed. **Figure 11.14** provides an example of an endoscope with a storage tag.

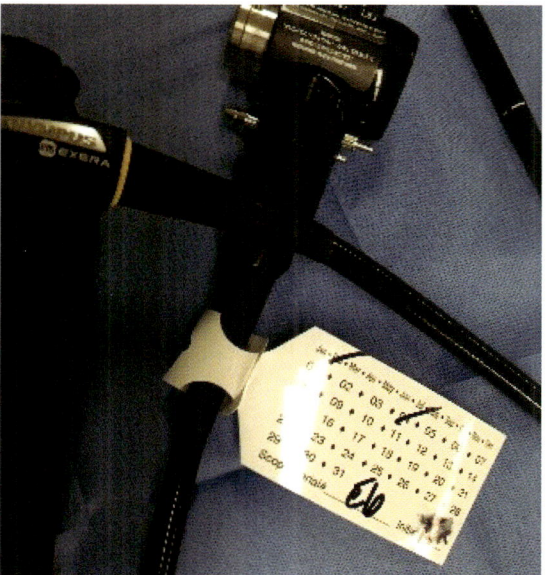

Figure 11.14

Endoscope Storage Timelines

Determining an appropriate expiration date or "hang time" (these terms are often used interchangeably) for reprocessed flexible endoscopes has been an ongoing discussion. Several associations and agencies provide guidance on hang time. This guidance can be helpful; however, different facilities have different endoscope storage conditions. Therefore, hang time should be determined by the individual facility, based on its actual storage conditions. To help guide the process, the following question must be asked by each facility: If the endoscope has been properly high-level disinfected and stored, how long is it able to be stored before needing to be reprocessed? Each facility should conduct a **risk assessment** to determine the quality of the storage conditions and develop policies and procedures to address storage hang time.

Endoscope reprocessing staff should also be knowledgeable about what resources such as the Association for the Advancement for Medical Instrumentation (AAMI), the Association of peri-Operative Registered Nurses (AORN), the Society of Gastrointestinal Nurses and Associates (SGNA) and the Centers for Disease Control and Prevention (CDC) have to say about hang time, as each provides valuable information that can assist with policy and procedure development regarding appropriate endoscope hang time.

> **Risk assessment** The process of identifying all risks to and from an activity, and assessing the potential impact of each risk.

It is difficult to assign a hang time of a specific number of days if storage conditions at a facility are lacking or do not meet the requirements. In some cases, events may occur that will shorten a stored endoscope's hang time. The following are some important points to consider: What if the endoscope isn't dry when it is placed in storage? What if the endoscope is hung in an open space with heavy traffic in the area? What if the endoscope is placed on a cart in a procedure area? Many scenarios and events can affect potential contamination of an endoscope after it has undergone the HLD process; therefore, all endoscope staff must be fully aware of what is recommended in guidelines, and also be well versed on the specific storage conditions for the reprocessed device. Each person who retrieves or dispenses endoscopes must be able to identify when breaches in storage and handling requirements have occurred.

CLEAN ENDOSCOPE TRANSPORT

Endoscopes that have been reprocessed and stored correctly still face potential risks during transport. Removing an endoscope from a controlled storage situation and delivering it to its point of use

increases the risk of contamination. This risk can be reduced by handling the endoscope with new, clean gloves.

All patient-ready flexible endoscopes should be transported to the procedure area using a transport device, such as a clear plastic bag or a labeled container. **Figure 11.15** provides an example of a container designed to transport clean endoscopes.

Figure 11.15

STORAGE OF PACKAGED, STERILE ENDOSCOPES AND ACCESSORIES

Endoscopes that have been packaged and sterilized should be stored in the same manner as other sterile packages. Each package should be stored in a traffic-controlled environment that meets temperature and humidity requirements assigned to other sterile storage areas, such as the Central Service/Sterile Processing Department. Wrapped sterile endoscope and accessory packages should not be stacked and should be handled with care to maintain the integrity of packaging and protect the contents from contamination. Sterile packages should be inspected for package integrity (the absence of package damage, moisture, holes or tears) before being dispensed. The integrity of sterile packages should also be checked again before packages are opened for use.

CONCLUSION

Each endoscope must be delivered to the procedure area in safe and good working condition. Using care when storing, handling and transporting endoscopes reduces the risk of an unsafe endoscope being used in a procedure. Proper endoscope handling, storage and transport creates a safer environment for patients and staff alike.

RESOURCES

Centers for Disease Control and Prevention. 2016. CDC HICPAC, *Essential Elements of a Reprocessing Program for Flexible Endoscopes*. https://www.cdc.gov/hicpac/pubs/flexible-endoscope-reprocessing.html.

Association of periOperative Registered Nurses. AORN Endoscope Recommendations: January 2016, doi: 10.6015/psrp.16.01.675. Published in: Guidelines for Perioperative Practice. Vol. 1. 2016.

Association for the Advancement of Medical Instrumentation. ANSI/AAMI ST91:2015 *Flexible and semi-rigid endoscope processing in health care facilities*.

American Society for Gastrointestinal Endoscopy. *Technologies for monitoring the quality of endoscope reprocessing*. 2014.

Rutala WA, Weber DJ, and the Healthcare Infection Control Practices Advisory Committee. 2008. *Guideline for Disinfection and Sterilization in Healthcare Facilities, Recommendations from CDC and the Healthcare Infection Control Practices Advisory Committee*.

TERMS

Risk assessment

Chapter 12

Rigid and Semi-Rigid Endoscopes

Learning Objectives

Upon completion of this chapter, readers will be able to:

1. Recognize the common standard and specialty endoscopes

2. Summarize the typical uses and anatomy viewed with common rigid endoscopes

3. Define the basic optical system and components of rigid endoscopes

4. Demonstrate proper rigid endoscope handling techniques to prevent endoscope damage

5. Describe the pre-cleaning, washing, rinsing and sterilization processes for rigid and semi-rigid endoscopes

6. Perform a basic rigid endoscope inspection, including proper cleaning of the distal and proximal lenses and inspection of the distal image and lighting system

INTRODUCTION

Although the primary focus of this publication has been on flexible endoscopes, it is equally important to be familiar with rigid and semi-rigid endoscopes as they have their own special cleaning and handling requirements. These endoscopes, used in minimally invasive surgery (MIS), are designed for examination of various anatomy either through a small incision or through an existing orifice, such as the urethra, vagina, nose, etc. Unlike a flexible endoscope that is designed to have flexibility for maneuvering in and around anatomy, the rigid endoscope is, as the name implies, "rigid" in design and not meant to be flexed. (See **Figure 12.1**) One exception would be the semi-rigid ureteroscopes that are used for examining the ureters. These endoscopes are mostly rigid in design, but allow for slight flexing.

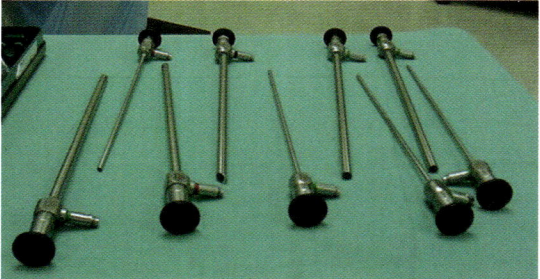

Figure 12.1 Rigid Endoscopes

Many rigid endoscopes also have flexible endoscope counterparts that can be used for viewing and/or treating the same anatomy. For example: cystoscopes can be either rigid or flexible. Ureteroscopes can either be semi-rigid or flexible. A healthcare professional must understand the distinction.

Another distinction is where the procedures are performed. Many flexible endoscope procedures are performed in the Gastrointestinal (GI) Lab or Endoscopy Department, whereas rigid endoscopes are widely used in general and minimally invasive surgery (MIS) departments in hospitals, surgery centers and in departments and facilities that specialize in urology, ear, nose and throat (ENT), orthopedics, women's health and bariatric centers. On a routine basis, endoscope reprocessing professionals will likely encounter rigid endoscopes, along with their corresponding instrumentation. Endoscopes are much more expensive and delicate than most other surgical instrumentation; therefore, it is crucial that reprocessing professionals understand and practice proper endoscope handling, care and inspection.

COMMON RIGID ENDOSCOPES AND PROCEDURES

There are many different types of endoscopes designed for viewing specific anatomy—from small structures, such as joints or ureters, to the large abdominal cavity. Although most endoscopes are fabricated in a similar fashion, the diameter, length and degree of the endoscope are the primary criteria used to determine suitability for examination of specific body structures. A large laparoscope would be used to examine large body structures, such as the abdominal cavity, whereas small, short endoscopes are used to view small cavities, the sinus cavity, or small joints, such as the knee or shoulder. **Figures 12.2** and **12.3** provide examples of the most common rigid, semi-rigid and rigid specialty endoscopes, along with their common sizes and lengths. *Note: Endoscope sizes and lengths may vary slightly from manufacturer to manufacturer.*

Many rigid endoscopes are the same, or similar, in size and length; therefore, it is important for the reprocessing technician to become familiar with the various surgical applications. For example: Arthroscopes and sinuscopes are often the same length and diameter, but used in different applications. *Note: Many common endoscopes are also available in pediatric sizes (smaller in diameter or shorter in length) and bariatric length (longer in length). The smaller the endoscope, the easier it is to become damaged.*

Common Rigid Endoscope Procedures

Arthroscopy: Examination, diagnosis or treatment of a joint (e.g., knee, shoulder, hip).

Common arthroscopic procedures include:

- Anterior cruciate ligament (ACL) reconstruction of the knee;

- Rotator cuff surgery;

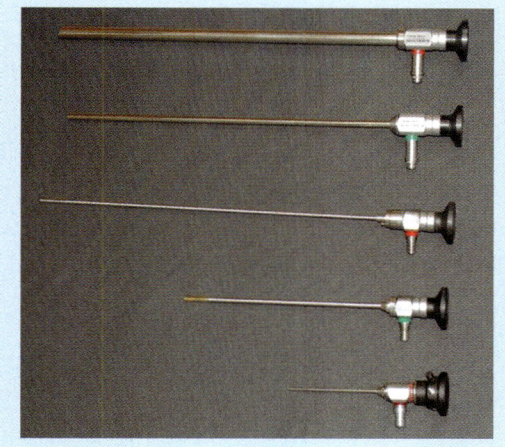

- **Laparoscopes** (top 2 images)
  5-10mm diameter, 280-330mm length

- **Cystoscope / Hysteroscope**
  2.7- 4mm diameter, 290-300mm length

- **Arthroscope / Sinuscope**
  4mm diameter, 175-180mm length

- **Small Joint Scope**
  1.9-3mm diameter, 90-180mm length

Figure 12.2 Common Standard Rigid Endoscopes

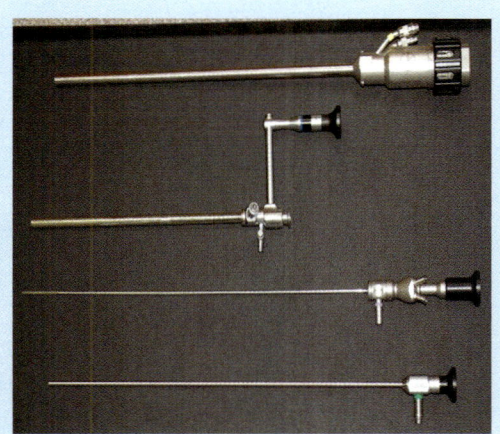

- **Robotic Scope**
  8.5-12mm diameter, 295--375mm length

- **Operating Laparoscope**
  8-12mm diameter, 280-330mm length

- **Semi-Rigid Fiber Ureteroscope**
  6.5-8.5 Fr, 330-450mm length

- **EVH/Bariatric Laparoscope**
  5-10mm diameter, 450-480mm length

Figure 12.3 Specialty Rigid and Semi-Rigid Endoscopes

- Repair/resection of torn cartilage (meniscus) or torn ligaments;

- Removal of inflamed lining (synovium); and

- Removal of loose bone or cartilage.

Small joint arthroscopy (arthroscope): Examination, diagnosis or treatment of small joints (e.g., wrist, jaw, ankle). (See **Figure 12.4**)

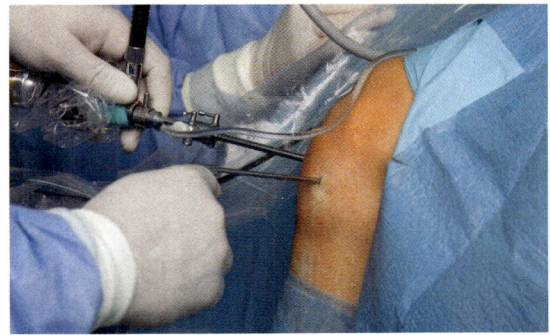

Figure 12.4 Knee Arthroscopy

Examples of common small joint arthroscopic procedures:

- Carpal tunnel release; and

- Temporomandibular joint (TMJ).

Sinuscopy/Functional Endoscopic Sinus Surgery: Examination, diagnosis or treatment of the inside structures of the nose and sinus cavity; often referred to as FESS or ESS Examples of common sinuscopic procedures:

- FESS or ESS;

- Treatment of sinusitis;

- Removal of bone, tissue or nasal polyps or tumors; and

- Treatment of deviated septum.

Cystoscopy: Examination, diagnosis or treatment of the urethra & bladder or prostate gland

Examples of common cystoscopic procedures:

- Blockage or tumor in the bladder;

- Stones, polyps, tumors or cancer in the urethra or bladder;

- Treat strictures, a narrowing of the urethra;

- Benign Prostate Hyperplasia (BHP) for enlarged prostate; and

- Retrograde pyelography – X-ray procedure with contrast medium to evaluate urinary flow.

Hysteroscopy/Mini-hysteroscopy: Examination, diagnosis or treatment of the vagina, cervix and uterus

Examples of common hysteroscopic procedures:

- Polypectomy;

- Myomectomy – for uterine fibroids;

- Cyst aspiration; and

- Tubal reversal.

Note: Mini hysteroscopes are 2.7mm to 3mm in diameter and can be used in an office setting, without general anesthesia.

Laparoscopy (laparoscope): Examination, diagnosis or treatment of the abdominal and pelvic organs (See **Figure 12.5**)

Examples of common laparoscopic procedures:

- Laparoscopic cholecystectomy - removal of the gallbladder;

- Hernia repair;

- Laparoscopic appendectomy - removal of the appendix;

- Colectomy - removal of part of the colon; and

- Laparoscopic hysterectomy - removal of the uterus.

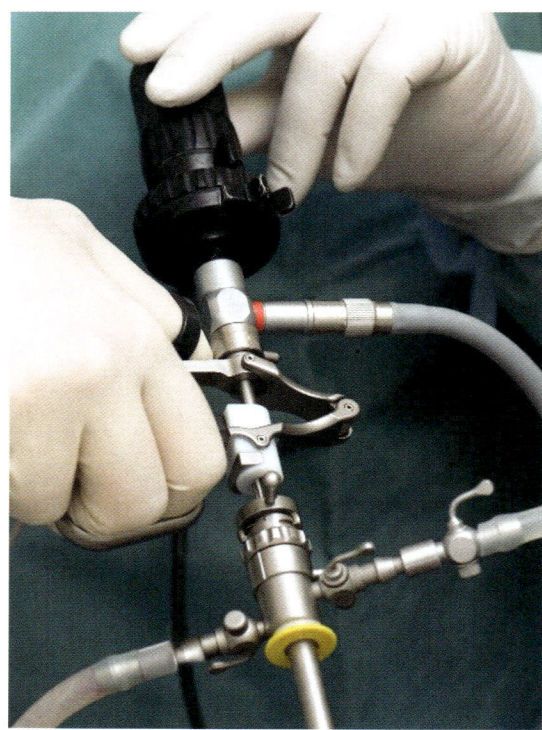

Figure 12.5 Laparoscopy

Semi-Rigid Ureteroscopy (Semi-rigid ureteroscope): Examination, diagnosis or treatment of the ureter

Examples of common ureteroscopic procedures:

- Stone removal or manipulation (with a stone removing basket);

- Laser lithotripsy - breaking up of large stones from a ureter or kidney with a laser beam for easier removal;

- Stent placement; and

- Remove or treat abnormal tissue, polyps or tumors.

Nephroscopy (nephroscope): Examination, diagnosis or treatment of the kidney

Percutaneous nephrolithotomy – removal of kidney stones through a tube via a small incision in the back;

Percutaneous nephrolithotripsy – Involves the surgeon breaking up the kidney stone and then removing the stone fragments through a tube. The distal end of the endoscope may or may not have threaded balloon tip;

Endoscopic vein harvest (EVH) (vein harvesting endoscope): Harvesting of the saphenous vein from the leg, or the radial vein from the arm to use as coronary graft.

- EVH endoscopes are specifically used for coronary artery bypass graft (CABG) surgery.

Robotic-Assisted Surgery

Some procedures are now accomplished with the assistance of a robot that uses instruments and endoscopes mounted on a robotic arm. A surgeon views a 3-D image and directs the robotic arm from a computer terminal. (See **Figure 12.6**) Such procedures may include:

- Urological: Prostatectomy (removal of the prostate);

- Gynecological: Hysterectomy (removal of the uterus);

- General Surgery: Laparoscopic cholecystectomy (removal of ther gallbladder);

- Cardiac: Mitral valve prolapse repair;

- Thoracic: Lobectomy (removal of the lung lobe); and

- Colorectal: Colectomy (resection of the colon).

Advancements in the minimally-invasive surgical field are continuously leading to the development of other types of innovative procedures and endoscopes for specialized treatment (e.g., heart, spine, plastic surgery, etc.)

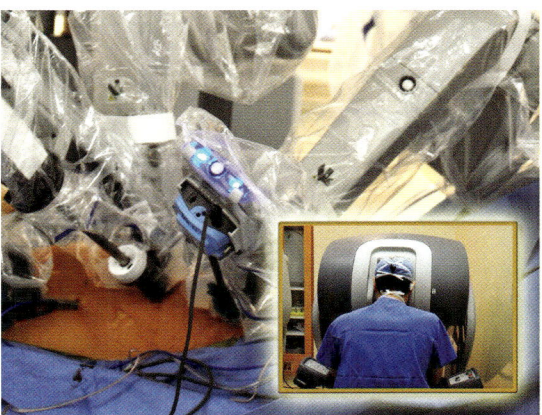

Figure 12.6 Robotic Endoscopic Surgery Set up (Inset: Surgeon's console)

RIGID ENDOSCOPE COMPONENTS AND TERMINOLOGY

While rigid endoscopes are designed in a simpler fashion than flexible endoscopes, they are by no means simple devices. Like flexible endoscopes, they are designed to perform specific functions and, if not handled and cared for correctly, they can be damaged. **Figure 12. 7** Provides a look at the basic design of a rigid endoscope.

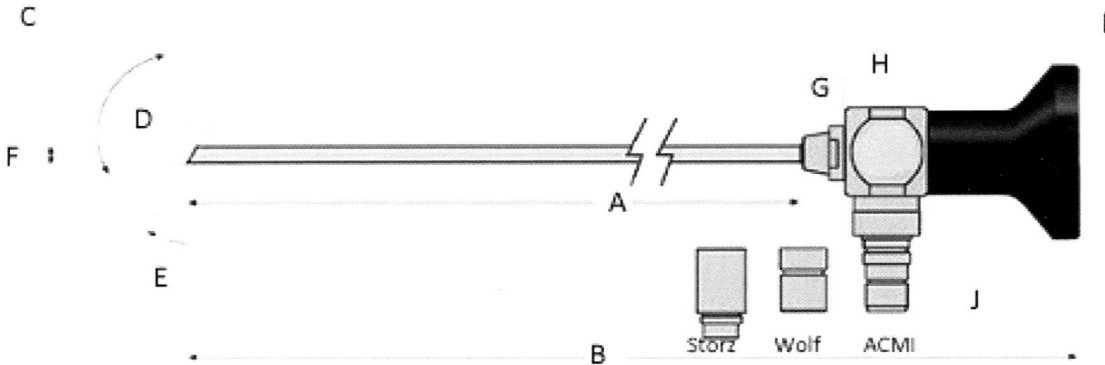

A. Working Length (mm)
B. Length (mm)
C. Distal End
D. Field of View (FOV)
E. Angle of View (AOV)
F. Outside Diameter (mm)
G. Sheath Mount / Bayonet
H. Body
I. Proximal End
J. Light Post Adaptors

Figure 12.7

Working length refers to the length of the shaft/insertion tube that enters the patient. The working length is measured in millimeters from the base of the sheath mount to the longest point on the distal tip.

Length refers to the overall length of the endoscope from eyepiece to tip.

Distal end refers to the end of the endoscope farthest away from the eye or point of attachment (e.g., video camera).

Diameter refers to the outside diameter of the scope shaft/insertion tube. Diameter is typically measured in millimeters, or French on semi-rigid endoscopes.

Sheath mount/bayonet is the locking mount at the base of the endoscope body that connects to instrumentation, such as a sheath or bridge. Sheath mounts vary by manufacturer; this makes the mating instrumentation brand-specific and not interchangeable between manufacturers.

Proximal refers to the eyepiece end of the endoscope, closest to the eye or point of attachment (e.g., video camera).

Light post adaptors allow for attachment of the fiber optic light cord to the light post of the endoscope. The various adaptors offered mate to specific manufacturer connections.

Field of view or real field of view (FOV) Refers to the angle from one edge of the maximum viewable area to the other edge.

Apparent field of view (AFOV) is the image seen within the black-bordered circle when one looks through an endoscope. Illustrated by constructing an imaginary angle, beginning at the eye and extending to the right and left sides of this circle, the resulting angle is the AFOV. The AFOV determines the size of the image on the monitor.

Direction of view (DOV) is the sight line or the direction the endoscope or optical system is looking, relative to the distal tip of the endoscope. The inclination (expressed in degrees) of the center of the real FOV with respect to the shaft of the endoscope determines the angle or direction of view. (e.g., the scope's angle of view is 0°, 30°, 70°, etc.)

Forward - 0° angle of view – Forward, straight viewing.

Forward Oblique – 5° to 70° angle of view - Forward, angled viewing.

Right Angle - 90° - Right-angled viewing.

Retrograde – 110° to 120° angle of view - Backward, angled viewing.

Unlike a flexible endoscope where direction of view can be manipulated by angulating the distal tip of the endoscope, most rigid endoscopes have a fixed direction of view. Depending upon the procedure, the surgeon may use one or more endoscopes with a specific DOV to enable the proper viewing of the anatomy.

Image resolution is the detail an image holds. Resolution quantifies how close lines can be to one another and still be visibly resolved. Resolution is typically measured in lines per millimeters/lines per inch, both horizontally and vertically. Resolution refers to an image's degree of clarity. Monitors with higher resolution have higher pixel counts. High-definition images have more than 2.1 million pixels. **Figure 12.8** provides an example of resolution testing.

Depth of field (DOF) refers to the ability of the endoscope to resolve the image in the foreground and background. An endoscope with good depth of field will allow the surgeon to clearly see both. In optics, DOF is also called focus range and is the distance between the nearest and farthest object in view.

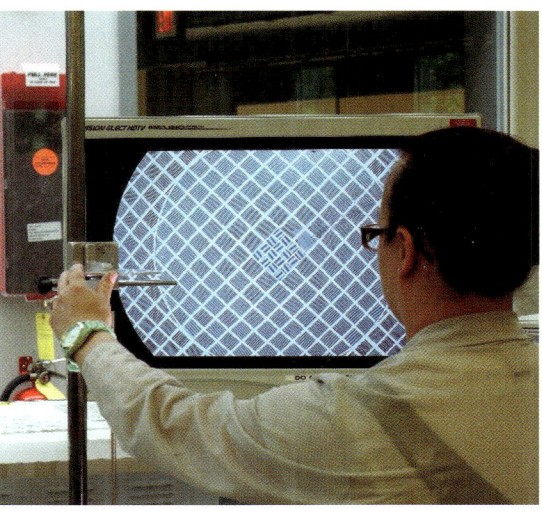

Figure 12.8 Inspecting resolution

THE RIGID ENDOSCOPE OPTICAL SYSTEM

All endoscopes (rigid and flexible) have two main functions:

1. Illuminate the anatomy; and

2. Transfer the reflected image back to the surgeon's eye or to an attached video camera system.

Some endoscopes also have a third function: allowing operative procedures to be performed through a working channel.

Two separate components within the endoscope, optical and lighting, must work in harmony to produce a clear, bright image for the surgical team. The rigid endoscope itself plays a crucial role, but it is not the only piece of equipment used by the surgical team. Additional video equipment and accessory instrumentation are necessary to complete the surgical procedure.

Endoscope reprocessing staff should be able to identify the various components of the endoscope and the endoscopic system, and understand their function, so staff can communicate clearly and accurately with the surgical team, vendors, biomedical staff and others within the healthcare facility.

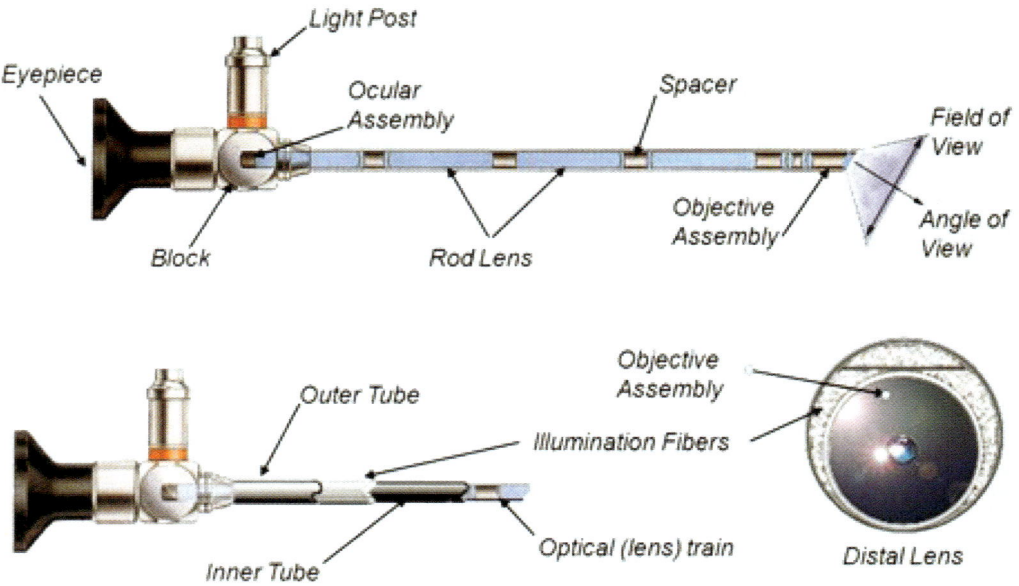

Figure 12.9.

Internal Optical Lens System & Scope Components

The optical system of an endoscope relays the image from the objective lens assembly through the rod lenses and to the ocular assembly. These precision, mostly glass optical components are housed inside the endoscope's inner optical tube. Most rigid endoscopes today use the same Hopkins rod lens design (refined by Professor Harold Hopkins in the late 1960s). The individual components in the optical system are outlined in **Figure 12.9**.

Objective Lens Assembly: In optics, the objective lens is the component located at the distal end of the endoscope, (the end opposite the eyepiece), that gathers light from the object being viewed and focuses the light rays to produce a real image. The objective lens assembly is typically comprised of several glass optical components, including an achromatic lens, prism or negative lens. The latest technology incorporates an aspherical lens in the objective assembly, which results in a better image. (See **Figure 12.10**) The objective lens assembly is usually the most expensive optic in the endoscope. The objective lens can be easily damaged by shavers,

lasers or mishandling.

Figure 12.10

Distal Window: The distal window may be part of the objective lens or a separate lens covering at the distal end. Because the distal window comes in contact with bioburden, fluids and chemical sterilants, it should be inspected under magnification and cleaned carefully after every procedure to ensure the window is clean and intact. Evidence of improper cleaning is seen as a white film covering all or part of the distal window. (See **Figure 12.11**) Water quality issues, if present, will appear on both the distal and proximal windows. If clouding is evident only on the distal window, this indicates that the endoscope was not properly cleaned prior to sterilization.

Figure 12.11 Distal Window with Residue

Figure 12.13 Rod Lens Spacers

Rod Lenses: Multiple rod lenses produced from the purest quality glass are positioned between the objective (distal end) and ocular (proximal) lenses through the interior of the endoscope. (See **Figure 12.12**) The lenses have curvature (concave or convex) achromat on the ends that limit the effects of chromatic (color) and spherical (shape) aberration, thus improving image quality. Rod lenses are separated by very small hollow tubes, called spacers, which keep the rod lenses from contacting one another. (See **Figures 12.13** and **12.14**) If the lenses were not separated by spacers and were allowed to touch, the image would lose clarity. Rod lenses transmit and refocus the image as it passes from one rod lens to the next through the endoscope. Anti-reflective (AR) coatings on the lens also help reduce reflection and stray light. Glass rod lenses are very delicate and can easily break or chip if the endoscope is bent or dropped. Lens separation (separation of the achromat) can also occur if exposed to excessive heat, temperature changes or moisture, resulting in an unclear or hazy image.

Figure 12.14 Assembly of a Rod Lens/Spacer System

Ocular Lens: The ocular lens (see **Figure 12.15**) earned its name because it is the closest lens to the eye. It is the last lens in the optical train that focuses and magnifies the image. The ocular lens is typically comprised of two lenses, which are optically adhered together. These can separate over time from heat or moisture exposure, or can become loose from physical trauma.

Figure 12.12 Rod Lens

Figure 12.15 Ocular Lens

Proximal/Eyepiece Window: The eyepiece window is the glass lens covering on the eyepiece that keeps the eyepiece watertight.

Optical Fibers: Optical fibers (not to be confused with light fibers) made from fused quartz are used in specialty endoscopes, such as semi-rigid and some small-diameter flexible endoscopes, to transfer the image through the endoscope from the objective to the ocular instead of rod lenses. This design enables slight flexing of the rigid shaft of the endoscope to access the ureters for viewing; a rigid rod lens cannot be flexed. Optically clear glass fibers are aligned precisely throughout the image bundle to allow correct image transfer and projection.

Additional Endoscope Components

Eyepiece: The eyepiece attaches to a video camera. Most rigid endoscopes on the market today have an eyepiece with a standard eye cup (See **Figure 12.16**). This attaches to a coupler on the video camera.

C-Mount Video Scopes: These endoscopes either have an integrated camera head or a connection on the eyepiece that attaches directly to the camera head, thereby, circumventing the coupler. (See **Figure 12.17**) The video scope will have the focus mechanism built into the endoscope instead of the coupler.

Cartridge Scope: Some brands of rigid endoscopes offer a cartridge-style connection where the endoscope pops into the camera head. (See **Figure 12.18**)

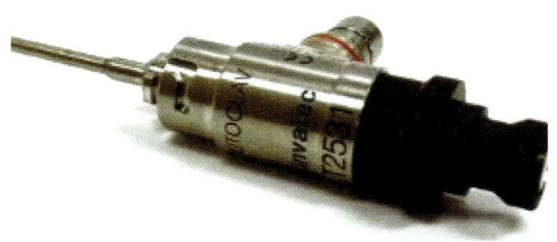

Figure 12.18 Cartridge or Snap Mount

Outer Insertion Tube: The outer insertion tube is the part of the endoscope that contacts the body or cannula used with the endoscope. The light fibers are sandwiched between the outer insertion tube and the inner optical tube. Some manufactures utilize a third tube design, which contains the optical lens system. The third tube makes the assembly process easier and also adds strength to the design. All the tubes are rigid; thus, any bending, dropping, kinking or flexing can damage the endoscope.

Hermetic Seals: Rigid endoscopes must be airtight and impervious to moisture or gases that could enter the optical system and cause damage. The endoscope is hermetically (airtight) sealed in various places, such as the distal window, light fibers, eyepiece, eyepiece window and body seams, using medical-grade epoxy/adhesives, solder or laser welds. These seals, if broken, can allow moisture, such as water or chemical sterilants, into the system during cleaning and sterilization. Visible water droplets, water spots and/or a foggy image can be an indication of moisture invasion and seal failure. *Note: A leaking endoscope cannot be effectively sterilized and must not be used for patient care.*

Figure 12.16 Standard Eye Cup

Figure 12.17 Video C-Mount

Working Channel: As stated, some rigid endoscopes also include a working channel (see **Figure 12.19**) that allows the surgeon to perform a procedure. Operative endoscopes, such as operating laparoscopes and semi-rigid fiber ureteroscopes, have a working instrument channel that allows for passage of instrumentation through the endoscope. Without a working channel, additional instruments used in the procedure are passed into the patient through multiple trocar entry ports.

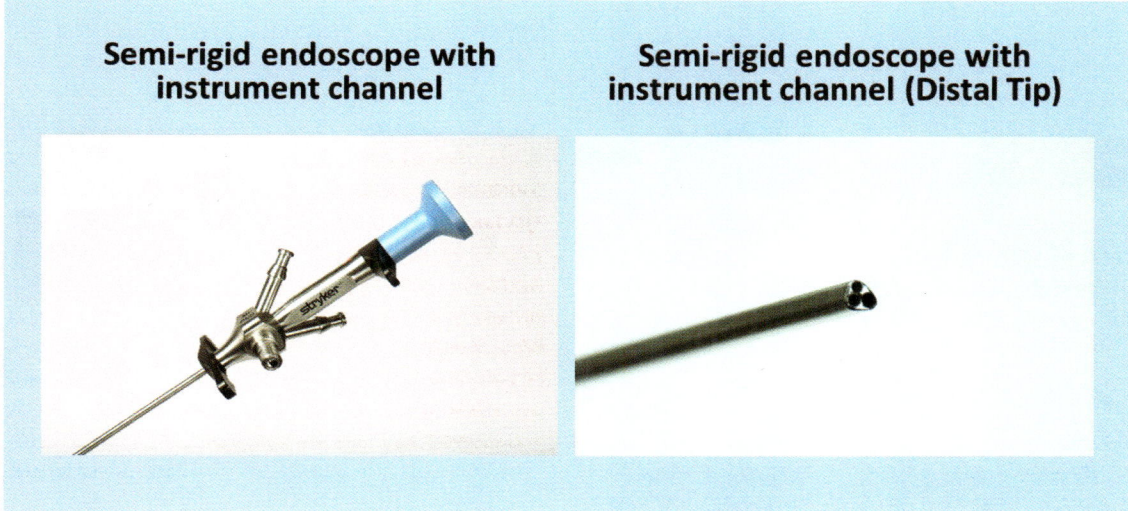

Semi-rigid endoscope with instrument channel

Semi-rigid endoscope with instrument channel (Distal Tip)

Figure 12.19 Semi-rigid Endoscope with Working Channel

The Lighting System

Illumination/Light Fiber Optics: Small strands of light carrying fiber optics made from glass (silica) transmit light through the endoscope and provide illumination to the surgical site. In a rigid endoscope, the light fiber optics are positioned between the inner optical tube and outer insertion tube. These fiber optic strands are about the size of a human hair. Although imperceptible to the human eye, these strands are bent slightly at the distal end of the endoscope to match the angle of view. This bend causes the light to be evenly spread over the field of view. Improper placement during the manufacture (see **Figure 12.20**) of the endoscope, or damage to the light fibers, can cause hot and cold spots in the illumination of the surgical site, resulting in poor image quality. The fibers are made of glass (see **Figure 12.21**) and are sensitive to moisture, heat and physical trauma. If such damage occurs, reduced lightput from the endoscope will result.

Figure 12.20 Installation of Raw Fibers

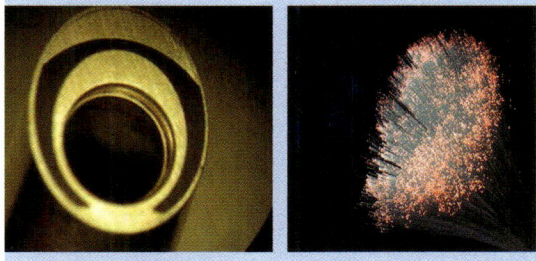

Figure 12.21 Distal End Fibers after Polishing

Light Post/Fiber Cone: The light post is the point of connection for the fiber optic light cord and the point where the illumination fibers begin. Adaptors on the light post enable the attachment of various brands and types of fiber optic light cords. The light post may or may not include an additional lens, light intensifier or fiber cone that helps direct the light from the light cord to the light fibers within the endoscope. Some manufacturers recommend and supply various sizes of light cords. They also recommend matching the size of the light cord to the endoscope. In general, smaller-diameter light cords are used with 4mm and smaller endoscopes. Larger light cords are used with 5mm and larger endoscopes. Matching the light cord to the endoscope per the manufacturer's instructions helps protect the light fibers from excessive heat, burns and moisture.

The Path of Light Transmission

Figure 12.22

It is important to remember that the internal optics, lighting system and video system all work together, but are nonetheless separate parts of the system. For example, a surgeon may complain that the "scope is dark." While one may assume that a dark image would be a result of the illumination fibers, a dark image could be a result of any number of issues, including damaged optics in the endoscope; damaged illumination fibers; light loss in another part of the lighting pathway, such as the light source or light cord; or even a damaged camera or coupler. The endoscope reprocessing technician should understand the complete system and know how to evaluate and troubleshoot the various parts of the system to better identify the cause of the light loss.

In addition to the light fibers in the endoscope, the lighting system consists of several other important lighting components that make a path of light transmission. (See **Figure 12.22**)

The light source is an external box on the video tower that houses a light bulb [xenon, halogen or light-emitting diode (LED) that can be adjusted in terms of intensity. As noted, a laser generator may also be included for special procedures. Although not commonly used, the light source may also be a portable battery-powered LED light stick that attaches directly to the endoscope.

A fiber optic light cable plugs into the light source at one end and attaches to the light guide post of the endoscope at the other end. The light cable houses illumination light fibers from tip to tip, like those in the endoscope. If too many individual fiber strands become damaged, light loss can result.

Advancements in Technology

Newer LED light sources produce less heat and have a much longer life span than xenon or halogen bulbs. It is recommended to replace xenon bulbs after every 5,000 hours of use. It should also be noted that xenon bulbs produce less light over time; therefore, adjustment to the light source may be necessary to adjust for this decrease in light output. *Note: Excessive heat buildup in the endoscope may cause damage to the endoscope and create a potential fire hazard. The cooler light emitted from LED light sources reduces the risk for overheating.*

Caution must still be used in the Operating Room (OR) regarding light source-generated heat. There are numerous reported cases of fires being caused by a light cable or endoscope after coming into contact with draping materials. Newer light source/light cable technology automatically causes the light source to go into standby mode whenever the cable is not attached to an endoscope. This helps reduce the risk of the cable causing a fire and it also eliminates bright light flash when disconnecting the light cable from the endoscope.

Video System

Before the advent of the video system, a surgeon had to look through the endoscope directly to view the anatomy. Now, most MIS procedures are performed with the endoscope attached to a video camera system for viewing on a monitor. The advantages of video imaging are:

- The entire surgical team can see the operative site and anticipate the surgeon's needs;

- Surgeons can easily point out anatomy for training purposes; and

- Images can be transmitted to alternate sites around the world and then recorded and stored for later viewing and recordkeeping.

Advanced features can be incorporated into the start-up menus for the video system. This may include patient information, time-out procedures and lab and imaging results that can be pulled from the hospitals electronic files. Today's highly advanced ORs even allow for live images to be sent to other locations within the hospital or around the world for the purpose of teaching or consultation.

High Definition (HD) Video: HD images are those that produce at least 1920×1080p (or 2,073,600 pixels). Each pixel is a dot of color in the image, as seen on the monitor. The higher the image resolution, the better the image quality. With the advent of HD video for the OR, endoscope quality becomes more important. If the endoscope is not preforming to the manufacturer's specifications, any flaws in the endoscope will be seen on the image. As such, the endoscope reprocessing technician's job of inspecting the endoscopes and light cables becomes even more important.

Video Tower Components (See **Figure 12.23**)

- **Camera Control Unit (CCU)**: The camera control unit is an external device that either the camera or the video endoscope plugs into. It receives the digital image and modulates it before passing the digital signal along to the monitor for viewing.

- **Camera Head and Endo Coupler**: The camera head attaches to the endoscope either directly (with a C-mount video scope) or with an endo coupler. The coupler has a focus adjustment so the image can be focused to the camera to optimize the image viewed on the monitor.

- **Monitor**: The surgeon views on a video monitor images relayed through the endoscope, camera and camera control unit. Displaying images on a monitor allows the surgical team to observe the surgical procedure and anticipate the surgeon's needs.

- **Additional Equipment**: Other equipment may also be on the tower. This equipment may include insufflators; suction devices; video enhancement hardware [used to enhance images for color, clarity and advanced imaging capabilities, such as indocyanine green (ICG), a pharmaceutical product that is injected into the patients' blood stream for illumination]; and an image capture device or video recorder for taking still shots of video images.

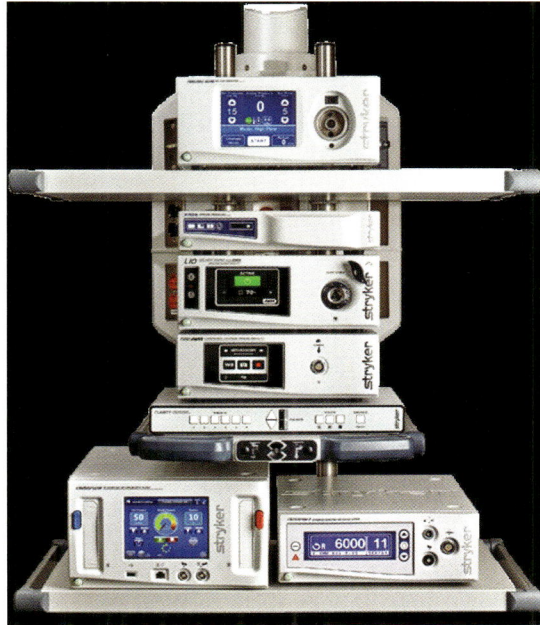

Figure 12.23 Video Tower

Accessory Instrumentation

Surgical instrumentation, such as sheaths, bridges, etc., attach to the endoscope at the sheath/bayonet mount. Other instrumentation and equipment, such as trocars (see **Figure 12.24**) and cannulas, laparoscopic graspers, forceps, suture passers, shavers and lasers, are also used to perform various functions (e.g., cautery, irrigation and drainage), while also providing access to the surgical site. It is very important that reprocessing professionals carefully inspect all accessory instruments and ensure that the components fit together properly. The endoscope, when inserted, should also slide in with little or no effort. *Note: It is important to never force an endoscope into an accessory instrument. If force is required, this is an indication that one of the components is damaged or incorrectly attached. Forcing an endoscope into an accessory can damage the endoscope.*

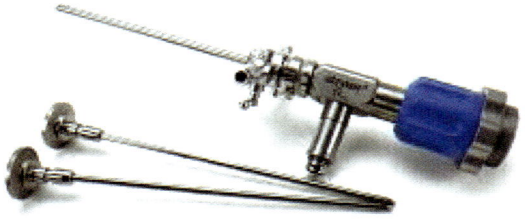

Figure 12.24 C-mount Arthroscope with Sheath and Trocars

CLEANING PROCESS

For effective sterilization or high-level disinfection, (HLD) the endoscope must be effectively cleaned with all visible debris removed.

Pre-Cleaning

1. Pre-cleaning begins as soon as the surgical procedure is completed. OR staff should carefully remove the video equipment from the sterile field and disconnect the components, video camera, light cord and endoscope. The light guide adaptors on the endoscope (if present) and the video camera coupler (if designed to be removable) should be removed. Each should be wiped down with a lint-free towel moistened with clean, cool water to remove all visible debris.

2. Next, the nurse or technician should carefully place the endoscopes back into their protective containers, ensuring they are properly secured and that no other instrumentation is placed on top of them.

3. The final pre-cleaning step is to apply a manufacturer-approved pre-cleaning enzymatic to the instruments. The use of the enzymatic helps break down bioburden that remains on the endoscope following patient use and keeps the instrument moist, thereby, preventing bioburden from drying on the device prior to cleaning and reprocessing. *Note: A towel moistened with clean, cool water can also be laid over the instruments to help prevent debris from drying and impeding the cleaning process.*

4. Finally, the instruments should be covered and promptly and properly transported to the decontamination area so the cleaning process can begin.

Note: Prolonging the life of endoscopes and protecting them from contamination, such as the drying of soil and the formation of biofilms, is everyone's responsibility. The OR and reprocessing staff should work together to help ensure that endoscopes are kept in the best condition possible.

Manual Cleaning Processes

1. Following the manufacturer's instructions for use (IFU), prepare a bath of enzymatic solution. Care must be taken to ensure that the correct amount of enzymatic and water -- at the correct temperature, per the enzymatic manufacturer's recommendation -- are mixed to create the cleaning solution. Enzymes may be less effective in removing debris if the temperature or concentration of the solution is not correct.

2. Ensure that all removable components are removed [e.g., light guide post adaptors, camera coupler (specific models only)], secure any water caps (certain camera models) and place the devices into the enzymatic bath. Soak the instruments for the recommended time, per the manufacturer's IFU.

3. Using a soft cloth or sponge, wash the entire instrument, paying special attention to the distal end of the endoscope. The distal end of the endoscope frequently comes in contact with blood and body fluids. Heat from light emitted from the endoscope warms the tip of the endoscope and contributes to the drying of debris, which makes cleaning more challenging.

4. If the endoscope has a working channel, use a proper sized brush, per the manufacturer's IFU. It is also important to follow the manufacturer's recommendation for the number of brushes and the number of recommended flushes with the enzymatic solution (if required).

Note: Do not immerse rigid endoscopes in any kind of liquid for longer than 20 minutes, or longer than what is recommended in the IFU.

Note: Enzymatic solutions do not disinfect the product being cleaned. Check with the manufacturer's IFU on approved steps for disinfecting devices cleaned only with enzymatic solutions (if facility policies require this for safe handling). The use of unapproved chemicals may damage the device. Residual chemicals may interact negatively with sterilization chemicals, and residual chemicals may cause patient harm.

Rinsing

Proper and thorough rinsing is critical to successful preparation of the instrument for sterilization.

1. Follow the manufacturer's IFU for the recommended water quality for rinsing.

2. The rinse must be thorough to remove all debris and enzymatic solution from the entire instrument. Any debris or enzymatic solution left on the instrument will prevent successful sterilization of the instrument.

3. Failure to thoroughly rinse cleaning agents off the instrument may lead to chemical reactions with subsequent sterilization methods, and these residuals may cause patient harm.

There is a higher risk of this occurring when hand washing instruments versus automated washing due to a variability of cleaning techniques.

4. If the endoscope contains a working channel, follow the manufacturer's IFU and flush the channel with clean water.

5. After rinsing, thoroughly dry and inspect the instrument for any debris.

Automated Washing

Automated washing provides the following benefits:

- Automated wash cycles are consistent, timed and documented. There is no variability with times and processes between loads, which cannot be said for hand washing.

- Reducing hand washing in the decontamination department will save processing time and minimize damage because the process around hand washing exposes the rigid endoscope to many factors that lead to damage (dropping, bending, heavy objects dropped or placed on top of them, improper chemical usage, improper rinse, etc.). *Note: endoscopes must still require some manual cleaning to remove gross soil and clean the operating channel, if present, prior to automated washing.*

- Automated washers can disinfect via heat or chemicals. Hand washing in enzymatic solution does not disinfect the device. A disinfected device is safer to handle by reprocessing staff.

Follow the manufacturer's IFU to determine if a device is approved for washing in an automated washer. *Note: Many rigid endoscopes are NOT compatible with automated washers.*

If the device is approved for automated washing and if the instrument is devoid of visible debris and packaged appropriately to prevent damage, the device can then be washed in an automated wash cycle.

INSPECTION OF RIGID ENDOSCOPES

A critically important role of the endoscope reprocessing technician is to validate the optical and functional integrity of the endoscope after each use and prior to sterilization. This helps ensure a safe and functioning endoscope for the next patient.

This section outlines important inspection steps to follow after the endoscope has been washed and before it is subjected to sterilization or high-level disinfection (HLD). The manufacturer's IFU should always be consulted for additional cleaning and inspection details related to the brand and type of endoscope being reprocessed.

If defects to the image, distal end or lighting components are identified, the rigid endoscope should be removed from service and repaired or replaced. Consult the repair provider for additional information. **Figure 12.25** provides a step-by-step overview of the process.

FIGURE 12.25

Before cleaning

After cleaning

Step 1 - Clean Lens Surface

Prior to checking the image quality, ensure all optical surfaces are cleaned (distal end, eyepiece end, light post) using a non-abrasive cloth. Use only a non-abrasive cloth, gauze or swab with alcohol or acetone. Films that cannot be easily removed with alcohol must be removed using a manufacturer-provided polishing paste or water-based lens cleaner. If this type of film is only found on the distal end of the endoscope, it is evidence of improper cleaning and the problem should be addressed with staff. When washing, special attention must be paid to the distal window to ensure removal of all debris. Devices that are not clean cannot be effectively sterilized. If lens paste is used, the paste must be carefully rinsed away to prevent additional build up. Tip: A pencil eraser is an effective tool for safely removing build up from the lens surface.

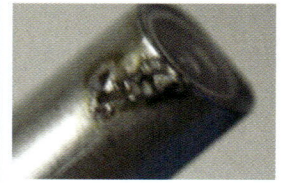

Step 2 - Overall Check

Visually examine the overall exterior of the scope. Look for signs of damage, including light post damage, improper cleaning, shaver/laser damage, missing or loose parts, bent insertion tube, etc.

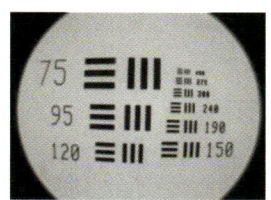

Step 3 – Visual Image Check

Visually inspect the image by looking through the endoscope.

The correct method to inspect the image is to look down at an object, such as print on a white piece of non-glossy paper, to simulate the focal distance (usually 8 to 10 cm) to anatomy during the surgical procedure, and to pick up on fine image detail.

The image should be round, clear and in focus from the center to the outside edges (in all directions).

Defects such as shadows, lines, haziness, distortion or partial or no image, may indicate damage to the internal optics or distal window.

Note: Inspecting by looking at the ceiling light or across the room will not provide adequate visualization for inspection.

Step 4 –Inspect Distal End

A critical part of the inspection process is to inspect the distal end under magnification (such as a magnifying glass, jeweler's loupe or microscope). Look at the glass, seal and surrounding light fibers for signs of damage, including scratches, chips, shaver/laser/cautery damage, missing sealant and damage to the distal light fibers. The distal end should be inspected for burrs or sharp edges.

If the lens appears dirty, clean (See Step 1) and then re-inspect. It may be necessary to clean multiple times to remove build up.

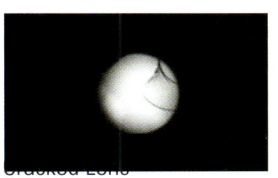

Cracked Lens

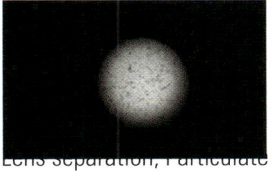

Lens Separation, Particulate

Step 5 - Inspect Internal Optics

An often-overlooked step in the inspection process is to carefully examine the internal optics. Using a jeweler's loupe or optic scanner, one can look into the internal optics to inspect for damage, such as broken, chipped or separated lenses, moisture, particulate or other optical defects. Place the loupe or scanner to the eyepiece and pull back to reveal the internal lenses.

Note: Some level of particulate is acceptable as long as it doesn't affect the image quality.

Tip: Lightly shake the endoscope to ensure there are no loose optics.

Burnt light fibers at the light guide post

Damaged light fibers viewed from the distal end

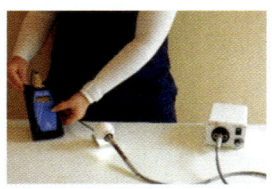

Measuring Light output using a light meter

Step 6 – Inspect Light Fibers

Light fibers run between the inner optical tube and outer insertion tube, from the light post to the distal end, in order to provide illumination.

Visually inspect these fibers by pointing the light guide post toward a source of light, while looking at the distal end of the endoscope. Broken fibers (visible as black dots) can be seen, as well as burns or fibers that are not sealed. Always check both the distal end fibers and the light post fibers for damage.

To go beyond a visual inspection, use a light testing meter, such as a lux meter or light tester, for quantitative measurement of light output.

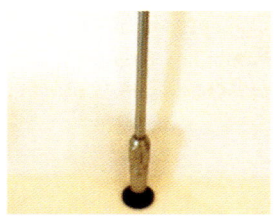

Step 7 – Inspect Shaft

The insertion tube may become misaligned or damaged if the endoscope is mishandled or used for torque during the procedure. Carefully inspect the shaft to ensure the shaft is not bent or out of alignment. Feel the shaft and distal end for dents or dings that may affect the passage of the endoscope through mating instruments or cannulas.

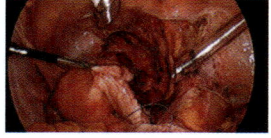

Good Image

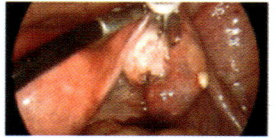

Image Hazy and out of Focus

Step 8 – Additional Troubleshooting/Testing

If unsure of the image quality, hook up the rigid endoscope to a video camera and light source, and examine the image on a monitor.

Note: Video endoscopes cannot be visually inspected unless attached to a video camera. No image will be visible by simply looking through the scope.

BASIC RIGID ENDOSCOPE HANDLING, STORAGE AND TRANSPORT

Practicing good handling, storage and transport of rigid endoscopes protects them from inadvertent damage; this can prevent costly repairs and extend the life of endoscopes. The following are some simple DOs and DON'Ts for rigid endoscope handling:

Do:

- Carry the endoscope carefully, holding it by the body/eyepiece.

- Protect the shaft from trauma.

- Keep rigid endoscopes separate from other instrumentation. (See **Figure 12.26**).

- Secure the endoscope in a tray or container, so it cannot move around.

- Manually clean, as instructed by the manufacturer. Remove light post adapters and clean instrument channels on rigid endoscopes (e.g., operating laparoscopes, ureteroscopes, etc.).

- Follow the manufacturer's recommended sterilization instructions.

- Use low-temperature sterilization (if approved by the manufacturer) to extend the life expectancy of the endoscope.

Do Not:

- Carry the endoscope by the shaft.

- Drop, ding or crush the endoscope.

- Place other instrumentation on top of the endoscope (See **Figure 12.27**).

- Push or pull on the insertion tube while placing or removing the endoscope from its tray.

- Place endoscopes in automated washers (unless approved by the manufacturer).

- Place endoscopes in an ultrasonic unit.

- Overmix cleaning agents as these can etch the glass.

- Immerse endoscopes in any liquid for longer than 20 minutes.

- Subject endoscopes to immediate use steam sterilization (IUSS) cycles, unless specifically approved in the endoscope manufacturer's IFU.

Figure 12.26

Figure 12.27

COMMON CAUSES OF RIGID ENDOSCOPE DAMAGE

Rigid endoscopes are comprised of stainless steel and glass and are fragile pieces of surgical equipment. The cost of a new rigid endoscope will typically range from $3,000 to more than $15,000 (for endoscopes used in conjunction with surgical robots). Repair costs can range from several hundred to several thousand dollars. It is not uncommon for a large hospital to spend $60,000 to

$100,000 per year on rigid endoscope repairs. Even worse, a damaged device may distort the physician's view and delay a procedure. Because of these risks, preventing damage to these devices is critical.

Common causes of damage include:

1. **Lapses in good care and handling practices.** Dropping, bending, crushing or rough handling can result in damage to the endoscope.

2. **Improper cleaning.** Poor cleaning will leave debris or biofilm attached to the endoscope. Evidence of improper cleaning is often seen by viewing the distal window of the endoscope. A cloudy or foggy appearance of the distal window indicates that the endoscope was not properly cleaned.

3. **Improper storage.** All trays used must secure the rigid endoscopes and hold them in place. Placing a rigid endoscope in a tray without brackets to hold the instrument in place is similar to riding in a car without wearing a seat belt. (See **Figure 12.28**) If an accident occurs, chances of injury are greatly increased.

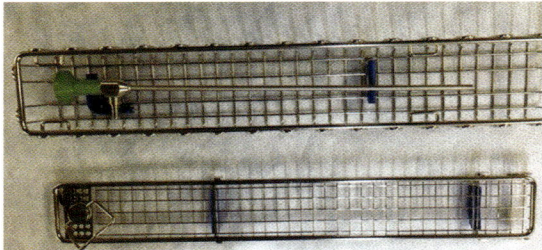

Figure 12.28

4. **Improper use of chemicals.** When cleaning an endoscope, only the chemicals indicated in the manufacturer's IFU should be used. Also important is using the appropriate ratio of water to chemicals when mixing solutions; an over concentration of cleaning agents can cause chemical etching of the glass.

5. **Excessive heat.** Heat caused by using the wrong size light cable or using the light source at its highest power can cause damage to epoxies that secure the light fibers.

6. **Improper sterilization.** Some rigid endoscopes are validated for multiple types of sterilization, including steam autoclave. Technicians should check the IFU to ensure that the chosen method of sterilization is appropriate for the endoscope being reprocessed.

ADVANCEMENTS

Newer technology incorporates laser light as an option for the surgeon. This new video technology requires special light cords capable of transmitting the laser light be used with the endoscope. The endoscope must also have special capabilities to transmit the laser light. A laser is a high-frequency wave of light that carries more energy than white light. A laser is used in surgery in conjunction with ICG (a pharmaceutical product that helps provide fluorescence), which is injected and transported via the blood. ICG glows green (See **Figure 12.29**) when hit by certain frequencies of laser light. Surgeons use ICG to identify anatomy, such as the biliary tree, as well as blood profusion through tissue. Endoscopes and light guides used for these procedures are specially designed to transfer laser light. Endoscopes and light guides will have special designations by their manufacturer to clearly state the devices are designed for use with a laser.

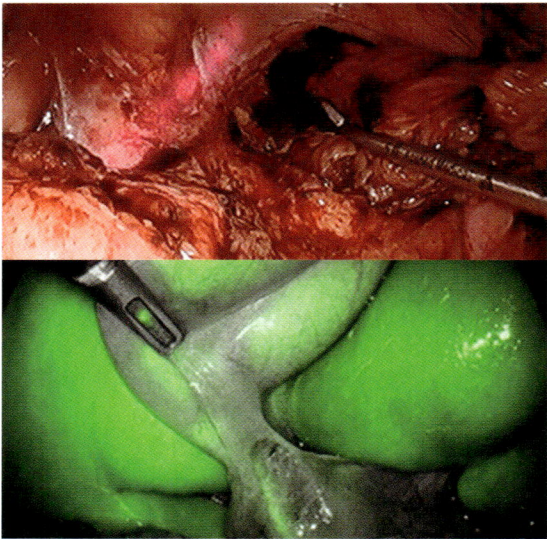

Figure 12.29

Note the red illumination of the ureteral stent in the first photo and the green illumination of the bile ducts in the second. This is accomplished through advanced video imaging technology, along with the use of products or pharmaceutical agents. This technology makes surgery safer for the patient because the surgeon can more easily identify anatomy.

There are several other technologies that use special rigid endoscopes, light cords and light sources for viewing anatomy. Near infrared and blue light laser are two examples. Near infrared allows the endoscope to pick up color given off by stents placed in the ureter or esophagus. Blue light cystoscopy allows the surgeon to detect cancerous cells in the bladder. Blue light cystoscopy utilizes a pharmaceutical optical imaging agent indicated for use in the cystoscopic detection of non-muscle invasive papillary cancer of the bladder (among patients suspected or known to have lesion(s) based on a prior cystoscopy).

CONCLUSION

Rigid and semi-rigid endoscopes have their own special cleaning and handling requirements and certain steps must be diligently followed to prevent endoscope damage, prevent microorganisms and biofilm from remaining on the instrument, and mitigate patient safety risks. Endoscope reprocessing technicians must carefully follow the rigid endoscope manufacturer's IFU for proper cleaning and sterilization. Careful inspection is also critical, along with proper handling, transport and storage. This helps ensure that endoscopes remain protected and in good working condition, and facilitate safe patient use.

RESOURCES

Association for the Advancement of Medical Instrumentation. ANSI/AAMI ST91:2015 *Flexible and semi-rigid endoscope processing in health care facilities.*

International Association of Healthcare Central Service Materiel Management. *Central Service Technical Manual, Eighth Edition.* 2016.

Mobile Instrument Repair. *Safe Handling and Reprocessing of Rigid Endoscopes.* 2014.

Rutherford, CJ. **Differentiating Surgical Instruments, Second Edition**. 2012. F.A. Davis.

Chapter **13**

Endoscope System Maintenance

Learning Objectives

Upon completion of this chapter, readers will be able to:

1. Review requirements, guidelines and recommendations for a flexible endoscope management program

2. Describe inspection strategies to identify functional and physical damage that renders an endoscope unsafe for use

3. Define recordkeeping expectations for inspection

4. Outline the processes for care of a damaged flexible endoscope being sent out for repair

5. Outline the processes for care of a repaired flexible endoscope when returned from service

6. Outline processes for working with loaned flexible endoscopes

7. Define quality management measures to track for recurring, avoidable repairs

INTRODUCTION

Like all medical device systems, the endoscope system requires support on several levels. The devices must be kept in good working order, and inspection, maintenance and repairs must be documented. Devices must also be tracked to provide information in the event of a recall. If there is reason to believe a process has failed, or if an incident occurs or an outbreak is suspected, documentation is critical for tracing specific endoscopes to the patients and procedures in which they were used.

Like most medical devices, flexible endoscopes will require repair at some point in their use life. Repairs may range from minimal fixes to major ones. To ensure endoscopes are safe and well-functioning for each and every patient and procedure, healthcare facilities must develop a system that will:

- Protect endoscopes from damage;

- Routinely inspect and test endoscopes to identify issues;

- Ensure endoscopes undergo prompt and appropriate repair;

- Receive and properly place endoscopes back into service (cleaning, inspection and disinfection or sterilization); and

- Track and document endoscope usage and repair.

Because flexible endoscopes are extremely complex and sophisticated devices, it is important to note that any repair(s) made to a flexible endoscope must be performed by a qualified endoscope repair technician. Endoscope reprocessing staff should never attempt to repair an endoscope. **Figure 13.1** and **Figure 13.2** show flexible endoscopes disassembled for repair.

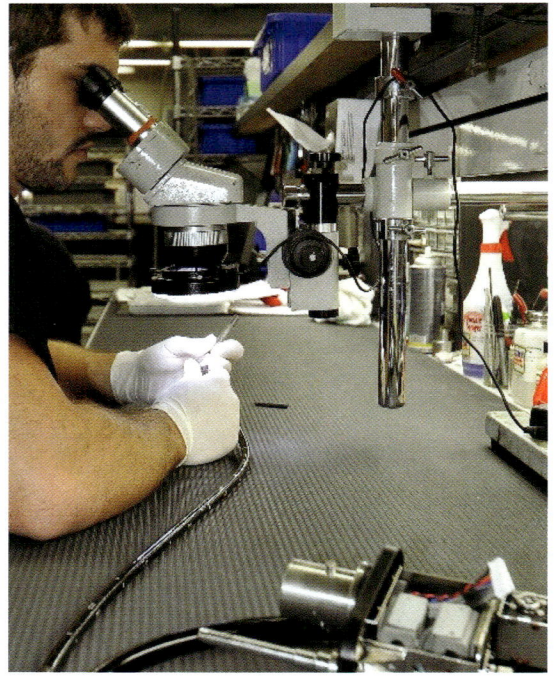

Figure 13.1

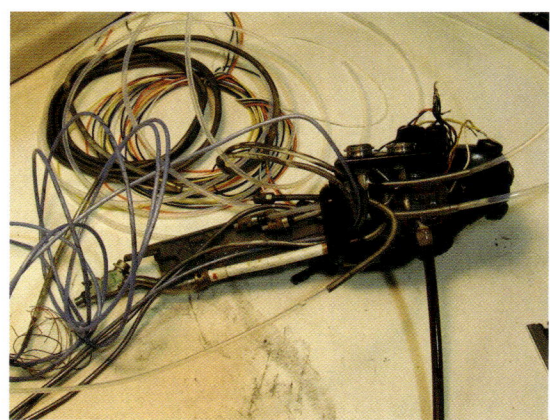

Figure 13.2

REQUIREMENTS, GUIDELINES AND RECOMMENDATIONS FOR FLEXIBLE ENDOSCOPE MANAGEMENT PROGRAMS

Each facility is required to have a medical equipment management program, which includes the functions and activities to maintain flexible endoscopes for safe patient care. According to the Code of Federal Regulations, equipment must be maintained to ensure an acceptable level of safety and quality if the facility is to meet the Center for Medicare and Medicaid Services' (CMS's) condition of participation. Activities, functions and responsibilities to meet these conditions are written within American National Standards Institute and Association for the Advancement of Medical Instrumentation (ANSI/AAMI) standards; recommended practice for a medical equipment management program and guidance for the use of medical **equipment maintenance** strategies and procedures. Policies and procedures include instructions on tracking of inventory, equipment safety, inspection, planned maintenance and repairs. Policies and procedures also outline quality indicators that reflect performance of scheduled inspections and repairs.

> **Equipment maintenance** Processes used to keep equipment and devices, including flexible endoscopes, working properly and safely and restore them to their original performance standards.

While much of the equipment management function, beyond the endoscope of reprocessing, may be performed by others, endoscope reprocessing staff are responsible for knowing about the facility's equipment management program and how to comply with it. Accreditation auditors/ surveyors may ask anyone involved in the use or care of flexible endoscopes the following questions:

- The number of endoscopes in the department;

- Which department or service line uses them;

- How frequently endoscopes are inspected and/or maintained and by whom;

- How to determine if an endoscope needs repairs; and

- What processes are in place to document the need for repairs.

Any endoscope reprocessing professional may also be asked to demonstrate or explain how departmental protocols for damaged endoscope care are implemented. They may also be asked about the care and documentation needed when an endoscope returns from repair.

INSPECTION STRATEGIES TO IDENTIFY ENDOSCOPE FUNCTIONAL AND PHYSICAL DAMAGE

A preemptive inspection program for all endoscopes should be developed, performed and documented. Clinical engineering may be the record keeper for this process. Preventive maintenance (PM) inspections for performance and integrity may be performed by reprocessing staff, the contracted repair vendor or another designated service provider. Many opportunities for flexible endoscope inspection come during the reprocessing steps that take place after every use cycle of the endoscope.

It Takes a Multi-disciplinary Team

Developing an effective system for endoscope use and handling requires input and communication with several teams within the healthcare facility. Users, reprocessing staff, infection preventionists and clinical engineering staff must develop a process that meets all requirements. They must also continue to communicate to the group to help ensure that all involved are following procedures -- and that those procedures reflect current requirements and best practices.

General practices for leak testing were identified in Chapter 6. Leak testing is a fundamental inspection step that allows the observer to determine whether the tubes and/or channels are intact; therefore, this process is a critical component of the flexible endoscope maintenance program. A successfully performed leak test prevents a range of endoscope damage and extends the useful lifespan of the endoscope. A hole can be detected by the application of positive pressure (either manually or mechanically) to the endoscope. It is imperative that each step is performed in its ordered sequence and that careful, uninterrupted inspection is performed. Other elements of performance during the leak test can be considered steps of physical and functional inspections. By slowly and individually rotating each directional knob to each extreme position while the endoscope is pressurized, the observer can determine whether the O-rings or seals that support those knobs are properly seated. A monomeric drop (witnessed as bubbles forming around the knobs) alerts reprocessing professionals to an issue that, if left untreated, will lead to fluid invasion. While rotating the knobs during the leak test, the observer is also able to determine whether there is over tightness, looseness or an incapacity to attain the expected range of angulation. An endoscope with an elevator or forceps raiser should also be challenged during the leak test by moving its lever in both directions; a leak in this system is determined by a drop in pressure during a manual test, or bubbles forming around the lever or metal elevator during an underwater mechanical test. If the endoscope is a video scope, the video function buttons can be massaged in a circular motion during the leak test. If there is an unseen hole in one or more of the switches, a pressure drop or bubbles will be detected. **Figure 13.3** shows an example of damage resulting from an undetected leak.

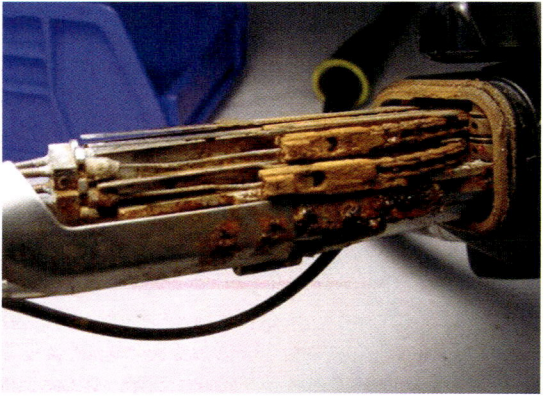

Figure 13.3

Following the leak test and during the cleaning process, the reprocessing technicians are responsible for examining the endoscope for debris and bioburden and also damage. A cleaning brush in good condition and of the appropriate size for each endoscope channel should have no difficulty navigating the suction and biopsy channels to clean effectively. Any restriction of brush movement could indicate a kink in the channel. Some facilities use a small-diameter borescope to enhance their ability to inspect the endoscope's internal channels.

In a well-lit environment with magnification, technicians should carefully inspect each component at the distal end for integrity. Lenses should be inspected for chips or cloudiness. Inspecting for

dents or cracks in any surface, peeling of the outer coating, and/or looseness of parts should also be part of the inspection protocol following every use of an endoscope.

Removable endoscope parts, such as biopsy port covers and function valves, should also be visually inspected for integrity during the cleaning process.

Facility policies regarding endoscope maintenance should include any instructions by the repair service provider to direct the reprocessing professionals on how to care for and prepare a damaged endoscope for repair. A facility protocol should also be in place to instruct reprocessing staff on which altered conditions are acceptable for returning the endoscope to routine use, which endoscopes should be tagged for observation, and which should be removed from circulation until repairs can be made.

RECORDKEEPING EXPECTATIONS FOR INSPECTION

Records of PM inspections and repairs should be maintained according to regulatory and accreditation standards, and in a manner consistent with facility policy. Service agents providing PM and repairs should meet the requirements set forth in facility policy. The policy should detail inspection intervals; the function/condition checks unique to the endoscope; make and model parameters; and the disposition of endoscopes that fail inspection.

Documentation of the endoscope's inspection by reprocessing staff should be incorporated into departmental records. The outcome of a successful leak test and notation that the cleaned endoscope met safety and functional parameters can be included on logs that track other elements of that episode (e.g., the result of the chemical indicator used during high-level disinfection or sterilization).

Documentation of an employee's orientation, training and competency verification of endoscope inspection (by make and model) should be maintained according to facility policy.

Record retention may be governed by state and local regulations.

PROCESSES FOR CARE OF THE DAMAGED FLEXIBLE ENDOSCOPE BEING SENT OUT FOR REPAIR

An endoscope and any accessories requiring repair should be identified prior to the disinfection or sterilization process. Once the issue is identified, it is important to determine which reprocessing protocol is warranted, in accordance with facility policy and in consensus with the repair provider. Often, the modified reprocessing cycle for flexible endoscopes requires positive air pressure to be maintained on the endoscope through all phases of the process to prepare the endoscope for transport for repair. This protocol is developed with two main goals:

- Rendering the endoscope safe to handle by removing all bioburden; and

- Not causing further damage to the endoscope.

Once reprocessed, the endoscope and/or accessories should be placed in a shipping container for transportation to prevent additional damage. The U.S. Code of Federal Regulations (CFR) outlines the requirements for shipping and some basic packaging requirements. Department of Transportation (DOT) requirements reflect these regulations. Facility policy will direct whether these requirements are the responsibility of reprocessing staff, clinical engineering or another entity.

*Note: Each endoscope must be packaged in a manner that protects it from additional damage during the shipping process. **Figures 13.4 and 13.5** provide examples of incorrect packaging and acceptable packaging. It is essential to check with the repair provider for specific requirements.*

Figure 13.4

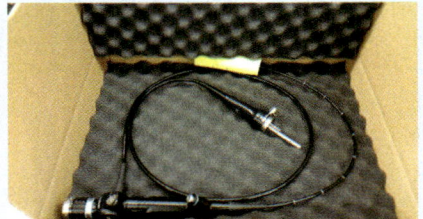

Figure 13.5

Endoscope reprocessing staff should label the malfunctioning device prepared for shipping by its make, model, serial number or unique identifier. This notation/documentation should meet the requirements for facility recordkeeping and facilitate clear communication with the repair service provider. Many service providers offer a form to make it easier for users and endoscope reprocessing professionals to be comprehensive and compliant with communication needs. A description of the problem, defect or malfunction should be noted and the method of reprocessing should be included on any communication with the repair provider. **Figure 13.6** provides an example of a communication form used to clearly and concisely identify endoscope issues for repair technicians.

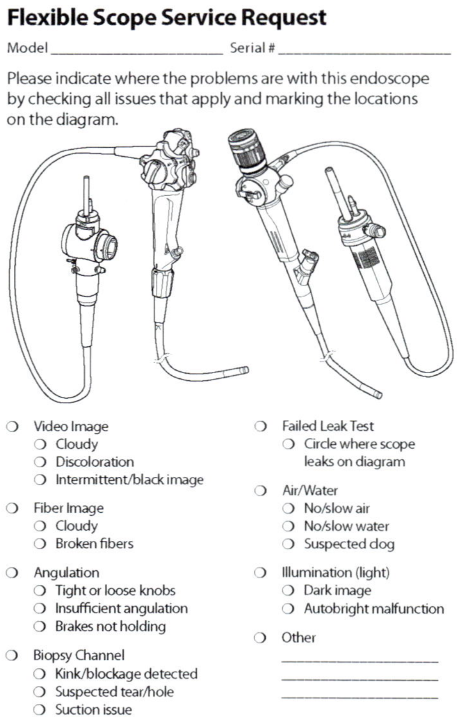

Flexible Scope Service Request

Model _____ Serial # _____

Please indicate where the problems are with this endoscope by checking all issues that apply and marking the locations on the diagram.

- ◯ Video Image
  - ◯ Cloudy
  - ◯ Discoloration
  - ◯ Intermittent/black image
- ◯ Fiber Image
  - ◯ Cloudy
  - ◯ Broken fibers
- ◯ Angulation
  - ◯ Tight or loose knobs
  - ◯ Insufficient angulation
  - ◯ Brakes not holding
- ◯ Biopsy Channel
  - ◯ Kink/blockage detected
  - ◯ Suspected tear/hole
  - ◯ Suction issue

- ◯ Failed Leak Test
  - ◯ Circle where scope leaks on diagram
- ◯ Air/Water
  - ◯ No/slow air
  - ◯ No/slow water
  - ◯ Suspected clog
- ◯ Illumination (light)
  - ◯ Dark image
  - ◯ Autobright malfunction
- ◯ Other
  - _____
  - _____
  - _____

Figure 13.6

A contact name and method for communication should also be logged on the accompanying paperwork. If the facility anticipates the repair will be made under warranty or as part of a recall, that information should be noted on the form.

When transporting an endoscope, it is critical to ensure the safety of all involved in the process. Because some damaged or defective endoscopes may not be able to be fully reprocessed, it is important to ensure that all involved in the transport and repair of each endoscope are aware of the risk of contamination. Many repair facilities request that the healthcare facility verify the level of reprocessing that the endoscope has received. Such communication reduces the risk of unnecessary exposures. **Figure 13.7** provides an example of a document used to verify decontamination of an endoscope being shipped out for repair.

LOANED ENDOSCOPES

A facility policy and procedure should be in place for borrowing flexible, rigid or semi-rigid endoscopes. The policy and procedure should be developed in conjunction with Infection Prevention, Risk Management, Materials Management, Perioperative Services, Gastrointestinal/Endoscopy (GI/Endo), Clinical Engineering and others, as necessary.

Endoscope reprocessing professionals should be knowledgeable of the facility's policies and agreements for loaned endoscopes. A facility should only request a loaned endoscope to be used during the repair period after facility policies have been carefully reviewed and considered. These policies should clearly indicate how records should be maintained to ensure endoscopes can be properly traced back to the patients on whom they were used.

When a loaned endoscope is received by the healthcare facility, the device should be inspected for damage, consistent with the inspection protocols for that endoscope. In addition, the manufacturer's instructions for use (IFU) must be available for the specific make and model of the loaned endoscope.

If any differences exist between the loaned endoscope and other endoscopes in the facility's inventory, all staff members who will reprocess or dispense the endoscope should be inserviced, with competencies

Dear Customer:

As part of our enhanced repair process documentation, we are requesting that a facility representative complete and sign this letter. Completion of this certification will help to ensure the safety of all who come in contact with devices used in medical procedures as well as enable a streamlined repair process.

Reprocessing Verification

By signing this form, you are certifying that unless shipped in biohazardous packaging in accordance with OSHA1 and DOT2 regulations, all equipment shipped for service will be cleaned and disinfected or sterilized, and that all federal, state and local laws and regulations regarding decontamination of medical equipment for shipment will be adhered to per your facility's protocol prior to shipment.

Facility Name /Customer Number_____

Print Name_____

Signature, Title, Date _____

If Service Request Notification (SRN) document does not include an acknowledgement that your instrument or device was properly cleaned and disinfected prior to shipment, our lab will decontaminate the instrument or device and your facility will be charged a fee for decontamination.

We thank you for your support in this effort to further ensure the safety of our employees and all individuals who come in contact with medical devices that have been used in patient procedures. We look forward to serving you in the future and thank you for your continued business.

1 - 29 CFR Part 1910.1030, Blood-borne Pathogens Regulations, U.S. Occupational Safety and Health Administration.

2 - 49 CFR Parts 171-178, Hazardous Materials Regulations, U.S. Dept. of Transportation

Figure 13.7 – Sample Verification of Decontamination Document

verified for processing the loaned endoscope, before it can be placed into circulation for patient use. Before requesting or accepting a loaned endoscope, it is essential to confirm that corresponding processing accessories and connection adapters are available for effective processing and that automated systems are validated for that endoscope by make and model.

If any damage is noted when inspecting the incoming loaned endoscope, reprocessing professionals should contact the loaned endoscope's provider to report the damage and request a replacement device. It is also important to document the endoscope by manufacturer, model, date received and serial number, as well as any other condition, function and reprocessing parameters.

Prior to returning the loaned endoscope, the device and any attachments or accessories that may have accompanied it should be completely reprocessed and inspected for damage. The endoscope's condition should be documented, along with the date the endoscope and any attachments or accessories were returned.

PROCESSES FOR CARE OF THE REPAIRED FLEXIBLE ENDOSCOPE WHEN RETURNED FROM SERVICE

When a flexible endoscope is returned from repair, endoscope reprocessing professionals should:

- Review documentation returned with the repaired endoscope;

- Confirm that the issue for which the endoscope was sent to the service provider was addressed; and

- Communicate the information provided and file all documents returned with the endoscope, in accordance with facility policy.

The repair provider should include information regarding the type of repairs performed, any components that were replaced, any adjustments that were made, and the outgoing quality inspection results. The warranty period for the repair process and/or replaced components should also be provided by the service agent. Recommendations to keep the device in good working order and prevent future damage and recurring repair needs may also be included on the documentation provided by the repair provider.

Before placing the repaired endoscope back into circulation for use, the device should be carefully inspected and reprocessed in a manner that meets all reprocessing steps defined by facility policy and the device's IFU. This process should then be documented and maintained in accordance with facility policy.

QUALITY MANAGEMENT MEASURES TO TRACK AND REDUCE REPAIR

Current and comprehensive protocols are necessary for ensuring quality device care and minimizing repair needs. Training, continuing education and competency verification on an ongoing basis play an important role as well. A list of employee training and competency offerings that impact the condition of the endoscope may include, but not be limited to:

- Training according to the manufacturer's written IFU on the design, function, care and potential failures of all endoscopes in inventory and of new models as they are added to inventory; and

- Competency verification of leak testing, inspection for cleanliness and damage, channel identification, utilization of cleaning chemistries, and accessories and articulation.

Outcomes of monitoring and management, based on performance indicators, provide tangible evidence that reprocessing professionals can use to ensure process quality and device integrity. Effective management also includes **action plans** to review processes, the environment of care and performances that contribute toward negative trends, and a process to make appropriate modifications. Performance indicators may include:

- Completeness of auditing tools that document that processing steps were performed, (including, but not limited to, leak test outcome and cleaning verification);

- Completeness of auditing tools that document inspection and maintenance for all endoscopes and reprocessing equipment;

- Documented repair history to alert reprocessing staff of repeating, preventable repair needs; and

- Repair cost per procedure by endoscope type or user group. For example: The total cost of repairs to ureteroscopes by all repair providers over a designated period of time (month, quarter) divided by the number of procedures for which that endoscope type was used during the same period.

Trends may be impacted by user group, make/model of endoscope; employee; process; reprocessing method and/or environment. As an example, a repeating occurrence of fluid invasion could be the result of an employee not following proper protocol, malfunctioning leak testing equipment, or use of a small sink in a poorly-lit environment.

> **Action plan** A sequence of steps that must be taken, or activities that must be performed well, for a strategy to succeed. An action plan has three major elements: 1. Specific tasks: What will be done and by whom? 2. Time horizon: When will it be done? 3. Resource allocation: What specific funds are available for specific activities?

CONCLUSION

Ensuring that endoscopes are well maintained, well-functioning and safe for patient use is a primary responsibility of every individual who manages and reprocesses these complex devices.

Tracking and managing quality indicators that are designed to reduce the cause and effect of recurrent repairs is critical, as is ensuring that all individuals who reprocess and manage endoscopes consistently follow endoscope proper care, handling, transport and management policies and requirements, as set forth by their facilities, state regulatory agencies, loaned equipment providers and repair providers.

RESOURCES

Centers for Disease Control and Prevention HICPAC, *Essential Elements of a Reprocessing Program for Flexible Endoscopes*. https://www.cdc.gov/hicpac/pubs/flexible-endoscope-reprocessing.html. 2016.

Association of periOperative Registered Nurses. *AORN Endoscope Recommendations: January 2016*, doi: 10.6015/psrp.16.01.675. Published in: Guidelines for Perioperative Practice, Vol. 1. 2016.

Association for the Advancement of Medical Instrumentation. ANSI/AAMI ST91:2015, *Flexible and semi-rigid endoscope processing in health care facilities*.

American Society for Gastrointestinal Endoscopy. *Technologies for monitoring the quality of endoscope reprocessing*. 2014.

International Association of Healthcare Central Service Materiel Management. *Central Service Technical Manual, Eighth Edition*. 2016.

TERMS

Equipment maintenance

Action plan

Chapter 14

Regulations, Standards and Resources

Learning Objectives

Upon completion of this chapter, readers will be able to:

1. Explain the difference between regulations, voluntary standards and regulatory standards

2. Explain the roles and responsibilities of the regulatory agencies that impact endoscope reprocessing

3. Discuss organizations and associations that develop standards that impact endoscope reprocessing

4. Explain how surveying agencies improve quality in healthcare facilities and, specifically, in endoscope reprocessing areas

5. Discuss the role of best practices in endoscope reprocessing

6. List industry resources that can be used to enhance endoscope-related knowledge and enable readers to keep abreast of change

INTRODUCTION

Endoscope reprocessing requirements are changing and new technologies are being introduced at a rapid pace. Some might assume that careful adherence to manufacturers' instructions for use (IFU) would be the only requirement for effective endoscope reprocessing; however, there is much more involved in developing appropriate, effective endoscope reprocessing systems and processes to keep patients safe. Endoscope reprocessing staff must be aware of and comply with several reprocessing requirements designed to improve quality and reduce the risk of endoscope-related infection and injury. This chapter will review the agencies and associations that impact endoscope reprocessing policies, provide information about current **regulations** and **standards**, and provide resources to keep abreast of new requirements and developments in endoscope reprocessing.

Regulations and standards impact every healthcare professional, including those working in endoscope reprocessing. These regulations (laws) and guidelines establish minimum levels of quality and safety. When these laws and guidelines are not followed, the results can vary from poor patient outcomes to legal consequences.

There are two types of standards that endoscope reprocessing areas must consider: **regulatory standards** and **voluntary standards**. Regulatory standards provide a comparison benchmark that is mandated by a governing agency. Noncompliance with regulatory standards may lead to citations and legal penalties. Voluntary standards provide guidelines or recommendations for **best practices** to provide better patient care. A voluntary standard does not enforce the rule of law and is optional; however, some **accrediting agencies** use voluntary standards as a condition of their surveys. When a voluntary standard becomes a requirement of an accrediting agency, a facility that wishes to achieve accreditation will be required to adhere to that voluntary standard.

> **Regulation** Requirements issued by administrative agencies that have the force of law.
>
> **Standard** A uniform method of defining basic parameters for processes, products, services and measurements.

> **Regulatory standards** A comparison benchmark that is mandated by a governing agency. Noncompliance with regulatory standards may lead to citations and legal penalties.
>
> **Voluntary standards** Guidelines or recommendations for best practices to provide better patient care. Industry, nonprofit organizations, trade associations and others develop these.
>
> **Best practice** A method or technique that has consistently shown results superior to those achieved by other means.
>
> **Accrediting agency** An agency that surveys healthcare facilities to determine if minimum standards for patient safety are being met. Accreditation is awarded to facilities that comply with identified standards.

REGULATORY AGENCIES THAT IMPACT ENDOSCOPE REPROCESSING

U.S. Food and Drug Administration

The U.S. Food and Drug Administration (FDA) is the federal agency responsible for ensuring that foods, cosmetics, human and veterinary drugs, biological products, medical devices, and electronic products that emit radiation are safe and effective for public use.

The FDA functions within the Public Health Service of the U.S. Department of Health and Human Services. The FDA regulates the manufacture of all medical devices and requires premarket clearance of new medical devices. The agency also regulates the sterilants and high-level disinfectants used to process critical and semi-critical devices. Rigorous testing with a broad range of microorganisms is required prior to marketing these chemicals. Packaging materials, sterilizers, automatic endoscope reprocessors (AERs), and quality monitors, such as biological indicators, are also regulated by the FDA.

FDA regulations help ensure medical devices are safe for patients and healthcare workers by requiring the device manufacturer to provide IFU with each product. The IFU should contain detailed instructions on how to properly reprocess and use the product; this includes disassembly, cleaning, assembly, disinfection and sterilization instructions.

Caution

Only products and equipment that have been approved by the FDA should be used in the reprocessing of endoscopes. Endoscope reprocessing managers should ensure that applicable items purchased for the endoscope system are approved. Once those items enter the facility, they must be handled and reprocessed according to the manufacturers' IFU.

U.S. Food and Drug Administration Labeling Document

The FDA has expressed concern about the potential for infectious disease transmission through the use of improperly reprocessed medical devices. In 2015, the FDA released an updated document, *Reprocessing Medical Devices in Health Care Settings: Validation Methods and Labeling*. This document provides guidance for FDA reviewers who evaluate premarket approval applications for medical devices. The document requires manufacturers to comply with certain criteria (mostly involving reprocessing instructions) when they submit medical device applications to the FDA for evaluation. The FDA places the responsibility for safe and effective medical device reprocessing with both the device manufacturer and device users. Reprocessing requires clear and detailed IFU from the manufacturer and then requires the healthcare facility to consistently and appropriately follow those instructions. The FDA released the updated document, in part, because some IFU had been difficult for users to obtain. Having ready access to detailed IFU not only provides users with the guidance needed to reprocess the devices effectively in their facility, but can also help them determine whether they have the necessary equipment – such as ultrasonic cleaners, AERs, washers and sterilizers, and cycle capabilities — to reprocess the devices within their department and in accordance with the manufacturers' IFU.

Per FDA requirements, the manufacturer is responsible for:

- Supporting the claim of reuse with adequate labeling and ensuring the labeling has sufficient instructions on how to prepare the device for the next patient; and

- The validation and documentation of tests, which show that the instructions are adequate and can be reasonably executed by users.

Users are responsible for:

- Confirming they have the equipment and resources to properly follow the instructions, and

- Verifying the manufacturer's instructions and ensuring the instructions are followed.

Medical Device Reporting Requirements

The Safe Medical Devices Act of 1990 requires healthcare facilities to report medical device malfunctions to the FDA. Before the passage of this Act, only medical device manufacturers were required to notify the FDA whenever they learned of a patient death or serious injury that may have been caused by, or was attributed to, their devices— and whenever they learned of a device malfunction that could cause death or serious injury if it recurred. Medical device reporting regulations require user facilities (hospitals, ambulatory surgical facilities (ASC's), endoscopy clinics and outpatient treatment facilities) to report suspected medical device-related deaths to the FDA and device manufacturers within 10 days of the event. User facilities must also report medical device-related serious injuries to the manufacturer within 10 days of the event. If the manufacturer is unknown, the injury should be reported to the FDA.

A serious injury is defined as "an injury or illness that is life-threatening; resulting in permanent impairment of a body function or permanent damage to body structure; or necessitates medical or surgical intervention to preclude permanent impairment of a body structure." A semi-annual report of deaths and serious injuries must also be submitted to the FDA on January 1 and July 1 of each year. The Safe Medical Devices Act is important to endoscope reprocessing departments because process failures may have to be reported if they can be linked to patient illness.

The FDA **MedWatch** program is designed for the voluntary reporting of device-related problems. It provides a vehicle by which healthcare professionals can notify the FDA about medical device malfunctions, labeling inadequacies and other problems, including ineffective or inadequate IFU.

In recent years, the FDA has used both voluntary and mandatory reporting programs to collect information about specific potential problems. Forms to report either voluntary or mandatory device issues may be obtained from the FDA website at www.fda.gov/safety/medwatch.

> **MedWatch** A safety information and adverse event reporting system that serves healthcare professionals and the public by reporting serious problems suspected to be associated with the drugs and medical devices they prescribe, dispense or use.

In 2009, the FDA, in conjunction with the Centers for Disease Control and Prevention (CDC) and the Department of Veterans' Affairs (VA), issued a Safety Communication identifying improperly processed flexible endoscopes as a health risk to patients. The Safety Communication can be accessed at: http://www.fda.gov/MedicalDevices/Safety/AlertsandNotices/ucm190273.htm.

Since that time, the FDA has carefully monitored endoscope reprocessing challenges and risks and has issued several communications to both manufacturers and users regarding endoscope safety. Endoscope reprocessing managers should keep abreast of FDA communications via the FDA website (www.fda.gov).

Medical Device Recalls

A recall is an action taken to address a problem with a medical device. This action can be initiated when a device is defective and/or poses a health risk. Recalls can be instituted voluntarily by the manufacturer, distributor or other interested party, or they can be required by the FDA. A recall does not always mean the affected product can no longer be used. Instead, it could mean that the product must be checked or repaired. For example, if an implant, such as a pacemaker, is recalled, it may not have to be removed from the patient; however, the risks of the removal decision should be discussed with the patient. The FDA monitors all required recalls to ensure the actions taken by the manufacturer are adequate to protect the public.

There are three categories of FDA recalls:

- Class I: High Risk – There is a reasonable chance the product will cause serious health problems or death. The manufacturer must notify customers and direct them to notify the product recipients. The notification must include the name of the device being recalled, the lot or serial numbers, the reason for the recall, and instructions to correct, avoid or minimize the problem. The manufacturer must also issue a press release to notify the public. In addition, the FDA may also issue its own press release or public health notice. The FDA posts applicable information on its medical device recalls website: www.fda.gov/safety/recalls.

- Class II: Less Serious Risk – There is a possibility that the product will cause a temporary or medically-reversible adverse health problem or there is a remote chance that the device will cause serious health problems. The manufacturer must notify customers and, sometimes, ask them to inform the product's recipients. Generally, neither the FDA nor the manufacturer issues a press release.

- Class III: Low Risk – Use of a product is not likely to cause adverse health consequences; however the product violates FDA regulations and action must be taken to address the problem. The manufacturer must notify customers and neither the FDA or the manufacturer will issue a press release.

Recent FDA Recall Example

In 2015, the U.S. Food and Drug Administration (FDA) announced that it ordered Custom Ultrasonics to recall all its automated endoscope reprocessors (AERs) because of persistent regulatory violations that "could result in the increased risk of infection transmission."

FDA Enforcement Requirements for Facilities Reprocessing Single-Use Devices

In August 2000, the FDA released its guidance document, *Enforcement Priorities for Single-Use Devices (SUD) Reprocessed by Third Parties and Hospitals*. As of August 2002, all healthcare facilities and **third-party reprocessors** who reprocessed SUDs were required to follow the premarket and postmarket requirements outlined in the enforcement document. These requirements state that facilities (including hospitals, ambulatory surgery centers and clinics) must obtain and comply with FDA **510(k)** directives to reprocess SUDs. A 510(k) is a premarket submission made to the FDA to demonstrate that the device to be marketed is at least as safe and effective, that is, substantially equivalent, to a legally marketed device (21 CFR 807.92(a)(3)). Submitters must compare their device to one or more similar legally marketed devices, and make and support their substantial equivalency claims.

Faced with the FDA regulatory requirements, healthcare facility administrators may consider outsourcing their SUD reprocessing to a third-party reprocessor. While outsourcing does relieve the hospital of the burden of the actual work, it does not relieve the facility of legal and ethical responsibilities applicable to the reprocessing of SUDs. It is necessary to provide safe and effective medical devices, regardless of who does the processing or where the processing takes place.

As previously stated, facilities that choose to reprocess SUDs must obtain a 510(k) to do so. To obtain approval, the facility must prove it can properly clean and sterilize the product to the original manufacturer's standards each time the product is reprocessed. The facility must also show it can test the product to prove the standards have been met in all reprocessing areas, including decontamination, disinfection and/or sterilization.

> **Third-party reprocessors** Vendors that have received FDA approval to reprocess certain medical devices and supplies that are labeled as single use. Most third-party reprocessors transport used items to their facility, reprocess them according to strict specifications, and return them to the user facility.
>
> **510(k)** A premarket submission made to the FDA to demonstrate that the device to be marketed is at least as safe and effective (substantially equivalent) to a legally marketed device (21 CFR 807.92(a)(3)). Submitters must compare their device to one or more similar legally marketed devices, and make and support their substantial equivalency claims.

To reduce operating costs, some facilities may be tempted to reprocess SUDs within their facility. Reprocessing single-use endoscope accessories and supplies is not allowed, unless the facility applies for and receives a 510(k) approval to do so.

For more information on the FDA's impact on endoscope reprocessing, visit: www.fda.gov.

Centers for Disease Control and Prevention (CDC)

The Centers for Disease Control and Prevention (CDC) is a federal agency organized within the U.S. Department of Health and Human Services. It works to promote health and quality of life by preventing and controlling disease, injury and disability, and by responding to health emergencies.

CDC personnel developed the first practical recommendations for isolation techniques and guidelines for infection control. Although CDC guidelines are not considered regulatory (law), other agencies rely heavily on them and review healthcare facilities for compliance.

Many CDC guidelines are incorporated into the policies and procedures of healthcare facilities, including their protocols for instrument processing following exposure to prions (see www.cdc. gov/ncidod/dvrd/cjd/qa_cjd_infection_control.htm and the CDC's Bioterrorist Readiness Plan www. bt.cdc.gov/). Prions are infectious protein particles that, unlike a virus, contains no nucleic acid, do not trigger an immune response, and are not destroyed by extreme heat or cold. Prion diseases are rapidly progressive and always fatal.

In 2008, the CDC released its document *Guideline for Disinfection and Sterilization in Healthcare Facilities*. This document presents evidence-based recommendations on the preferred methods for cleaning, disinfection and sterilization of patient care medical devices, and for cleaning and disinfecting the healthcare environment. This document is widely used by other agencies and healthcare facilities. Central Service (CS) departments use this document to help develop their standards, practices, policies and procedures for cleaning, disinfection and sterilization of medical devices. This CDC document can be downloaded free of charge at: http://www.cdc.gov/hicpac/pdf/guidelines/ Disinfection_Nov_2008.pdf.

In 2015, the CDC released its document, *Interim Duodenoscope Surveillance Protocol*, which provides information on endoscope surveillance. It can be downloaded free of charge at: http://www. cdc.gov/hai/organisms/cre/cre-duodenoscope-surveillance-protocol.html.

In 2016, the CDC released its document, *Essential Elements of a Reprocessing Program for Flexible Endoscopes – Recommendations of the Healthcare Infection Control Practices Advisory Committee* which provides specific information on endoscope reprocessing and system management. That document can be downloaded free of charge at: https://www.cdc.gov/hicpac/pdf/Essential_ elements.pdf

The CDC also provides information about proper use of personal protective equipment (PPE) and handwashing. It has several educational materials that may be helpful to endoscope reprocessing staff. This document is available at: https://www.cdc. gov/HAI/prevent/ppe.html

For more information on the CDC's impact on endoscope reprocessing, visit: www.cdc.gov search: endoscope.

U.S. Environmental Protection Agency

In 1970, Congress created the U.S Environmental Protection Agency (EPA) as a regulatory agency for the purpose of protecting human health and the environment by writing and enforcing regulations based on laws passed by Congress. The EPA is responsible for minimizing greenhouse gases and toxic emissions, regulating the reuse of solid wastes, controlling indoor air pollution and developing and enforcing pesticide regulations.

> **Greenhouse gases** Gases that trap heat in the atmosphere are called greenhouse gases. Such gases include carbon dioxide, methane, ozone and fluorocarbons.

The EPA administers two acts that are important to endoscope reprocessing staff: the Federal Insecticide, Fungicide and Rodenticide Act (FIFRA) and the 1990 Clean Air Act Amendments.

FIFRA regulates pesticide safety and effectiveness, and it impacts all antimicrobial products, including disinfectants, sanitizers and ethylene oxide (EtO). Every disinfectant and sanitizer manufacturer must obtain an EPA registration number for every covered product. The manufacturer must submit data relating to labeling claims, effectiveness and safety data to a division of the EPA's Office of Pesticide Program. If the data is approved and accepted, a registration number is issued. All EPA-approved products must contain the following label information:

- Product ingredients;

- Directions for use;

- Product precautions and warnings;

- Directions for storage and disposal;

- EPA registration number; and

- Expiration date (if applicable).

Note: Endoscope reprocessing technicians must always read and consistently follow the information provided on all chemical labels.

The EPA also administers the 1990 amendments to the Clean Air Act Amendments, which created a regulatory program to achieve air quality goals. As of December 14, 2014, the Clean Air Act bans the sale of most hydrochlorofluorocarbon (HCFC) products. This left 100% EtO as the only option for healthcare facilities.

The 1990 Clean Air Act Amendments also established National Emission Standards for Hazardous Air Pollutants (NESHAP). These regulations established emission standards for industrial EtO sterilization facilities. Several states have developed standards for the allowable amount of EtO a facility may emit into the atmosphere. To date, there are no national emission standards for EtO sterilization within the healthcare industry.

Since the EPA regulates disinfectants, all disinfectants used in endoscope reprocessing must be EPA approved.

For more information on the EPA's impact on endoscope reprocessing, visit: www.epa.gov.

U.S. Department of Transportation

The U.S. Department of Transportation (DOT) is a federal government agency dedicated to ensuring a fast, safe and efficient transportation system. Laws relating to healthcare include those concerning the transportation of minimally-processed instrumentation for repair, and the transportation of hazardous and radioactive wastes. The DOT inspects and cites organizations for statute violations.

When endoscope departments transport soiled or minimally-processed endoscopes or instrumentation between healthcare and repair facilities, DOT regulations for labeling and packaging must be followed. These requirements include proper biohazard labeling and containment. Endoscope departments should contact their state's DOT for specific requirements.

Note: State or local regulations may be more restrictive than federal regulations and, in all cases, regulations with the most stringent provisions apply.

For more information on the DOT's impact on endoscope reprocessing, visit: www.dot.gov

Occupational Safety and Health Administration (OSHA)

Created in 1971, the Occupational Safety and Health Administration (OSHA) operates under the U.S. Department of Labor. Its primary role and responsibility is to protect workers from occupationally-caused illnesses and injuries.

Many of OSHA's regulations and standards are represented in laws passed by U.S. Congress. Endoscope reprocessing professionals should be aware of OSHA regulations pertaining to their work areas.

The Occupational Exposure to Bloodborne Pathogens Standard is a comprehensive guideline that outlines employee safety in all areas of the facility as they relate to potential exposure from bloodborne pathogens. OSHA's Bloodborne Pathogen information can be accessed at: https://www.osha.gov/SLTC/bloodbornepathogens/index.html.

Note: Endoscope reprocessing staff must follow bloodborne pathogen guidelines when handling contaminated endoscopes. Noncompliance with this standard, such as not following the guidelines for transportation of contaminated instruments or not complying with the personal protective equipment (PPE) requirements, carries heavy fines.

If EtO is used as an endoscope sterilant, workers must be educated about EtO hazards and safety, and trained to use EtO safely. OSHA's Guidelines for the use of ethylene oxide sterilization can be accessed at: https://www.osha.gov/SLTC/ethyleneoxide/standards.html.

The General Duty Clause of the Occupational Safety and Health Act requires that each employer furnish each employee a place of employment that is free from recognized hazards that are causing, or are likely to cause, death or serious physical harm to employees; this means that OSHA may intervene in a matter of worker protection, even if there is no specific regulation that covers the situation.

OSHA personnel conduct announced and unannounced facility inspections. The need for inspections is based on complaints through the OSHA Whistle Blower Program, the rate of workplace accidents, high hazard targets, referrals, and follow-ups of previous visits. Some of the OSHA penalties are as follows:

- An employer who "willfully or repeatedly violates the requirements of section five of this Act" or rules promulgated under section six of this Act may be assessed a penalty of up to $126,000 for each violation.

- An employer who received a citation for a serious violation under section five of this Act or rules promulgated under section 6 shall be assessed a "penalty up to $12,600 for each such violation."

- An employer who received a citation for violating section five or six and is not one of "a serious nature" may be assessed a penalty up to $12,600 for each violation.

- Repeat - A violation of any standard, regulation or rule where, upon reinspection, a substantially similar violation is found.

- Failure to abate - Failure to correct a prior violation may result in high financial penalties.

OSHA representatives may enter a facility for a specific reason; however, once inside the facility, they have the right and obligation to investigate any violation in any department they may find.

Recent penalties and citations may be viewed by accessing the OSHA website at www.osha.gov/ oshstats/ and listing search criteria, such as zip code, facility size or citation type.

For more information on OSHA's impact on endoscope reprocessing, visit: www.osha.gov search: endoscope

The Centers for Medicare & Medicaid Services (CMS)

The Centers for Medicare & Medicaid Services (CMS) operates under the U.S. Department of Health and Human Services. CMS is responsible for the operation of **Medicare**, **Medicaid** and the State Children's Health Insurance Program. CMS is also one of the agencies that administers the standards of the **Health Insurance Portability and Accountability Act (HIPAA)**. HIPAA is the act that established national standards to protect patients' medical records and other personal health information. CMS is important to endoscope reprocessing managers and staff because the agency performs both announced and unannounced surveys of hospitals, long-term care facilities, ambulatory surgery centers and laboratories. Failure to follow CMS standards may result in the loss of federal funding to a facility, including Medicare and Medicaid payments. Nonpayment for the amount of time the patient is in the hospital due to healthcare-associated infection (HAI) means less operating funds for the facility. This loss of funds may result in fewer instrument and equipment purchases that could impact the reprocessing department's workload. For healthcare employees, violating HIPAA rules may result in loss of employment.

> **Medicare** A federal medical insurance program that primarily serves those over age 65 (regardless of income), people under age 65 with certain disabilities, and people of all ages with end-stage renal disease.
>
> **Medicaid** A federal and state assistance program that pays covered medical expenses for low-income individuals. It is run by state and local governments, within federal guidelines.
>
> **Health Insurance Portability and Accountability Act (HIPAA)** The HIPAA Privacy Rule provides federal protections for individually identifiable health information held by covered entities and their business associates, and gives patients an array of rights with respect to that information.

The CMS Center for Clinical Standards and Quality/Survey & Certification Group issued an alert related to outbreaks of *Carbapenem-resistant enterobacteriaceae* (CRE) during gastrointestinal endoscopy, particularly Endoscopic Retrograde Cholangio-Pancreatography (ERCP). The memo contains new instructions for all survey and certification staff when surveying hospitals, critical access hospitals (CAHs) and ambulatory surgical centers (ASCs).

CMS surveyors are now required to ask during the entrance conference whether duodenoscopes are used. If duodenoscopes are used, surveyors must request a copy of the manufacturer's instructions for use for the duodenoscope(s), as well as any automated endoscope reprocessors, the facility uses in reprocessing the duodenoscope(s). Surveyors may observe endoscopes being reprocessed and should ask the responsible staff to demonstrate and explain how they are adhering to manufacturers' IFU and standards and recommendations. Hospitals, CAHs and ASCs must also follow the FDA *Recommendations for Facilities and Staff that Reprocess ERCP Duodenoscopes*. Any noncompliance identified by surveyors must be cited accordingly and the increased risk to patient safety resulting from improper reprocessing taken into consideration when determining the appropriate level of citation.

For more information on CMS's impact on endoscope reprocessing, visit: www.cms.gov search: endoscope.

STATE REGULATORY AGENCIES

State agencies may also be involved in the regulation of healthcare facilities and the endoscope reprocessing areas within them. *Note: State requirements may be more or less stringent than federal standards. The more stringent requirement (either federal or state) must be followed.*

Department of Health Services (DHS) Many states look to their DHS to establish local health safety standards. A few states include DHS surveyors in The Joint Commission (TJC) survey process. DHS surveys are often random and unannounced. It is important that facilities and endoscope reprocessing staff understand and follow their specific state requirements.

Department of Transportation (DOT) Several states have their own regulations for transporting

healthcare wastes from the facility to landfills or other final disposal sites. DOT regulations may affect technicians working in the decontamination area and those responsible for packing endoscopes that will be sent for repair.

Environmental Protection Agency (EPA) Some states have EPA offices that regulate issues that concern their jurisdiction. State regulations regarding biohazardous waste and drain discharge are important to reprocessing staff. State EPA offices monitor chemicals poured into the main sewer lines, and there may be regulations against pouring blood and disinfectants into drains in endoscope decontamination areas.

Occupational Safety and Health Administration (OSHA) Approximately 25 states and two territories have state OSHA offices. These offices typically follow the same penalty criteria as those at the federal level.

Again, standards and regulations of state agencies may be more restrictive than, but cannot be less restrictive than, those of their federal counterparts. The requirements of the most restrictive agency always apply.

Endoscope professionals must be aware of and consistently comply with applicable state and other localized standards and regulations.

PROFESSIONAL ASSOCIATIONS

Professional associations may develop and promote voluntary standards that provide a foundation for processes and practices performed in the endoscope reprocessing area.

Association for the Advancement of Medical Instrumentation

Founded in 1967, the Association for the Advancement of Medical Instrumentation (AAMI) is a nonprofit voluntary consensus organization whose membership is comprised of healthcare technology professionals, many of whom sit on one or more technical committees and working groups. These healthcare professionals may be manufacturers, scientists, healthcare organizations, independent healthcare personnel, or members of another organization, such as the FDA, with an interest in the development, management and use of safe and effective medical technology. These committees and workgroups research and develop new **AAMI standards** and **Technical Information Reports (TIRs)** that address the use, care and processing of devices and systems, or revise existing standards and TIRs. Committees also develop standards for manufacturers, which recommend the labeling, safety and performance requirements for the products they produce.

> **Standards (AAMI)** Voluntary guidelines representing a consensus of AAMI members that are intended for use by healthcare facilities and manufacturers to help ensure that medical instrumentation is safe for patient use.
>
> **Technical Information Reports (TIRs)** Reports developed by experts in the field that contain valuable information needed by the healthcare industry. TIRs have not undergone the formal approval system that standards are submitted to and may need further evaluation by experts. TIRs may be revised or withdrawn at any time because they address a rapidly-evolving field or technology.

AAMI currently publishes several standards and TIRs. Many of these address functions that affect endoscope reprocessing, including cleaning, high-level disinfection, sterilization, packaging and equipment testing.

In 2010, AAMI released its best-selling healthcare document, *ANSI/AAMI ST79: Comprehensive guide to steam sterilization and sterility assurance in health care facilities*. This document quickly became one of the most widely used documents in sterile processing. ST79 is used to write policies and procedures and serve as a reference for best practices. Although the title states the document is related to steam sterilization, many sections of this document address processes that affect all types of sterilization, such as cleaning, packaging, quality indicators, product verification, education, and departmental work flow and design. This document became more important to central service/sterile processing departments in 2011 when TJC surveyors began referencing ST79 during facility surveys.

In 2015, AAMI published ST91: 2015 *Flexible and Semi-rigid endoscope reprocessing in health care facilities*. This document provides guidance for several areas of endoscope handling and reprocessing.

Other AAMI documents that may be helpful to endoscope reprocessing areas include:

- AAMI ST58: *Chemical sterilization and high-level disinfection in health care facilities;*

- AAMI ST41: *Ethylene oxide sterilization in health care facilities: Safety and effectiveness; and*

- AAMI TIR34: *Water for the reprocessing of medical devices.*

Although AAMI is a voluntary organization, AAMI standards are considered a key resource for healthcare guidelines, as many of their documents have been approved by the American National Standards Institute (ANSI). Noncompliance with these standards is cited by regulatory organizations that inspect healthcare facilities. Endoscope reprocessing managers and technicians should be familiar with current AAMI guidelines that address many of these processing and sterilization practices.

For more information about AAMI, visit: www.aami.org.

Association of periOperative Registered Nurses

The Association of periOperative Registered Nurses (AORN) is a professional organization consisting of perioperative nurses and others who are dedicated to providing optimal care to the surgical patient. AORN's committees are comprised of AORN members and allied association members who develop nationally-recognized, evidence-based standards, recommended practices and guidelines. AORN's Guidelines for Perioperative Practice currently have several sections devoted to topics directly affecting the reprocessing area. These include sections on cleaning, high-level disinfection, packaging, flexible endoscope processing and sterilization.

AORN published *Guideline for Processing Flexible Endoscopes*, which contains evidence-based information on endoscope reprocessing.

Although AORN standards are reprinted annually, most standards are on a five-year review cycle. AORN, like the other professional associations being outlined in this chapter, is not a regulatory agency; however, regulatory officials look for compliance with AORN recommended practices. Endoscope reprocessing technicians should be aware of AORN recommended practices and guidelines that relate to endoscope and endoscope accessory processing, these documents may also be utilized by surveying agencies during reviews of the reprocessing area.

For more information about AORN, visit www. aorn.org.

Society of Gastroenterology Nurses and Associates

The Society of Gastroenterology Nurses and Associates (SGNA) is a nonprofit organization of nurses and associates dedicated to the safe and effective practice of gastroenterology and endoscopy nursing. SGNA collects information and establishes standards and guidelines relating to the processing of flexible endoscopes. The following standards and guidelines are available for free download at http://www.sgna.org/Education/Standards-Practice-Guidelines:

- *Standards of Infection Prevention in Reprocessing of Flexible Gastrointestinal Endoscopes (2016);*

- *Standard of Infection Prevention in the Gastroenterology Setting (2015);*

- *Standards of Clinical Nursing Practice and Role Delineation Statements (2014); and*

- *Guideline for Use of High Level Disinfectants & Sterilants for Reprocessing Flexible Gastrointestinal Endoscopes (2013).*

For more information about SGNA, visit www. sgna.org.

The Joint Commission

The Joint Commission (TJC) is a private, independent, nonprofit organization that develops standards for healthcare facilities. TJC personnel evaluate healthcare organizations and programs in the U.S. by conducting on-site surveys at least every three years. TJC teams will arrive unannounced at a facility and spend two to five days studying virtually every aspect of care within the facility. TJC-accredited healthcare facilities are recognized as those that are dedicated to quality practices. TJC standards are voluntary; however, they carry significant weight. Failure to comply with these standards as evaluated through the TJC survey process may result in loss of accreditation by federal and state governments. This, in turn, may result in the forfeiture of millions of dollars in Medicare and Medicaid program payments.

Endoscope reprocessing managers and staff must understand and cooperate with their facility's procedures to comply with TJC. They must know and promote the hospital's mission and consistently comply with all safety standards, including those specific to their department. They must attend all mandatory facility inservice sessions, assist with quality improvement goals for their specific functions and follow all directives of Infection Prevention personnel. TJC emphasizes continuous quality improvement for patient care, and endoscope reprocessing staff plays a key role in improved patient outcomes. TJC standards may be incorporated by reference into federal, state and/or local statutes and then become binding on healthcare facilities.

In an effort to help facilities improve their performance and educate staff, TJC offers "Booster Paks" that provide information about best practices. In 2015, TJC developed a Booster Pak called, "High-Level Disinfection (HLD) and Sterilization." The goal of the High-Level Disinfection (HLD) and Sterilization Booster Pak is to ensure practices are carried out following regulatory standards and evidence-based guidelines for HLD and sterilization in order to minimize the potential risk of infection transmission to patients.

For more information about TJC, visit www. jointcommission.org.

The Association for Professionals in Infection Control and Epidemiology

The Association for Professionals in Infection Control and Epidemiology (APIC) is a voluntary international organization whose members work to prevent HAIs in healthcare facilities. APIC members work in conjunction with other agencies, such as the CDC, to adopt standards for infection/disease prevention. APIC publishes *Guidelines for Infection Prevention Control in Flexible Endoscopy*, which provides information on endoscope reprocessing. TJC holds the Infection Prevention department, in conjunction with endoscope management staff, responsible for endoscope reprocessing outcomes.

For more information on APIC, visit www.apic.org.

CONCLUSION

Standards and regulations are designed to keep both patients and employees safe. Endoscope reprocessing management and staff should become familiar with the agencies and organizations that develop the requirements that impact their jobs. They should also strive to keep abreast of changes impacting endoscope reprocessing as they happen; doing so creates an environment of safety and competency.

RESOURCES

U.S. Food and Drug Administration. *Code of Federal Regulations, Title 21, Part 813 — Medical Device Reporting, Subparts A, B, C.* U.S. Government Printing Office. 2000.

U.S. Environmental Protection Agency. Data *Requirements for Registration*. Federal Register 49, No. 207: 42881-42905. October 24, 1984.

U.S. Environmental Protection Agency. *Clarification of HIV (AIDS Virus) Labeling Policy for Antimicrobial Pesticide Products.* Federal Register 54, No. 26:6288-6290. February 9, 1989.

U.S. Environmental Protection Agency. *National Emission Standards for Hazardous Air Pollutants for Source Categories,* Code of Federal Regulations, Title 40, Part 63, Subpart 0 (Updated 1996). Washington, D.C. 1994.

Centers for Disease Control and Prevention. *Guidelines for Disinfecting and Sterilizing in Healthcare Facilities. Guidelines for Hand-washing and Hospital Environmental Control.* 2008.

Occupational Safety and Health Administration. Occupational *Exposure to Ethylene Oxide.* Federal Register 49, No. 122: 25734-25809. Code of Federal Regulations, Title 29, Part 1910.1047. 1984.

Occupational Safety and Health Administration. *Occupational Exposure to Ethylene Oxide.* Federal Register 53, No. 66: 53:11414-11438. Code of Federal Regulations, Title 29, Part 1910.1047. 1988.

Occupational Safety and Health Administration. *Hazard Communication Standard.* Code of Federal Regulations, Title 29, Part 1910.1200.

Occupational Safety and Health Administration. *Occupational Exposure to Blood-borne Pathogens: Final Rule.* Federal Register 56, No. 235: 56:64004. Code of Federal Regulations, Title 29, Part 1910.1030. 1991.

Occupational Safety and Health Administration. Occupational *Exposure to Bloodborne Pathogens: Final Rule.* 29 CFR Part 1910.1030. 1992.

Occupational Safety and Health Administration. *Occupational Exposure to Bloodborne Pathogens; Needlestick and Other Sharp Injuries; Final Rule.* Amended and effective April 18, 2001; and 29CFR 1910.1035 Occupational Exposure to Tuberculosis, Proposed Rule. October 17, 1997.

The Joint Commission. *High-Level Disinfection (HLD) and Sterilization* December 2015. https://www.jointcommission.org/standards_booster_paks/ .

TERMS

Regulation

Standard

Standards (regulatory)

Standards (voluntary)

Best practice

Accrediting agency

MedWatch

Third-party reprocessors

510(k)

Greenhouse gases

Medicare

Medicaid

Health Insurance Portability and Accountability Act (HIPAA)

Standards (AAMI)

Technical Information Reports (TIRs)

Chapter 15

Human Factors That Impact Endoscope Reprocessing

Learning Objectives

Upon completion of this chapter, readers will be able to:

1. Explain the role that individuals play in the successful reprocessing of endoscopes

2. Define human factors and the impact they can have on successful process outcomes

3. Discuss factors that impact work practices in endoscope reprocessing

4. Identify common errors in endoscope reprocessing and the impact each can have on patients, co-workers and the environment

5. Identify the responsibilities of staff members who reprocess endoscopes

6. Identify the responsibility of managers and administrators who supervise endoscope reprocessing

INTRODUCTION

Throughout this textbook, emphasis has been placed on the information, tools and techniques necessary to successfully reprocess endoscopes. One crucial factor still needs to be addressed: how human factors impact endoscope reprocessing. No amount of equipment, supplies or planning can overcome the behaviors of those responsible for the safety of endoscopes. While having the proper tools to perform reprocessing duties is certainly essential, focused attention must also be given to the people who work within the complex endoscope system. This chapter will address the human factors that impact endoscope reprocessing.

WHAT ARE HUMAN FACTORS?

Human factors examine the relationship between human beings and the systems with which they interact. For medical device manufacturers, incorporating human factors into a medical device design may make the device more intuitive for the user or it might make the device easier to clean and inspect for reprocessing staff. For healthcare facilities, human factors also include facility systems and the people who work within those systems. For example, a facility may invest in an endoscope tracking system; however, if the employees working in the area do not receive proper training, the effectiveness of the tracking system can be diminished.

The success of endoscope reprocessing and the safety of every endoscopy patient depends on the human beings responsible for performing the task and the tools and equipment provided to complete the task. The physical work environment and the information available to help reprocessing professionals understand each step in the process are also key factors.

This text has examined scientific information, standards, regulations and guidelines pertaining to endoscopes. It would seem that a well-designed endoscope reprocessing system that follows standards and best practices would be foolproof; however, that is not the case. Many factors impact each employee's performance and those factors can then impact the reprocessing function and outcomes.

Cause for Concern

In 2010, Ofstead and Associates conducted a study to examine the impact of human factors on endoscope reprocessing. Steps in endoscope reprocessing were observed at facilities that had written information on proper endoscope reprocessing. Employees indicated they were aware of the reprocessing protocols; however, during an observation of manual cleaning processes, only 1 of 69 flexible endoscopes was processed properly using all steps of the manual processes. Reprocessing professionals had the tools and information needed to perform the task, but they still failed to perform the task correctly.

In 2014, the International Association of Healthcare Central Service Materiel Management (IAHCSMM) conducted a member survey on endoscope reprocessing. Of the 1,000 respondents, 29% revealed flexible endoscope reprocessing at their facility needed improvement.

ECRI Institute, a nonprofit patient safety organization, identified "inadequate cleaning of flexible endoscopes before disinfection" as the number one health technology hazard in ECRI Institute's Top 10 list for 2016. Flexible endoscopes were also included on the organization's 2014 and 2015 health technology hazard lists.

The intricacy and sophistication of these devices and the complexity of the instructions for reprocessing them point to the need to examine all factors, including human factors, that may impact endoscope reprocessing outcomes. There could be many reasons for failure. **Figure 15.1** provides an illustration of some possible human factors that could lead to reprocessing errors.

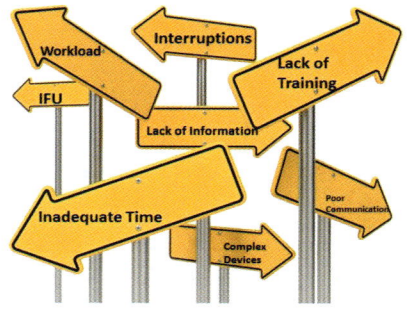

Figure 15.1 – Human Factors Can Impact Outcomes

Human factor errors may result from issues outside the workplace. For example, staying up all night with a sick child may cause a technician to feel drowsy at work and overlook a key component of the instructions for use (IFU) while cleaning an endoscope. Other examples of human factors outside the healthcare facility that may impact reprocessing outcomes include:

- Personal problems;

- Substance abuse;

- Mental or emotional issues;

- Complacency or boredom;

- Stress; and

- Physical pain or illness.

How Do Human Factors Impact Endoscope Reprocessing?

A 2010 study of endoscope reprocessing conducted by Ofstead and Associates found that proper IFU steps were not followed when technicians did not like the task. Other factors that impacted the process included technician confusion regarding the task and misunderstanding of the importance of the task. Unlike machines, people perform differently depending upon several factors. For example, an automated endoscope reprocessor (AER) runs the same cycle and in the same timeframe, even when the endoscope is needed immediately. On the other hand, technicians performing cleaning tasks may cut corners or skip steps if they feel pressured in a **turnaround** situation. Unlike humans who can become distracted or tired over the course of a shift, a properly managed and maintained AER will work consistently throughout the shift, without its function becoming compromised.

> **Turnaround** A situation where a medical device, such as an endoscope or surgical instrument, is used on one patient and then needed immediately for another procedure.

COMMON HUMAN FACTORS THAT MAY IMPACT ENDOSCOPE REPROCESSING

Failure to Follow Good Work Practices

The complex configuration of flexible endoscopes can make the cleaning process very difficult. A review of any flexible endoscope's IFU provides many steps that must be executed exactly as written. As discussed in previous chapters, many other details—such as equipment and chemical IFU—must also be diligently followed. Making matters even more difficult, there are many types of endoscopes with many types of configurations, so one process will not work for all endoscopes. Technicians must understand that endoscope reprocessing is a complicated process that cannot be altered or shortened. Failure to complete IFU steps exactly as written by the manufacturer because of user confusion or a desire to hasten the process may lead to process failures that can jeopardize patient safety.

Staff Responsibilities

Staff assigned to endoscope reprocessing functions must ensure they follow manufacturers' IFU and established work best practices – each and every time. There is never an excuse to cut corners. An old reprocessing adage states, "Prepare the device as if it was to be used on someone you love." All endoscope reprocessing staff must follow that (very human) thought.

It is also every staff member's responsibility to ask questions and request additional training if they are unsure how to properly perform any reprocessing steps. Every medical device reprocessing professional must strive to create a culture where every staff member feels comfortable asking questions and is willing to help others learn and enhance their skills. Reprocessing endoscopes and any other medical device should be done in a spirit of collaboration — where every endoscope reprocessing professional understands the main goal of patient safety and the need to work as a team to reach that goal.

Common Errors and Omissions

While few people (if any) set out to perform a procedure incorrectly, errors do happen. Even the smallest error can have a major impact on the overall process and the safety of patients and staff. Skipping a step or taking a shortcut can also have serious consequences. It is important to remember that the manufacturers of the devices being cleaned and the products being used have performed extensive testing and have developed their specific IFU after careful consideration. Regardless of the experience of someone working in the reprocessing area, their knowledge and understanding of the product or item being processed will never supersede that of the device or product manufacturer; therefore, endoscope reprocessing staff should never second guess instructions or deviate from manufacturer-required processes. The following sections review common errors in endoscope reprocessing and explore the impact that each error can have on reprocessing and patient outcomes.

Point-of-Use (Procedure Room)

Endoscope reprocessing begins at the point-of-use. Failure to complete the required point-of-use pre-cleaning can impact the success of the cleaning processes that follow. The following are common errors observed at the point-of-use:

Error	Impact
Not wearing proper personal protective equipment (PPE)	• OSHA violation • Danger of exposure to possibly infectious microorganisms • Danger of cross contamination in work and public areas
Not having or following manufacturers' IFU for the process	• Danger of improper processing that could result in the formation of biofilm and soil that is allowed to dry • Danger of improper processing that could damage the device
Reprocessing delays (e.g., too busy to perform task or procedures performed at night or on the weekend)	• Formation of biofilm that is very difficult to remove • Dried soil will make the endoscope more difficult to clean
Failure to pre-clean all channels (even if unused)	Unused channels may still become contaminated during use and handling of the endoscope
Transporting without using a closed container that is properly labeled	Transporting a soiled endoscope without a closed container increases the danger of cross contamination
Transporting the endoscope in a manner that may cause damage to it	Endoscopes are expensive, precision devices. Failure to transport the endoscope safely may result in damage and expensive repairs

Leak Testing

Leak testing is a critical step that should occur as soon as the endoscope reaches the decontamination area. This test determines whether the endoscope can be processed further and continue to be used. Common errors in leak testing include:

Error	Impact
Not having or following manufacturers' IFU for the process	Failure to leak test according to specific IFU could lead to fluid invasion and damage the device
Use of a damaged water-resistant cap	Could lead to fluid invasion and device damage
Overlooking pressurization of the endoscope prior to immersion	Could lead to fluid invasion and device damage
Incomplete angulation of the distal tip in all directions during the leak test	Failure to angulate the distal tip in all directions may jeopardize accurate leak test results
Using water with enzymatic already added	It is easier to detect leaks in clear water. Water with chemicals added may make it more difficult to detect leaks
Not fully submerging the endoscope underwater	Some leaks may not be detected
Not leak testing for the full time recommended by the endoscope manufacturer	Some leaks may not be detected

Manual Cleaning

Manual cleaning is a critical part of endoscope reprocessing. Soil that is not removed during this process will impede future disinfection or sterilization processes. Common manual cleaning errors and their impact include:

Error	Impact
Failure to fully submerge endoscope	Inadequate cleaning process due to low to no contact with detergent or enzyme
Failure to wash external surfaces of the endoscope	Inadequate cleaning process due to low to no contact with detergent or enzyme
Failure to submerge for the required length of time	Inadequate cleaning process due to low to no contact with detergent or enzyme and inadequate contact time
Neglecting to dilute and use the detergent per the detergent manufacturer's IFU	Detergent may not work optimally
Using water that is not at the correct temperature	Detergent may not work optimally
Using worn, damaged or improper brushes	Improperly-sized or -styled brushes will result in inadequate cleaning. Worn brushes may leave bristles behind that can enter the patient during a procedure
Failure to brush all internal lumens	Lumens that are missed during cleaning will prevent the endoscope from being successfully disinfected or sterilized
Failing to use manufacturer's validated cleaning adapters	Cleaning adapters that are not specifically fit to the endoscope being reprocessed will result in inadequate cleaning
Using damaged or improperly processed adapters	Inadequate cleaning. (See above)
Failure to manually clean accessories (buttons, etc.) thoroughly	Improperly cleaned accessories can lead to microbial growth and infection

Manual High-Level Disinfection (HLD)

Steps in the manual high-level disinfection process must be performed exactly as indicated in the endoscope and high-level disinfectant IFU. Common errors include:

Error	Impact
Failure to use a basin large enough to safely accommodate the endoscope	• Damage from coiling the endoscope too tightly • Risk of the endoscope not being completely covered by the solution
Using a high-level disinfectant (HLD) solution after its expiration date	The solution may not work properly resulting in an unsafe endoscope
Not testing a solution before use	The solution may not work properly resulting in an unsafe endoscope
Using a HLD at a temperature lower or higher than the requirements in the solution's IFU	The solution may not work properly resulting in an unsafe endoscope
Not submerging the complete endoscope (including the head) in the HLD solution	Lack of direct contact with the HLD will result in a failed disinfection process
Not exposing internal channels to the HLD solution	Lack of direct contact with the HLD will result in a failed disinfection process
Failure to expose the endoscope for the minimum contact time required by the solution manufacturer's IFU	The HLD solution will not have the time it needs to be effective
Failure to properly rinse the endoscope according to the solution manufacturer's IFU	Residual disinfectant solution may cause injury to patients and possible damage to the endoscope
Failure to properly dry the endoscope according to the endoscope manufacturer's IFU	Moisture remaining in an endoscope will increase the chance of microbial growth during storage
Failure to flush alcohol through all internal lumens according to the endoscope manufacturer's IFU	Alcohol is a drying agent. Failure to use it may result in inadequate drying
Failure to perform a quality check on test strips per IFU and facility policy	The solution may not work properly resulting in an unsafe endoscope
Failure to properly use minimum recommended concentration (MRC) test strip	Inadequate testing will fail to identify solution issues. The solution may not work properly resulting in an unsafe endoscope
Failure to document required steps (MRC, quality control (QC), temperature, patient identification, etc.)	Documentation is required by standards and it is critical in the event of a recall

Automated Endoscope Reprocessor (AER)

Automatic endoscope reprocessors are efficient only if the items processed are prepared correctly and the AER is operated exactly as specified in the IFU. Common errors include:

Error	Impact
Failure to manually clean and rinse the endoscope before placing in the AER	Faulty preparation will impede the AER's process and may result in an unsafe endoscope
Temperature of the solution not monitored	Some HLD chemicals are designed to be used at a specific temperature. Failure to achieve and maintain that temperature will impact the process. Documentation must be completed to create a quality record
Failure to connect endoscope properly per AER and endoscope manufacturer IFU	When connections are not correct exposure to the HLD and the following rinses may not be adequate resulting in an unsafe endoscope
Endoscope not validated for the specific AER	Processing an endoscope that has not been validated for a specific AER risks a failed HLD process and, in some cases, damage to the endoscope
Failure to manually clean accessories per manufacturer IFU before placing in the AER	Soil remaining on endoscope accessories and detachable components may result in a failed HLD process
Failure to set minimum exposure times properly	Minimum exposure times are exactly that — minimum exposures. When minimum requirements are not met, the process will not be successful
Failure to test MRC during appropriate cycle time	Each AER is designed and tested to meet specific requirements. Users who fail to follow IFU risk poor outcomes
Failure to follow AER manufacturer's IFU for cleaning and disinfecting the AER	The AER must be kept ready for use. Failure to performs appropriate maintenance of the AER increases the risk of process failure
Failure to perform recommended maintenance on the AER (filter changes, preventive maintenance)	The AER must be kept ready for use. Failure to performs appropriate maintenance, cleaning and disinfecting of the AER increases the risk of process failure
Failure to maintain required document for properly reprocessed endoscope	Documentation is a critical component of endoscope reprocessing. Failure to document results in a lack of specific information for possible recalls and reviews

Storage

Preparing an endoscope for use is critical; however, it is also critical to maintain the endoscope in a ready-to-use state until it is ready to be dispensed. Common errors in storage include:

Error	Impact
Failure to remove all valves and water-resistant cap when storing the endoscope	Keeping caps and valves in place during storage impedes air circulation and may trap moisture that can create an environment where microorganisms can grow
Neglecting to ensure that endoscopes are stored with all locks in the free position	Storing endoscopes with locks closed impedes air circulation and may trap moisture that can create an environment where microorganisms can grow
Crowded and unsecured endoscope storage areas	Cross contamination may occur when endoscopes touch one another in storage. Using an unsecured storage area enables unauthorized personnel access to endoscopes and increases the risk of contamination
Failure to properly dry endoscope before storage	Moisture can create an environment where microorganisms can grow
Failure to identify when the endoscope was last processed	Failure to identify the last reprocessed date makes it impossible to rotate endoscopes and ensure that each endoscope is within its established shelf life
Failure to connect endoscope to connectors (if using a cabinet with this feature)	Failure to connect an endoscope properly may result in inadequate drying

Common Pitfalls

Along with failure to perform each step in endoscope reprocessing, there are also other issues that can have a negative impact on reprocessing outcomes.

Misinformation

Misinformation can lead to failed processes and damaged endoscopes. Endoscope reprocessing staff must take care to ensure that the information used within the reprocessing system is accurate and current. Several scenarios can spread incorrect information. It may come from a co-worker or colleague who does not understand the process and its importance.

Misinformation may come from outside the department as well. It is important that process changes do not occur unless those changes are verified as appropriate for the item being reprocessed. Outside vendors or company representatives who are the facility's direct contact for most device and product-related issues and information should never direct a facility to deviate from the original IFU, unless the IFU has been updated and the vendor can provide a

written copy of the new IFU that supports the change. Manufacturer's IFU and departmental policies for reprocessing endoscopes should be written and only updated by authorized personnel. Reprocessing technicians should ask questions and request documentation from the vendor, as needed.

Outdated information can also cause process failures. As more information becomes available, as IFU are updated, and as standards, guidelines and regulations change, it is imperative that the information used in endoscope reprocessing be kept current. Failure to follow the most current information can increase the risk to patients.

Lack of Communication

Even the smallest communication breakdown can be very dangerous in endoscope reprocessing. For example, failure to notify the reprocessing area when a procedure has finished and the endoscope is ready to be cleaned can delay reprocessing and make the endoscope much more difficult to clean. Other communication failures may occur when processes change, an IFU is updated or other information is not conveyed to the appropriate people in a timely manner.

Pressure to Reduce Reprocessing Time

A 2015 survey of IAHCSMM members asked, "How often do you reprocess endoscopes in a STAT or turnaround situation?" Of 1,000 respondents, 26.9% indicated they reprocessed endoscopes in STAT or turnaround situations every day. In recent years, emphasis has been placed on meticulous cleaning that follows detailed IFU. Following the IFU for endoscope reprocessing is a lengthy process and there are no safe ways to shorten the process. Unfortunately, occasions arise where pressure to shorten processes is placed on endoscope reprocessing staff. That can be an intimidating and difficult situation because no one wants to delay a procedure or frustrate a physician. Reprocessing staff may feel challenged with deciding to process an item correctly or give in to a demand for rushed (inadequate) reprocessing. It is the responsibility of every reprocessing technician, however, to never deviate from standards or IFU, regardless of who is making the request for faster device turnaround, because doing so could jeopardize patient safety.

The Impact of Fatigue

A well-maintained piece of equipment can perform specific tasks consistently, regardless of its hours of operation in a given day. Equipment does not require breaks. Numerous repetitive motions and steps undertaken by an individual, however, can lead to fatigue and, subsequently, errors that can impact outcomes.

Lack of Prioritization

Successful reprocessing and customer satisfaction relies on effective, ongoing communication. Users should communicate changes in needs to the endoscope reprocessing staff so proper prioritization can take place. In situations where multiple procedures are performed, knowing the procedures and their scheduled times make it much easier to prioritize.

MANAGEMENT RESPONSIBILITIES

When addressing an endoscope reprocessing error, it is often easy to blame the reprocessing staff for their failure to meet requirements. While reprocessing professionals sometimes are the ones responsible for errors, they share the responsibility for safe and successful endoscope reprocessing with those who manage the endoscope reprocessing system. Management must ensure that those performing reprocessing duties have the proper tools to do the job, adequate time to complete the process, and the proper training to do it correctly.

Managers should also create a culture where patient safety is paramount and employees are encouraged to bring questions, suggestions and concerns forward at any time.

A successful endoscope reprocessing system also requires support from the facility's administration. Requirements for equipment, supplies, staffing and education may be necessary to develop an endoscope reprocessing system that is able to meet customer needs. That increased cost will sometimes require approval from administrators who are under pressure to contain costs. Reprocessing area managers should honestly share with their administrators information about the challenges of reprocessing endoscopes correctly. This communication should take place on a routine basis, not just when an issue arises. Managers should also provide endoscope reprocessing information to the facility's Infection Control and Preventionist (ICP). ICPs have extensive education of microbiology and disease processes and prevention, and can provide valuable advice and access to resources. They may also support the need for additional resources the reprocessing department requires to safely reprocess and store endoscopes.

Audits

When training has been provided and quality expectations have been clearly defined, it may be necessary to conduct process audits to help ensure the performance of tasks aligns with facility policies and the manufacturers' IFU. **Figure 15.2** provides an example of an audit checklist.

Sample Endoscope Cleaning Audit Checklist

Task	Completed	Comments
Receives endoscope, reviews manufacturer's IFU and begins the cleaning process within 15 minutes		
Performs leak testing according to leak testing protocol		
Soaks, scrubs, brushes and rinses all removable parts as outlined in the IFU		
Immerses and cleans exterior of scope		
Brushes and flushes entire channel system taking care to thoroughly brush each channel		
Rinses endoscope thoroughly taking care to flush channels until all residues are removed		
Inspects the scope for any debris, repeat the manual cleaning process if debris remains		
Performs protein soil detection on endoscope and repeats cleaning process if there is an indication of protein		
Dries endoscope		
Safely transports the endoscope to the high-level disinfection area		

Technician: _____

Audited by: _____

Date: _____

Figure 15.2

Employees should be inserviced

Upon hire or transfer

Annually for existing technicians

When a process changes

When equipment or supplies change

When a new endoscope is introduced into the system

When IFU, standards or guidelines change

When breaks in protocol are discovered

Figure 15.3

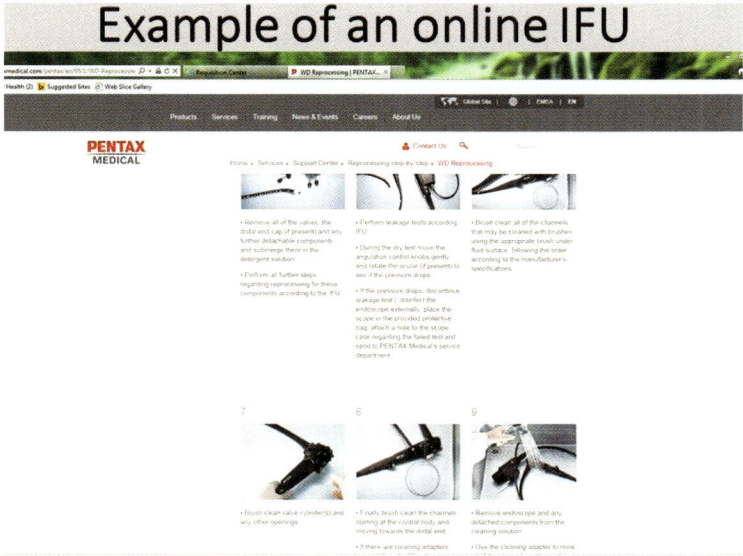

Figure 15.4

TRAINING AND CONTINUING EDUCATION

No one can properly reprocess an endoscope without training. It is not a process that should be carried out using guesswork and it is not a skill that can be picked up by reading an IFU. Those responsible for endoscope reprocessing must be well trained in the process and understand the impact that steps in that process can have on the patient. Endoscope education should begin before an employee first handles an endoscope, and the education should continue throughout the time the employee performs endoscope reprocessing duties. **Figure 15.3** provides an overview of circumstances when employees should receive training and continuing education.

Staying Current in a Busy Working Environment

Education remains one of the greatest challenges in today's endoscope reprocessing area. When time, staffing or budgets are tight, education is often the first area to suffer. Changes in standards, guidelines, regulations and IFU happen and it is imperative that each endoscope be reprocessed using the most current information available. Reprocessing staff should have access to current standards, guidelines

and IFU. **Figure 15.4** provides an example of an IFU retrieved from the internet.

Formal Inservices

Formal inservices and training can help introduce new equipment, devices and processes to reprocessing professionals. Inservice attendance should be mandatory for anyone working with the items, and employee attendance records should be maintained. Employees files should also include all records of education and training. **Figure 15.5** is an example of a notice for a formal endoscope inservice.

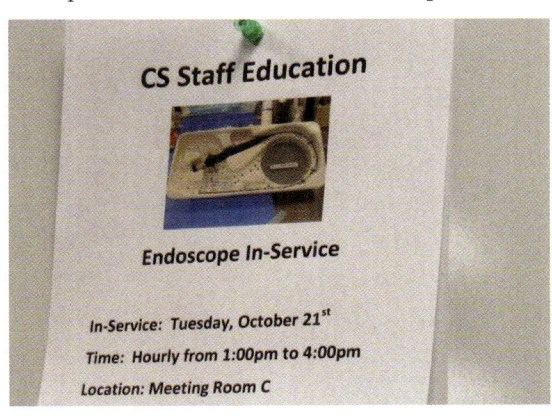

Figure 15.5 Notice of a Formal Education Program Scheduled for Employees

When changes occur or errors are identified, informal reminders may be used to immediately notify staff of changes and prevent recurrence of errors. These simple, yet effective information posts in the immediate work area help quickly spread the word of an issue, thereby reducing the risk of recurrence. **Figure 15.6** provides an example of a post that reminds employees to follow a specific protocol.

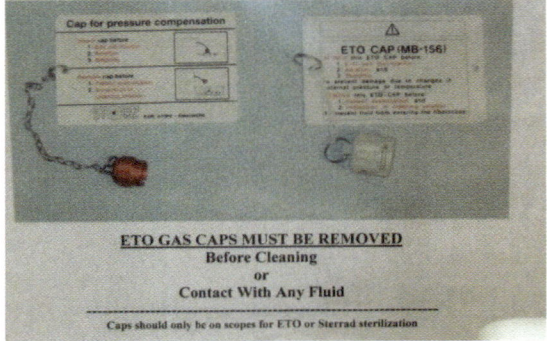

Figure 15.6 Reminder Posted to Prevent Recurrence of an Error

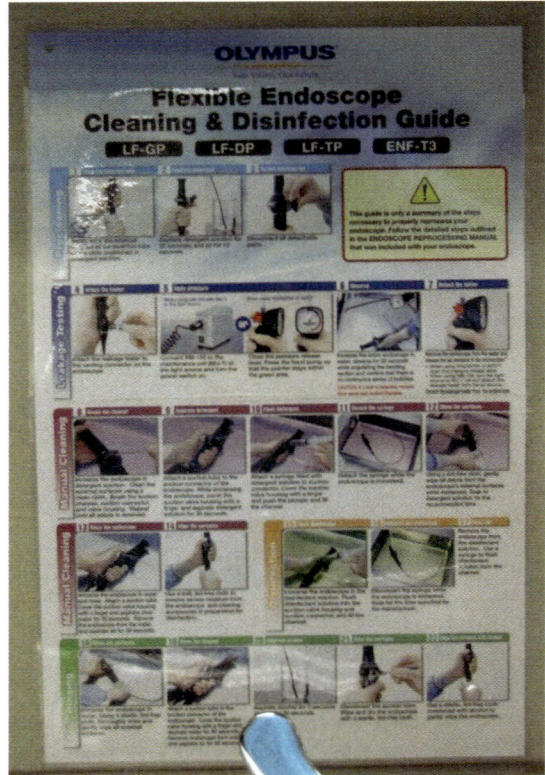

Figure 15.7 Poster Placed in a Work Area to Help Employees Follow a Step-by-Step Process

Some manufacturers provide posters or other informational materials that can be placed in the work area to help ensure employees follow specific processes. (See **Figure 15.7**)

Safety

No endoscope management program would be complete without a safety component. Throughout this textbook, the focus has been primarily on patient and employee safety. The need for proper use of personal protective equipment (PPE) and the reasons for wearing it have been addressed, for example, as have the importance of airflow, air monitoring and ventilation systems. Reprocessing technicians should practice good work practices that reduce the risk of exposure to chemicals and contaminants and they should understand why such practices are necessary. **Figure 15.8** provides an example of a spill kit that employees should know how to use in case of emergencies.

Figure 15.8 – All Employees Should Understand How to Handle Spills

CONCLUSION

Healthcare is a very human process that is delivered to humans by humans. Numerous human factors can impact quality service, care and outcomes. The goal of every healthcare professional should always be to provide the best care possible and to remain vigilant on the job to ensure human factors are identified and addressed, so they do not get in the way of quality outcomes. Every patient and each member of the endoscopy team relies on endoscope reprocessing professionals to deliver safe, effective endoscopes and related equipment to help make quality care possible. A commitment to continuing education and training, and staying vigilant on the job to ensure that standards, guidelines, best practices and IFU are consistently followed will allow endoscope reprocessing technicians to fulfill their quality commitment.

RESOURCES

Association for the Advancement of Medical Instrumentation. *ANSI/AAMI ST91: 2015. Flexible and semi-rigid endoscope processing in health care facilities.*

International Association of Healthcare Central Service Materiel Management. *Central Service Technical Manual, Eighth Edition.* 2016.

Carayon, Pascale, *Handbook of Human Factors and Ergonomics in Health Care and Patient Safety.* CRC Press. 2011.

Faa.gov. *Handbook of Human Factors*, Chapter 14. https://www.faa.gov/regulations_policies/handbooks_manuals/aircraft/media/AMT_Handbook_Addendum_Human_Factors.pdf .

Ofstead CL, et al. *Endoscope Reprocessing Methods; A prospective Study on the Impact of Human Factors Gastrointestinal Nursing.* Society of Gastrointestinal Nurses and Associates. Am J Infect Control. Volume 33, Volume 4. August 2015.

TERMS

Turnaround

Glossary

510(k) A premarket submission made to FDA to demonstrate that the device to be marketed is at least as safe and effective, that is, substantially equivalent, to a legally marketed device (21 CFR 807.92(a)(3)). Submitters must compare their device to one or more similar legally marketed devices and make and support their substantial equivalency claims.

A

AAMI Abbreviation for Association for the Advancement of Medical Instrumentation.

abrasive Any of a wide variety of natural or manufactured gritty substances used to grind, wear down, rub away, smooth or scour.

accrediting agency An agency that surveys healthcare facilities to determine if minimum standards for patient safety are being met. Accreditation is awarded to facilities that comply with identified standards.

acid fast stain A special stain to identify mycobacteria and nocardia. Also called a Ziehl-Neelsen stain.

action level The level of exposure to a harmful substance or other hazard at which an employer must take required precautions to protect workers. It is normally one half of the permissible exposure limit.

action plan A sequence of steps that must be taken, or activities that must be performed well, for a strategy to succeed. An action plan has three major elements (1) Specific tasks: what will be done and by whom. (2) Time horizon: when will it be done. (3) Resource allocation: what specific funds are available for specific activities.

activated (activation) Process by which a solution is combined with an activating chemical before use. Glutaraldehydes must be activated before initial use.

adhesions The holding together of two surfaces or parts; a band of connective tissue between parts that are normally separate; the molecular attraction between two contacting bodies.

aeration A process by which sterilized packages are subjected to moving air to facilitate removal of toxic residuals after exposure to a sterilizing agent, such as ethylene oxide.

aerosols A suspension of ultramicroscopic solid or liquid particles in air or gas; a spray.

airborne Suspended or carried in a gas or air stream.

air exchanges A measurement of air movement within a specific space. A minimum of 10 total air exchanges per hour is recommended for areas housing EO sterilizers and aerators.

air flow The rate and direction of exhaust air flow in the immediate vicinity of sterilizers should be measured to verify that there is adequate air flow away from sterilizer operators and other personnel in the sterilization area.

aggressive (bacteria) The ability of a microorganism to invade, survive, and multiply in the tissues.

alimentary canal Pathway that food takes through the body's digestive system.

anaerobes Bacteria that do not require free oxygen.

ANSI Abbreviation for American National Standards Institute.

antibiotic Substance produced by one microorganism that will kill or inhibit another microorganism.

antibiotic resistant The ability of pathogens to resist the effects of antibiotics that would normally be used to kill the microorganism.

antibody Protein produced in the body which reacts against a specific foreign molecule (antigen).

arthroscopy Examination, diagnosis or treatment of a joint.

asepsis Absence of microorganisms that cause disease.

asepsis (medical) clean technique Procedures performed to reduce the number of microorganisms to minimize their spread.

asepsis (surgical) surgical technique Procedures to eliminate the presence of all microorganisms and/ or to prevent the introduction of microorganisms to an area.

aseptic Free from pathogenic organisms; a means of preventing infection.

aseptic technique Activity or procedure that prevents infection or breaks the chain of infection.

autoclave Equipment that uses steam under pressure to sterilize, usually at temperatures of 250° or 270°F (121°C or 132°C).

B

bacilli Rod shaped bacteria.

bacteria Single celled microorganisms that multiply by splitting. There are helpful bacteria such as those that help with food digestion in our intestines or those used in sewage treatment plants. There are also those that cause disease called pathogens or germs. (Note: if there is just a single one it is called bacterium).

bacterial capsule A gel-like coating that surrounds some bacteria. The capsule hides the identifying marks on bacteria making them almost invisible to the immune system, making it difficult for immune cells to mount a successful attack.

bacterial spore (endospore) stain A stain used to identify the presence of spores. IF they are still covered with the membrane of the original bacteria, they are referred to as endospores.

bactericide Substance that kills bacteria.

bacteriology Science of the study of bacteria.

bacteriostatic Inhibition of bacterial growth without their destruction.

barrier packaging Minimum package that prevents ingress of microorganisms and allows aseptic presentation of the product at the point of use.

best practice A method or technique that has consistently shown results superior to those achieved by other means.

bioburden The number of microorganisms on a contaminated object; also called bioload or microbial load.

biocide A substance or microorganism that kills or controls the growth of living organisms. Examples: antibiotics and disinfectants.

biodegradable Readily decomposed by bacteria or enzymatic actions.

biofilm A collection of microorganisms that attach to surfaces and each other and form a colony. The colony produces a protective gel that is very difficult to penetrate with detergents and disinfectants.

biohazardous waste Wastes containing infectious agents that present a risk or potential risk to human health either directly through infections or indirectly through the environment.

biological indicator (BI) Sterilization process monitoring device consisting of a standardized, viable population of microorganisms (usually bacterial spores) known to be resistant to the mode of sterilization being monitored.

borescope A device used for visual inspection in areas that are inaccessible by other means. Some borescopes are equipped with cameras that provide still images or video of inaccessible areas within endoscope lumens.

Bowie-Dick (Daily Air Removal) Test Test run daily to validate the vacuum cycle of a steam sterilizer. The test should be run in an empty load at the same time each day.

bronchoscopes A device used to examine the examine throat, larynx, trachea and lower airways. There are two types of bronchoscopes; flexible and rigid.

C

capsid A viral capsid is the protective protein structure housing the virus DNA or RNA.

capsule stain A stain used to identify the presence of a capsule surrounding individual bacterium.

cell Basic unit of life; the smallest structural unit of living organisms capable of performing all basic life functions.

Centers for Disease Control and Prevention (CDC) The Centers for Disease Control and Prevention (CDC) is a federal agency that conducts and supports health promotion, prevention and preparedness activities in the United States with the goal of improving overall public health. Established in 1346 and based in Atlanta, GA., the CDC is managed by the Department of Health and Human Services (HHS).

certification Association and industry recognition given to individuals with educational and/or work experience requirements who successfully complete an examination process that demonstrates their knowledge of subject-matter to be mastered for success in the position.

chain of infection A way of gathering the information needed to interrupt or prevent an infection. Each of the links in the chain must be favorable to the organism for the infection to continue. Breaking any link in the chain can disrupt the infection. Which link is most effective to target will depend on the organism.

chains Bacteria that are cocci shaped, appearing in single file chains like a necklace.

chelating agents Chemicals that hold hard water minerals in solution and prevent soaps or detergents from reacting with the minerals.

chemical indicators (CIs) Devices used to monitor the presence or attainment of one or more of the parameters required for a satisfactory sterilization process.

chemical sterilization Process using a chemical agent to render a product free of viable microorganisms.

choledochoscope A flexible endoscope used to visualize the interior of the biliary tract.

CJD (Abbreviation for Creutzfeld-Jakob Disease) A debilitating, fatal brain disease; see prions.

cleaning The removal of soil from the item being reprocessed.

cocci Spiral or ball-shaped bacteria.

colon Main portion of the large intestine.

colonoscope A flexible endoscope used to examine the lower gastrointestinal tract (GI).

colony Visible growth of microorganisms seen in culture medium; usually obtained from a single organism.

contagious Highly communicable; easily transmitted.

contaminate To render unfit for use through introduction of a substance which is harmful or injurious.

contamination State of being soiled or infected by contact with infectious organisms or other material.

copious Present in a large amount (such as large volume of rinsing water).

critical devices Refers to the Spaulding medical device classification system. Instruments or objects introduced directly into the bloodstream or other normally sterile body areas.

cross contamination Migration of contaminants from one person, object or work location to another.

cuboid Bacteria that are cocci shaped, appearing in groups of eight like a box.

cycle (sterilization) Defined sequence of operational steps designed to achieve sterilization; carried out in a sealed chamber.

cycle time Total elapsed time of a sterilization cycle from when the sterilizer door is closed and the cycle is activated until the cycle is completed and the door is opened.

cystoscope, flexible An endoscope used to examine the inside of kidneys and urinary tract organs.

cystoscope, rigid An endoscope used to examine inside the bladder.

cystoscopy Examination, diagnosis or treatment of the urethra and bladder or prostate gland.

D

decontamination Removing or reducing contamination by infectious organisms or other harmful substances.

deflection The ability of the tip of a flexible endoscope to bend (using control knobs) to increase the area that can be accessed by a physician, visually or with an instrument.

decontamination area Location within a health care facility designated for collection, retention and cleaning of soiled and/or contaminated items.

deionized (DI) water Water that has had all minerals removed by using an ion exchange process.

delayed processing Reprocessing activities that are started over one hour after an endoscope's use. A delay in reprocessing enables soil to dry on endoscope components and biofilms to form.

denatured alcohol Alcohol that has been rendered unfit for use as a beverage by the addition of substances which impart an unpleasant odor and taste. Examples: wood alcohol and benzene.

detergent Cleaning agent composed of a "surface wetting agent" that reduces surface tension; a "builder" which is the principle cleaning agent, and a "sequestering" or "chelating agent" to suspend the soil; detergents may also have additional additives, such as blood solvents or rust inhibitors; any chemical that causes oil or grease to dissolve in water and cleans the item on which it is used. Unlike soap, detergent does not contain fats and lye.

detergent/germicide Combination of a cleaning agent and a disinfectant.

detergent/sanitizer Combination of chemicals that possesses antibacterial and cleaning properties.

diagnostic The process of attempting to determine or identify a possible disease or disorder.

diploid (diplococci) Bacteria that are cocci shaped, appearing in pairs.

disease State of illness characterized by marked symptoms caused by an infectious agent producing a definite pathological pattern.

disinfectant Chemical that kills most pathogenic organisms, but not all spores.

disinfectant/detergent Chemical compound that contains both detergent and disinfectant. Usually, the action of both is compromised because of the combination.

disinfection Destruction of nearly all pathogenic microorganisms on an inanimate (non-living) surface.

distal The end of an item that is farthest away from the point of origin; the end of the instrument farthest away from the operator; the distal end of the femur is closest to the knee.

distilled water Water that has been heated to boiling point, vaporized, cooled and condensed into liquid form. Distillation removes impurities and like gases and organic material, it also removes some bacteria.

DNA Deoxyribonucleic acid that carries the genetic information of the organism.

droplet nuclei Droplet nuclei develop when the fluid of pathogenic droplets evaporates. They are so small and light they may remain suspended in the air for several hours. Airborne droplet nuclei can be widely dispersed by air currents.

duodenoscope A flexible endoscope used to diagnose and treat abnormalities in the duodenum.

duodenum First portion of the small intestine.

E

ECRI institute A nonprofit organization dedicated to using applied scientific research to discover which medical procedures, devices, drugs and processes are best to improve patient care. ECRI Institute aims to keep healthcare professionals abreast of challenges and concerns regarding medical devices.

endoscope Specially designed medical instrument used to view the interior of a hollow organ or body cavity. The endoscope can be Flexible, Rigid or Semi-Rigid and vary by function, design, and size depending upon the area of the body being examined.

endoscope accessories Separate components used with a flexible endoscope. Examples include water bottles, biopsy forceps and basket forceps.

endoscopic vein harvest (EVH) Harvesting of the saphenous vein from leg or radial vein from the arm to use as a coronary graft.

endoscopist A medical specialist trained in the use of an endoscope.

endoscopy A medical procedure done with an instrument called an endoscope. The endoscope is put into the body to look inside Endoscopy is sometimes used for certain kinds of surgery.

endoscopy or GI Lab A Department dedicated to the performance of common endoscopic procedures.

endoscopy technician A technician who supports and assists the endoscopists by setting up or taking down endoscopic procedures.

endospore A tough dormant structure that some bacteria are able to form when cells find themselves in such extreme conditions that they are in peril of dying. The endospore allows the survival of bacteria's cell lines through harsh conditions that would kill a normal member of the species.

endospore stain A stain used to identify the presence of spores. If spores are still covered with the membrane of the original bacteria, they are referred to as endospores.

enteroscope A flexible endoscope used to examine the small intestine to investigate irregularities such as blocked bowel passages and small bowel tumors.

enzymatic solution Solution containing special enzymes that dissolves proteinaceous materials.

enzyme Substance that initiates chemical changes, such as fermentation, without participating in them; a catalyst, usually protein, produced by a living cell with a specific action and optimum activity at a definite pH value.

epidemiology Study of the occurrence and distribution of disease; usually refers to epidemics.

equipment maintenance Processes used to keep equipment and devices, including flexible endoscopes, working properly and safely and restore them to their original performance standards.

excursion limit The exposure level of EO above which no employees may be exposed to under normal workplace conditions.

expiration date Date calculated by adding a specific period of time to the date of manufacture or sterilization of a medical device or component that defines its estimated useful life.

expiration statement Statement indicating that the contents of a package are sterile indefinitely, unless the integrity of the package is compromised.

exposure time Time in which the sterilizer's chamber is maintained within the specified range for temperature, sterilant concentration, pressure and humidity.

F

fahrenheit Thermometer scale in which the space between the freezing point and the boiling point of water is 180°; 32° is the freezing point and 212° is the boiling point. To convert from Fahrenheit to Centigrade scales: 5/9 (°F - 32) = °C.

FDA Abbreviation for U.S. Food and Drug Administration.

FESS functional endoscopic sinus surgery Examination, diagnosis or treatment of the inside structures of the nose and sinus cavity. Also known as sinuscopy.

filter Device secured to a rigid sterilization container's lid and/or bottom that allows passage of air and sterilants, but provides a microbial barrier.

filter retention system Mechanism on a rigid sterilization container that secures disposable filters in place.

flexible endoscope An optic instrument that transmits light and carries images back to the observer through flexible transparent fibers, and used to inspect and treat interior portions of the body.

fluid invasion A situation where fluid invades internal sections of an endoscope. Fluid damage causes damage to working components of the endoscope and creates a situation where microorganisms are introduced to areas of the endoscope that cannot be cleaned. 6

fungicide Substance that kills fungi.

fungus A diverse group of microorganisms and plants that include the microscopic fungi and yeasts such as Candida albicans, and Aspergillus fumigatus. Fungus also includes mold, mushrooms, mildews and smuts.

G

gasket Pliable strip on sterilization containers that seals the lid and container to prevent entry of microorganisms.

gastroenteritis Inflammation of the stomach and intestines with symptoms similar to enteritis and dysentery; often caused by enteric group of bacteria (e.g., Salmonella paratypih and Salmonella schottmuller).

gastrointestinal (GI) lab Department dedicated to the performance of common endoscopic procedures.

gastroscope A flexible endoscope designed to view the interior of the stomach.

germ Microorganism that causes disease.

germicidal Related to destroying germs.

germicide Agent that kills germs.

germinate Refers to the spore process moving from the dormant, highly protected spore state, to become an active bacteria in a favorable environment again. Also explained as moving from the spore form back to a vegetative (non-spore, vulnerable) form.

gram negative Bacteria that cannot hold on to the purple color after a gram stain and are instead counter-stained red or pink.

gram positive Bacteria that maintain a purple color after a gram stain is completed.

gram stain Gram staining is usually the first test on a sample (specimen) taken from the patient when trying to identify bacteria that might be causing an infection. Most bacteria are either gram positive (hold on to a purple color) or gram negative (turn red or pink) when the staining is completed. The stain does not work for other non-bacterial microorganisms.

greenhouse gases Any of the gases that absorb solar radiation are responsible for the greenhouse effect, including carbon dioxide, methane, ozone and fluorocarbons.

H

HAI See "healthcare-acquired infection."

hand hygiene Act of washing one's hands with soap and water or using an alcohol-based hand rub.

hardness (water) Amount of dissolved minerals in water, which alters the effectiveness of many disinfectants, detergents and soaps.

hazardous waste Substances that cannot be disposed of in the facility's normal trash system.

Health Insurance Portability and Accountability Act (HIPAA) The HIPAA Privacy Rule provides federal protections for individually identifiable heath information held by covered entities and their business associates, and gives patients an array of right with respect to that information. www.hhs.gov.

healthcare-associated infection (HAI) An infection that is not present when a patient is admitted to a hospital or healthcare facility. If the infection develops in a patient on or after day three of admission to the hospital or healthcare facility, the infection is referred to as hospital-acquired or healthcare-associated.

Healthcare Infection Control Practices Advisory Committee (HICPAC) The Healthcare Infection Control Practices Advisory Committee (HICPAC) is a federal advisory committee assembled to provide advice and guidance to the Centers for Disease Control and Prevention (CDC) and the Secretary of the Department of Health and Human Services (HHS) regarding the practice of infection control and strategies for surveillance, prevention, and control of healthcare-associated infections, antimicrobial resistance and related events in United States healthcare settings. The primary activity of the Committee is to provide advice on periodic updating of existing CDC guidelines and development of new CDC guidelines.

hepatitis Inflammation of the liver; usually caused by the hepatitis virus.

high-level disinfection The destruction of all vegetative microorganisms, mycobacterium, small or non-lipid viruses, medium of lipid viruses, fungal spores and some bacterial spores.

HIPAA See Health Insurance Portability and Accountability Act.

HIV Abbreviation for human immunodeficiency virus; an HIV infection is a chronic viral infection characterized by progressive destruction of the T-cell, which impairs the body's immune system; disease severity is relates to the degree of immune suppression.

hysteroscope A flexible endoscope used for visualization of the uterus.

hysteroscopy Evaluation, diagnosis, treatment of the vagina, cervix and uterus.

I

IAHCSMM Abbreviation for International Association of Healthcare Central Service Materiel Management.

immediate use steam sterilization (IUSS) Process designed for the cleaning, steam sterilization and delivery of patient care items for immediate use. Previously known as flash sterilization.

immune Exempt from a given infection.

inactivation To stop or destroy activity.

inanimate Not endowed with life or spirit; not alive.

incompatible Not capable of being mixed without undergoing destructive chemical changes or antagonism.

incubate To maintain under optimum environmental conditions favorable for growth.

incubator Apparatus for maintaining a constant and suitable temperature for the growth and cultivation of microorganisms.

infection Invasion of body tissue by microorganisms that then multiply. The invading microorganism may be a recognized pathogen (germ) or a normally helpful microorganism (like one that normally lives in your intestine) that invades a different part of the body such as the bloodstream, kidneys or lungs. Things that cause infections are often called infectious agents.

infection, opportunistic An infection caused by microorganisms (bacteria, viruses, fungi, or protozoa) that take advantage of an opportunity not normally available, such as a host with a weakened immune system. See opportunistic infection.

infection control Control of active infectious disease; requires (a) working knowledge of the usefulness and applications of physical and chemical agents that suppress or kill microorganisms and (b) familiarity with the sources of potentially dangerous microorganisms, routes by which they spread, and their portals of entry into the body.

infectious Having the ability to transmit disease.

inferior Below or lower.

inflammation Reaction of the tissues to an injury; a protective mechanism to an irritant on tissues.

instructions for use (IFU) See manufacturer's instructions for use.

integrating indicator Chemical indicator (CI) designed to react to all critical parameters over a specified range of sterilization cycles, and whose performance has been correlated to the performance of the relevant biological indicator (BI) under the labeled conditions of use.

intermediate-level disinfection The destruction of viruses, mycobacteria, fungi and vegetative bacteria, but not bacterial spores.

intubation scope, flexible An endoscope used to visualize the airway either through an eyepiece or a screen.

IUSS See immediate use steam sterilization .

J

jejunum Second portion of the small intestine.

julian date The Julian day or Julian day number (JDN) is the number of days that have elapsed since January 1 of a specific year.

K

L

laparoscopy Examination, diagnosis and treatment of the abdominal and pelvic organs.

large intestine (colon) Digestive organ that dehydrates digestive residues (feces).

latex Common form of rubber used in the manufacture of hospital and medical supplies.

latex sensitivity Sensitivity (allergic reaction) of some people to latex caused by exposure to latex that is improperly processed; symptoms range from skin rash, primarily on the hands, to an anaphylactic reaction.

leak test (endoscope) Endoscope processing procedure that ensures the device's flexible covering and internal channels are watertight.

LED Abbreviation for light emitting diode, a semiconductor diode that emits light when voltage is applied.

load control number Label information on sterilization packages, trays or containers that identifies the sterilizer, cycle run and date of sterilization.

loaner instrumentation Instruments or sets borrowed from a vendor for emergency or scheduled surgical procedures that will be returned following use.

lot (load) control number Numbers and/or letters by which a specific group of products can be traced to a particular manufacturing or sterilization operation.

low-level disinfection The destruction of vegetative forms of bacteria, some fungi, and lipid viruses, but not bacterial spores.

lumen Interior path through a needle, tube or surgical instrument.

lungs Main organs of the respiratory system whose function is transporting oxygen into the blood and removing carbon dioxide from the blood.

lux A unit of illumination equal to one lumen per square meter.

M

manufacturer's instructions for use (IFU) Written recommendation provided by the manufacture of a medical device providing instructions for safe and effective methods to correctly reprocess that device.

manufacturer Maker or producer of items or equipment.

medicaid A federal and state assistance program that pays covered medical expenses for low-income individuals. It is run by state and local governments within federal guidelines.

medicare A federal medical insurance program that primarily serves those over age 65 years of age (regardless of income), and people under 65 with certain disabilities and people of all ages with end-stage renal disease.

MedWatch A safety information and adverse event reporting system that serves healthcare professionals and the public by reporting serious problems suspected to be associated with the drugs and medical devices they prescribe, dispense or use.

methicillin-resistant Staphylococcus aureus (MRSA) Staphylococcus aureus bacteria that have developed a resistance to methicillin, the drug of choice; usually occurs with patients who have had antibiotic therapy for a long time.

microbes Organisms of microscopic or submicroscopic size generally, including viruses, rickettsiae, bacteria, algae, yeasts and molds.

microbiology The study of microorganisms.

micron Unit of measurement; 1/1000 of a millimeter or 1/25,000 of an inch or one millionth of a meter. Note: meter equals 39.37 inches.

microorganism Organisms that can only be seen with the aid of a standard or electron microscope.

mil Unit of length or thickness equal to .001 of an inch.

minimally invasive Causing no significant trauma to the patient, requiring little of no incision.

minimally invasive surgery (MIS) Minimally invasive surgery uses state-of-the-art technology to access body cavities and reduce the damage to human tissue during procedures.

minimum recommended concentration (MRC) Minimum concentration at which the manufacturer of a liquid chemical sterilant or high level disinfectant (HLD)tested the product and validated its performance.

mixture Blend of two or more substances.

MRC Abbreviation for minimum recommended concentration; minimum concentration at which the manufacturer tested the product and validated its performance.

MRSA See methicillin-resistant staphyloccus aureus.

N

negative air pressure Situation that occurs when air flows into a room or area because the pressure in the area is less than that of surrounding areas.

noncritical devices Refers to the Spaulding medical device classification system; devices that come in contact with intact skin.

nontoxic Not poisonous; not capable of producing injury or disease.

nephroscopy Examination, diagnosis, treatment of the kidney.

O

olestra A synthetic fat used in some foods labeled as reduced fat or fat free. Olsetra may leave a waxy substance in the colon that may stick to the channels of an endoscope.

operative endoscope Used to perform procedures. (i.e. the removal of a rectal polyp).

opportunistic infection An infection by a microorganism that normally does not cause disease but becomes pathogenic when the body's immune system is weakened by a genetic condition, surgery, traumatic injury, chemotherapy, or certain diseases such as AIDS or cyctic fibrosis. Even being on antibiotics is a risk factor for some infections like Clostridium difficile (C.diff).

organic Describing compounds containing oxygen, carbon and hydrogen; characteristic of, pertaining to or derived from living organisms.

P

packaging Application or use of appropriate closures, wrappings, cushioning, containers, and complete identification up to, but not including, the shipping container and associated packing.

parasite Organisms that live off of, or in, another organism (called the host), obtaining nourishment and protection from the host, but giving no benefit in return. Parasitic infections in human hosts often cause disease.

parts per million (PPM) The volume of EtO per volume of air. One part per million means that there is one part of EO in every million parts of air sampled.

pasteurization Process of heating a fluid to a moderate temperature for a definite period of time to destroy undesirable bacteria without changing its chemical composition.

pathogens Capable of causing disease. For example, disease causing bacteria, fungus, viruses, protozoa and helminths are called pathogens.

peracetic acid (PA) Liquid oxidizing agent that is an effective biocide at low temperatures; used in a sterilization system that processes immersible diagnostic and surgical instruments (primarily flexible and rigid scopes); items must be used immediately after sterilization because they are wet and cannot be stored.

permissible exposure limit (PEL) The maximum amount of concentration of a chemical that a worker may be exposed to under OSHA regulations.

personal protective equipment (PPE) Specialized clothing or equipment worn by an employee for protection against a hazard.

pH Measure of alkalinity or acidity on a scale of 0 to 14; pH of 7 is neutral (neither acid or alkaline); pH below 7 is acid; pH above 7 is alkaline.

point-of-use processing That which occurs when a medical device is processed immediately before use and/or close to the patient care area.

preconditioning Treatment of product prior to the sterilization cycle in a room or chamber to attain specified limits for temperature and relative humidity; see conditioning.

prion An infectious protein particle that, unlike a virus, contains no nucleic acid, does not trigger an immune response and is not destroyed by extreme heat or cold.

procedure area An area within the healthcare facility that conducts invasive and minimally invasive procedures requiring instruments, supplies and equipment.

process challenge device (PCD) Object that simulates a predetermined set of conditions when used to test sterilizing agent(s).

process indicators Devices used with individual units (e.g., packs or containers) to demonstrate that the unit has been exposed to the sterilization process, and to distinguish between processed and unprocessed units.

processing area Area in which decontaminated, clean instruments and other medical and surgical supplies are inspected, assembled into sets and trays and wrapped, packaged or placed into container systems for sterilization; commonly called the "preparation and packaging area" if part of Central Service, and "pack room" if textile packs are assembled there.

product family Collection of products determined to be similar or equivalent for validation purposes.

Q

quality Consistent delivery of products and services according to established standards. Quality "integrates" the concerns for the customers (including patients and user department personnel) with those of the department and facility.

R

regulation Requirements issued by administrative agencies that have the force of law.

reprocessing The process of rendering a clinically used device safe and ready for reuse.

reverse osmosis (RO) A water purification process by which a solvent, such as water, is removed of impurities after being forced through a semipermeable membrane.

rhinolaryngoscopes A flexible endoscope used to examine upper airways such as nasal passages, nasopharynx, oropharynx and larynx.

rigid container system Instrument containers that hold medical devices during sterilization and also protect devices from contamination during storage and transport.

risk assessment The process of identifying all the risks to and from an activity and assessing the potential impact of each risk.

RNA Ribonucleic acid is the messenger nucleic acid that normally carries the instructions from the DNA to the actual assembly line for proteins. RNA viruses are the only entities that carry only RNA (no DNA).

robotic assisted surgery Surgery performed with the assistance of instruments and scopes mounted on a robotic arm.

S

safety data sheet (SDS) A written statement providing detailed information about a chemical or toxic substance including potential hazards and appropriate handling methods. An SDS is provided by the product to the product buyer and must be posted or made available in a place that is easily accessible to those that will use the product.

sanitary Relating to health; characterized by or readily kept in cleanness.

sanitize To reduce the microbial flora in materials or on articles, such as eating utensils, to levels judged safe by public health standards.

SDS Abbreviation for safety data sheet.

secondary container A generic container that is filled from a primary container or filled with a diluted solution; secondary containers must be clearly labeled with content.

semi-critical devices Refers to the Spaulding medical device classification system; devices that come in contact with non-intact skin or mucous membranes.

semi-rigid ureteroscopy Examination, diagnosis, treatment of the ureter.

sentinel event An unexpected occurrence involving death, serious physical or psychological injury, or the risk thereof.

septic Relating to the presence of pathogens or their toxins.

sequestering agent A substance that removes ions from a solution system by forming a ring which does not have chemical reactions with the ion which is removed. Sequestering agents are commonly used for removing water hardness.

shelf life Period of time during which product sterility is assumed to be maintained.

shelf life (disinfectants) Length of time a disinfectant can be properly stored after which it must be discarded.

sigmoid colon Last portion of large intestine.

simethicone An ingredient found in over-the-counter anti-gas medications. Simethicone drops are sometimes injected into water bottles or endoscope channels to reduce bubbles that can impede visibility. Residue from simethicone can remain in an endoscope even after reprocessing.

single-parameter indicator Designed for one critical parameter that indicates exposure to a sterilization cycle at a stated value of the chosen parameter.

sinuscopy Examination, diagnosis or treatment of the inside structures of the nose and sinus cavity. Also known as FESS or functional endoscopic sinus surgery.

small intestine Digestive organ where the greatest amount of digestion and nutrient absorption into body cells occurs.

small joint arthroscopy Examination, diagnosis or treatment of small joints (e.g., wrist, jaw, ankle).

SMS (spunbond-meltblown-spunbond) Nonwoven packaging material that is the most popular flat wrap.

soap Compound of one or more fatty acids, or their equivalent, with an alkaline substance.

Spaulding classification system A system developed by Dr. E.H. Spaulding that divides medical devices into categories based on the risk of infection involved with their use.

spirals Bacteria that are curved, spiral or corkscrew shaped.

standard A uniform method of defining basic parameters for processes, products, services and measurements.

standard (AAMI) Voluntary guidelines representing a consensus of AAMI members that are intended for use by healthcare facilities and manufacturers to help ensure that medical instrumentation is safe for patient use.

standard, regulatory A comparison benchmark that is mandated by a governing agency. Noncompliance with regulatory standards may lead to citations and legal penalties.

standard, voluntary Guidelines or recommendations for best practices to provide better patient care. Industry, nonprofit organizations, trade associations and others develop these.

staphylococci Gram-positive bacteria that grow in grape-like clusters.

statute A written law adopted by a legislative body that governs a city, county, state or country.

sterilant/sterilization Physical or chemical entity, or combination of entities, that has sufficient microbicidal activity to achieve sterility under defined conditions.

sterile Completely devoid of all living microorganisms.

sterile field Immediate environment around trauma site or surgical incision; includes all materials in contact with the wound, gowns worn by the surgical team (front panel from chest to the level of the operative field and sleeve from the cuff to two inches above the elbow), patient drapes (area adjacent to the wound) and table covers (top surface).

sterility (event-related) Items are considered sterile unless the integrity of the packaging is compromised (damaged) or suspected of being compromised (damaged), regardless of the sterilization date; sometimes referred to as ERS (event-related sterility).

sterility (time-related) A package is considered sterile until a specific expiration date is reached.

sterilization Process by which all forms of microbial life, including bacteria, viruses, spores and fungi are completely destroyed.

sterilization wrap Device intended to enclose another medical device to be sterilized by a healthcare provider, and maintain sterility of the enclosed device until used.

sterilizer Equipment to sterilize medical devices, equipment and supplies by direct exposure to sterilizing agent.

sterilizer (ethylene oxide) Sterilization equipment that utilizes ethylene oxide under defined conditions of gas concentration, temperature and percent relative humidity.

sterilizer (steam) Sterilization equipment that uses saturated steam under pressure as the sterilant.

sterilizer (steam, dynamic-air-removal type) Steam sterilizer in which air is removed from the chamber and the load by means of pressure and vacuum excursions, or by means of steam flushes and pressure pulses.

streptococci Bacteria which divide to form chains; members of the genus streptococcus which are Gram-positive, chain-forming bacteria.

surfactant A substance that lowers the surface tension of the water and increases the solubility of organic compounds.

surgical drape Device made of natural or synthetic materials and used as a protective patient covering. Its purpose is to isolate a site of surgical incision from microbial and other contamination.

surgical gown Devices worn by Operating Room personnel during surgical procedures to protect the patient and Operating Room staff from transfer of microorganisms, body fluids and particulate matter.

surgical site infection An infection that occurs after surgery in the part of the body where the surgery took place.

surgical towel Absorbent product, typically made of cotton, intended to be used in a patient care procedure.

sustainability Processes designed to reduce harm to the environment or deplete natural resources, thereby supporting long-term ecological balance.

symbiosis Living together or close association of two dissimilar organisms with mutual benefit.

symbiotic bacteria "Good bacteria" that help us in some way. A symbiotic relationship means that both benefit: bacteria can live and the human is helped.

T

tamper-evident seals Sealing methods for sterile packaging that allow users to determine if the packaging has been opened. Tamper-evident seals allow users to determine if packages have been opened (contaminated) and help users identify packages that are not safe for patient use.

tap water Treated water that is acceptable for drinking.

Technical Information Reports (TIR) Reports developed by experts in the field that contain valuable information needed by the healthcare industry. TIRs have not undergone the formal approval system that standards are submitted to and may need further evaluation by experts. TIR may be revised or withdrawn at any time because they address a rapidly-evolving field or technology.

terminal sterilization The process by which medical devices are sterilized in their final containers, allowing them to be stored until needed.

tetrad Bacteria that are cocci appearing in groups of four.

therapeutic/operative Used to perform procedures (e.g. the removal of a rectal polyp) , tumor ablation, dilatation.

thermal disinfection Use of heat to reduce the amount of microorganisms (excluding spores) on a medical device.

third-party reprocessors Vendors that have received FDA approval to reprocess certain medical devices and supplies that are labeled single use. Most third party reprocessors transport used items to their facility, reprocess them according to strict specifications and return them to the user facility.

time-weighted average (TWA) The amount of a substance that employees can be exposed to over an 8-hour day.

toxin Poisonous substance produced by and during the growth of certain pathogenic bacteria.

treated water Water that has been processed to reduce impurities using filtration, distillation, deionization or reverse osmosis (RO) processes.

tuberculocidal Having the ability to kill tubercle bacilli.

tuberculosis Highly variable and communicable disease of man and some animals caused by the tubercle bacillus (Mycobacterium tuberculosis) and characterized by the formation of tubercles in the lungs or elsewhere.

turbidity Occurs when water contains sediments or solids that, when stirred, make the water appear cloudy.

turnaround A situation where a medical device such as an endoscope or surgical instrument is used on one patient and is needed immediately for another procedure.

turnover/turnaround Term used to describe instruments or equipment that must receive priority reprocessing in order to be made available for another procedure.

U

ureters Tube-like structures extending from the kidneys to the urinary bladder that move urine between these organs.

ureteroscope A flexible endoscope designed to provide visualization of the urinary tubes that connect the kidney to the urinary bladder.

urethra Tube that discharges urine.

urinary bladder Reservoir for urine.

V

validation Documented procedures, used by manufacturers, for obtaining, recording and interpreting test results required to establish that a process will consistently yield produces complying with predetermined specifications.

vancomycin-resistant enterococcus (VRE) Enterococcus bacteria that are no longer sensitive to vancomycin; transmission can occur either by direct contract or indirectly by hands.

vegetative bacteria Non spore-forming bacteria or spore-forming bacteria in a nonsporulating state.

vegetative stage State of active growth of microorganisms (as opposed to resting or spore stages.)

virulence Ability of a microorganism to overcome a person's immune defenses and cause disease. The faster the infection progresses, or more severe the symptoms are, the ore virulent the pathogen is rated.

virus One of a group of infectious agents that can only reproduce using the mechanisms inside a living cell. They can cause infections ranging from the common cold to hepatitis (A,B,C), to Ebola and small pox. Because they connot reproduce outside a living cell, viruses are not considered to be alive. They are too small to be seen using a standard microscope, so an electron microscope must be used.

virus, enveloped Viruses that have a delicate membrane around the capsid.

virus, non-enveloped Viruses without an envelope around the capsid.

VRE Abbreviation for vancomycin resistant enterococcus. When enterococcus bacteria are no longer sensitive to vancomycin, treatment is a challenge. Transmission occurs by direct contract or indirectly by hands.

W

wetting agent Substance that reduces the surface tension of a liquid and allows the liquid to penetrate or spread more easily across the surface of a solid.

wicking material Approved absorbent material that allows for air removal and steam penetration, and facilitates drying.

X

Y

yeasts Any of several unicellular fungi of the genus, Saccharomyces, which reproduce by budding.

Z

Index